Indigenous Peoples and Politics

Edited by

Franke Wilmer
Montana State University

A Routledge Series

Indigenous Peoples and Politics

Franke Wilmer, *General Editor*

The Globalization of Contentious Politics
The Amazonian Indigenous Rights Movement
Pamela L. Martin

Cultural Intermarriage in Southern Appalachia
Cherokee Elements in Four Selected Novels by Lee Smith
Kateřina Prajnerovã

Storied Voices in Native American Texts
Harry Robinson, Thomas King, James Welch, and Leslie Marmon Silko
Blanca Schorcht

On the Streets and in the State House
American Indian and Hispanic Women and Environmental Policymaking in New Mexico
Diane-Michele Prindeville

Chief Joseph, Yellow Wolf, and the Creation of Nez Perce History in the Pacific Northwest
Robert R. McCoy

National Identity and the Conflict at Oka
Native Belonging and Myths of Postcolonial Nationhood in Canada
Amelia Kalant

Native American and Chicano/a Literature of the American Southwest
Intersections of Indigenous Literature
Christina M. Hebebrand

The Present Politics of the Past
Indigenous Legal Activism and Resistance to (Neo)Liberal Governmentality
Seán Patrick Eudaily

The Ecological Native
Indigenous Peoples' Movements and Eco-Governmentality in Colombia
Astrid Ulloa

Spiraling Webs of Relation
Movements Toward an Indigenist Criticism
Joanne R. DiNova

Negotiating Claims
The Emergence of Indigenous Land Claim Negotiation Policies in Australia, Canada, New Zealand, and the United States
Christa Scholtz

Collective Rights of Indigenous Peoples
Identity-Based Movement of Plain Indigenous in Taiwan
Jolan Hsieh

The State and Indigenous Movements
Keri E. Iyall Smith

Speaking with Authority
The Emergence of the Vocabulary of First Nations' Self-Government
Michael W. Posluns

Speaking with Authority

The Emergence of the Vocabulary of First Nations' Self-Government

Michael W. Posluns

Routledge
New York & London

Routledge
Taylor & Francis Group
270 Madison Ave,
New York NY 10016

Routledge
Taylor & Francis Group
2 Park Square,
Milton Park, Abingdon,
Oxon, OX14 4RN

Routledge is an imprint of Taylor & Francis Group, an Informa business

Transferred to Digital Printing 2010

International Standard Book Number-10: 0-415-94653-0 (Hardcover)
International Standard Book Number-13: 978-0-415-94653-7 (Hardcover)

Library of Congress Cataloging-in-Publication Data

Posluns, Michael.
Speaking with authority : the emergence of the vocabulary of First Nations' self-government / Michael W. Posluns.
p. cm.
Includes bibliographical references and index.
ISBN 0-415-94653-0 (alk. paper)
1. Indians of North America--Canada--Government relations. 2. Indians of North America--Canada--Politics and government. 3. Indians of North America--Canada--Ethnic identity. 4. Self-determination, National--Canada. 5. Communication in politics--Canada. 6. Canada--Ethnic relations--Political aspects. 7. Canada--Politics and government. I. Title.

E78.C2P76 2006
323.1197'071--dc22 2006014054

ISBN10: 0-415-94653-0 (hbk)
ISBN10: 0-415-88261-3 (pbk)

ISBN13: 978-0-415-94653-7 (hbk)
ISBN13: 978-0-415-88261-3 (pbk)

Visit the Taylor & Francis Web site at
http://www.taylorandfrancis.com

and the Routledge Web site at
http://www.routledge-ny.com

For my grandchildren,
Rebecca, Brittany, Austin, Shane, Camryn and Yossi
And
In memory of my parents
Rebecca Brenzel Posluns and
Samuel Posluns

Contents

Foreword

During the near-decade of the 1970s in which I was the full-time editor of *Akwesasne Notes*, Mickey Posluns was one of those committed volunteers whose support made *Notes* possible. He often arrived at the reserve on his motorcycle, and without prompting dug into the nearest mountain of work waiting attention. Neither he nor I were then aware that the thesis which accompanies this foreword was within him and would emerge a third of a century later.

Notes was published in the heart of Akwesasne, with the hearts of the traditional people of Akwesasne. Into that close setting came a wonderful and rich variety of helpers from the outside world, some more easily fitting in than others. At first glance, Michael's fit was more difficult to imagine. He was very urban and urbane in the reserve's rural and rustic setting, devoutly Jewish amongst traditional Mohawk families, highly literate in an oral culture, coming from comfort into spartan living in an economically-challenged community. The times were militant, sometimes hostile to outsiders. Being accepted was not to be taken for granted. The fact is that Michael's inherent incongruity melted with each visit to the reserve.

Every test was met. He developed friendships with extended families and respected elders. He helped in the kitchens, gardens, and workshops. He found legal support for persons dealing with the complications of "being Indian". He became a welcome guest in many humble homes. Most of all, he listened. And he learned.

There are various strategies available for us to accommodate dramatically new life experiences into our ongoing existence. Some abandon the past and embrace the new. Others add the new as an appendage and carry on with life as it was. Still others live the new experience for a time and then leave it behind as if it had never happened. Michael's style was to merge the experience with previous interests, and to use it as a vital ingredient in experiences yet to happen.

This book is evidence of the strategy Michael adopted simply because that is the way he is. His approach is to merge life experiences. He has combined his love and knowledge of all things parliamentary with a talent for intensely detailed scholarship and his experience growing up Jewish with what he learned from Mohawk elders, Cree leaders, and such icons as George Manuel. As a producer of radio programs for CBC, he developed listening skills for the careful splicing of tape, the equivalent of retyping Senate transcripts to find meaningful detail, providing essence that otherwise might be overlooked.

The value of this thesis would be diminished with the loss of any one of these ingredients, because each has been used skillfully to complement the others.

And what is the value? It is twofold which together offers a third benefit. A reader impatient with the necessarily-ponderous first section may do well to set it aside and proceed to the second section which can stand on its own as historical background helpful to understand the 21st century dynamic of industrialized Canada with indigenous peoples of Great Turtle Island. It is startling to read the remarks of Ernie Benedict and George Manuel in 1970 as reverse echoes of contemporary presentations by First Nation leaders to new generations of parliamentarians and the Canadian public. The reading of the second part will whet an interest in returning to the scholarly discourse on the discourse of habitual colonizers and peoples who must combine the decolonizing process with strategies for cultural and physical survival, one of which is to carry on the decolonizing in a manner which is consistent with cultural values.

Or the reader may push on in ordinary fashion from start to finish. This choice has the advantage of permitting the reader to see the historical materials in the second half of the book through crystal-clear lenses which magnify and focus the details of the distorted (and at times disgraceful) discourse which has characterized the relationship of First Nations peoples with Euro-Canadians. (Attaining expertise in this discourse will be essential in the decades to come in understanding what I predict will be an inevitable shift in approach as Euro-Canadian advocates and proponents of 19th Century policy and attitudes are replaced by Canadians with roots in Africa and Asia.)

In whichever order, the rewards of a thorough reading of this book will include gaining expertise in political linguistics, the Talmudic approach of examining the roots of key words, ultra-detection of such tactics as burden-shifting, and the interplay of language, policy, and ethics.

Study of this book will enable readers also to become sensitive to language inversion, in which the plain meaning of words is twisted to mean quite the opposite. "Assimilation" for example, may be a sought-after goal for persons from other parts of the world who look forward to becoming "Canadians". The meaning is inverted for First Nations peoples, however. As Dr. Posluns points out by quoting a presentation to a parliamentary committee, "assimilation" is "a peculiar euphemism meant to describe a series of actions in which individuals and communities are displaced from their lands, deprived of their property and cultural rights, reduced to a further level of deprivation without any particular prospect of improving their lot. A synonym for assimilation in this context is cultural genocide."

To a new generation of both Canadians and First Nations peoples, Dr. Posluns is passing on the background of the formative policies of assimilation, enfranchisement, and the 1969 White Paper which are the unspoken pillars of today's policies. This is a background of facts which often were hardly noticed even when they were fresh and which might otherwise be lost, and yet are matters important to be understood by Canadians who might not know the origins of contemporary muddled thinking and by First Nations people who will learn their views are rested on a solid historic foundation. A reading of the statements made to Parliamentary committees reveals the frequent use of what today is called "the *S* word" – sovereignty, a term which is forbidden in official discourse. Even the use of the word "Treaty" has been known to cause entire federal delegations to get up and walk out of negotiations.

The theme of "finding voices, finding ears" was central to the work of Dr. Vine Deloria, Jr., who went on his spirit journey as this manuscript was being prepared for publication. Vine's clarion *We Talk, You Listen; New Tribes, New Turf* (New York: MacMillan) was published in 1970, the beginning of the decade which is scrutinized in Dr. Posluns' work, following the publication of the good-humored *Custer Died For Your Sins. God Is Red* came later. All were provocative works which helped indigenous people the world over find new ways of clearly expressing aspirations and intent.

"Finding voices" is not easy for oppressed peoples, generally, and particularly not easy for indigenous peoples who must express in another language abstract concepts which are not present in their own cultures, or the reverse: abstract concepts capsulized in one word in their own language but which requires extensive explanation for their non-indigenous listeners. "Finding ears" an equally difficult task when those ears are located in a society with deeply ingrained stereotypes and self-serving mythologies which serve to entrench the status quo. *Genuine dialogue cannot take place without genuine listening*. Without dialogue, constructive change cannot take place.

As Dr. Posluns points out, "Feasibility of change depends upon the ability of the colonizers to hear what indigenous people have been saying all along more than on the colonized peoples learning to express their aspirations."

For change to occur, then, the burden of learning to listen lies with the colonizers. Indigenous people frequently have developed highly acute listening devices. After all, they are expected to listen, not to speak. This offers the opportunity for indigenous people to develop skills in "hearing" nonverbal expression, particularly since the colonized are more comfortable in cross-cultural situations than the colonizers.

Employment of the Posluns tests and analytical methods to understand how the ways in which two peoples are prevented from working together to dismantle colonialism will, however, create a new dilemma. Once we have become expert in detecting prevarication, of locating language inversion and burden shifting, how do we approach the prevaricators? What do we say to them? How do we know if the prevarication is unconscious or deliberate? In the ideal world, the tests and methods would be applied to one's own discourse so that it might be self-decontaminated. Is that a dream too far-fetched to imagine? Remember: successful prevarication often results in a self-deception.

Of all areas of government policy, the First Nations discourse with the people and parliamentarians of Canada is best seen through the prism of "metapolicy", described by Dr. Posluns as "the ways in which a larger world view creates a general framework within which policy might be made." Considering metapolicy creates awareness about *how* we think even more than *what* we think. Finding metapolicy requires us to answer the question, "What is really happening here?" He suggests asking certain diagnostic questions:

> Language plays a major role in the shaping of policy and particularly metapolicy. Ethics is the crux of the interplay between language and policy. Are the characterizations of both situations and the persons accurate and fair? Is there an analysis built upon this fair description, and if so, is it rational? Do the assessments of severity of the problem and prospects to relieve it appear realistic and consistent with experience? Has the person advocating a position discharged the burden of proof regarding facts and the burden of persuasion for the analysis?

To help answer those questions, Dr. Posluns has provided a full kit of analytical tools. The reader can use these practical tools in analyzing current or past media utterances – Canadian media in general and the *National Post* in particular offers a rich lode to be mined. Speeches from the Throne from the 1970s to the present day will provide many jewels to the analyst armed with the tests set out in this book. Platforms from governing parties will offer revealing insights. Under the microscope, even school textbooks will be found to be conveying hidden messages.

We can also use these devices to look back at recent history. We will see the period of the '70s was an emergence, the decade of activism, the occupation by protestors of Indian Affairs offices in both the United States in Canada, Wounded Knee, and waves of lesser known events across the continent. The '70s marked the emergence of articulate thoughtful voices, of new hope for honest dialogue.

At the beginning of the 1980s, there was tangible reason for hope. There were frank, often heated discussions by indigenous delegates and federal and provincial officials in preparing for the First Ministers' Conferences called for in the just-patriated Canadian Constitution. The same year, Roberta Jamieson, representing the Assembly of First Nations, was appointed an *ex officio* member of the House Standing Committee on Indian Affairs traveling extensively throughout Canada in a study on "Indian Self-Government." In the 14 months of that study, Parliamentarians found their assumptions challenged and their views tested. Gradually genuine respect and genuine dialogue emerged. The "Penner Report" which emerged remains today a solid starting point for making self-government a reality in Canada. (Despite the success of this unique cross-cultural initiative, the true story of its creation lies in prevarication. It was the Government's intention to use the Committee's tour as a showcase for the *Indian Band Government Legislation* which had been secretly and unilaterally crafted by bureaucrats for several years. The government had fervently denied the *Band Government Bill* even existed. The Committee received its mandate to travel, but Justice Department drafters were unable to get the Bill into shape for release. The Committee set out without it, and once it had taken wind, continued on, forcing Minister John Munro to continue with the denial the bill existed.)

Although the *Penner Report* received the unanimous endorsement of all parties in the House of Commons, unfortunately, this shining example of honest dialogue never was implemented. As well, there was the failure of the nationally-televised now-forgotten series of post-patriation First Ministers' Conferences to reach any agreements. (In an example of corporate memory loss, the 2005 meeting of First Ministers and "aboriginal leaders" in Kelowna was billed as the first-ever such meeting.)

That was followed in the 1990s by Oka I and the resulting Royal Commission on Aboriginal Peoples Report and its now-forgotten, always-ignored, thoughtful recommendations. That decade saw the emergence within the Department of Indian Affairs of the "SWAT team" – Special Words and Tactics providing professionalism and structure in the discourse of prevarication designed to discredit First Nations leaders and activities which countered government objectives.

The 2000-2003 period is best characterized by the derailing of the Liberal Government's *First Nations Governance Act* which had been bravely promoted by Minister of Indian Affairs Robert Nault using every tactic of prevarication described in this book in a futile attempt to get his Bill passed.

This foreword is being written on the eve of Stephen Harper's Conservative Government taking office in Canada. That party's policy in opposition used the same "code" that has been typical of articulations since the 1960s. Setting out in 2006 an objective to "replace the *Indian Act* to provide for devolution of full legal and democratic responsibility" is a true copy of the *White Paper* code talk articulated by the Liberal Government in 1969 and used ever since. The Posluns tools will help scrape the gloss to show that "devolution" implies that Indian Affairs has control and may be willing to share it with the colonized. The use of the future tense implies First Nations people do not now have "legal and democratic responsibility." There is no mention that the *Indian Act*, despite its obviously colonialistic underpinning, also provides the legal protections for reserves, nor that the First Nations goal is to replace the *Indian Act* with self-government rather than with the "democratic responsibility" of other Canadians.

Such "code talk" is commonly used by parents conversing about a matter in the presence of their children when they do not want the children to understand what they are saying. It is the "nudge-nudge wink-wink" which is frequently used among bureaucrats in discussions with less-sophisticated First Nation peoples. It is a "code talk" which resonates in the minds of Canadians who want to be fair and just and "to do the right thing" in their dealings with indigenous peoples and who feel frustrated and rejected when their offering is resoundingly rejected.

Dr. Posluns' how-to manual for analysis of political utterances is certain to become well thumbed in the years to come.

Rarihokwats
Four Arrows
Ottawa, June 2006

Acknowledgments

A great many people helped me in one way or another that contributed to this work. The dedication of this work to my grandchildren and the generations still coming toward us is a small advance on the debt of gratitude that I owe to each of the many people whose teachings and encouragement have helped me see this work through to a conclusion. Were I far less absent-minded I would still be unable to mention by name each person to whom I am indebted. Those who I do mention by name are not responsible for the uses to which I have put their gifts.

I am particularly grateful to the Social Science and Humanities Research Council of Canada for their support of this work.

Following the Bridge Blockade at Akwesasne in December 1969, Ernie Benedict invited me to assist in organizing a legal defense for the Akwesasne people who had been charged with offenses related to standing on their own land. Since then, many of our conversations have touched on language and its social and political uses as well as many of the specific political issues discussed in this book. Rarihokwats has been a mentor in political thought, First Nations history and political linguistics since I began to follow and sometimes to assist his work on *Akwesasne Notes*. Many of the people with whom I worked at *Notes* deepened my appreciation of the interplay of language, policy and ethics.

George Manuel, the second president of the National Indian Brotherhood of Canada (the precursor of the Assembly of First Nations) extended the privilege of co-authoring his memoirs,[1] and building them into an historical reflection on First Nations relations from British Columbia's entrance into Confederation in 1871, to the post-1969 *White Paper* period. The privilege of writing a number of briefs with Art Solomon and of co-editing his two books[2] was a further course in the contrast of Native and mid-Atlantic language styles.

Mary Bernard's early encouragement and guidance enabled me to become a "mature student" after being away from school for several decades. Several professors at the Faculty of Environmental Studies and at Osgoode Hall Law School at York University also encouraged my interest in relating my earlier research and writing on First Nations political concerns to broader and deeper currents. I am particularly grateful in this respect to Prof. Doug Hay, Prof. John Borrows and Prof. Joe Sheridan. My time in the Government Documents Library at York University was made both pleasant and profitable by continuing help from Elizabeth Watson and other members of the library staff.

Prof. Liora Salter, of Osgoode Hall Law School and the Faculty of Environmental Studies at York University, on examining my proposal, remarked that I would honour my grandfathers by following a Talmudic approach of examining the roots of each key word. Prof. David Bell, the former Dean of the Faculty of Environmental Studies, the foster parent of the idea of *political linguistics* and my dissertation supervisor, was unfailingly generous in sharing his library, a gesture that assured me that others had trod this ground before me.

Prof. Kent McNeil, a distinguished scholar of First Nations law and Indigenous Rights at Osgoode Hall Law School,[3] has been unfailingly patient in his readings of my legal discussions.

I have also benefited from discussions of these ideas with numerous other professors, colleagues and friends including Dr. David McNab, an Aboriginal historian and land claims researcher and Dr. Kris Groberg, a friend, a museum curator and historian and the late Tom Jewiss, a dear friend who is sorely missed.

I also want to acknowledge a particular debt to three professors with whom I studied during my wayward years as an undergraduate at Carleton University: Dr. Naomi Griffiths with whom I studied French history, Dr. Vaclav Mudroch who introduced me to mediaeval history and Dr. Eleanor Swallow with whom I studied Greek and Latin literature in translation. Each of these distinguished professors conveyed to their students a sense of awe at the historical processes that were unraveled through the course of studies and a sense of delight at the literature and artifacts around which the history was composed.

I also owe a special debt of gratitude to various people at Routledge and at IBT Global for pulling my manuscript into presentable form. I am particularly grateful in this respect to Benjamin Holtzman, Erica Wetter, Amber Stein and Alicia Solsman. I am also grateful to the many people in the background whose labour and good will helped to turn my manuscript into this book. I am also indebted to Judith Brand for her preparation of a thorough and, I trust, very useful index.

My indebtedness to Rabbi Zalman Schachter-Shalomi, former professor of Jewish Mysticism at Temple University, founder of B'Nai Or and "the grandfather of the Havurah movement in contemporary Judaism" is evident throughout my discussions of Four Worlds Theory.

Dr. Bryan Dobbs, a former professor of Jewish Studies and of Canadian Studies at the University of Texas at Austin has been a steadfast friend as well as a mentor on language, Kabbala and literature for eighteen years. Our weekly meetings, our daily talks and his patient editing have all exemplified his teaching that slow reading will carry the reader farther than speed-reading.

Marilyn Eisenstat has been a companion, a partner and an inspiration. She has also been an amazing editor.

Introduction

GAINING A PURCHASE: AN INTRODUCTION TO THE PUBLIC EMERGENCE OF THE VOCABULARY OF FIRST NATIONS' SELF-GOVERNMENT

> These beliefs about how life should be lived, what men and women should be and do, are objects of moral inquiry; and when applied to groups and nations, and, indeed, mankind as a whole, are called *political philosophy*, which *is but ethics applied to society.*
>
> Isaiah Berlin, "The Pursuit of the Ideal" in *The Crooked Timber of Humanity*, Princeton, N.J., Princeton University Press, 1990

THE SCOPE OF THIS BOOK

In 1971–73, when I was collaborating with George Manuel, who was then president of the National Indian Brotherhood of Canada, on his memoir, *The Fourth World: An Indian Reality,*[1] he was of the view that an explicit discussion of self-government aspirations would not benefit either his constituents or his career. In 1980, Manuel's successor, Noël Starblanket,[2] in testimony before the Commons Indian Affairs Committee shortly after the founding of the Assembly of First Nations, set out a detailed vision of self-government. Two years later the Commons mandated a subcommittee of the Indian Affairs Committee to conduct an inquiry which became the *Penner Report on Indian Self-Government.*

What I describe as "the vocabulary of First Nations' self-government developed as the building blocks of a unique political discourse during those ten or twelve years. This work examines the emergence of that discourse into the public arena.

The emergence of the vocabulary of First Nations self-government is an important historical question for a number of reasons. First, although First Nations had, been self-governing communities each with their own political and social organization before European contact and for a long period after European settlement had begun, the vocabulary with which the various First Nations carried on the business of government was the vocabulary of their respective indigenous languages. Treaties, we are told, were a well known practice in settling affairs between nations.

The term "chief," on the other hand, appears to have been devised as a one-size-fits-all title in the British Colonial Office. The Mohawk term *Rotiyaner* was not necessarily an equivalent of the Cree or Anishinaabe term, *Mukwa*. Both the tenure and the duties might have differed significantly, much as a president is neither a king nor a prime minister. Efforts to translate key political terms from indigenous languages to English and French have repeatedly foundered on the prejudices of translators or their clients. Many of the names by which various First Nations are most commonly known in English or French discourse today–Maliseet, Mohawk, Sioux, and Eskimo–originated as epithets of a neighbouring First Nation. "Trade languages" such as Chinook and Michief might have risen above their commercial origins if political discourse among First Nations people had not been generally criminalized under Canadian law.

Secondly, in the 1920s when there was a growing grassroots movement to bring "Indian nations" from across Canada together under a common umbrella, Parliament passed, in 1927, legislation making the raising of funds for the purpose of pressing Indian land claims a punishable offence.[3] This civil disability[4] was imposed on Indians across Canada in 1927 largely in response to a campaign led by Andrew Paull, to whom George Manuel would apprentice 20 years later, to have the land claims of the Interior Tribes of British Columbia referred to the Judicial Committee of the British Privy Council.

In the course of collaborating with George Manuel, and, more particularly, narrating Andrew Paull's experience, before a Joint Committee of the Senate and House of Commons, mandated to study Paull's petition on behalf of the Interior Tribes I became struck by the enormity of the civil disabilities imposed by Canada on First Nations by federal statutes enacted between 1882 and 1927.

Parliament had already enacted legislation prohibiting various giveaway ceremonies such as the so-called "potlatch."[5] Gatherings of more than three Indians constituted another offence under Canadian law. Leaving the reserve of one's band without a pass, much like the later pass laws in South Africa, also constituted an offence. At some First Nations communities where land had been leased to cottagers, it was an offence for Indians to set foot on their own islands.[6]

Developing an English or French toponymy was an important step in eliminating immigrant consciousness of a people existing prior to European migration while also eliminating the sense of place that is often said to be central to most First Nations' world views. Indigenous names such as "Akwesasne" had been replaced by English or French names, often at the direction of a Christian Church. Akwesasne was known as "St. Régis" from early in the 19th century until late in the 20th century. Pronunciation of names such as *St. Régis* became the site of a continuing contest between French and English in a struggle for cultural supremacy. Neither the French nor the English from the late 18th century through the 20th century gave much thought to the possibility that the Mohawk community which had occupied that natural town site for some centuries might also have had a name for it.

Eliminating cultural consciousness went far beyond toponymy. Federal police[7] had arrested the leaderships of the traditional Longhouse governments of the Five Nations of the Haudenausonee at Kanesatake, Kanawake, and Akwesasne.

Canada and its clerical partners left few stones unturned in their effort to suppress indigenous cultures. An Indian man, who gained an education and found permanent employment, became a civil servant or a minister of a Christian religion was forcibly "enfranchised." Likewise, a woman married to such a man, and their children, were also "enfranchised." Indeed, the co-option of the term "enfranchised" so that, in the context of Canadian Indian policy, it came to represent *the loss of membership* in one's native community rather than the usual meaning of *gaining a right to vote* is emblematic of the Orwellian speech that runs throughout the bureaucratic and parliamentary discourses on Indian policy in Canada.

The residential schools, about which so much has been said and written since the Royal Commission on Aboriginal Peoples[8] account ended the taboo against public discussions of those institutions, represent a bundle of civil disabilities over and above those set out in federal statutes. Much attention has been paid to the physical and sexual abuse that occurred in those "schools." Much less attention has been paid, in the past decade, to the enormous mortality rates which, through the efforts of Dr. P.H. Bryce, the medical officer of the Indian Affairs Branch and others, were the subject of some interest and concern as early as 1907.[9]

The significance of these disabilities in shaping the course of First Nations relations[10] in Canada can hardly be overstated. The depth of their influence, both in the years when they were in effect and for the decades when they continued to influence both the thinking of First Nations leaders and the ill-founded assumptions and attitudes of Canadian political leaders,[11] has yet to receive the study on which a thorough assessment might be built. Various provincial statutes imposed further disabilities.

These prohibitions, taken as a whole, constituted a longer and more severe set of sanctions than any of the more famous Canadian impositions of civil disabilities, including those against Ukranian-Canadians in World War I, Japanese Canadians and German refugees (including German Jewish refugees) in World War II. It has somehow become important to acknowledge these other egregious errors, and even to admit that the evidence placing these ethnic communities under suspicion was flimsy at best. Meanwhile the disabilities imposed on First Nations, with no rationale beyond the pretence of "civilizing" the savages continue to be overlooked, minimized and denied. The "need" to civilize the Indians was a matter of policy and did not require evidence in the sense that a charge such as treason or lesser charge of collaborating with an enemy in a time of war might raise an expectation of a burden of proof falling on the Crown.

It may seem curious that the vocabulary of First Nations' self-government only emerged in English political discourse in the 1970s. One important consideration is the fact that the exercise of such a vocabulary, in a discourse of First Nations' autonomy was a punishable offense from 1927 to 1951 when most of the civil disabilities in the *Indian Act* were repealed.

My concern here is not to construct a history of these disabilities but simply to note the part they played in suppressing any kind of political discourse amongst First Nations leaders, and particularly the development of a shared vocabulary of First Nations self-government. The first Indian witnesses to walk into a committee room to ask for a guarantee of Indian rights in a patriated Canadian Constitution were well aware that they were breaking new ground. Likewise, the whiff of condescension in the response of parliamentarians conveyed a clear impression, in the early 70s, that Indian testimony was not something for which it was necessary to do one's homework before coming to class.

The third factor is a dilemma that arises in the idea that what emerged in the 1970s is a new vocabulary. Basic concepts such as self-government and autonomy derive their meanings from words that have international definitions, are widely discussed academically and on which there is also a significant legal literature. However, the use of these and other key terms in a First Nations context has proven to be highly contested. Nominally friendly parliamentarians and academics, even in the

21st century demonstrate the greatest difficulty speaking of "peoples" and "nations." A few take some comfort in learning that George III, in the *Royal Proclamation of 1763* spoke of "those Indian nations with whom we are allied."

John Marshall, then Chief Justice of the U.S. Supreme Court, observed in the 1832 decision *Worcester v. Georgia,*

> The words "treaty" and "nation" are words of our own language, selected in our own diplomatic and legislative proceedings, by ourselves, having each a definite and well understood meaning. We have applied them to Indians, as we have applied them to other nations of the earth. They are applied to all in the same sense.

Such a straightforward, plain sense interpretation of language, if ever it was embraced, has long since been abandoned in the realm of Canadian Indian policy. Challenges to the ordinary or plain sense meaning of words runs through federal Crown legal arguments in court no less than in the testimony of senior officials before parliamentary committees, and, in such negotiations and consultations as take place between Canada and various First Nations from time to time.[12]

Government officials have found it convenient to endorse and even to adopt terms such as "the inherent right to self-government" and then proceed to "read them down," i.e., to ascribe, for instance, to self-government, far less meaning than it has in most other contexts. The "suite of bills" introduced by Robert Nault, Jean Chrétien's Minister of Indian Affairs, in 2001 and 2002 stand as models of the co-option of language. Under his leadership departmental officials spoke glowingly of "the inherent right to self-government" but insisted that they and their minister would decide just what was included in this "inherent right."

After the publication of *The Fourth World* I worked for some time with *Akwesasne Notes* which was then becoming the journal of record in "the Indian world." In 1976, when Noël Starblanket succeeded George Manuel, I went to work for him developing a parliamentary relations programme for the N.I.B.

My personal involvement with both Manuel and Starblanket led me, both at the time and later in my academic work, to reflect on the evolution of the idea of First Nations self-government during the decade of the 1970s and to reflect on ways to document both its articulation and the response of Canadian parliamentarians.

The formal development of this study began as a curiosity about how a vocabulary–indeed, an entire rhetoric–that had been forcibly muted for several decades emerged into the public domain during the decade of the 1970s. The muting of self-government aspirations through federal legislation imposing civil disabilities is discussed in Chapter Two, an overview of the history of First Nations relations before 1970. The centerpiece of this work–Chapters Three, Four and Five –chronicles the testimony of First Nations witnesses and other witnesses addressing issues related to First Nations self-government before a series of parliamentary committees from 1970 to 1980. I will refer to these three chapters collectively as "the narrative." A brief description of the background of each committee is provided at the beginning of the narrative of that committee.

My analysis of the significance of the 1969 *White Paper* is discussed at the end of the chapter on the history prior to 1970, Chapter Two because I see it as the end of the era epitomized in Mackenzie King's declaration that a person could not have both "Indian rights" and the rights of Canadian citizenship. I have chosen to begin the narrative in 1970, after the *White Paper* because the drive to create a national resistance to the *White Paper* policy resulted in the formation of the National Indian Brotherhood, the relocation of the N.I.B. from Winnipeg to Ottawa and the determination to make the N.I.B. a significant presence in the Ottawa scene. In short, the new era began with the reaction against the *White Paper.*

In order to better understand what was happening in the proceedings of these committees, I found it necessary to develop a conceptual framework that might serve as a prism through which I might gain a perspective on the dynamics developing in the relationship between the parliamentarians and the various witness groups who addressed them including First Nations leaders, ministers and their officials, academics and leaders of various non-indigenous social movements.

The conceptual framework that I have developed for this purpose is set out in Chapter One, "The Interplay of Language, Policy and Ethics." I am equally interested in the vocabulary and rhetoric of the First Nations witnesses and the responses of the parliamentarians (MPs and Senators) on each committee. A number of conceptual tools that I have found helpful for analyzing political discourse are laid out in chapter I including: (1) burdens of proof; (2) licensing; (3) prevarication; and, good faith. It is clear, even at a quick glance, that these terms are all closely related. It is also clear that they have a peculiar application to the particular policy arena that I describe as "First Nations relations," a term that I use to embrace both contemporary and historic "Indian policy" and the prospects of a healthier and more authentic relationship between the dominant cultures and the First Nations in North America.

The narrative chapters (Three, Four and Five) each conclude with a review analyzing the changes in the discourse of First Nations relations during the period convered by that chapter and based on my reading of the accounts of the committees reviewed in that chapter, i.e., the sum of public and administrative discourse about the relationship between First Nations and the Crown in right of Canada, i.e., the federal government.

The historical materials that form the basis of the narrative chapters are the proceedings of two Joint Committees on the Constitution and the Standing Commons Committee on Indian Affairs and Northern Development mandated during this decade, one in 1970–72 and the second in 1978. Other primary materials which are examined are the *Indian Act* and related statutes from 1857 to 1980 and the major legal decisions regarding Aboriginal and treaty rights from *St. Catharines Lumber and Milling*[13] to *Sparrow.*[14] The judicial decisions occurring during the decade of the 1970s, e.g., *Calder,*[15] *Kanatewat*[16] form an immediate backdrop to the parliamentary committee proceedings under examination. The earlier cases are discussed in Chapter Two, "An Historical Overview Prior to 1970." The language used by the courts from *St. Catharines* to *Sparrow* is a major influence in the development of an overall framework for this study.[17]

The secondary sources that I reviewed in developing the conceptual framework fall into three broad categories: (1) the literature on attitudes of dominant cultures to colonized peoples, (2) particularly works on North American settler attitudes and public policies regarding Native societies; and, (3) selected readings on political ethics with an emphasis on questions of dialogue, authenticity, good faith and deception.

After I had written the narrative chapters and proceeded to draft a chapter on the *meaning* of these events, I became preoccupied with the idea that the discourse of First Nations' autonomy could not be properly appreciated through the existing literature on political discourse. What was at issue was not so much a policy question in the ordinary sense but what I have come to call a metapolicy, i.e., the ways in which a larger worldview creates a general framework within which policy might be made. The worldviews at issue here are those that caricature First Nations and provide a rationale for policy attitudes of the settler societies in North America. Although these views have often ascribed a childlike status to Indians, they have also frequently exempted the Crown from the obligations of a parent. Having identified the existence of this worldview and documented it in the narrative chapters, I argue that such a worldview stands in opposition to anything resembling a genuine dialogue in the proceedings of parliamentary committees.

In the course of considering the matter of worldviews, I developed and explored the application of two sets of tools for analyzing the language of both witnesses and parliamentarians. One of these sets of tools I describe as a *Four Worlds analysis*. The four worlds analysis, in my doctoral dissertation, was of such a length that I have excised it from this book and hope to see it published in a volume of its own in which I will also be able to examine its application to other policy arenas.

What remains to be done in this introduction is to begin the discussion of the second set of tools, a group of analytical concepts: prevarication, licensing, spectrum and fulcrum. One can not look at the history of First Nations relations without reflecting on the dark side of the discourse of First Nations' autonomy: the determination of successive governments to undermine and dissolve the last vestiges of First Nations' autonomy.

Throughout the history of First Nations relations, Canadian since Confederation, there has been a tendency of significant persons amongst the settler population to describe First Nations in terms calculated to bring the host nations into disrepute, to foster hostility and suspicion and to exclude First Nations people from participation in the dominant culture and its institutions. To deal with this result, I have coined a new term, *the Discourse of Prevarication.*

By prevarication, I mean a statement or a line of argument that tends to deceive. In this sense, prevarication is broader than some conceptions of lying. Within the framework of formal discourse by elected political leaders, senior officials, professionals and academics, in formal testimony, I take statements that tend to deceive as being intended to deceive or as reflecting a serious issue of competence.

Prevarication can, then, be seen to cover a wide range of statements. The characterization of First Nations by U.S. Chief Justice John Marshall, in *M'Intosh*[18] ("fierce savage Indians whose occupation was war") are, as was pointed out by Hall J., in *Calder*[20] "ill-founded," i.e., statements that are not true. A more subtle example of a prevarication would be a statement by Jean Chrétien, then Minister of Indian Affairs that he proposed to promote the NIB-AFN program of *Indian Control of Indian Education* if he has not made provisions to begin what will surely be a difficult and complex set of legislative and administrative processes. Marshall's statement differs from Chrétien's in that it confirms a caricature of Indians as dangerous, fierce, and savage while Chrétien's prevarication simply fosters a belief that his department will follow certain policies when with historical hindsight we can see that there was never any intention of implementing those policies.

The notion of the dark side of the discourse is strongly reinforced by a current tendency to doubt the reality of "the plain sense," i.e., the world that is described by language that describes external referents. The discounting of the reality of "plain sense meaning" is bound up with the tendency in post-structural and critical analysis which centres reality in language while doubting or disparaging the notion that language refers to realities external to the discourse.

"Nietzsche denigrates the 'impulse to truth' crucial to a metaphysics of presence," according to the entry on "influence" in *The New Princeton Encyclopedia of Poetry and Poetics*.[21] Walter Truett Anderson's anthology of postmodernism, *The Truth about the Truth*[22] favours those who doubt that the pursuit of truth can produce substantial results—Derrida, Foucault, Rorty, Kuhn, and bell hooks–in contrast to those who hold that the pursuit of truth is necessary precisely because, despite truth being elusive, it is, nonetheless, fundamental both to scholarship and to social change–Isaiah Berlin, Umberto Eco, Václav Havel, Martin Marty and Arthur Schlesinger, Jr. George Lakoff and Mark Johnson, in *Metaphors We Live By*[23]push the idea of the world as a metaphor (hence lacking a plain sense meaning) to a further extreme.

In contrast, the notion that 'the impulse to truth' is crucial to a metaphysics of presence goes to the heart of any discussion of political ethics in two distinct senses. First, coming from a background in paralegal work, I do not understand making charges against persons without allowing that the contest over those charges is a struggle to come closer to the truth about a stated set of events.

An event that ostensibly happens time and again under state auspices or with the sanction of the state can be seen as an indicator of policy. Much of what was known in the 1990s about Indian residential schools was documented in reports that were published as early as 1907. The inability of the state to institute reforms that would, at the very least, reduce the mortality rates in these supposed schools demonstrates an acceptance of the mortality rate as a "collateral effect" of government and church policy. If, however, one views either the events or the reports as less than factual it is not possible to respond appropriately to a report that state sponsored, church run institutions achieved a mortality rate of close to 50%, a rate described by Dr. P.H. Bryce, in 1907, as higher than "most wars."[24]

Secondly, 'the metaphysics of presence' is fundamental to any study of policy discourse, and especially to the work of receiving submissions and examining witnesses as a member of a public or parliamentary inquiry. In examining committee proceedings over several decades, and particularly in relation to this immediate study, I have become concerned with issues of *active listening* on the part of panels of parliamentarians.

Some Members' questions reflect a deep and active attention to testimony being addressed to them. Some questions are intended only to put the Members' own interests on the record and are unrelated to the opening remarks of the witness then testifying. Martin Buber regarded active listening as the most elementary feature of genuine dialogue.[25] One can be present to another without speech, but not without listening. Jean-Paul Sartre describes the consequences when the requirements for authenticity are lacking as *une dialogue du sourd*.[26]In an essay entitled "The Place of Genuine Dialogue in the Judicial Discussion of Aboriginal and Treaty Rights,"[27] I discussed a similar need for a metaphysics of presence on the part of judges and looked at a line of cases in which judges evidenced a strong sense of being present to the court and another line in which such evidence was not apparent. For all their many differences, the need to be present to the witness and to the overall process is fundamental to the role of judges, commissioners of public inquiries, and parliamentary inquirers.

This study is premised on a concern for situations in which other people live and die, prosper and are diminished. I have no doubt that these situations can be vividly portrayed through language. Neither policy nor law can have meaning unless some description of external reality is possible. I have already introduced the notion of the Discourse of Prevarication. It seems self-evident that there can be no prevarication if there is not, at the very least, a possibility of "getting it right."

To deal with the way that language is used in a representational sense, the rabbis of the Talmud offer an account of *peshat*, the Hebrew term which is commonly translated as "plain sense."[28] The Supreme Court of Canada continues to find the term useful, though they speak of a "modern idea of plain meaning."[29] Careful consideration and comparison shows that these two understandings–the rabbinic and the contemporary juridical–intersect. While the subtle distinctions that lead the justices to refer to the "modern idea of plain meaning" are, undoubtedly important, the fundamentals remain throughout. I have attempted to make my observations from the roundabout of that intersection.

The emergence of the vocabulary of First Nations' self-government into *the public domain* is an important question for a number of reasons. What I mean by "public domain" is that the objectives of diverse First Nations are expressed in a common language and in a forum where their views are available both to an Aboriginal constituency across Canada, and to a non-Aboriginal cross-Canada constituency.

Historically, federal Indian policy has infantilized Indians, i.e., it has taken the view that Indians *qua* Indians were both childlike and incompetent. A variety of specific regulations served largely to make this policy self-fulfilling, e.g., punishing people who showed leadership tendencies, requiring a pass to leave a reserve, dispatching the RCMP when people gathered in sizeable numbers, prohibiting spiritual and religious practices other than those endorsed by the dominant culture.

"Indians" did not become part of "the public" [30] in Canada until some time after 1951, perhaps in 1960 when Indians were granted the unqualified right to vote in federal elections in Canada. Until 1951, those who became civil servants, ministers of a Christian religion or were regularly employed were described as "enfranchised" because they gained the right to vote. In keeping with Indian Affairs' peculiar way of speaking, this was called "enfranchisement."

This use of a term–enfranchisement–seen as an unqualified good in every other minority community–to represent the removal of a person from his or her ancestral community is emblematic of the discourse of prevarication running throughout the history of Canadian Indian policy.

At least one teacher, Emily General, was fired when she refused to take an oath to the King out of loyalty to the Mohawk nation.[31]

"Native," as a term, appears to have had its origins as a category which was intended to stand over against "man" or "human" or "person."[32] "Naïf," a French contraction of "native," takes the matter full circle: while "Natives" are said to be childlike, we now describe those whom we see as "childlike" as "naïve."[33]

Most important, the repeated efforts to suppress free speech and free assembly of First Nations people from the first prohibition of traditional ceremonies until the 1950s did not stop the discourse of First Nations' autonomy; it simply forced it underground.[34] Canada's decision to circumscribe its persecution of indigenous people who expressed normal human aspirations did no more than to allow a discourse which had never altogether ceased to emerge into the light of day.

As that discourse began to emerge into English, those of us who have not been immersed in a language indigenous to the land where we live have, nonetheless, become privileged to gain access to this discourse.

A series of parliamentary committees allowed Indian leaders, usually those representing national or regional political organizations, to make presentations which put their political agendas and their policy critiques into the most public of Canadian records. However poorly these presentations were understood at times, the decision that they might be heard represented a tentative beginning of a new political direction in Canada in which First Nations leaders were included, in at least some nominal way.

This did not achieve self-government. It did, however, put into the public record *a vocabulary of First Nations self-government.* Almost all the innovative language that occurs in the 1982–83 Penner Committee on Indian Self-Government or in the First Ministers' Meetings on self-government had their initial appearances before the Commons Indian Affairs Committee or the two Joint Committees on the Constitution. It also allowed some recognition that First Nations were communities in Canada, that their leaders were adults and that their representations could not be altogether ignored.

On several occasions, in the course of my writing I was asked whether this work is a study of discourse theory or a study of policy. The best answer I can offer is to say that this is a study in the history of a political idea, the idea variously described as *First Nations Self-Government*, *First Nations Self-Determination, First Nations sovereignty* or *First Nations jurisdiction*. These various terms represent important variations, but they are variations on a common idea: First Nations interests can best be served by institutions, customs and constitutions devised by the various First Nations.

My interest in this idea focuses on the extent to which *the possibility of genuine dialogue between First Nations leaders and Canadian parliamentarians* coincides with elements of decolonization and a reduction of the imposition of civil disabilities[35] and the consequent human suffering.

These proceedings record what First Nations leaders have had to say to Parliament in regard to self-government ranging from broad overviews relating First Nations self-government to patriation of the Canadian Constitution to those discussion of a dysentery epidemic and the death of children resulting from the non-fulfillment of *James Bay and Northern Quebec Agreement*. Indeed, the testimony of First Nations leaders before the Indian Affairs Committee through the 1970s and before other committees including a succession of joint committees on the Constitution, the Commons Committee on Forestry and Fisheries and the Senate Committee on Legal and Constitutional Affairs constitutes a genre of political literature that has not received the attention that it deserves. The genre is characterized, in part, by the frequent movement from statements of aspirations to analyses of departmental estimates, and disputes as to the presence and extent of disease. I have often watched parliamentarians as they listened to First Nations leaders who had mastered the bureaucratic jargon and were replying, line by line, to earlier testimony of senior officials of the Indian Affairs Branch.

As I worked my way through a decade of testimony, possibly the most significant change in my own thinking came from an appreciation of the change that occurred amongst parliamentarians as a small handful of non-Aboriginal political leaders learned to listen to First Nations speakers and to seek a sustained and genuine dialogue with those leaders.

The feasibility of social change with a minimum of violence does not depend upon a colonized people learning to express their aspirations in the language of the colonizer as much as it depends upon the ability of the colonizers to hear what indigenous people have been saying all along.

A METHODOLOGICAL OVERVIEW

What I mean by a narrative is primarily the presentation of historical material in much the same way that it might be presented in a radio documentary. The narrative, in a narrower sense, is the voice that introduces and interprets the action which occurs through the medium of the tape clips. Here, I have worked to adapt that method to the selection of those quotations from the *Proceedings* which I consider to be most revealing of one or another development.

The downside of this approach is that it produces a bulky manuscript. Its strength is that, when it succeeds, it provides a dramatization of the historically most noteworthy statements and exchanges, at least in the opinion of the narrator who has made the selection.

To rein in my own enthusiasm I have sought editorial assistance to better control the quoted material. I have also sought assistance in assuring that the significance of each passage is properly discussed.

METHODS FOR A NARRATIVE ON FIRST NATIONS TESTIMONY

Because the methods used in the narrative part of this dissertation are primarily historical they can be sorted into the following categories:

1. Gathering materials;
2. Recording and organizing research;
3. Selecting events for the narration;
4. Historical and Parliamentary terminology;
5. Verifying biographical information.

HISTORICAL RESEARCH: GATHERING MATERIALS

The focus of my research was the *Proceedings* of three Joint Committees on the Constitution and the *Proceedings* of the Standing Committee on Indian Affairs and Northern Development and its sub-committees.

I used these sources primarily because, from my own recollections, they had the makings of a good story which had not previously been told. There were also, fortunately, a number of scholarly advantages.

All these *Proceedings* could be found in the Government Documents Library at York University. There was little competition for access to these materials. Several of the volumes appeared never to have been cracked open.

A further advantage is that, apart from a tendency of *Hansard* to complete sentences and correct minor grammatical errors, there is no serious contestation as to the veracity of these *Proceedings* as transcripts.

In addition, I considered it an important advantage that the presentations and other testimony of First Nations leaders were statements that they had each chosen to present to committees of the Parliament of Canada. In some other contexts, the lack of spontaneity, or the careful consideration for political purposes might be considered to detract from these statements. I was particularly interested in those statements which were the result of careful deliberation. If a First Nations leader chooses to introduce a concept which is central to his thinking, or the positions of his or her organization and which have historically been anathema to the Parliament of Canada, I expect that he or she will give the matter careful consideration. In a number of instances, the witnesses refer to decisions taken in their own assemblies on which they are basing their position.

I brought to the study of these *Proceedings* several decades of experience in the study of Parliamentary papers. Often in the course of the narrative, I venture an opinion that a certain phrase or lexical unit is being introduced for the first time. These opinions bring together my close reading of these *Proceedings* with my previous experience. Nonetheless, I do tend to favour qualified statements, e.g., "appears to be the first time."

I have, in my previous writing, been reticent about the use of materials given to me by a First Nations teacher or elder lest someone consider that their use was a kind of appropriation. Testimony of First Nations leaders, and their advisors, that drew on discussion and resolutions from their own assemblies, is, I trust, beyond that kind of criticism.

SELECTING MATERIAL FROM THE PROCEEDINGS

The overriding criterion in selecting quotations was whether they represented, one way or another, a further articulation in the emergence of the vocabulary of self-government. This, of course, was often open to interpretation. Despite the large volume of material I have used, I can assure readers that I have, in fact, chosen just the highlights from many volumes of committee proceedings.

This process became somewhat more complex as I came to appreciate more fully the significance of the role played by the parliamentary audiences in influencing the presentations. The inability to address witnesses by their proper names, to frame questions from opening statements or to carry key concepts from one sitting to the next suggested that these parliamentarians–viewed as one might view a class of students–were often conflicted about the material being presented and ill-equipped to grasp what was being offered. Toward the end of my reading of these proceedings some progress in overcoming these obstacles on the part of certain parliamentarians became evident. Taking note of this progress became no less critical to my understanding of the dynamic between parliamentarians and First Nations leaders than my original interest in the evolution of the vocabulary of First Nations leaders. Likewise, there was occasional testimony from non-Aboriginal witnesses whose testimony touched on Aboriginal matters.

The two major groups of such witnesses were law professors and members of territorial councils. The view of the law professors evolved considerably over the decade. By and large, the recurring theme followed by all the law professors can be summed up by the phrase "Citizens Plus," first introduced in the 1967 *Hawthorn Report* and adapted as the title of Harold Cardinal's reply to the *White Paper*, more generally known as the *Red Paper*.

SECONDARY HISTORICAL SOURCES

In the course of narrating the events through which the vocabulary emerged, it was frequently necessary to provide essential historical background of a more general kind. As a rule, I have sought to limit this background to brief descriptions of the issues influencing the work of the Committee. The work of these parliamentary committees took place in the context of larger parliamentary events and other political developments. The first Joint Committee on the Constitution, for instance, was given a mandate (officially termed an "Order of Reference") based on *the Victoria Charter*. Although that Committee's mandate was of a general nature, the second Joint Committee was established to study Bill C-60 of the third session of the 30th Parliament (1978), Pierre Trudeau's first patriation legislation.

I have generally provided a brief background on each of the First Nations leaders and each of the parliamentarians (Members of Parliament or Senators).

I have tried to keep these background discussions to a minimum. At the same time, I have cited a series of excellent reference works which will provide the interested reader with all the background one might want.

In addition to the published works, I have also drawn extensively on a large collection of administrative memoranda from the Department of Indian Affairs and Northern Development and from the then Ministry of State for Social Development which was released under Access to Information in the late 1980s. The portions of this collection in which self-government and related issues are discussed formed the basis of my master's dissertation, *The Bureaucratic Response to the Penner Report.* The complete collection of these materials is in my files.

READING AND ORGANIZING RESEARCH MATERIALS

My primary objective when I began reading these committee proceedings was to experience, as far as one can from reading historical documents in general and transcripts in particular, the experience of the witnesses. Several of the key witnesses were First Nations leaders for whom I had worked: George Manuel, Noel Starblanket, and Sol Sanderson. Ernest Benedict is a long time friend and colleague. Most of the others were people with whom I was acquainted from attending meetings. I had read their written work and had corresponded with their advisors.

When I started my library research at York University's Government Documents Library, I *previewed* the parliamentary materials, i.e., looked over what was available and determined that the *Proceedings* for which I was looking were in the library's holdings. I had not recalled, until I began to look over the collection, the work of the first Joint Committee on the Constitution. I recognized its importance when I looked through its *Final Report* and the list of witnesses.

The method I used for *gathering* materials, in 1997 and 1998 is one that some scholars may consider obsolete a few years later. I transcribed all the testimony that appeared to be of any interest at all. I chose this approach for two reasons: First, I was advised by a senior official in the *Hansard* Branch that Parliament had begun the work of putting *Debates* and Committee *Proceedings* in digitized form in 1986, six years after the end of the period I wished to cover.

Secondly, when I observed that this was a slow and tedious process, a member of my dissertation committee kindly pointed out old-fashioned copy work was an efficient way to learn the material. Copying indeed gave me an intimate knowledge of these texts. Thirdly, I did consider scanning. As I understood the technology of that time and the resources then available in the York libraries, would not have materially saved time.

The advantage of having the materials, at the end of the exercise, in electronic form was self-evident. As I transcribed, I made a point of entering the page numbers, issue number (the number of the sitting) and the session number.

HISTORICAL AND PARLIAMENTARY TERMINOLOGY

In writing the narrative, I have tried to use the language that was used, at that time, by the persons whose work I was narrating and describing. I consider that this was an essential part of illustrating the process of language change. On those occasions when I am speaking entirely in my own voice, rather than paraphrasing statements of, or otherwise portraying the activities of an historical character, I have used more contemporary language.

I have applied this principle not only to language related to First Nations issues but also to parliamentary terminology. The presiding officers of these committees were addressed as "chairman." In fact, when Senator Joan Neiman became the first woman to chair the Senate Legal and Constitutional Affairs Committee, in 1980, she used the term "chairman" throughout her tenure. This usage continues in the Senate with the apparent approval of numerous women committee chairmen and other women senators.

As a general rule, I have used the term "Indian" to refer to persons registered or entitled to be registered under the *Indian Act*. I follow this usage because this was the usage of the National Indian Brotherhood (N.I.B.) until it began to develop the "First Nations" terminology, e.g., the Assembly of First Nations (A.F.N.).

I use "Native" to mean the people represented by the Native Council of Canada during this decade, i.e., persons of Aboriginal ancestry who do not claim an entitlement under the *Indian Act* and who, largely, do not identify with an Indian band or a First Nations community.

I acknowledge, but I do not follow, a broader use of the term "Native" elaborated by Harry Daniels' statement in which he equates "Native" with "constitutional Indian," as that expression was used by legal scholars of the day, i.e., everyone who might claim to be an Indian within the meaning of section 92(24) of the *Constitution Act, 1867*, including "registered Indians, urban Indians, non-status Indians, Inuit, Métis, treaty Indians, non-treaty Indians, etc."[36] "Constitutional Indian" is, I believe, interchangeable with the term "Aboriginal" as it is used in section 35 of the *Constitution Act, 1982*.

Peter Cumming made a similar point in arguing that the federal government could, if it wished, "continue to legislate for enfranchised Indians."[37] Inuit have been "constitutional Indians" since 1939 when the Supreme Court found that "The exclusive legislative jurisdiction of the dominion Parliament under s.91(24) . . . over Indians extends to Eskimos."[38] Indeed, the Court found that Inuit had been "constitutional Indians" since Confederation.

I have chosen to restrict my use of the term "Native" to those represented by the Native Council of Canada for two reasons. First, in the prairies, when treaties were being made in the late 19th century, certain communities chose to enter into treaties and others chose script that was, supposedly, intended to be used for the purchase of land in fee simple, i.e., they would hold their land in the same manner as settlers. Generally speaking, this was the distinction between those represented by the National Indian Brotherhood and those represented by the Native Council in the 1970s.

Secondly, many Indian leaders, in the 1970s, held that certain ministers of the government preferred the term "Native" because it was consonant with the government's desire to avoid dealing with promises, obligations and relationships set out in the treaties. Lastly, I have chosen to refer to the two major groups of actors in the proceedings that I review as "parliamentarians" and "First Nations leaders" or, in the earlier periods as "Indian leaders." These terms appeared to be the most neutral terms by which to describe these two groups of people according to their roles that would be readily understood.

REFERENCES AND CITATIONS

In citing Parliamentary committee proceedings, I have followed a citation style that is common throughout Parliamentary committee reports. Page numbers are commonly prefaced by the issue number, i.e., the issue of the *Proceedings*. Daniels' statement, for example, may be found at *MacGuigan-Lamontagne* at 5:40. (An "issue" typically, but not always, represents the proceedings of a single day.) *Proceedings* of committees whose mandate runs over more than one session are commonly cited by the session number plus the issue number plus the page number, e.g., John Turner's testimony at the outset of the *MacGuigan-Molgat Proceedings* occurs at 2:1:26.

Mark MacGuigan was the Commons co-chairman of two joint committees on the Constitution. Maurice Lamontagne was the Senate co-chairman of both committees at their inceptions. He resigned his chairmanship of the first committee and that position was taken up by Senator Gildas Molgat. To resolve the confusion that I myself experienced,

I have designated the earlier of these two Joint Committees on the Constitution as "*MacGuigan-Molgat*" and the second as "*MacGuigan-Lamontagne 30,*" i.e., because Maurice Lamontagne co-chaired the first of these committees for a very brief period at the beginning of its work, I have added the number of the Parliament in which the second of these committees did its work to the names of the presiding officers.

I have put these names in italics because the reference is to the *Proceedings*. For example, *MacGuigan-Molgat* is the short form I use for the Joint Committee on the Constitution of 1970–1972. Lastly, I have used the term "*Proceedings* " because it is the term by which the publication is described on the cover. The term *Hansard* occurs, in small type, under the main title of the *Debates* of both Chambers, i.e., the *House of Commons Debates* and *The Debates of the Senate.*

References to *House of Commons Debates* and *Debates of the Senate* from the 36th Parliament onward rely on the text posted to the Parliamentary web site, "www.parl.gc.ca." Although these texts do not have page numbers, they do have the time stamps which occur every five minutes throughout each sitting. Since these time references also occur in the paper versions of *Hansard* and represent approximately two pages of double column text in the paper copy, I consider this the most specific reference available through the two media.

In the analytical discussions at the conclusion of each of the narrative chapters and particularly in Chapter Seven, the major analysis, reference to quotations from the proceedings are to the places where the quotations may be found in the narrative chapters.

ETHICS AND REFERENCES

There is one ethical question which needs to be highlighted at this point: There are two statements from offhand observations, though not strictly off-the-record, remarks made during interviews.

One instance was a statement George Manuel made while we were collaborating on his biography. I believe that positions George took later in his political career combined with his passing allow me to refer to his comment without breaching a confidentiality. The second instance was a reflection of Senator George Isaac (Ike) Smith, a Conservative Senator and former Premier of Nova Scotia, when he was chairman of the Senate Committee on National Transportation, about the practices of the Nova Scotia cabinet while he was premier. The passage of time, Senator G. Isaac Smith's own passing, in 1982, and the corroboration of the practice he described by former ministers in a variety of other governments allow that this statement–which was not made in confidence at the time–might be recorded here.

Any other conversations to which I make reference are interviews conducted for my master's thesis. The tapes and notes remain in my files.

METHODS FOR "THE INTERPLAY OF LANGUAGE, POLICY & THE DISCOURSE OF PREVARICATION"

Methodologically, I began my work on the analytical and theoretical discussions with the question, "How do I understand these *Proceedings*?" This is admittedly a largely subjective question. I brought to this question a certain amount of experience both in reading parliamentary papers and in writing about the history of First Nations relations. I first began reading parliamentary debates and committee proceedings in 1960, the last year I was in high school. My longstanding interest in parliamentary papers focused on discussions of "Indian Affairs" when I began to work with *Akwesasne Notes*, in 1970. In 1976, I began to develop a Parliamentary Liaison Programme for the National Indian Brotherhood and continued in that programme through the metamorphosis of the N.I.B. into the Assembly of First Nations (A.F.N.) until 1982. I continued to do parliamentary relations for various regional First Nations organizations until 1985.

In 1998, the year in which I did most of the research on policy discourse for this project, very little of the existing work addressed the history of the discourse on First Nations relations. Some very helpful work had been done on discourse within various First Nations, particularly the work of Keith Basso[39] and Julie Cruikshank. Basso is at his most interesting in his studies of how Apache speech puts together various ideas including ideas with strong political overtones. Cruikshank looks at the relationship of Athapascan people, particularly a group of women informants, with various *places* with which their stories are indelibly linked. Nobody had looked at either formal speeches or discussion in a formal setting in which First Nations leaders addressed influential non-indigenous audiences.

A number of distinguished theorists of policy discourse are deeply concerned with democratic principles. They focus, quite reasonably, on issues or arenas in which the persons at whom a policy might be primarily directed are also a part, albeit often a marginalized part of the electorate. I was interested, however, in a situation in which policy, developed primarily for influential stakeholders, acts on people and communities who have been excluded from the political process and, in some instances, prohibited from normal means of participation.

Although I was interested in policy discourse in general, I had (and continue to have) an abiding interest in the evolution of a particular discourse, viz., the discourse of First Nations self-government. A policy discourse on First Nations relations, in its mature state, may not be a policy discourse, in the ordinary sense of that phrase, so much as it will be a meta-policy of affirmation and recognition, coupled with *a no-policy*, i.e., *a federal policy of not making decisions on behalf of first nations.* Almost any federal policy, which goes much beyond that is likely to be inconsistent with the very idea of self-government. The exceptions are those areas which are, like some land management matters, either under joint management or, following various Supreme Court decisions, subject to a Crown duty to consult and a corollary duty to disclose.[40]

The historical narrative which follows is not a study of a policy discourse so much as it is a history of one early decade in the history of an idea that, by its nature, is not so much a policy as a a meta-policy. This narrative focuses neither on the day-to-day policies of the Department of Indian Affairs and Northern Development (DIAND)[41] nor on the discussions of those policies in Parliament, but on the fundamental, underlying attitudes expressed in political terms that shaped and largely determined those policies.

A series of legal, ethical and epistemological terms are introduced throughout my discussion of language, policy and ethics in Chapter I. These are then applied in the conclusions to the historical narratives in Chapters Three, Four, Five and Six and, again, in Chapter Seven, the concluding analysis.

Legal concepts, such as *the burden of persuasion* and *the burden of proof* are important to the study of the discourse of First Nations relations because they represent norms that are widely accepted throughout formal discourses of all kinds but which have their origins and their most rigorous examinations in the courts.

A Jewish adage has led me to view ethics as a body of thought directed at "doing more than the law requires," i.e., achieving a systematic body of thought at a higher standard than is legally required. So far as the study of the historical record of the Discourse of First Nations relations relates both to other parliamentary discourses and to the possibility of "forging new relationships,"[42] the discussion of ethics was fundamental.

My primary sources for definitions of legal terms has been the usage of the Supreme Court of Canada and the appeal courts together with two major legal dictionaries: *Black's Law Dictionary* and *The Oxford Companion to Law.* [43] For definitions of ethical and religious terms, wherever possible, I have drawn on standard English language reference works, particularly the *Oxford Companions to Philosophy, Law, World Religions, the Bible and Politics* together with other major reference works including *The Princeton Encyclopedia of Poetry and Poetics*, *The Oxford English Dictionary*, *The Encarta Dictionary* and *The Encyclopedia of Philosophy*. On a very few occasions, in dealing with Jewish sources which are not discussed in standard English reference works, I have gone to English language Jewish reference works. Almost all of these are scholarly paperback publications. On a very few fundamental questions, I went behind these secondary sources to the original Talmudic and classical Greek references in translation.

On matters of usage and style I have generally followed the *Oxford Guide to Canadian English Usage*, a work that is familiar both with scholarly usage and with parliamentary, legal and public service usages.

I have included a Glossary which focuses on terms that are particular to the discourse of First Nations relations in Canada or to Canadian politics and Canadian political institutions. The Glossary begins on pagae 267.

Chapter One

The Interplay of Language, Policy and Ethics in the Discourse of First Nations' Relations

> The words "treaty" and "nation" are words of our own language, selected in our own diplomatic and legislative proceedings, by ourselves, having each a definite and well understood meaning. We have applied them to Indians, as we have applied them to other nations of the earth. They are applied to all in the same sense.
>
> Chief Justice John Marshall,
> United States Supreme Court,
> *Worcester v. Georgia*

HOW AND WHY FIRST NATIONS RELATIONS ARE UNLIKE ANY OTHER ARENA OF PUBLIC POLICY

Several factors make the dynamics of this policy arena different from the interplay of ethics, language and policy development in other policy arenas. First, Aboriginal rights are, as Dickson C.J.C. observed in *Guérin*, *sui generis*,[1] i.e., they constitute "their own kind or class" and are "unique."[2] The contestation of the meaning, nature and reality of these unique rights has been a major theme running throughout the history of First Nations relations[3] and forms the major part of the discourse for which an analytical framework is wanted here. Secondly, there is, to my knowledge, no other field in which senior officials have testified before parliamentary committees that it is the objective of government policy to end the presence of an ethnic group or nationality in Canada.[4]

Thirdly, the discourse has been radically shaped by the division of powers in the Canadian constitution which provides that "Indians and lands reserved for the Indians"[5] are exclusively federal jurisdictions. This point is particularly significant in an examination of federal parliamentary committee proceedings. Most of the matters discussed in the Indian Affairs Committee are matters which, in respect of non-Indian persons and communities in Canada, would be matters of exclusively provincial jurisdiction: health, education, infrastructure, community development, band councils and their powers under the federal *Indian Act*. Legal scholars outside the federal government seem widely agreed that "Indians" and "lands reserved for the Indians" are two distinct powers, both federal. As recent as 2005, however, Indian Affairs officials told a Senate Committee, in hearings on a bill to establish a procedure for recognition of First Nations self-government on Aboriginal Peoples that "education off-reserve" would fall under provincial jurisdiction.[6]

This is more than a jurisdictional difference. Whatever democratic deficit may be apparent in historic or contemporary provincial governments, the people whose health, education and municipal institutions are subject to the jurisdiction of that legislature are the same people who elect that legislature.[7] There is a common cultural ground between governed and governors.

The terms of political discourse are largely shared by legislators, journalists and academics. Senior officials, the most frequent witnesses before parliamentary committees, must have some expectation that their vocabulary will be understandable to their major clients, other stakeholders and even to the members of parliamentary committees. In contrast, new members on the Commons Indian Affairs Committee, in the period under examination, were typically unfamiliar with both the geography of "Indian country" and the terms of Indian political discourse. Yet, it was these same new MPs who often cast deciding votes to sustain government spending priorities and to ignore the criticisms offered of First Nations political leaders.

Fourthly, the public discussion of "First Nations relations" in Canada has, in reality, been a discussion of *federal* Indian policy. Historically, and especially prior to the period about which I am writing, there had been little or no consideration of the perspectives of First Nations leaders. On the contrary, for large parts of the history of this discourse, federal statutes have prescribed severe punishments for certain types of expressions by First Nations viewpoints, including the potlatch prohibitions, the pass laws, and the 1927 prohibition against the raising of funds for the purpose of pressing land claims.

When large parts of political discourse by First Nations citizens have been subject to criminal sanctions, the terms of *identity politics*,[8] as they have been conceived in other contexts do not constitute a satisfactory analytical framework for First Nations relations, although they remain useful background to which reference may be made. Indeed, in Chapter Two, "An Overview of First Nations Relations before 1970," I will argue that this history has been characterized by three interwoven themes: (1) assimilation and termination; (2) civil disabilities; and, (3) language inversion.

Lastly, a discourse of autonomy might well be said *not* to be *a policy discourse* if policy is understood to mean what the federal government *does* rather than what it *says*. Conversely, the corollary of the federal insistence on making policy is a refusal to allow First Nations to exercise their autonomy. The most substantial components of a discourse of autonomy are about the development of institutions of self-government, developments which preclude the further articulation of policy on the part of the federal or provincial governments and the failures of federal policies in specific areas which are, according to opinions reviewed in this study, calculated, in part, to undermine the development of First Nations institutions.

Imposition of federal policies without consultation, or contrary to the advice received in consultations, even when not illegal[9] has been characterized, both by First Nations leaders and by the courts, as violating Aboriginal and treaty rights. One form of federal imposition, which has elicited particularly vehement First Nations opposition, is the transfer of various aspects of Indian policy to provinces. The administrative transfer of federal powers to provincial governments necessarily runs counter to any constructive pursuit of First Nations' autonomy.[10]

The full development of self-government, as envisaged in *The Report* of the *Special Committee* on *Indian First Nations Self-Government (Penner* 1983),[11] *The Report of the Royal Commission on Aboriginal Peoples* (*RCAP*)[12] (1996) and in *Forging New Relationships*, a 2000 report of the Senate Committee on Aboriginal Peoples, would represent a federal **no-policy** in respect to any particular field of jurisdiction, i.e., the federal role would consist, not of making and administering policy but of refraining from developing policy beyond protecting a First Nation's occupation of a group of legislative fields.[13]

In a very real sense, this is not a study of a policy discourse but a study of *a metapolicy discourse* centred on *the recognition of First Nations' autonomy*, the development of the institutions of First Nations' government, and the fiduciary obligation of the federal government to protect those institutions.

In this section I will briefly touch on the works of William Connolly (*Identity/Difference)*, Coleman and Skogstad (*Policy Communities and*

Public Policy in Canada), Deborah Cameron (*Researching Language*) and David Bell (*Power, Influence and Authority*) as well as a number of encyclopedic references regarding discourse and concepts related to discourse. My purpose is not to provide a comprehensive review of these materials but to indicate that, although they have been helpful, there is a need to look beyond them if the discourse of First Nations' autonomy is to be better understood.

ETHICS, POLICY AND LANGUAGE

The most fundamental relationship between ethics and policy arises from the idea that politics is basically about power relationships. *Policy is an attitude manifested*, through both words and by direction actions, *by those with some claim to having power* to effectively influence the direction in which decisions of a given agency proceed. The term "attitude," as the dictionary indicates, includes both mental attitudes, "a way of thinking," and physical attitudes both of persons and of vessels in relation to the horizon.[14] The integration of mental and physical states is what makes the term peculiarly appropriate to describe policy. A minister's statement may reflect an objective, to which he aspires; however, if the machinery[15] of the department is not engaged in accomplishing that objective, the statement might better be described as a "policy goal" rather than an existing policy or even a policy objective.

The perception of *policy as an attitude manifested in the actions of a department or agency* has three advantages for the discussion of a metapolicy such as First Nations relations. First, it distinguishes between *what is said* and *what is done*. The history of federal Indian policy is rife with examples that demonstrate that the mere publication of a *policy statement* does not establish policy. Secondly, it is a definition that keeps one eye on *departmental practices* while keeping the other on *overall direction*. What actual steps toward the winding down or restructuring of the Indian Affairs Branch were initiated by the introduction of the 1969 *White Paper*, a document actually entitled *Statement of Indian Policy*? What actual changes resulted from the supposed 1971 withdrawal of the *White Paper*? Or, from the 1973 statement of the then Minister of Indian Affairs, Jean Chrétien, that the NIB position paper, *Indian Control of Indian Education* would become departmental policy? In none of these cases is it evident that the mere uttering of a policy statement established a policy direction. Thirdly, when several departments have a role in a given policy arena there is little historical evidence to support an expectation that all departments will follow the same policy. C.S.I.S. and the

R.C.M.P. do not have consistently uniform policies. Legislative chambers, line departments and central agencies frequently disagree quite openly.

The claim to make policy supposes the power to significantly influence the course and direction of policy. Removing criminal sanctions against Indians' attempt to influence federal Indian policy did not mean that Indians actually acquired influence. Persons, such as the heads of client industries of Indian Affairs and Northern Development are likely to wield much more influence.

For purposes of federal Indian policy, I would regard the **policy network** as *the persons with power, authority or influence to affect the course of actual federal policy.* Whether First Nations leaders are possessed of such influence is a much debated question, the exploration of which leads one into the contests over such terms as "consultation" and "partnership." It is not self-evident that the opportunity to submit briefs to public and parliamentary inquiries or attend "consultations" with middle ranking civil servants constitutes a palpable influence on the actual course of policy.

People, including the greater part of First Nations communities whose lives are largely governed by such policy making, do not have power and are effectively outside the policy community. "Policy communities are institutions in themselves and become integrated to greater or lesser degrees by developing a set of shared values, norms and beliefs which shape . . . the policy outcomes in the given sector."[16]

This asymmetrical power relationship creates ethical obligations on, or at least raises ethical questions about those with a policy capacity for which there is not a reciprocal set of questions for those without power.

BUREAUCRATIC PRAGMATISM AND A LACK OF ETHICAL CONCERN

In *Identity/Difference*, William E. Connolly, says, in regard to the question, "Why be ethical?"

> Not *why* be ethical, then, for if someone really . . . poses that as the question to be answered first, he or she is probably beyond the effective reach of ethical concern.[17]

The significance of Connolly's observation that those who do not understand the need for ethics are probably beyond the reach of ethical concern has particular significance for First Nations relations in contemporary as well as historical terms. The history of First Nations relations is a long and complicated narrative in which those in positions of power, influence or authority were exempted from ethical concerns.[18] This lack of ethical concern is exemplified in numerous memoranda and voluminous correspondence amongst public servants in both the Department of Indian Affairs and the central agencies to which those officials are allied. Senior officials, in recent years, have characterized such concerns as "purist" and "naive" while elevating their own posture by the term "pragmatic."[19]

The range of examples of those who may be "beyond the effective reach of ethical concern" while participating in some aspect of First Nations relations, even today, appears quite endless. A school system which achieved a mortality rate approaching 50% through neglect and malnutrition might well be thought to be "beyond the reach of ethical concern."[20] In 2001, the Anglican Church of Canada and other Christian churches asked the government to limit their liability for damages suffered by children under their care.[21] Any such limitation imposed by the legislature would be tantamount to imposing a civil disability[22] since it would bar Indians from access to the courts and limit their right of petition.[23] This is a curious companion piece to the recent apologies from the same churches. The apparent support for their lobby in all corners of both Houses assures us that such logic chopping is not limited either to the clerical professions or to the professionally religious.

> These beliefs about how life should be lived, what men and women should be and do, are objects of moral inquiry; and when applied to groups and nations, and, indeed, mankind as a whole, are called *political philosophy*, which *is but ethics applied to society.* [24]

If we accept Isaiah Berlin's view that "political philosophy is but ethics applied to society," then there is, indeed, no other place to begin a theory of discourse relevant to First Nations' relations than to address the question of "why be ethical?" Far from such an approach being merely academic, it is quite consistent with methods used in program evaluations and policy reviews both of which attend closely to a set of objectives which were stated at the outset of the program in question. An evaluation measures whether or not the program fulfilled originally *stated* the objectives. A policy review considers whether or not the objectives ought to be revised or renewed *in a mandate* for the upcoming period. Neither program evaluations nor policy reviews can happen without a discussion of "how life should be lived," at least in reference to the program and objectives in question. Every such exercise is, in effect, an in-house exercise in "ethics applied to society."

Every such exercise must also begin with reference to *a written authority* and conclude with the production of a *new text.*

The analysis of the relationship of language, policy and ethics in the particular context of First Nations relations in this chapter is founded on a three-fold premise:

1. Language plays a major role in the shaping of policy and particularly of meta-policy;
2. The elements of language, policy and ethics interact differently in the field of First Nations relations than they might either in a conventional domestic policy field or in foreign relations; and,
3. Ethics is the crux of the interplay between language and policy.

Language and ethics are always intertwined, the more so in politics where a great deal of power is exercised through *speech acts*. The first ethical questions to be asked in most political discourses are (1) Are the characterizations of both situations and the persons accurate and fair; (2) Is there an analysis built upon this fair description and, if so, is it a rational, i.e., a logical analysis; and, (3) Do the assessments of the severity of the problems and the prospects for relief appear both realistic and consistent with previous experience? Each of these sets of questions falls within what we broadly mean by truth, i.e., do we consider that the persons leading this discourse (typically ministers or senior officials) are telling the truth so far as it can be known?

Implicit in all these questions is a procedural question which can best be understood in terms borrowed from the courtroom, "Has the person advocating a policy position discharged both the burden of proof regarding the *facts* and the burden of persuasion in his (or her) analysis?" These questions are much harder to answer in regard to First Nations relations than in regard to local road networks in one's own neighbourhood. In 1980, when the Opposition critic charged that there was an outbreak of dysentery among children in the Cree communities of James Bay, a relatively remote area of the country, urban citizens had no empirical way of evaluating either the critic's charge or the minister's denial. The news media were not yet ready to travel to a remote part of the country to do their own independent coverage.

Whether the burdens of proof and persuasion have been met is a further test of "truth." Even if an account seemed plausible, were there no evidence offered, or if the analysis was entirely intuitive and without reason we should consider this view to be entirely personal, i.e., it would be more suitable for choosing ice cream flavours than for establishing public policies applicable through a public agency upon an entire citizenry.

I have found that in a highly contested arena of federal policy such as First Nations the ethical dimension of this discourse might be better understood by the introduction of three concepts: (1) *burdens of persuasion,* (2) *licensing* and, (3) *the discourse of prevarication.* If you trust me and find my three propositions about the relationship of language, policy and ethics to be plausible then I would ask you also to trust that our reading of the history which is the main concern of this work will benefit from learning about these three concepts.

This chapter will largely be devoted to these three concepts and their application to public policy and, more specifically, to First Nations relations. The concept of *burdens of proof and burdens of persuasion* is, to my mind, the most fundamental of these notions.

BURDENS OF PERSUASION IN FIRST NATIONS RELATIONS

There are three parts to this discussion: (1) the definition of **the burden of persuasion** contrasted with the **burden of proof**; (2) **the significance of the concept of burden** to academic discourse and to parliamentary discourse; and, (3) the uses of **burden shifting.** [25]

The burden of persuasion is a vital key in the use of language as an attitudinal indicator in policy discourse. This concept, that is so central to the common law, is also a primary indicator of ethical proceedings in discussions of public policy both academically and legislatively. Burden shifting—the effort to shift a burden that properly falls onto the party making a motion onto an opposing party—is often one of the earliest and most certain indicators that the quality of discussion may be falling below an ethical Plimsoll line.[26]

The common practice of using the term "burden of proof" to cover two different burdens that arise both in legal discourse and in other formal discourses has been a source of some confusion. The definitions that I am about to set out are intended to clarify the use to which the terms "burden of proof" and "burden of persuasion" will be put here. I follow the definitions set out in the *United States Federal Rules of Evidence*, a source that was both reliable for this purpose and accessible.

Conventionally, two burdens are placed on a plaintiff: first, **the burden of proof**; and subsequently, **the burden of persuasion.** The **burden of proof,** sometimes called "the burden of going forward"[27] refers to **the obligation to present factual evidence in support of the plaintiff's claim. The burden of persuasion** is a broader concept and refers to **the obligation of the plaintiff**

to persuade the court of its view of the facts. The burden of persuasion has also been referred to as **the risk of non-persuasion.**[28]

The burden of going forward (a term we might adopt simply to avoid the term "burden of proof" for the moment) begins with the plaintiff. This burden quite properly shifts to the respondent following the plaintiff's (or proponent's) presentation offering the respondent a corresponding burden of "establishing the non-existence of the presumed fact." *The risk of non-persuasion*, i.e., the burden of persuasion, however, remains "throughout the trial upon the party on whom it was originally cast,"[29] i.e., the plaintiff.[30] What this means is that each side has an opportunity (and an obligation) to present evidence but *the onus of persuading the court of the legal significance of the evidence* remains with the plaintiff/proponent."

Running throughout the history of First Nations relations is a tendency, on the part of successive governments and parliaments and, often, on the part of the courts, to place the burden of proof on First Nations in regard to land claims, in regard to a right and capacity to govern themselves, indeed, even in proving their humanity and their historic existence as nations. In considering the relationship of language, ethics and policy in First Nations relations, this tendency to **burden shifting** is one of the most common and most conspicuous features.

Although the term "burden of proof" has been widely adopted both in popular and in non-legal academic discourse, when this term is seen in its narrower sense of *the production of evidence,* the counterpart in other academic disciplines includes the documenting and presentation of research.

Even the most recent proposal for a land claims commission[31] maintains the unwillingness of Parliament to recognize that various First Nations historically had certain boundaries within which their claim to land could be taken as a given. Current federal policy continues to put the burden of proof of historic ownership upon a First Nation plaintiff.

The burden of persuasion as the duty to persuade a court of *the significance of the facts* in light of an established set of rules has a much broader counterpart in other academic disciplines. The burden of persuasion encompasses *the questions of the value and meaning to be attributed to the factual research presented.* It is, for instance, common in social science discourse to observe that *facts are theory laden.* Facts become theory laden when we choose those facts which, singly or collectively, serve to demonstrate a claim based on an accepted standard, norm, ethic, rule or law.

One of the corresponding issues that I will examine is the extent to which parliamentarians, in the various committees under examination, are responsive either to the evidence or to the arguments as to its significance both in their individual replies in committee proceedings and in the final reports of their committees. The earliest Canadian Indian legislation, *An Act for the Gradual Civilization of the Indians, 1857,*[32] asserted the incompetence of Indians in its very title. Among other provisions, the *Act* set out the means by which exceptional Indians might demonstrate their competence. To what extent do the parliamentarians of the 1970s, the period under examination here, succeed in working their way past the cultural attitudes inherited from their predecessors?

The discharging of the burden of persuasion, and so far as it applies, the burden of proof, is at the very core of every rational procedure. Both the burden of persuasion and the burden of proof are properly placed, at the outset, on the party who brings a motion or an application. The burden of proof, i.e., the burden of going forward with evidence, later shifts to the respondent. *The burden of persuasion,* on the contrary, *does not normally shift.* As the alternative descriptor, *the risk of non-persuasion* suggests, respondents do not have an obligation to persuade the court of an alternative view beyond discrediting the motion.

Improper burden shifting is a form of prevarication,[33] a term I will develop later to describe the *deceptive rhetoric* characterizing the dark side of federal Indian policy. By improper burden shifting I mean *any move* by a party on whom a burden properly falls *to place that burden onto another party.* How burden shifting is accomplished and the ends to which it is attempted are the primary concern of this discussion of burdens of persuasion in First Nations relations.

JUDICIAL PROCEDURE AS A MODEL OF PRACTICAL REASONING

Without glossing over the essential difference between judicial proceedings and public inquiries,[34] it is apparent that they share a common ground in the duty to establish and to follow a coherent, communicable and rational procedure with specific roles assigned to key players and a sharp focus on a defined question. Although some inquiries in recent years have reduced the level of formality in their proceedings, the tendency to follow a procedure, which has been deeply influenced by common law culture, remains readily apparent.[35] Richard Gaskins, in *Burdens of Proof,*[36] sees judicial procedure as a model of practical reasoning.

Gaskins, however, argues that dubious burden shifting, i.e., shifting the burden of persuasion[37] from where one might normally expect to find it, is a strategic move which first achieved contemporary prominence in legal argumentation but has since become a major feature of critical theory in all academic disciplines. After an examination of a series of American legal cases, Gaskins considers the tendency to burden shifting in philosophy and science. In American legal history, Gaskins says, the earliest recent effort at burden shifting arose out of benign and progressive motives in the fight against racial segregation on the part of plaintiffs in *Brown v. Board of Education*[38] but was, after 1969 in the Burger Court, adopted as an effective strategy by conservative forces.[39] Gaskins argues that this co-option for conservative purposes of a strategy introduced by progressive elements runs through the contemporary history of burden shifting.

In a scientific context, inappropriate burden shifting has been seen, historically, to constitute *poor science*. Gaskins, however, argues that burden shifting has in recent decades become a significant issue in both science and philosophy.[40]

Gaskins follows Kant[41] and several of his successors in looking to legal argument as a rhetorical model to be applied in other fields. The difference which he claims for himself is that although Kant and others have treated law rather metaphorically for their philosophical purposes, Gaskins pursues the analogy between law and other disciplines based on practical reason in some depth. He begins with an examination of reasoning in a series of ground-breaking U.S. Supreme Court decisions and an examination of the work of legal philosophers including Dworkin and Rawls.

An examination of both the *bona fides* and the strategic *argument-from-ignorance* will prove helpful in an analysis of the parliamentary discourse of First Nations relations. The question to which we will need to return is whether, if indeed burden shifting is a characteristic of that discourse in the instances at hand, the burden shifting arises from appeals to higher authority or is it a mere rhetorical sleight of hand executed with the acquiescence of an audience? If the burden shifting relies on a higher authority, we also need to ask whether that authority is one on which the discussant community is generally prepared to rely.

The strategy of burden shifting by a proponent is commonly accomplished through *an argument from ignorance*. Indeed, these may be two names for the same phenomenon viewed from a different perspective. Gaskins describes ***an argument-from-ignorance*** as:

> an affirmative inference from the lack of knowledge . . . [I]t requires some kind of decision rule (usually unstated) about how the parties to a discussion should proceed in the face of uncertainty or indeterminacy.[42]

The Oxford Companion to Philosophy[43] defines ***argumentum ad ignorantiam*** as "the argument that because a particular proposition has *not* been proved true (false), we may conclude that it is [the opposite, i.e., false or true]." *Black's Law Dictionary* defines *argumentum ad ignorantiam* [44]as "an argument based on an adversary's ignorance of the matter in dispute."

Taking note of **the argument from ignorance** in a brief review of burden shifting allows us to observe that *burden shifting is accomplished through a device that has long been recognized as a fallacy.*

Much academic discussion of methodology draws analogies with legal discourse. If judicial procedure is, indeed, a model of practical reasoning, then we will do well to follow Gaskins in a more careful consideration of the parallels that have been attempted in references to figurative courts in philosophic literature (and in academic examinations) from Kant to the present.

Gaskins' great strength is two-fold. First, in his demonstration of the importance of observing—both in litigation and in any major question of policy, philosophy or social science—who has the primary burden of making out a particular part of a case and whether the decision making rules are clear or opaque or unstated. Secondly, in arguing that the customary burdens of persuasion have come to be increasingly subject to *burden shifting* both in litigation and in academia.

Burden shifting in academic discourse, Gaskins argues, is not different from the kind of *argumentum ad ignorantiam* made in a variety of legal cases. Gaskins states that the essential argument in *Brown v. Board of Education*, in the United States Supreme Court bypassed psychological evidence from one of the trial decisions on appeal and rested on the fundamental principle that "Separate can not be equal."[45] Another lofty principle, proclaimed by Anna Freud and others, has become standard in child custody litigation: "the best interests of the child." Gaskins reviews family law literature to suggest that this argument was cultivated in the 1970s by Joseph Goldstein, Anna Freud, and Albert Slant whose definitions were largely adopted by the U.S. courts. However,

> Goldstein reduced the abstraction of best interests to a temporal 'community of care,' an inertial concept that says children are best off staying with those adult(s) with whom they have already formed a psychological bond.
>
> . . .
>
> Goldstein's approach thus supplied a missing ingredient in the Supreme Court's due process jurisprudence: an affirmative reason, in the form of an ostensible scientific theory, for shifting the burden of proof.

This example suggests that some significant part of judicial burden shifting begins as burden shifting within an academic discipline, e.g., psychology.

Acceptance of these arguments by the courts, presumably, has the incidental effect of reinforcing them by raising their status within the academic community.

The fundamental question raised by Gaskins' work is whether the burden shifting which has become commonplace as a result of critical studies is appropriate or whether it has the effect of turning the traditional discourse of a discipline on its ear.

BURDEN SHIFTING AND THE RHETORIC OF COLONIALISM

Examining the allocation of burdens in the rhetoric of colonialism in general and "Canadian Indian policy," in particular, allows us to inquire whether these are reasoned discourses. A discussion of burden shifting will illuminate the workings of the discourse of prevarication. Burden shifting is, I suggest, crucial to stereotyping statements and to statements which draw upon **unfounded accounts** of acts, events and happenings to negate or to deny the civility of entire peoples or to denigrate or disparage their culture, in effect denying that there is a culture.

The burden of persuasion is particularly significant to First Nations relations because much Indian policy has historically been made through one or another rhetorical sleight which placed the burden of persuasion on a First Nation or upon individual First Nations persons. *Much of what I will describe as "the discourse of prevarication" is accomplished largely through burden shifting.* Indeed, the success of prevarication depends upon burden shifting.

I have long been fascinated with the variety of prevaricating strategies—statements calculated to deceive—that run throughout the discourse on federal Indian policy. In Chapter Two, the particular **modes of prevarication** will be highlighted.

In the narrative chapters I will consider the role played by burden shifting in each of the various rhetorical sleights that will be identified in the analysis. I will also consider the ideas of *good faith*, of *genuine dialogue* and of *licensing*, each of which is explained in later parts of this chapter.

The most extreme version of burden shifting as a bald assertion of a claim for which there is no supporting evidence is "The Great Lie Theory" expounded in *Mein Kampf*.[46] Although the comparison of Hitler's outrageous notions to metapolicy discourse in our own democratic societies may be unpalatable, if we follow the kind of burden shifting found in official discourse on Indian policy to its extreme we will find ourselves not very distant from Hitler's "Great Lie Theory."

Further, the Great Lie Theory did not originate with Adolph Hitler.[47] Although the uses to which Hitler put his lies were, possibly, more gross in sheer numbers, the illogic on which his strategic theory is founded runs throughout the rhetoric of colonization. The strategy consists of this: the leader or his agent makes a sufficiently outrageous statement characterizing those people against whom he wants to foment hatred that *neither justification nor evidence is sought by his immediate audience.*

For the Great Lie to succeed, it must go unchallenged not only at the time that a speech is made at a great public gathering or in Parliament but in the ostensibly serious media in the days that follow and, indeed, even by scholars. *Statements of vilification, in particular, cannot succeed unless the audience acquiesces.* Acquiescence cannot happen unless the audiences, those to whom the strongest statements of vilification are addressed, suspend their prior knowledge of those being vilified. This is most evident when crowds are aroused by provocative oratory to wreak havoc on neighbours or on adjacent communities with whom they have long made accommodation. 17th and 18th century missionaries and government officials appear to have been far more knowledgeable about neighbouring First Nations than their successors a century later. Arguments in favour of civil disabilities are always easier to purvey when local leadership is less knowledgeable. It also appears, however, that people can, and often do, become less knowledgeable *as a matter of convenience.*

When a state imposes civil disabilities on minority communities[48] without arousing their neighbours to resistance, that state has gained the acquiescence of the dominant (domineering) communities.

An examination of acquiescence by parliamentarians in the statements of ministers and officials is a continuing theme in the chapters chronicling the public emergence of the vocabulary of First Nations' self-government.

THE TEST OF THE REASONABLE PARLIAMENTARIAN

Typically, the burden of persuasion in a policy context falls into three broad categories: (1) that a proposal addresses a significant problem; (2) that the policy proposed is likely to provide the desired benefits; and (3) as a further proof that the *stated* policy is the policy being implemented. If policy is a behavioural attitude construed from the cumulative effect of statutes, regulations, ministerial statements, guidelines and methods of enforcement, one might ask just what the policy actually is at any given moment and then consider its relationship, if any, to legal obligations of the minister or to ministerial statements as to policy.[49]

The test I want to apply to the discourse of First Nations' autonomy, and particularly to statements of ministers and senior officials before parliamentary committees is whether it meets a burden of persuasion. Specifically, the following questions might be asked:

1. Does the minister or senior official (or other witnesses before such a committee) address a significant problem?
2. Does the (ministerial or official) witness offer reasons and cite evidence?
3. Are the standards of logic or the quality of the evidence of a different order than would normally be offered from other ministries or witnesses before other parliamentary committees?
4. Are the apparent meanings of words different than the meaning that those words enjoy in normal usage, in parliamentary usage or in legal usage?
5. Are the answers given by the witness actually responsive to the questions asked?
6. Are the witnesses' remarks addressed (through the committee) only to a narrow constituency that does not include the people spoken about?

If we are to apply a burden of persuasion test to the testimony before parliamentary committees, there needs to be a reciprocal set of questions with reference to the questions and remarks of parliamentarians:

1. Are the questions or remarks raised by parliamentarians responsive to the testimony offered?
2. Are the questions or remarks directed at eliciting further details, verifying information, or seeking to clarify doubts or do they appear to serve a purpose extrinsic to the testimony?
3. Does the parliamentarian have command of the vocabulary commonly associated with the topic?
4. Does the parliamentarian retain a command of the name of the witness and the organization that the witness represents?

If we were to conceive of a reasonable parliamentarian we must imagine that he or she is subject to the same basic rules as to the allocation of burdens of proof and burdens of persuasion as one would expect in any other forum:

1. The burden of "going forward" with evidence, or the burden of proof, is incumbent upon the party who brings a motion.
2. This burden shifts to the respondent, opponent or critic.
3. The burden of persuasion, the obligation to lend weight, significance, value or interpretation to the evidence stays with the mover or applicant throughout and does not shift.
4. Persons bringing amendments or sub-amendments, however, take on a burden of persuasion in respect to their own motion.

Arguments for the development of new policy instruments, as far as they are rational, are also an attempt to show that certain past or ongoing events resonate with the proposed policies. A well reasoned policy discussion must address three points: (1) that the proposals address problematic historical events; (2) that the expressly desired outcome is likely to be achieved; and, (3) that the objectives on which the proposals are based are not adequately addressed in existing law or other policy instruments. In contrast, *policy proposals that rely on rhetorical sleights are typically those that cannot be sustained in a reasoned discourse.* Surveys of cabinet minutes and administrative memoranda suggest that regulations and statutory instruments that are adopted without public scrutiny have very often received no reasoned discussion in cabinet.[50]

One example of burden shifting in provincial law is found in sections 12–14 of the British Columbia *Evidence Act, 1960*[51] regarding testimony given by Indians. These provisions are particularly instructive for several reasons. The *Evidence Act* is the statute governing the taking of evidence in any court dealing with a provincial matter including both provincial offenses and civil litigation.[52] Sections 12–14, as they appeared in the B.C. *Evidence Act* until 1977 provided as follows:

> **12.** In any proceeding over which the Legislature has jurisdiction, it is lawful for any Court . . . to receive the evidence of any aboriginal native, or native of mixed blood, of the continent of North America or the islands adjacent thereto, *being an uncivilized person, destitute of the knowledge of God and of any fixed and clear belief in religion or in a future state of rewards and punishments,* without administering the usual form of oath to such aboriginal native . . . upon his solemn affirmation to tell the truth . . .

> [Indian testimony, how taken] In the case of any proceeding in the nature of a preliminary inquiry, the substance of the evidence . . . of any such aboriginal native . . . shall be reduced to writing and signed . . . by his name or mark.
>
> 14. [Preliminary caution] The Court, Judge, Coroner . . . shall, before taking any such evidence . . . caution every such aboriginal native or native of mixed blood as aforesaid, that he will be liable to incur punishment if he does not as aforesaid tell the truth.

The civil disability imposed on Indians who testified under the B.C. *Evidence Act* when that procedural law deemed Indians to be (a) "destitute of the knowledge of God"[53] and (b) therefore needing instruction in the meaning of truth was likely to reduce the weight of evidence offered by Indian witnesses.

The offensive nature of this provision does not entirely depend upon the equation of a belief in God with a tendency toward truthfulness but on the presumption that *only a Christian knowledge of God* tends toward truthfulness. Wilson Duff, an anthropologist who had, before becoming provincial archivist of B.C., read all of Franz Boas' notes from the turn of the 20th century, held that the First Nations were "philosophically more advanced at first contact" than were Europeans.[54] Even a much more modest evaluation would recognize that a belief in some form of higher authority could be found in the culture of every First Nation in British Columbia. Only the objection that the traditional knowledge of a higher authority was not a Christian knowledge could justify the characterization of First Nations people following their own way as "destitute of the knowledge of God."[55]

A close reading of this text resonates both with the metaphysics of Indian hating, a term Richard Drinnon borrows from a chapter title in Herman Melville's *The Confidence Man*[56] for the sub-title of his book on American Indian policy, *Facing West: The Metaphysics of Indian Hating and Empire Building*.[57] The presumption that Indians are savages reaches its full depth when "native" is used over against "person."[58] The claim of the British-Israelites, in their testimony to the *MacGuigan-Molgat* Joint Committee on the Constitution[59] is the last gasp of a political theology that justified the British Empire by equating the royal family with the biblical line of David. Whether in its Anglican or Puritan forms, the rhetoric growing from this political theology runs throughout the discourse of First Nations' autonomy.

It is reasonable to read the B.C. *Evidence Act* within this tradition because this provision repeats what that tradition had held throughout the history of colonization. It may be imprecise to say that the provision was calculated to reduce the weight of evidence offered by Indian witnesses. It did, nonetheless, sanction a dynamic in which Indian witnesses began their appearances as witnesses by receiving an admonition about the importance of truth.

If there is a normal expectation a judge has a duty to extend to a witness the benefit of the doubt until the witness gives reason for him to do otherwise, then this provision reverses that norm. It requires that the witness be demeaned or that he demonstrate his humanity before offering other testimony. This provision placed on Indian witnesses an obligation to demonstrate their humanity.

So far the description of the proper allocation of burdens in a parliamentary context has been useful primarily to aid the interested observer to figure out what is really happening and "to follow the play" more thoroughly. At the very least, classifying statements and allocating burdens should help determine the shell under which the pea is most likely to be found from moment to moment. These elements also highlight the need for a procedure under which some acknowledgement of the proper burden allocation is reflected in the rules of every legislative chamber.

Brian Slattery, in "A Theory of the Charter"[60] argues that senior officials and legislators, in drafting legislation and regulations, have a duty to serve as the first lines of defense for Charter principles and, indeed, for constitutional principles generally. Senior officials and parliamentarians who honour Slattery's constitutional ethic effectively take upon themselves the burden of ensuring that their proposals comply with the Constitution in all respects, particularly in regard to the rule of law, the distribution of powers, *The Rights of the Aboriginal Peoples* and the *Charter of Rights and Freedoms*.

Parliamentary committee proceedings are, to my mind, the single most useful source for putting all parties to Slattery's test, i.e., of ascertaining whether or not senior officials, ministers and parliamentarians have fully considered whether or not a legislative or regulatory proposal is consistent with the *Charter of Rights* and with other constitutional principles. Committee proceedings are more worthwhile than *Hansard*–the *verbatim* record of debates in the Senate and the House of Commons–for a number of reasons: (1) senior officials testify and are subject to questioning by MPs and Senators; (2) ministers are more closely questioned in committee than in the House of Commons[61]; (3) all parties have an opportunity to invite expert witnesses in addition to officials and ministers. That said, it is also eminently worthwhile to find out whether consistency with constitutional principles was raised as an issue in the debate in either House.

This is not to overlook the very wide variation in interpretations of the Constitution. The wide range of constitutional interpretations can, however, be divided into two broad ranges. One range consists of *good faith interpretations*. The other range is characterized by memoranda of members of a Deputy Ministers' Committee that distinguished between "purists" and "the practical minded" in the following manner:

> Purists might insist on obtaining guidance from the highest order context (the Constitution), but on the other extreme, the practical-minded would have us proceed to the future incrementally. The AFN [Assembly of First Nations] is on one extreme, the federal bureaucracy on the other, and the Parliamentary Special Committee probably straddles the middle.[62]

My experience in parliamentary relations for First Nations political organizations as well as my scholarly research indicates that this attitude is common through much of the public service but is nowhere more prevalent than in the Department of Indian Affairs and Northern Development.

Almost every instance in which officials attempt to circumvent Parliament or to disregard a fundamental constitutional principle is paralleled by an attempt to shift or, at least, to sidestep, the burden of proof which properly falls to their minister.

INTENTION IN PUBLIC POLICY DISCOURSE

> in·tend
> **1** have in mind as a purpose; plan: We intend to go home soon. He apologized and said he had intended no insult.
> **3** Archaic. direct: to intend one's course.
> DME < OF < L intendere < in- toward + tendere stretch[63]

The concept of intention is particularly critical for an understanding of the history of First Nations relations. To some significant degree it is essential to any metapolicy discourse. Governments may not always fulfill their stated objectives but they rarely do better than the goals that they have set out. But publicly stated goals, particularly in First Nations relations, are often quite different from those that emerge when cabinet documents are released, typically many years after the meetings where those documents were discussed. Further, policy objectives, i.e., intentions, are often quite different in one agency, branch, department or ministry than another. Indeed, there are often conflicts between the goals and intentions of the Indian Affairs Branch and the intentions of the Privy Council Office, the public service department headed by the Prime Minister.

What I mean by intention is, necessarily, more than a wish. If a minister tells a parliamentary committee that "Indian Control of Indian Education" will become departmental policy but there is no indication of plans being put into place to achieve that change then *fulfilling that statement was not something that the minister intended to happen.*

The question of a failure to develop appropriate intentions takes on a whole different order when we move from the personal realm to the professional, from personal discourse to policy discourse. The failure to develop appropriate intentions, and the inclination to make unfounded assumptions have far greater consequences when they become characteristic of positions of power, authority or influence.

The benefits of an office carry with them certain burdens. One such burden is an obligation to demonstrate the development of proper intentions not as wishful thinking but as a substantial plan designed (intended) to achieve the stated objective. If there is no indication that the minister and his officials are *stretching toward a goal* then there is no reason to think that they intend to reach that goal. Although such goals may be stated as policy they are not actual policy objectives.

Intentions are exemplified both in the Golden Rule and in the Kantian imperative. Both Jesus' Golden Rule—"Do unto others as you would have them do unto you"[64]–and Hillel's dictum–"What is hateful to you, do not do unto others"[65,66]–depend on an element that is not readily susceptible to rules of evidence but that directs the listener *to form and acts upon* proper intentions. In most discussions of Hillel's dictum there is a tendency to emphasize the second clause, "do not do unto others." However, the first clause, "that which is hateful unto you," is critical to *the formation of intention*. Intention, in turn, relates a contemplated action to conscience, a bundle of higher principles including equity, love, *caritas*, care, and duty. Intention likewise connects to a set of negative values including greed (inequity), hate, oppression, and other deadly sins.

The formulation of principles begins with the recognition and cultivation of intentions. Kant considered categorical imperatives to appeal to a higher authority; they are essentially transcendental.[67] Principles are "held to be self-evident" when they are not susceptible to ordinary rules of evidence. It is, of course, possible to demonstrate, *post facto,* that the world is a better place, measured against certain standards, when certain principles are honoured. *Behaviours* flowing from principles can be shown either to cause harm or to confer or foster benefits but behaviours that are adduced from principles are, nonetheless, behaviours.

Intentions are inferred from behaviour. "Good intentions," the variety with which the road to hell is proverbially paved, are those which are not actualized and have, at least in retrospect, no air of reality. *Behaviour is the meeting ground of intention and consequences.* There are abundant examples in personal contexts in which one becomes persuaded of a course of action by considering the most likely outcome. There are also examples, both in law and in policy of questions that are necessarily treated as *pro*spective questions rather than as *retro*spective questions.[68] Child custody decisions, based on "the best interests of the child" are a foremost example in both law and public policy[69] of a question resolved prospectively and one germane to First Nations relations. I will refer to the resolution of prospective questions based on an informed and educated intuition, along the lines of a judge deciding the best interests of a child, as *future testing*.[70]

One merit of future testing is that it allows for a test of the *bona fides* in situations in which no more direct evidence or demonstration of the initial statement is possible. However, a proposition which depends upon future testing while calling for a more immediate response as a condition of that future requires a deeply intuitive answer on the part of the hearer.

What can be said about **burdens of persuasion** is three-fold:

First, that so far as abstract values—including both principles and intentions–can be applied to policy, they must, initially, be taken as either "self-evident" or as "speaking for themselves."

Secondly, that the opportunity or capacity for persuasion about intentions and about prospective or future actions is much more limited than the burden of proof for past acts. The listener either does or does not believe the speaker; more evidence is very often no help at all.

Thirdly, that in some important respects, the burden is quite properly shifted to a respondent. A person whose competence has been called into question may be required to demonstrate competence. A person on probation is required to account for their whereabouts. Members of licensed professions, for reasons we are about to discuss, are subject to analogous shifting of burdens.

LICENSING, BURDEN SHIFTING AND PUBLIC POLICY

In order to understand the policies underlying the mismanagement, wrongdoing and breaches of fiduciary duties running through the history of Canada-First Nations relations, we need to consider whether the persons acting on behalf of the Crown were subjected to the standards of competence by which a fiduciary might be judged in private fiduciary relationships. Will the persons carrying out the Crown's fiduciary duties to a First Nation strike you as attractive candidates to manage an educational trust on behalf of your own children?

Licensing is the grant of a privilege[71] to persons claiming special trust or competence on the part of the granting body. As a grant of authority a license (even a driving license) constitutes a kind of office, albeit possibly a minor office. For example, an armed forces commission, known as a "warrant," announces that the Queen places "an especial trust" in the newly appointed officer.

The trust that justifies a license cannot be based solely on technical competence, at least in the contemporary, narrow notion of "technical." *Technique*, in an older sense, however, refers to "the manner of execution or performance in any [art] discipline, profession, or sport."[72]

Intention is the beginning of technique. Technique is the actualizing of intention.

A respectable small craft pilot is more interested in the forecast of the weather for the trip back to port than in the weather he can see in front of his face. Anaesthetists have been heard to say, "Anyone can put someone to sleep. My job is to help them to wake up." Poor brakes can result in a careless driving charge even in a borrowed car. Poor acceleration, however, does not attract such a charge. Poor ignition is even safer.

Licensing is important to the discussion of burdens of persuasion because *with the benefits of a license come a certain degree of burden shifting*. A licensed professional whose decisions are called into question may be required to justify the chosen course by demonstrating that he (or she) conducted a given exercise according to specified standards. This is most frequently accomplished by matching case notes with established protocols.[73] In such instances, the fact of licensing shifts the burden of proof onto the licensee. This burden shifting is held to be reasonable because the license is *a benefit granted in recognition of especial competence.*

The privilege granted to a licensee by the state and grounded in a perceived competence and a corollary trust carries with it two related burdens. The first burden is to conduct one's practice in a generally ethical manner and, more particularly, in keeping with the ethical guidelines of an appropriate professional college or other licensing body.

The second burden is *the capacity to see likely consequences or outcomes* of an exercise or procedure peculiar to the licensed activity. Both motor vehicle drivers and surgeons are expected to foresee the outcomes of standard procedures. An argument that certain unlikely outcomes were not foreseeable must meet the burden of persuading a disciplinary panel that the failure to foresee and avoid an undesired outcome was not a result of negligence.

I call these obligations "burdens" because they carry with them the further obligation *to demonstrate to a licensing body* that these obligations were fulfilled. The most fundamental step in discharging this **burden to demonstrate care** is meticulous record keeping. The importance of this requirement becomes particularly evident when we track the frequency with which public officials and executives of major corporations under investigation for malfeasance, lost their remaining credibility when they are reported to have misplaced, lost or tampered with their records.[74]

A person acquiring a license crosses over the balance-point from being a private person to one who holds a privilege from the Crown, a college or some other delegated authority. In crossing the line, he or she acquires the benefits of the office and *the consequent burden of demonstrating* that licensed activities were carried out competently and according to established standards and procedures.

Licensing is the fulcrum between the role of a private person and the capacity of an office because the privilege bestowed on an otherwise private person allows the licensee to perform a public function under the authority or with the sanction of the state or college. Licensing, then, is not only a benefit in the conventional sense of a favour, kindness or good deeds, it is also a benefit in the legal sense (a) of an office held from the king and (b) at least for professional purposes, being held to a certain standard.[75]

What all such standards have in common is that they place on a licensee or a candidate for licensing, a burden to demonstrate to an appropriate panel that the work carried out under the license (or the candidacy) is consistent with both general professional norms and, quite often, highly specific standards. The failure to be familiar with established standards is often taken as the definition of incompetence.

A license is a privilege granted in recognition of a demonstrated or presumed competence. The privilege carries with it **a burden to demonstrate** that the privilege is exercised in keeping with the standards of the profession or trade or activity.

In addition to actual licenses, issued directly or indirectly by the state, there are also semi-formal and informal licenses granted by a community or the part of a community that presumes a person to have acquired or demonstrated a certain competence. The acquisition of a university degree, college diploma or certificate is often a prerequisite for a license but, by itself, it is rarely sufficient. Yet, there is often an expectation of a certain kind of competence on the basis of a degree. When this is seen to happen I would describe it as a "semi-formal license."

Examples of informal licenses range from the continued deference paid to former holders of high offices, e.g., judges, ambassadors, and senators, to the recognition and acceptance of unlicensed paraprofessionals such as Native courtworkers. In certain fields, an informal license allows a person to carry on a kind of practice based on the reputation and esteem conveyed by his or her title and previous accomplishments.

In considering the history of Canadian Indian policy we are entitled to invoke these same standards in evaluating the conduct of the public officials who were responsible, from time to time, for fulfilling the fiduciary duties of the Crown.

LICENSING IS A STATEMENT OF INTENTION

Licensing by the state is an instrument of policy. The possession of a license and the exercise of the privileges that it confers, however, suppose a *good faith* intention to fulfill the trust conferred by the Crown or the particular delegated authority. The most important point about licensing in the interplay of language, policy and ethics is that *licensing is a statement of good faith intention*, i.e., licensing is predicated upon a belief by the granting authority (on behalf of a community at large) not only that the person possesses a competence but that the person will also carry on the licensed work in a competent manner and in good faith.

Semi-formal and informal licenses are not normally subject to review by a granting authority but, nonetheless, carry with them a community's expectation of competence. When a community, or a significant part of a community changes its assessment, the lack of a forum in which to address complaints or allegations often make a situation more difficult for someone operating under an informal license. When a court of public opinion censures through gossip there is little or no effective reply.

INTENTION IN THE REALM OF POLICY DEVELOPMENT

Intention in the realm of policy is significantly different from personal intention. The idea that policy is formulated more by offices than by persons becomes critical when we find that a change of party makes less difference in fiscal policy than we anticipated.

I do not mean to suggest that there is not a significant measure of discretion available to each of these office holders. Each office does, however, come with a "book" which sets boundaries and rules of fair play and procedure. Astute and rational observers of any policy arena (in any of the three broad branches of government) are able to identify (at least within a certain margin of error) when the play goes out-of-bounds.

The intention to honour the book in whatever office one holds is different in kind from personal intention. The clearest example of honouring the book is found in the decisions of those judges whose first priority in interpreting the law is to give meaning to the plain sense of the statutes and cases before them. As Slattery points out,[76] if the judges' decisions are to have real value senior officials and ministers need to honour the book in much the same manner. If *Charter* rights (or Aboriginal rights) are honoured only when a case reaches a superior court then such rights face a continuing uphill struggle. Citizens and communities can only be secure in their rights when those rights are routinely honoured by senior officials and parliamentarians.

In the most important areas of personal life there often is no book, at least not one with any specificity. People continue to become parents without prior experience. The incidence of amateurism in parenting rises directly as the birth rate declines. In these truly personal dimensions we need to write the book as we go along.

While personality plays an important part in the formulation of policy, that part is very much filtered through the role that is embedded in the office and which, for all policy purposes, transcends individual personality. There are, of course, instances in which senior officials accomplish significant change through their own outstanding integrity and fortitude.

Public inquiries offer the best opportunity to examine the interplay of personality and office. Unfortunately, from this perspective, the inquiries which provide the most comprehensive accounts are those appointed to inquire into misadventures and, therefore, have additional powers to subpoena a wider range of evidence and to take evidence under oath.[77] Inquiries into wrongful convictions (of which there have been several in Canada in recent years) have focused, in their reconstruction of events, at least as much on the police and other parts of the public administration as on the judicial proceedings culminating in the conviction. Each one also looked at the broader policy context including the state of the law and attitudes modeled by ministers, parliamentarians and other community leaders.[78] The tendency for police to develop tunnel vision in the course of an investigation may largely result from their general training and the pressure on field officers from superiors and political leaders.

Parliament, a body constituted *pour parler*, speaks collectively *by enacting* statutes which embody policy, even when their intention is highly debatable and regardless of whether a particular statute is prohibitive or permissive. Much policy can be gleaned from appropriation bills allocating funds and authorizing their spending even if no other authority exists.[79]

Delegated legislation allows subordinate agencies to develop the details which breathe life into many general acts. Nowhere is the old saw about "the devil being in the details" more evident than in the struggle to control and shape the writing of regulations and statutory instruments (directives, guidelines and other such instruments) pursuant to a highly general act.[80]

All such *speech acts*, however, can be seen to express an intention, or a complex of intentions on the part of the legislator, minister, or official. Each such intention is, however, only realized in the external correlative, i.e., so far as it acts upon what is described in the statement.

Intention in policy development differs from personal intention in another respect. It is far more reasonable to project at least the most negative aspects of policy from the past into the future. If an agency has a history of disrespecting "the rules of natural justice"[81] or the *Charter*, then, at the very least, the most reasonable position is to ask what provisions have been taken to prevent a repetition. Similarly, if an agency's record of financial management is open to question, then it is fair enough to ask whether those questions have been anticipated within the agency and, further, to ask in Parliament or in public how those questions have been addressed.

In brief, the quality of administrative intention can be measured by the extent to which previously identified issues have been addressed. So far as it is sensible to speak of administrative ethics, they consist of a demonstration that an agency has addressed the ethical issues previously raised in respect both to it and to similar or parallel agencies.

Such a scrutiny can only be as credible as its public manifestation. In a federal Canadian context I can think of no other plausible public scrutiny except through Parliament, its committees or the extensions of Parliament known as public inquiries.

THE AUTONOMOUS DOUBLE BIND

Woodrow Wilson's Fourteen Points brought the right of self-determination into the mainstream of western European and North American thought and gave the legitimacy of the democratic imprimatur to the idea that cultural and political autonomy were necessarily bound up together. It did not, however, provide much decolonization outside of Western Europe. Indeed, its failure to do so emphasized the European (including the Euro-American) perception of non-Europeans as being "less than human," thereby ensuring that future struggles of colonized peoples to assert their humanity would necessarily fail. This perception enters formal European records with the debate at Valladolid in 1550 between Las Casas and Sepulveda as to whether Indians had souls equal to those of Europeans.[82] (So far as Sepulveda drew on Aristotle, the argument had very ancient roots.) Arguments against the full humanity of Indians recur in American[83] and British-Canadian[84] jurisprudence. A less scholarly version of this attitude came from the U.S. Cavalry major and former Methodist missionary, John Chivington, who justified the killing of infants by saying, "Nits make lice," a statement echoed, if not borrowed by leaders of the Third Reich.[85] This reasoning was explicitly rejected only in 1973 when Mr. Justice Emmett Hall., in *Calder*,[86] described the characterization of the Cherokees in an 1832 U.S. decision, *Cherokee v. Georgia*, as "ill-founded."

The right of self-determination came into the mainstream of western European and North American thought with Wilson's Fourteen Points and the subsequent founding of the League of Nations. The incapacity of the League to deliver on the promise of self-determination beyond the bounds of western and central Europe highlighted the perception of non-European peoples as *untermenschen*. This metapolitical double bind ensured that future struggles of colonized peoples to assert their humanity would necessarily take the form of asserting the need for both cultural and political autonomy.

The literature and records representing the colonized peoples as less than human constitute *a discourse of prevarication* that runs throughout the history of colonization and the struggle of colonized peoples. Any effort to portray the misrepresentative nature of this discourse requires some intertwining of political and psychocultural narratives. The American Revolution, the great political culmination of the European Enlightenment, became the very model of self-determination while the failure of the United States to join the League ensured the incapacity of the League to carry through on President Wilson's doctrine.

In terms of political discourse, the continuing colonization of the First Nations of North America represents the deepest fulfillment of this political irony. That the irony continues to evade many North American political actors is an indicator that "Indian Policy" continues to be the nadir–the low point—of both the American dream and of democratic administration.

THE DOUBLE BIND: AN OFFSHOOT OF BURDEN SHIFTING IN THE DISCOURSE OF PREVARICATION

A double bind is a statement, or set of statements that set up a situation in which a party, ostensibly receiving instructions, *is put into a situation in which they will be wrong no matter what course they follow.* "Don't be so obedient!" is an example cited in *Language, Behaviour & Psychopathology.*[87] Double bind statements, in First Nations relations and in colonial discourse generally are intimately bound up with **prevarication** and a lack either of competence or *of good faith* intention.

In psychology, double bind rhetoric has been associated with the social reinforcement of schizophrenia and a variety of less dramatic psychological disorders. The double bind concept was introduced to the study of political discourse by writers with a strong background in psychiatric literature including Frantz Fanon (*The Wretched of the Earth* and *Black Skin, White Masks, Toward the African Revolution*[88]) and Albert Memmi (*Jews and Arabs), The Liberation of the Jew, Racisme, and Portrait du colonisé*[89]).

Two other writers whose work has particularly influenced my thinking about the discourse of autonomy, and the discourse of prevarication as its negation, have long been friends with one another and, indeed, produced one of their early books together.[90] The respective subject matters of Sander Gilman's *Jewish Self-Hatred: Anti-Semitism and the Hidden Language of the Jews* and Ted Chamberlin's *Come Back to Me, My Language: Poetry and the West Indies*[91] may not, at first glance, seem closely related. The underlying connection between Gilman's work and Chamberlin's is their continuing interest in the psycho-political project of healing peoples who have been colonized or enslaved and the relationship of healing to literature.

CONCLUDING: THE HISTORY THAT LIES AHEAD

This chapter has explored a series of concepts that I believe to be useful for the study of political ethics generally and, more particularly, for the study of the Discourse of First Nations relations. I began by setting out some reasons why this discourse was different from political discourses that relate directly to the experience of the dominant culture as an electorate: the people characterized in the discourse are the people being addressed; they are able to respond as an electorate to characterizations that are, in their opinions, unfounded, insulting or unhelpful. In contrast, a colonized indigenous culture is not a part of the electorate addressed by leaders of the dominant culture; and, the dominant culture has typically imposed civil disabilities limiting their use of the limited means for responding at their disposal.

I then offered a definition of *policy* that centred on the *attitude* of a particular office or agency, i.e., its relationship to the indigenous colonized communities and to its primary client groups.

A major part of this theoretical discussion focused on the concepts of *burdens of proof* and *burdens of persuasion* as they are used in law and their significance for better appreciating political discourse. I am particularly concerned about inappropriate "burden shifting" and the extent to which such burden shifting is a feature running throughout the *discourse of prevarication* that has characterized so much of the history of federal Indian policy, both in Canada and in the United States.

I also coined the phrase "licensing" in order to look at issues of competence in the context of claims of states and public officials to exercise authority over colonized peoples. I then concluded that *good faith* intentions set a standard for normative behaviour in the Discourse of First Nations relations.

The major part of this dissertation is a two-part history. The first part of this history is a single chapter overview of the history of First Nations relations with Canada from Confederation in 1862, to 1970. The second part is a three chapter study of testimony of First Nations leaders about issues of self-government and First Nations' autonomy before parliamentary committees between 1970 and 1980.

I have imposed this theoretical exercise on the readers' patience because I have found that the concepts outlined in this chapter provide a set of standards and norms by which to better evaluate the attitudes and conduct of officials, ministers and parliamentarians who played a role in the history narrated in the chapters that follow.

It has, for instance, become fashionable, in defending residential schools to argue that these schools were established with the sincere intention of benefiting the students who were brought to them and the communities to which they would eventually return. Yet, as early as 1907 medical and legal authorities were warning the government of the unconscionable condition of the residential schools.[92] These evaluations can not be reconciled with the claim that the schools were operated with a primary intention of benefiting the students. An examination of the history of those schools can be better evaluated through the use of the norms and standards that I have discussed in this chapter.

Much the same can be said for each other major event, policy or pattern of political behaviour in the history of Canadian Indian policy.

One reason why these concepts have been particularly helpful to me may provide a helpful note on which to close this chapter. I have long been struck by the tendency of officials and ministers, in addressing issues of federal Indian policy to invoke standards that do not correspond either to the legal norms or to the social standards by which other political behaviours are judged. I found it most helpful to note that Chief Justice John Marshall of the United States Supreme Court made a similar observation in *Worcester v. Georgia*, in 1832:

> The words "treaty" and "nation" are words of our own language, selected in our own diplomatic and legislative proceedings, by ourselves, having each a definite and well understood meaning. We have applied them to Indians, as we have applied them to other nations of the earth. They are applied to all in the same sense.[93]

The Supreme Court of Canada addressed this same question of the "plain meaning" of words in two cases that are otherwise about taxation. The first of these cases is about taxation of Indians for moneys earned on reserve. In *Nowigijick*, Chief Justice Brian Dickson explained why a liberal construction of treaties and statutes was appropriate in dealing with Indian matters:

> . . . treaties and statutes relating to Indians should be liberally construed and doubtful expressions resolved in favour of the Indian. If the statute contains language which can reasonably be construed to confer tax exemption that construction, in my view, is to be favoured over a more technical construction which might be available to deny exemption. In *Jones v. Meehan*, 175 U.S. 1, it was held that "Indian treaties must be construed, not according to the technical meaning of their words, but in the sense in which they would naturally be understood by the Indians."[94]

The more recent of these cases is not about a First Nations matter but it does address the tendency of officials to develop esoteric definitions for terms that describe events with which most people are familiar from their everyday experience.

> The strength of the 'plain meaning' rule is its recognition that it is the words of the provision themselves that constitute the vehicle used by Parliament to convey its intent to the people who are trying to assess their rights . . . under the Act.[95]

I, at least, have been struck, in the course of my reading for this work and in earlier research that the discourse of First Nations relations has been particularly coloured by a tendency of government officials not to speak in keeping with these standards but to shift the meaning of key words to ones that could not be gleaned from a knowledge of the ordinary use of those terms. This re-jigging of well-defined terms has, as we will see in the next chapter, become intimately intertwined, in the history of Indian policy, with shifting the burdens of proof and persuasion.

I have referred to these and other such devices as rhetorical sleights, i.e., a clever rhetorical trick. Taken together, I refer to the tendency to reconstitute language in this way as *a discourse of prevarication.*

Whether or not this insight is sustained by the histories that follow I leave to you and each other reader to judge on your own behalf.

Chapter Two

Assimilation, Enfranchisement and the *White Paper*: An Overview of First Nations' Relations Before 1970

> We must, I think, in these cases have regard to substance and to the plain and ordinary meaning of the language used rather than to forensic dialectics.
>
> Mr. Justice Brian Dickson,
> *Nowegijick v. Regina*,
> (1983), C.T.C. 20, 46 N.R. 41.

THE BAGGAGE BROUGHT TO THE COMMITTEE ROOM

In this chapter I examine the historical context within which the proceedings examined in the next three chapters took place. This chapter explores the baggage that each of the personalities and player groups—First Nations representatives and parliamentarians alike–brought to the proceedings of the 1970s. The chronicles which follow begin with the Joint Committee on the Constitution of 1970. This overview will survey the historical background ending with the *White Paper* of 1969 and the Indian response to that statement of *Indian Policy*. (The reasons why I identify the *White Paper* with the preceding period rather than with this decade will be discussed later.)

The Indian witnesses and the academic witnesses whose testimony lent credence to the Indian witnesses were, by and large, far more aware of the historical baggage crowding the committee rooms than were most of the parliamentarians. This disparity of awareness—parliamentarians knowing so little about the subject matter under scrutiny by a committee on which they are sitting—is, I suggest, peculiar to the history of First Nations relations in Canada.

If it is commonplace to observe that the party in a one-down position is far more knowledgeable about the history shared with the other than is the dominant party this lack of historical awareness is quite uncharacteristic of parliamentarians in most other legislative fields. Parliamentary debates, of the 1970s, are peppered with references to previous debates, many of which go back much earlier than the speaker's own place in Parliament. Some of this disparity is illustrated in testimony in which these acts are discussed either by Indian witnesses or by academics.[1]

Indian witnesses, in contrast, were painfully aware of the traumas suffered by previous leaders and their nations as a whole as a result of one or another civil disability imposed by acts of the Canadian Parliament. There are not many direct references in the proceedings to the various disabilities. Further, the history of Parliamentary imposition of civil disabilities stands as the sharpest possible contrast to the agenda of Aboriginal and treaty rights recognition, autonomy and self-government that are the recurring themes of the testimony reviewed here.

The radical ignorance of historic policies and legislation about the history of Indian policy is, I suggest, characteristic of Canadian parliamentarians of the 1970s. The lack of basic background becomes one of the major obstacles to any kind of deeper discourse. Ernest Benedict, a Mohawk from Akwesasne, appearing before the MacGuigan-Molgat Committee on December 7, 1970, said of the 1969 *White Paper* that:

> It showed no sense of history and therefore no acceptable view of the future. As Indian people we will always see our special status and legal rights as flowing from the original sovereignty of our nations.[2]

Not only had the *White Paper* shown no sense of history, it also became clear, as the proceedings of the Joint Committee on the Constitution progressed, that the parliamentarians were also free of the properties of historical knowledge.

The baggage that the Indian witnesses brought with them included the traumatic cultural conditioning induced by a variety of civil disabilities imposed by Canadian legislation. This includes the 1927 *Indian Act* amendment which, by prohibiting the raising of funds for the purpose of pressing Indian claims made the very practice of petitioning for Indian rights a matter that might place a person in legal jeopardy.[3]

The baggage that the parliamentarians brought with them consisted of a lack of the historical awareness that is the usual stuff and substance of their work, combined with an attitude that held that "Indian policy" was not an arena that required knowledge. The parliamentarians' baggage allowed that Indian policy might well be formulated through an *argumentum ad ignorantiam.*[4]

This baggage, of which the Indian and academic witnesses appear to have been far more aware than the parliamentarians, can best be unpacked for the purposes of this inquiry through three discussion points: (1) the policy of assimilation; (2) the imposition of civil disabilities; and (3) the use of the term "enfranchisement" as an early example of the inversion and co-option of language in Canadian Indian policy and the effects of that inversion on public discourse. These three intertwining topics are basic threads running through the history of the century before 1970.

DOES "ASSIMILATION" EXPLAINS HISTORIC CANADIAN INDIAN POLICY?

The *Report of the Royal Commission on Aboriginal Peoples (RCAP)*, in its historical overview, argues that there has been a consistent federal policy of *assimilation* since Canadian Confederation, in 1867.[5] A brief consideration of this thesis will allow a broader overview than the question of Parliamentary knowledge of previous Indian legislation. There are two distinct but interwoven difficulties with the assimilation thesis. The first is that it suggests that there has been a consistent policy of one or another kind since Confederation. The second, which will be discussed later, is that *assimilation* appears to have had very different meanings to different officials (as well as to different historians). Only some of these uses relate directly to the conventional use of the term.

Even when Alan Cairns[6] has defended the (*RCAP)* assimilation thesis of a continuing policy of assimilation since Confederation, he concedes that this concept reflects primarily the government's perception of its own policy rather than describing consistency between agencies or within any one agency over an extended period of time. If, as I suggested in the previous chapter, "policy" is best defined not as the government's stated objectives but as *an attitude manifested, through both words and more direct actions*, then the claim by officials and ministers that assimilation has been their continuing objective leads not to the conclusion that this has been the historical Canadian policy but that the history might be written by contrasting the perception with the actual attitudes.

The fact that an entire doctrine might be drafted, printed, presented to Parliament and published on "Indian policy" that was entirely free of all the evidentiary observations, aspirations and recommendations of Indian elders, teachers and leaders is, quite possibly, the single most important indicator about the actual nature of *the policy as an attitude* shared by the Prime Minister and the senior officials in the Privy Council Office (PCO).[7] So far as such a move is entirely consistent with historically accepted procedures, it is also the single most important indicator of the nature and meaning of assimilation.

The purpose of this discussion will be to identify, so far as possible, a continuing theme running throughout historic Canadian Indian policy and, from that, to infer what it is that has been meant by "assimilation." This discussion will, then, also provide a foundation for the later consideration of the language (or rhetoric) of Indian policy.

The notion that the history of federal Indian policy is best characterized by "assimilation" depends upon a confusion of the two quite opposite meanings of the term "assimilate."

> assimilate
>
> I. To make or be like.
>
> II. To absorb and incorporate.
> 7. a. To convert into a substance of its own nature, as the bodily organs convert food into blood, and thence into animal tissue; to take in and appropriate as nourishment; to absorb into the system, incorporate. Cf. assimilation 4.
> b. *fig.*
> 8. a. *intr.* To become of the same substance; to become absorbed or incorporated into the system.[8]

The first meaning is about causing or allowing one person, group or thing to become *like* another. The second, is *to convert into a substance of its own nature*. In this second sense, "an assimilate" is a piece of food absorbed into the body. Thomas à Kempis spoke of being assimilated to the holy angels. John Donne spoke of the adversary coming to "assimilate him [the believer] and, make him like himself." The distinction is as vital is it is subtle.

For one entity to *become like* another is quite a different matter from *being absorbed into* that larger body. Federal Indian policy has moved back and forth from one to the other. Pierre Trudeau's 1969 *White Paper* is one of a series of pronouncements since 1919 of an intention *to dissolve* First Nations as identities and to absorb their memberships into the larger society, albeit usually only as a proletarian class. In contrast, policies that have imposed civil disabilities, such as making the pressing of land claims[9] and the observance of traditional religious ceremonies punishable offenses are measures more likely to isolate even while impoverishing the same cultures.

If the theory that assimilation has been the major theme of Canadian Indian policy has any validity, it is not to be found in the idea that such policy was directed at bringing Indians into the dominant culture. A theory that looks to explain Indian policy by the goal of assimilation must look to the notion of *assimilation* as *a political devouring* of one culture by another. This is the sense in which objects were described, in the 19th century and earlier, as "assimilates," i.e., as objects to be dissolved and absorbed into a larger body.[10] This archaic used of "assimilate" taken into the context of political history, describes a spiritual-political process quite opposite to any notion of encouraging one group to *become like* another.

Since 1857, Canada had offered what it might have intended as the incentive of **enfranchisement** to Indians *who renounced their entitlement under the Indian Act and their membership in their band*. By the passage of the *Indian Act*, 18 years later, in 1876, only one person had accepted this offer.[11] The tactic of inflicting punishment and imposing civil disabilities on those who refused the generosity of Parliament was not producing the voluntary assimilation of Indians. No social theorist of that day anticipated that such policies would bring Indians into the Canadian Dominion as full and equal citizens except so far as they renounced affiliation with their traditional culture. If this was an instance of assimilation, then "*assimilation*" does not mean allowing people to become full and equal citizens. *Enforced* enfranchisement represented *a shift of discretion* from the individual to the Indian agent and his superiors.

> Our object is to continue until there is not a single Indian in Canada that has not been *absorbed into the body politic* and there is no Indian question.[12]

Duncan Campbell Scott's famous statement to a Parliamentary committee of 1920 that he intended to work until there was not a single Indian left in Canada appears to have met with the general approval of the committee before which he appeared and with its successors for years to come. Indeed, one can only suppose that a promise of an *Indian-free Canada* so appealed to Scott's political masters as to assure his tenure as Deputy Superintendent General of Indian Affairs. Scott's statement is ambiguous insofar as he does not say into what part of the body politic the people who are to cease being Indians are to be *absorbed*. The "Indian question" that he wants to no longer be asked appears more to be a matter of reducing federal responsibility (or liability from the point of view of the committee he was addressing) than about anything resembling integration.

Three years after this statement to a Parliamentary committee, Scott engineered the forcible overthrow of the Grand Council of the Haudenosaunee at Ohsweken and the seizing of the Fire Council Wampum. He then caused a royal commission to be constituted which reported that *The Great Law of Peace* was incomprehensible because it was "unwritten." By the time he came to orchestrate the Joint Committee of 1926, with the blessings of the Minister and the Chairman of the Committee, Scott's place in Canadian history was already well etched.

Assimilation as an historic doctrine has not been about integrating Indians into the mainstream of Canadian society. Had that been the continuing and overarching goal of governments since Confederation, very few of the more specific measures that have characterized Canadian history would have been taken. Assimilation, as the term has been used since the 18th century, has not been about integration but about something quite different.

Assimilation, as an historical Indian policy has been about **displacement** of Indian communities from their remaining lands and creating situations in which they were less rather than more likely to prosper. The conditions created by historical policies are ones which were more likely to create a class of landless people devoid of marketable skills and without an education appropriate to any kind of authentic absorption into the dominant culture. A policy calculated *to integrate* Indians or to assimilate them in the more positive sense of the word, would not have forced successful farmers off arable land or failed to honour treaty promises of education.

This goes beyond the conventional debate about the relative merits of cultural retention versus integration. So far as the historical Canadian Indian policy has been one of assimilation it has consisted of a set of practices and impositions the most likely outcomes of which were *neither cultural retention nor integration.*

CIVIL DISABILITIES AS INSTRUMENTS OF CANADIAN INDIAN POLICY

The imposition of civil disabilities[14] on Indians runs throughout the history of Canadian Indian policy. The offer of enfranchisement that was introduced in the *Act for the Gradual Civilization of the Indians* of 1857 was, undoubtedly, intended as an incentive. That so few Indians accepted the offer of a right to vote and own property in Canada in exchange for a loss of membership in their home community and their nation suggests that it was seen, at best, as a null offer, one that simply had no attraction.

Once enfranchisement became something that could be imposed at the discretion of officials, it became a civil disability. The corresponding prohibitions against owning property and voting while retaining the statutorily recognized attributes of Indian identity were also civil disabilities. There was, under this regime, a double set of constraints and no incentives.

The prohibitions of the potlatch and other religious ceremonies are the one generally acknowledged set of disabilities. These, too, were not clearly accompanied by an alternative set of behaviours for which there was a consistent set of incentives. Indians were encouraged to become Christians but the country had been distributed as spheres of influence amongst a variety of Christian denominations. This had all the attributes of historic policies of *compelle entrare* of the Roman Catholic Church in Europe including the benefit of state support. The distinguishing Canadian feature was the distribution of Indians amongst competing and conflicted denominations. Amongst all these various denominations, however, there is little indication of an effort *to integrate* Indian congregations with those of neighbouring communities. Even in ostensibly spiritual matters, assimilation meant dissolution but not integration.

The imposition of civil disabilities began in the 19th century but it was not an exclusive attribute of that century. New impositions continued to be imposed well into the 20th century. Old disabilities were periodically reinvigorated. Almost all were carried over from one statutory revision, both federal and provincial, to the next over several decades. The idea that the imposition of civil disabilities has been a principal hallmark of Canadian Indian policy and a defining characteristic of assimilation is fundamental to the observation that the conditioning from these impositions was a principal part of the baggage brought into the Parliamentary committee rooms of the 1970s.

George Manuel, for instance, was an apprentice of Andrew Paull, the founder of the Allied Tribes of British Columbia, centred largely in the B.C. Interior, as well as the Native Brotherhood, a union of coastal fishers. Manuel was intimately familiar with the trials and tribulations Paull had faced. He was well aware of the petition of the Allied Tribes in 1926, of the show trial procedure entertained by the chairman, Hewitt Bostock, a Senator from British Columbia and then Speaker of the Senate. Bostock had essentially inverted normal procedure when he chaired a Special Committee to consider a petition of the Interior Tribes asking that their claim of an Aboriginal title be referred to the Judicial Committee of the Privy Council.[15] The Minister and his Deputy Superintendent General spoke first and generally dominated the proceedings. Andrew Paull was allowed a brief and belated statement. His lawyer, A.E. O'Meara, was denied the right to call witnesses or to examine witnesses. The final report of the Committee did not so much address the substance of the claim—other than to assert that the unexamined petition was without merit—but focused on extolling the excellence of government policy, an issue the petition had carefully avoided.

This low point of Parliamentary relations with First Nations—Manuel said "I do not know if it was the darkest hour in the history of the Parliament of Canada"[16]—was more than representative of the quality of the larger discourse. The prohibition against raising funds for the purpose of pressing Indian land claims[17] which resulted from that hearing, although less celebrated than the prohibitions against the potlatch, was, in certain senses, a more severe and hostile civil disability. The 19th century efforts to end paganism and foster Christianity might, conceivably, be rationalized as part of the program described, at that time, as the "gradual civilization" of the Indian tribes.

HISTORICAL POLICIES AND THE PLIMSOLL LINE OF SUBSTANTIVE FAIRNESS

Taken as a whole, the post-Confederation 19th Century parliamentary debates on Indian Affairs were characterized by a policy based on a presumption of conquest and an intention to force "Indian tribes" into a state of submission

So far as possible, Canada eschewed the violence which characterized the westering of the United States while willingly sharing in the benefits it yielded. When American policy fostered the destruction of the buffalo and an end to the food supplies of the First Nations of the prairies, Ottawa was ready to move west to occupy the lands which became available through the loss of the buffalo. Ottawa purchased the Hudson Bay Company's interest in Prince Rupert's Land and then proceeded to make treaties to extinguish the First Nation's interest in these lands.

In 1887, Mr. Samuel Henry Justice Strong dissented from the majority opinion in *St. Catharine Milling,*[18] the first case dealing with the nature and meaning of Indian treaties to reach the courts after Confederation. At issue was the question of whether the St. Catharines Milling and Lumber Company, in order to take timber in the Northwest Angle of Ontario, needed to obtain a permit from Ontario or from Canada. In other words, once Indian land was surrendered, which order of government had jurisdiction? The decisions of Chancellor Boyd in the trial court[19] and of Lord Watson in the Privy Council,[20] to which the case was appealed from the Supreme Court of

Canada are often quoted for the racial diatribes in which they indulged, the gist of which was both *obiter dicta* and obscene.

Mr. Justice Strong may have been one of the few sincere assimilationists of his time.[21] He was concerned that there be funds available to fulfill the Crown's obligations to the Saulteaux Ojibway under Treaty #3. Because he considered it unlikely that Parliament would vote such funds, he considered it essential that the royalties from the sale of timber and other resources be directed toward the fulfillment of the trust responsibilities taken on by the Crown through that treaty.

Mr. Justice Strong's dissent is the Plimsoll line[22] of substantive fairness.[23]

The residential schools that flourished from the 1880s to 1970 were notorious, particularly in the early years of the 20th century, for their frightful conditions. Their latterday defenders argue that contemporary criticism imposes the values of our day on those institutions. A study of the account of these institutions in *Looking Forward, Looking Backward*[24] suggests otherwise. Dr. P. H. Bryce, the Chief Medical Officer of the department in 1907, described the appalling mortality rates in these institutions. He said, "Even war seldom shows as large a percentage of fatalities as does the education we have imposed upon our Indian wards."[25] "S. H. Blake, Q.C., who assisted in negotiations for the 1911 contracts, observed that because the department had done nothing over the decades 'to obviate the preventable causes of death,' [it] brings itself within unpleasant nearness to the charge of manslaughter."[26]

These institutions can not be said to have been built in pursuit of assimilation in any *bona fides* sense. The mortality rate attributed to residential schools by Bryce and Blake were the consequences of a fiduciary's *failure to develop a bona fides intention.* Both the State and the churches continued to maintain institutions that their most senior officials had made clear were not capable of providing for the children's most basic needs.

They did, however, make an immeasurable contribution to the stated goal of Duncan Campbell Scott, the longtime Deputy Superintendent General of Indian Affairs[27] of an *Indian free* Canada. Seen from the perspective of Scott's goal "assimilation" includes *depriving persons of fundamental rights, imprisoning leaders who persist in feeding their communities, and creating institutional conditions for children which preclude the possibility of learning.*

Parliament responded to the Joint Committee on Indian Affairs of 1948 with the repeal, in 1951, of many of the civil disabilities accumulated in the *Indian Act* since Confederation. The repeal did little to change the rhetoric surrounding Canadian Indian policy. Indeed, policies of which the repeal was a part also included the settlement of Indian veterans on land excised from their own reserves. *Any economic opinion independant from Indian Affairs would reckon this as a loss*; only Indian Affairs would claim it as some kind of gain. In addition, the decision to administer benefits to Indian veterans through Indian Affairs, rather than through Veterans' Affairs, fostered a separation of the best integrated Indians in Canadian history. It also ensured that the administration of Indian veterans' benefits was done by persons selected for their attitude to Indians rather than their training in the administration of veterans' benefits.[28] If one accepts the RCAP interpretation of the disposition of the Indian veterans' benefits, the government's claim of having provided equal benefits is, at best, illusory.

CIVIL DISABILITIES, ASSIMILATION AND THE RHETORIC OF INDIAN POLICY

If civil disabilities are a major characteristic of the historic policy which others find to be characterized by an overall goal of assimilation, then there is a need to re-assess the meaning of assimilation. Assimilation did not involve an anticipation of Indians becoming upwardly mobile, holding positions of responsibility, acquiring wealth, attending the same religious meeting houses and marrying into the families of the influential or powerful members of the community.

It did involve displacing communities where prosperity was developing and forcing hard working people onto scrub land.[29] It did involve residential schools in which, in addition to their mortality rates and incidences of abuse, there was little attempt made to meet the curriculum standards of the day. It did involve prohibitions against leaving a reserve community as well as disincentives against seeking permanent employment off-reserve.

From this survey, assimilation appears to be *a peculiar euphemism meant to describe a series of actions in which individuals and communities are displaced from their lands, deprived of their property and cultural rights, reduced to a further level of deprivation without any particular prospect of improving their lot.* A synonym for assimilation in this context is cultural genocide.[30] Certain parts of these historic polices—particularly the displacement of communities and the taking of children from their parents and their communities—appear to be prohibited under the *United Nations Convention on the Prevention and Punishment of the Crime of Genocide.*[31] It may well be argued, on the contrary, that what is intended is better described in the title of the 1857 statute, *An Act for the Gradual Civilization of the Indians.* The distinction between "gradual civilization" and "assimilation" is that that statute offered incentives, including enfranchisement as a personal choice. It also allowed for community definition of membership. A word that equates to "cultural genocide" is not the same word that equates to "integration."

In 1876, federal policy responded to the rejection of enfranchisement by almost all eligible Indians by enabling the Minister and his officials to exercise the discretion to *impose* enfranchisement. To this day Canadian Indian policy remains the only political discourse in which "enfranchisement" represents a net loss in the minds of the supposed beneficiaries and a legal disability to independent scholars.

Scott's goals, although they may well have enjoyed widespread approval among the parliamentarians of his day, cannot properly be said to have held a monopoly as *the world view* in his day. Scott was a contemporary of Franz Boas, a founder of modern anthropology, who worked to replace 19th century race based ideas with a more rational understanding of culture. Likewise, Mr. Justice Henry Strong's dissent is as much a part of the world view of the day as were the majority opinions. Scott's capacity to blaze the trail down the crooked path of prevarication may have won the hearts and minds of his political masters; yet, we can hardly say that prevarication was a widely endorsed value of the day.

What we begin to notice, however, is that two other phenomena parallel the imposition of civil disabilities. One is the continual resistance of Indian leaders. The other is the tendency of officials and ministers to promote their policies with the use of language which is invested with meanings that are not found elsewhere in political discourse. "Enfranchisement" re-defined to mean the loss of membership and property rights in one's native community as well as the right to vote in an alien community is but the first of a strong of examples.

THE UNDERGROUND PERIOD OF THE DISCOURSE OF FIRST NATIONS' AUTONOMY

First Nations leaders and teachers never stopped talking about the idea that their peoples were nations or that as nations they were autonomous.[32] Neither did they stop saying that as autonomous nations they were entitled to create and maintain institutions of self-government. Or that they were also entitled to have those institutions of self-government recognized by Canada and, indeed, that Canada might best exercise its jurisdiction under section 92(24) of the *Constitution Act, 1867* by protecting those institutions rather than by undermining them. However, they ceased to say these things in "mixed company" when they were threatened with criminal prosecution by Canada for a variety of corollary activities.

Much of the discourse of First Nations' autonomy that survived the imposition of civil disabilities was carried on in First Nations' languages. Not only were these the "mother tongues" in which such matters might most comfortably be discussed, they were also languages lost on most administrative and police officials. What was constrained was the emergence of a vocabulary of First Nations' self-government in the official languages of Canada.

The first generation of witnesses whose testimony is reviewed in this work—Indian witnesses appearing before the MacGuigan-Molgat Committee such as George Manuel, Dave Courchene, and Ernest Benedict[33]—had all achieved oratorical skills in English as a second language. As witnesses this was a factor of which they were quite conscious. For example, Dave Courchene made reference to the ways in which language was used to trick their ancestors.[34] Donna Tyndall began her statement in her own language and reflected on the reception she received.[35] My reading of these proceedings, together with my personal acquaintance with these witnesses leads me to the conclusion that they brought into the first committee, especially, a wariness founded upon a combination of factors including a consciousness of the challenge of delivering a major statement in a second language and a recollection of specific persecutions, under federal authority, in their own recollections.[36]

THE CONTESTED MEANING OF "ENFRANCHISEMENT"

The peculiar use of "enfranchisement" runs through the history of Canadian Indian policy and the discourse to which it gave rise. It epitomizes the intertwining of the unclarified policies of assimilation, and the willingness to impose civil disabilities to achieve those policies. It is an example of language that builds a communication barrier between Indian leaders and prospectively concerned citizens to whom statements using these words have quite opposite meanings. Uwe Poerkson calls such terms *Plastic Words*.[37]

Only in the discourse of Indian policy does the term "enfranchise" have a negative value. In any other history the struggle to win the franchise constitutes a significant theme: the expansion of the franchise in English history from the *Great Reform Act* of 1832 to universal manhood suffrage in 1870 and women's suffrage in 1929; The extension of the franchise to Jews and other non-Christians; and the extension of the franchise to women in Canada and the United States.

In each of these instances, "enfranchise" means "to give the right to vote." Concurrently, it means, "to set free, release from slavery or restraint."[38] In Indian policy enfranchising entailed, as a condition of gaining the vote, surrendering (1) existing political rights, (2) property rights, i.e., one's personal share in the lands reserved for the band of which one was a member; and, (3) cultural affiliation. Although an Indian, by ceasing to be an Indian, did gain the right to vote, it is debatable whether there was a concurrent experience of being "set free." Scott and Oliver and others may well have imagined that Indians upon enfranchisement were "released from . . . restraint." The lack of voluntary enfranchisement strongly suggests that their view of the matter was not shared by those to whom these provisions applied.

There is, in this brief examination of a few key words, the suggestion that the turning of words from well defined meanings and values to meanings and values unique to the discourse and misleading to interested observers runs through the history of Indian policy. So far as these impositions of new meanings on previously well defined words served to mislead, to confuse and to deter participation, they are a type of prevarication.

"INDIAN POLICY," THE 1969 WHITE PAPER[39]

This discussion of civil disabilities, assimilation and rhetoric suggests that the 1969 *White Paper* might well have an affiliation with the history of the Discourse of First Nations' autonomy, and particularly of the bureaucratic discourse of Indian policy, that we have not yet explored.

From the perspective of First Nations' testimony before parliamentary committees, *The White Paper* was quite the opposite of the dawn of a new era, albeit this was certainly the claim of the Trudeau Government, particularly Jean Chrétien, the Minister of Indian Affairs and Northern Development, in introducing their statement on *Indian Policy*. So far as assimilation was the longstanding historical objective of federal Indian policy, the *White Paper* was the culmination of an era in which First Nations relations were dominated by the thinking of William Lyon Mackenzie King, Prime Minister from 1926 to 1930 and 1935 to 1947 and Duncan Campbell Scott, the Deputy Superintendent General of Indian Affairs through much of the interwar period. Both the Prime Minister and the Deputy Superintendent General had, of course, been dead for many years by the time of *The White Paper*. This, apparently, did little to lessen the influence of their attitudes on the 1969 *Indian Policy* statement.

Sally Weaver, in *Making Indian Policy*[40] documented how the final text of this document was largely the result of a struggle between the

Department of Indian Affairs and Northern Development (DIAND) and the Privy Council Office (PCO). George Manuel, the second president of the National Indian Brotherhood, who had previously sat on the National Indian Advisory Council and had closely followed the Ministerial Task Force (the Andras hearings) which gathered evidence in preparation for *The White Paper* said that he had not heard one Indian witness advocate the termination policies which became the stuff and substance of *Indian Policy* as it was finally presented to Parliament.

The White Paper was characterized by the persistence of an attitude which articulated government Indian policy from the PCO without regard to anything said by any Indian leader. In that sense, *The White Paper* continued Mackenzie King's historic policies, epitomized by the 1927 *Indian Act* amendment which made the raising of funds for the purpose of pressing Indian land claims a punishable offense. By section 6 of the 1928 *Act to Amend the Indian Act*,[41] a new section 149A had been created in the *Indian Act* which provided as follows:

> Every person who, without the consent of the Superintendent General expressed in writing, receives, obtains, solicits or requests from any Indian any payment or contribution or promise of any payment or contribution for the purpose of raising a fund . . . for the prosecution of any claim which the tribe or band of Indians . . . has or is represented to have for the recovery of any claim or money for the benefit of the said tribe or band, shall be guilty of an offense and liable upon summary conviction . . . to a penalty not exceeding two hundred dollars . . . or to imprisonment for any term not exceeding two months.

Following a number of significant Indian victories in the courts and elsewhere, Parliament chose to protect its position by virtually making it an offense to press Indian land claims so far as it was prohibited to appeal to Indians for support of the claims of their own band or tribe.

Prime Minister Pierre Trudeau's comment, at the time of the *White Paper* that "Aboriginal rights were too vague a concept"[42] to be the basis for negotiation was cut from the same cloth as Mackenzie King's famous statement that Indian veterans might have either Indian rights or citizens' rights.[43] They could not have both. Manuel's final reflection on the betrayal of Indian leaders' collaboration with the Andras process was that "*The White Paper* was written by the ghost of Mackenzie King."[44]

Trudeau's early policy statement is more akin to the Mackenzie King line than to the recommendations of the Parliamentary committees which were mandated during Trudeau's time as Prime Minister. In contrast, the committees which began to sit in 1970—the MacGuigan-Molgat Joint Committee on the Constitution and the Watson Subcommittee on Indian Education—both produced reports focused on strengthening Indian culture and recognizing it as a central part of the Canadian heritage and a key to the revival of Indian communities.

The 1969 *White Paper* continued longstanding policies much more than it presaged the new era proclaimed by Prime Minister Trudeau and his Minister of Indian Affairs, Jean Chrétien. It sought to reinvigorate the historic policies of assimilation in the sense described here. It employed a rhetoric that is unique to Canadian Indian policy but which bears sufficient similarity to conventional English that it causes confusion and misunderstanding amongst the concerned citizenry who attempt to follow the discourse at second hand.

Lastly, but most important, from the Aboriginal perspectives reflected in the testimony before various inquiries before and after the *White Paper*, the *White Paper* represented yet a further set of civil disabilities. That these disabilities were being imposed in the name of freedom, progress and prosperity was not new. These features had also characterized the rationale of U.S. Senator Henry Dawes promotion of the bill that became the *General Allotment* or *Dawes Act* of 1887.

The *White Paper*, however, was a repudiation of the call for "participatory democracy" by Trudeau's immediate predecessor, Lester B. Pearson, in favour of the termination and assimilation policies of earlier Liberal governments. Indian leaders who had put considerable energy into gathering evidence for the hearings held by Robert Andras and for the Indian Advisory Councils did so with some expectation that the policies would bear some resemblance to the reports resulting from the evidence gathered by these hearings. Not only was that still a normative idea at that time, the Trudeau image of "a just society" lent credence to the hope of an Indian policy that reflected Indian perspectives.

The decision to put together a *White Paper* that reflected an ideological view held by the Prime Minister and cultivated by the PCO but which ran counter to the great bulk of Indian testimony demonstrated how little the thinking of central agencies had changed since Mackenzie King rejected the pleas of the Indian veterans after World War II.

The authoritarianism underlying the *White Paper* proclaimed that *Indians would be enfranchised provided that they stopped being Indians*. The early Trudeau era brought a new technology to the old ideology of Mackenzie King. The claims of both "participatory democracy" and of a "just society," at least in the context of First Nations relations proved to be entirely hollow.[45]

This brief survey of the history of Canadian Indian policy and First Nations relations from Confederation to the 1969 *White Paper* and the 1971 *Victoria Charter*—Trudeau's first major effort *to patriate* the Canadian Constitution—introduced a series of conceptual terms as well as terms that are specific either to parliamentary or Canadian political discourse or to the specific discourse of First Nations autonomy. None of Trudeau's three patriation proposals made any reference to First Nations by whatever name. The MacGuigan-Molgat Committee, after two years of hearings across the country on the *Victoria Charter* devoted an entire chapter to ways to include Aboriginal peoples in a revised Canadian Constitution. The 1978 proposal, Bill C-60, ignored these recommendations and renewed the bitterness and distrust of First Nations leaders toward the Trudeau Government. Likewise, the 1980 proposal, as it was introduced by Trudeau, contained no recognition of Aboriginal peoples. Only after considerable lobbying by Aboriginal organizations and committees of influential Canadians and pressure from the New Democratic Party was section 35 added.

The purpose of this chapter is to provide an overview of **the baggage**—*the previous experience and preconceptions*—brought into the proceedings reviewed in the next three chapters both by parliamentarians and by witnesses.

I have challenged the standard historical theory that there has been a consistent policy of assimilation since the earliest Canadian Indian legislation, in 1857 on two grounds. First, that there has not been a consistent policy either between agencies or over any extended period of time. Secondly, that *this theory conflates two conflicting definitions of assimilation*: one looks to a genuine acceptance of a previously excluded population into the mainstream or dominant culture while the other form of assimilation is tantamount to cultural genocide.

One measure of non-acceptance of a minority that runs throughout the history of Canadian First Nations relations is a tendency to impose civil disabilities. Another is the co-option of language so that words lose their ordinary and plain sense meaning. That U.S. Chief Justice John Marshall felt obliged to warn against this practice in 1832 is an indication that it is not unique to Canadian First Nations relations. Enfranchisement is, perhaps, the most distinctive Canadian contribution to the co-option of language and the cultivation of plastic words[46].

Likewise, I have chosen to start with the first Canadian Indian legislation, *An Act for the Gradual Civilization of the Indians* passed by the pre-Confederation Parliament of the province of the United Canadas (later to become Ontario and Quebec at Confederation). Based on my view of assimilation I have argued that the Trudeau White Paper reflected and perpetuated policies that were present in the late 19th century and that ran throughout the period when Duncan Campbell Scott was Deputy Superintendent General between the wars and when William Lyon Mackenzie King was Prime Minister.

I end this chapter (and start the next) with the formation of the National Indian Brotherhood, largely as a response to the *White Paper* and the 1970 mandate of the Joint Committee of the Senate and House of Commons on the Constitution (MacGuigan-Molgat) to study the *Victoria Charter*, Trudeau's first public effort at **patriation**—*changing the Canadian Constitution from a British statute to a document with a Canadian amending formula*, and a *Charter of Rights and Freedoms*.[47] These two developments are fundamental to deep changes in the Canadian political fabric in general and, more particularly, to Canadian First Nations relations.

My major reason for this approach lies in the fact that the MacGuigan-Molgat Committee devoted an entire chapter of its *Final Report* to the need to recognize the place of First Nations in Canadian constitutional history and to respect the wishes of the First Nations regarding constitutional matters affecting First Nations. This perspective, in a report mandated to study the prospects for federal-provincial agreement on patriation, represents a greater conceptual change from earlier Canadian First Nations relations than anything offered before that report by the Government of Pierre Trudeau.

Chapter Three

Public Conversations on First Nations' Self-Government

> "The government policy paper of June, 1969 . . . showed no sense of history and, therefore, no acceptable view of the future."
>
> Ernest Benedict, to a Joint Committee of the Senate and the House of Commons on the Constitution, December 7, 1970.

PART ONE: FINDING VOICES, FINDING EARS

This is the first of three chapters that chronicle the public emergence of the vocabulary of First Nations' Self-Government between 1970 and 1980. The emergence of this vocabulary is an index of the corresponding willingness and capacity of First Nations leaders to articulate their peoples' aspirations to Canadian parliamentarians. No less important, for substantial change in the quality of First Nations relations is the capacity of Canadian parliamentarians to participate in a dialogue centred on this emerging vocabulary.

FINDING A BEGINNING

There was never a time when First Nations people did not speak of their own institutions or of their traditions of autonomy and self-government. There was also never a time when there was not a vocabulary of First Nations' autonomy. There was, however, an extended period when this vocabulary belonged to the various indigenous languages and when discussion of First Nations' autonomy rarely happened in English and did not happen in public, i.e., in places open to all people with access by non-Indians and Indians alike.

The phenomenon traced here is not so much the creation of a concept *as its emergence into the public domain* indicated by *the development of a public record* and *an increasingly specific vocabulary* in a common language. Nonetheless, the emergence of a vocabulary from underground into the light of day can foster dramatic changes. My purpose is not to privilege English over indigenous languages but to look for conditions under which people from all First Nations might engage in a dialogue regarding the autonomy of their various nations. It is also not my intention to overlook the Innu of eastern Quebec and the Malecite and Mi'kmaq near the Quebec-New Brunswick border whose European tongue is French. The development of an English (and French) centred vocabulary has allowed a much freer exchange of ideas amongst the "several First Nations" and between First Nations and prospective supporters both within Canada and abroad.

The basic fact that it became both possible and desirable to discuss with Canadian parliamentarians a matter long discussed in First Nations languages allowed a nascent dialogue in which attitudes of all parties might begin to shift. (There is also evidence that the public emergence of this discourse fostered an increasing resistance by senior officials and ministers. This resistance, in turn, has contributed, at times, to the co-option of the vocabulary of self-government while investing words in this vocabulary with peculiar and non-standard meanings.)

Most important, the emergence of a freer discourse in a common language allows the discussion of First Nations' self-government to be compared to the discourse on autonomy and self-government of other peoples and cultures. Indeed, there is an initial expectation that similar phenomena will be described by similar words and that the words will have analogous, and often similar meanings, in discussions of the institutions and practices of self-government of various cultures.

A vocabulary that has been kept underground is, quite literally, *suppressed*. It is also certain to show signs of having been constrained. The removal of those constraints and the vocabulary's emergence into the public domain is likely to be accompanied, or immediately followed by a broadening and deepening of the vocabulary. One way to highlight constraints is to examine the early or first stages of evolution of the language after it has thoroughly emerged into the public domain. The early evolution will be the second phenomenon to be traced in these chapters.

1970 MARKS THE BEGINNING OF A NEW ERA

There are several reasons for preferring 1970, rather than 1969, as the beginning of a new era in First Nations relations in Canada. On a time line charting the peaks and valleys of "the several Indian nations" in their political relations with Canada, a series of events that began in 1970 mark the beginning of a new era. These include the development of national Aboriginal political organizations with a significant Ottawa presence, the presentation of an approach based on recognition of indigenous rights by two parliamentary committees in 1970, and the apparent retreat of the Trudeau Government from the position set out in thes 1969 *White Paper*.

The formation of a Joint Committee of the Senate and House of Commons on the Constitution under Mark MacGuigan (Liberal, Windsor-Walkerville) and Senator Gildas Molgat (Liberal, Ste Rose, Manitoba) provided a forum which could develop a fresh and largely non-partisan parliamentary perspective on Aboriginal and treaty rights in addition to its primary mandate.[1]

The era that began in 1970 is the era in which indigenous voices could no longer be altogether ignored in the political process. This era is suitably represented, at least in part, by the presentations to the Joint Committee, the requests by Aboriginal witnesses before the Committee for recognition of indigenous rights and the experience of indigenous witnesses and Canadian parliamentarians learning to talk with one another.

Within two years of Manuel taking office, and moving the National Indian Brotherhood from Winnipeg to Ottawa, the National Indian Brotherhood (N.I.B.) had consolidated under its umbrella three essential ingredients for building a Canadian national Indian perspective: (1) a significant level of representivity of provincial and territorial Indian political organizations (PTO's)[2]; (2) an active and direct dialogue with both parliamentarians and civil servants; [3] and, (3) a research capability, the Indian Rights and Treaties Research Program, which provided an independent source of information to the N.I.B. and enabled it to provide a service to its member organizations and to interested academics, journalists and members of the reading public.

The House of Commons Standing Committee on Indian Affairs and Northern Development, under the chairmanship of Ian Watson (Liberal, La Prairie, Québec) dramatically expanded its role in 1970 when it received a mandate to establish a subcommittee on Indian Education.[4] The close collaboration between the Chairman of the Committee and the President of the N.I.B. resulting from the work of the Subcommittee on Indian Education led to a continuing relationship between the Committee and the Brotherhood over the next twelve years which culminated in the Special Committee on Indian Self-Government, as the Penner Committee was formally known at the conclusion of its work in 1983.

The expanded role that the parliamentary committee took on during that twelve-year period may have reached its peak before the self-government study when the Committee increasingly assumed the role of mediating between Indian political organizations and the Department of Indian Affairs and Northern Development. This mediating role was made possible by the presence of a core group of MPs who were able to function in a largely non-partisan fashion, many of whom represented ridings with large Indian electorates and others of whom represented secure urban ridings.

The relatively long term service on the Committee of a core group of MPs allowed these few Members to become conversant with the perspectives of key Indian speakers and the organizations which they represented. After 1984 this consistency of membership and the collective memory and command of the discourse that came with it were largely lost. Two of these core MPs, after some years on the Committee, became, in succeeding governments, the Minister of Indian Affairs and Northern Development. Both of them returned to the Committee after having been the Minister. There was also a considerable overlap in membership between the Standing Committee and the Joint Committee on the Constitution both in 1978 and in 1980–81.

Those MPs and ministers who were sensitive to Indian perspectives and who also read the literature which began to flow from both the official provincial and territorial Indian organizations as well as a burgeoning Indian press are of particular significance in the changes described here. The 1970s may have been the first decade in which Canada enjoyed the benefit of a group of parliamentarians who achieved a degree of functional literacy in regard to Indian issues and Indian rhetoric.

THE MACGUIGAN MOLGAT JOINT COMMITTEE ON THE CONSTITUTION: AN OVERVIEW

The *MacGuigan-Molgat* Committee is the most appropriate first site for examination of the public emergence of this vocabulary because it was the first parliamentary committee to relate Aboriginal rights and treaty rights to the Constitution. The Committee chose to go beyond the ordinary understanding of its mandate and to include an entire chapter of recommendations regarding "Native Peoples." The *Final Report* of this Committee is an explicit rejection of the 1969 *White Paper*, by an all-party Committee of both Houses. Also, this Committee on the Constitution took cognizance in its *Report* of the work of the Standing Committee on Indian Affairs Subcommittee on Education.

The Report of the Subcommittee on Indian Education was produced, in 1971, under the chairmanship of Ian Watson (Liberal, Laprairie), a bilingual Québec Anglophone who worked closely with George Manuel, the President of the N.I.B., and reviewed each chapter of his *Report* with him.[5] The report proposed allowing Indian communities to assume increasing control of their own education. This also laid the groundwork both for Manuel's *Indian Control of Indian Education* and the Indian Affairs Committee's evolution toward the Penner *Report on Indian Self-Government.*

Although the concepts that were articulated during the next decade are present in the MacGuigan-Molgat Committee's *Proceedings,* they are found in this first committee mainly by implication, indirect reference, and historical discussion. The *Proceedings* are also important for their illustration of the discomfort of parliamentarians in discussing the ideas of treaty rights, Aboriginal rights and self-determination. Indeed, a number of the parliamentarians found it difficult to conceive that not only the submissions of Indian organizations but even their names were carefully nuanced to accommodate a complexity of factors. Signs of this discomfort can be found even in the *Final Report.*

An order of reference, setting out the mandate of the Joint Committee on the Constitution, was adopted by the House of Commons on January 27, 1970, and by the Senate on February 17, 1970 the key provisions of which were a mandate

> to examine and report upon proposals, made public . . . by the Government of Canada, on a number of subjects related to the Constitution of Canada. . . . during the course of the comprehensive review of the Constitution of Canada, which review was agreed upon at the Constitutional Conference of the Prime Minister of Canada and the Premiers and Prime Ministers of the Provinces in February 1968, and alternative proposals on the same subjects.[6]

The proposals in question were what became known as the "*Victoria Charter,*" proposals for *patriating* the Constitution, i.e., finding and adopting an amending formula under the control of Canadian legislatures, terminating the amending power which had remained at Westminster as a specific exception in the *Statute of Westminster* of 1931. Neither this formula, which was the bedrock of the MacGuigan-Molgat mandate, nor the mandates of the two later Joint Committees on the Constitution established during Pierre Trudeau's administrations contained explicit references to Aboriginal or treaty rights. Interestingly, the Order of Reference to the Joint Committee[7] was given six months before the Victoria Conference at which the Turner-Trudeau refinement of the Fulton-Favreau formula was tentatively adopted by a first ministers' conference, and an agreement to hold annual meetings thereafter described as "first ministers' meetings"[8] was made. The decision of the Committee to devote a chapter of its *Final Report* to "Native Peoples" is all the more noteworthy because there is no mention in the *Victoria Charter* of Aboriginal interests, or "Indian rights," as they were better known at the outset of the Committee's work.

Clearly, a public process intended to gather support for a refined and enlarged variation on the Victoria formula and to move Parliament toward a consensus on patriation was a real and important mandate and, possibly, one with a more enduring value than most Cabinet positions during the same Parliament.

Conversely, even as we value and appreciate this Committee's function, it becomes increasingly evident that this function, as the Trudeau Government intended in its original mandate, had nothing to do with Indians, constitutional or otherwise. That the Committee should devote an entire chapter of its final report to issues "concerning Native peoples" is an indication that the Committee membership and particularly its presiding officers were prepared to take a creative view of their mandate. They were prepared to reach out, at least obliquely, on a different tack than the Government. On the other hand, as we will see in a closer examination of the MacGuigan-Molgat recommendations, the language with which the Joint Committee attempted to express support for Indian aspirations reflects the authors' great uncertainty as to the language in which this support might most appropriately be expressed; however well intended, that chapter has the gait of a new born colt.

The *MacGuigan-Molgat* Committee consisted of nine Senators and 19 Members of Parliament with representation distributed among the parties according to their standings at the time. The Members representing the different parties in each House changed over the Committee's three years' duration, thus enhancing the position of those who lasted for the duration and, particularly, the Commons chairman, Mark MacGuigan.

WORK STYLE AND SELF-IMAGE OF THE MACGUIGAN-MOLGAT COMMITTEE ON THE CONSTITUTION

A brief note on the work style and self-image of the Joint Committee will help to place in context the discussion of Indian and Native issues in the testimony and, ultimately, in the *Final Report*.

There is a dynamic tension inherent in sustained service on parliamentary committees mandated to study constitutional amending formulas or Indian education. Members who devoted serious time to this

Joint Committee, for instance, would have done well not to expect to win additional votes for this service. At the same time, the Victoria formula represented a pinnacle of consensus for all the years of federal-provincial negotiations around the issue of patriation since the federal-provincial conference of 1967. Even Québec Premièr Robert Bourassa had consented to this formula while he was at the Victoria Conference.[9] For those who care deeply about national unity, patriation, responsible government or democratic principles, the possibility of fostering a widespread understanding and possibly even a parliamentary consensus of a patriation proposal could, after all, compete favourably with a Cabinet portfolio.

Some of this tension was resolved through the work of a select group of Senators with a longstanding commitment either to constitutional studies (Muriel Fergusson, a Liberal Senator from New Brunswick, Jacques Flynn, PC, Rosemont, Québec, and Eugene Forsey, Liberal, Nepean, Ontario) or to social development (Donald Cameron, a Liberal from Banff; J.C. Haig, PC, River Heights, Manitoba; Maurice Lamontagne, and Paul Yuzyk, a Conservative from Ft. Garry, Manitoba).

The MPs who sat on this Joint Committee also included a number with a longstanding interest in constitutional issues: Lincoln Alexander (PC, Hamilton West), Warren Allmand (Liberal, Notre Dame de Grace), Andrew Brewin (NDP Greenwood), Walter Dinsdale (PC-Brandon-Souris), Gordon Fairweather (PC-Fundy-Royal), Edmund B. Osler (Liberal, Winnipeg South Centre) and Marcel Prud'homme (Liberal, St. Denis). Perhaps no less striking is the number whose seats were relatively safe (at least as measured by the ability of the incumbent to retain the seat over a series of elections while his parties' fortunes rose and fell) and who could, therefore, invest themselves in a project which might carry minimal electoral rewards. Among those whose seats might have been considered to fit that description would be Lincoln Alexander, Warren Allmand (Liberal, Notre Dame de Grâce), Martial Asselin (PC-Charlevoix), Andrew Brewin, Pierre de Bané (Liberal, Matane), Walter Dinsdale, Gordon Fairweather.

The only Indian person on the Committee was Len Marchand (Liberal, Kamloops-Cariboo) who was newly arrived in June, 1968, at the start of the 28th Parliament but who would, indeed, hold his seat until he was elevated to the Senate.

The Committee's *Final Report* describes the then new and untried methods of inviting statements from the floor in addition to formal briefs. It also describes how widely the Committee travelled. It estimates that 13,000 people attended the Committee's hearings and "1,486 Canadians appeared as witnesses." The Report's advertisement for the Committee's work appears, to those already familiar with the work of the Croll Senate

Committee on Poverty and the Davey Senate Committee on the Mass Media, slightly overstated, "No previous parliamentary committee has ever held such an ambitious series of hearings in order to acquaint itself with public opinion." It also confused "participation by the *man* (sic) *in the street*" with the benefits of hearing from people who could be "encouraged to speak extemporaneously at [Committee] meetings from microphones placed on the floor." Under the pressure of a parliamentary schedule, these innovations tested the chairmen and moved them to distinguish between "representative witnesses" and those who appeared "in their individual capacities." It seems, nonetheless, fair to acknowledge that the Committee did engage in procedures and processes which were, at that time, new and innovative ways for public inquiries to take evidence. The Berger Inquiry would take public participation in public inquiries to new lengths only several years later in 1974–76.

Another overstatement underlies the left critique of Trudeau's constitutional reform campaign which claims that there was a lack of openness and opportunity for public participation.[10] When the work of the three Joint Committees is combined, parliamentary committees held public hearings on the Canadian Constitution, and particularly on patriation related issues through seven of the twelve years from 1970 through 1982. Although it can be argued that many of the same witnesses were heard by each of the three committees, the claim that there was a lack of public participation is either overstated or dependent upon differing definitions of "participation."

John Turner, the Minister of Justice of the day, was the first witness before the MacGuigan-Molgat Committee. He observed that the constitutional conference of justice ministers had established "four committees of ministers to consider special questions: official languages, the judiciary, fundamental rights, and the Senate."[11] Aboriginal issues did not carry sufficient gravity or political pressure, from the Government's to warrant such a committee. "There was also a Committee of Officials set up by the Conference in 1968 to assist the Conference in its task."[12]

> Mackenzie King would have been proud.
> The height of his ambition
> Was to pile a Parliamentary Committee on a Royal Commission,
> . . .
> To let Parliament decide–
> Later.[13]

David Lewis, the New Democratic Party leader invited John Turner to comment on the social and economic development in Canada which made the present Constitution set up (sic) inadequate, if it is inadequate, so people of Canada can see this exercise of Constitutional review not as an exercise between governments vying for power . . . but rather as a review deriving from fundamental needs of the Canadian people. [14]

Neither John Turner nor H.F. Davis, Secretary of the Constitutional Conference, offered a direct response.

EARLIER INDIAN AND NATIVE TESTIMONY BEFORE THE COMMITTEE

On Friday, September 11, 1970, three months after the Victoria Conference achieved a momentary consensus, the MacGuigan-Molgat Committee heard its first Indian and Native witnesses at Fort Garry outside Winnipeg,. The symbolic value of holding this first meeting at Fort Garry would have been apparent to all of the key players. The first Indian witness was Dr. Dave Courchene, the President of the Manitoba Indian Brotherhood. The first Métis witness was Mr. Tom Eagle, Vice-President of the Manitoba Métis Federation.

DAVE COURCHENE, PRESIDENT, MANITOBA INDIAN BROTHERHOOD

In 1970, Dave Courchene probably had a higher recognition factor among his own people and also among those non-Native people who cared about Indian matters than any other Indian leader. Dr. Courchene was the first of a long line of Indian political leaders to receive honorary doctorates when universities began to become aware of the Indian leadership in Canada. Courchene had received his honorary doctor of laws from the University of Manitoba in 1970.[15] For an Indian leader to appear before a parliamentary committee in 1970 bearing any degree was still a rare and notable event.

Dr. Courchene began his presentation with a move which allowed him to combine his classical style with a move that was both strategic and pragmatic. He quoted at length from a recent speech of the President of the United States, Richard M. Nixon, in support of Indian self-determination:

> The first Americans—the Indians—are the most deprived and most isolated minority group in our nation.
>
> This condition is the heritage of centuries of injustice. From the time of their first contact with European settlers, the American Indians have been oppressed and brutalized, deprived of their ancestral lands and denied the opportunity to control their own destiny. Even the federal

> programs which are intended to meet their needs have frequently proven to be ineffective and demeaning.
>
> But the story of the Indian in America is something more than the record of the white man's frequent aggression, broken agreements, intermittent remorse and prolonged failure. It is also a record of endurance, of survival, of adaptation and creativity in the face of overwhelming obstacles. It is a record of enormous contributions to this country, to its art and culture, to its strength and spirit, to the sense of history and its sense of purpose.
>
> It is long past time that the Indian policies of the federal government began to recognize and build upon the capacities and insights of the Indian people. Both as a matter of justice and as a matter of enlightened society, we must begin to act on the basis of what the Indians themselves have long been telling us.[16]

It was Dave Courchene's judiciously quoting from Richard Nixon which allowed a series of oblique references to Indian self-determination, references which would be quite clear to a careful listener. Nixon's characterization of "the Indians" as "the first Americans" employed a category which relied heavily on juggling two quite different meanings of the same word. This archetypal anachronism was, however, the very rhetoric Dr. Courchene needed to plant the idea of "Citizens Plus."

He quoted Richard Nixon saying, "The time has come to break decisively with the past and to create the conditions for a new era in which, *the Indian future* is *determined* by *Indian acts* and *Indian decisions.*"[17]

Dr. Courchene's Nixon quote links the depredations of the United States Government and their role in imposing the hardships of poverty through their repeated breaches of trust to the need to allow Indians to manage their own affairs and for the United States to recognize the right of Indians to pursue their self-determination through autonomous institutions. Had anyone else given this speech, the contrast of the *mea culpa* of official wrong doing by the U.S. federal state over against the "record of enormous contributions to this country" by "the Indian" would have been characterized as a latterday version of the romantic notion of the noble savage. The Nixon speech gave Dave Courchene the ammunition he needed to hold the attention and gain the respect of the more conservative members of the parliamentary committee.

Having set the stage by tipping his hat to the American president who brought the cavalry back from Vietnam and into real "Indian country,"[18] Courchene was ready to talk about the Canadian Constitution. Thirteen years before the Supreme Court of Canada declared that both treaties and statutes should be interpreted according to their spirit and intent and "ambiguities resolved in favour of the Indians."[19] Dave Courchene explained to the *MacGuigan-Molgat* Committee the inequitable nature of treaty negotiations:

> 100 years ago my forefathers presumed to speak for Indian people in signing treaties with the Crown without the full knowledge of the ramifications of those treaties and often without any knowledge of the meaning of the words of an alien tongue used to communicate their intent.[20]

Having offered the rationale for resolving ambiguity in favour of the Indians, Courchene summed up his observation of the actual conduct of government,

> Laws have been passed under the Constitution to reflect generally what government interpreted as its obligations by right of treaty, with little if any reference to the interpretation placed upon these documents by the other signatory, the Indian people themselves.[21]

Dr. Courchene's concern with history had mainly to do with its capacity to teach the present players how to avoid those same pitfalls: "I am conscious that I do not want to go down in history as one who has contributed to a second tragedy through misinformation and misunderstandings."[22]

Courchene drew from his analysis two conclusions that in the hands of less adept speakers might have appeared as antithetical and mutually exclusive. On the one hand, "the treaties of 100 years ago were signed between two sovereign nations;"[23] on the other hand, the actual outcome of the treaty process "in the light of today's circumstances and today's laws would be classified as *unconscionable.*"[24] This duality results in two types of interrelated injustices which need to be redressed.

In offering a definition of justice—"We must address ourselves to *a just reconciliation* of the causes of discontent" [25]—he introduced not only the idea of reconciliation but also the assurance that he and, presumably, his colleagues and constituents, were prepared to be part of a process which had to do with embedding justice and reconciliation in the Canadian Constitution. "Reconciliation" is, in its root meaning, about "restoring a bond of union."[26] Such a *restored bond*, Courchene argued, must be put on such a high shelf that it is not likely to be trampled upon in the future. This is a future focus which requires enough attention on the past to see the treaties as bonds between nations. The notion of "a restored bond" also reinforced the idea that there was, at some historical point, a healthier more positive relationship characterized by bonds of friendship.

Courchene was among the Indian leaders who, for rhetorical purposes at least, were prepared to take the promise of "a just society" at face value. It was fortunate that he was appearing before a committee chairman as scholarly and thoughtful as Mark MacGuigan.

Courchene had two basic requests. First, that "no amendments with respect to Indian people be recommended or undertaken until such time as we have had an opportunity to negotiate honestly and honourably a reconciliation of differences between our people and their government"[27] while, secondly, the reconciliation of which he was speaking should result in constitutional amendments. One condition of "honest and honourable negotiation" was the opportunity, including the means, to do thorough and complete research. He specifically warned against "Arbitrary changes in the Constitution that do not satisfy, in the final analysis, the moral and legal obligations as seen by both parties to the treaties."[28]

A number of Dave Courchene's recommendations surface in the *Final Report.* So does a significant number of the rhetorical devices in the speeches of both Dr. Courchene and Walter Gordon, including lexical items which occur not in their own words but in Courchene's extended quotation from Richard Nixon.[29] "First Canadians" as an effort to honour First Nations without using such politically complicated words as "nations" or "peoples" is a prime example.

The use of the term "first Canadians" may have been meant, in the drafting of the *MacGuigan-Molgat Final Report* as an ennobling term. It is a term without substance, *an ersatz term.* "Ganada" is a Mohawk term from which "Canada" may have evolved but its meaning is very different. "Canadiens" was adopted into French, and later into English, to refer to francophone fur traders, *couer du bois*, and settlers. There was no thought of including indigenous peoples as Canadians until the late 1940s, when Indian veterans, recently home from WWII, told a joint parliamentary committee that they should have both "Indian rights" and the rights of citizens. Governments did not accept this idea until the Diefenbaker Government amended the *Elections Act* to allow Indians the vote in 1961.

For a joint parliamentary committee to refer to indigenous peoples as "the First Canadians" a mere ten years later takes historical revisionism to an extreme. The term "first Canadians" is surely as good an example of *plastic language* as we are likely to find. It does not honour indigenous peoples to impose upon them yet another concocted label in which they are unlikely to recognize themselves. The term may well have appealed to members of the government which had, only three years earlier, introduced a policy paper proposing to abolish all vestiges of distinctive legal rights for indigenous people in Canada. If it was a term intended to honour peoples while denying recognition of their legal rights to land, culture and community, it is an honour without currency. I have been unable to identify any later text in which this term is used.

Courchene's own discussion of reconciliation resonated with a gradualism which, in contrast to Nixon's radical rhetoric appeared both responsible and Canadian. Courchene quoted Nixon saying "The time has come to break decisively with the past and to create the conditions for a new era."[30] In his own words he offers a much more modest observation: "It is unfortunate that the Constitution to date makes very little reference to the rights and privileges of Indian people."[31]There was at least an apparent contradiction in Courchene's suggestion that there is a need for a constitutional recognition while he also asked that no provision be made until there was further consultation. This kind of extreme democratic thought was not likely within the grasp of many of the Committee members.

He also appeared to recognize that one culture's impatience might foster the other culture's impatience. He asked, "How content are your people with the orderly approach that you are advocating?"[32]

Osler, like others who followed him, continued to speak in a zero plural[33] form i.e., to attribute traits and attitudes to "the Indian" and to "the white man."[34] Indeed, the stereotyping grammar persisted even among those parliamentarians whose substantive remarks indicated a wish to be basically supportive. "The Indian traditionally has had a different attitude towards natural resources than has had the white man."[35] Indeed, this grammatical conundrum prefaced a truly profound question, "Can an acceptable way of life be *guaranteed* to *Indian people* with the divergent philosophy that *it* has taken from the majority?" There is, of course, an assumption that there is a "majority" and that it is essentially identical, in the way of life to which it aspires, as "the mainstream" or "the dominant culture."

Dave Courchene took some of the starch out of this "either-or" by saying, "We want the same good things that Canada makes available to its citizens. *We do not have to lose our identity in the process though.*"[36] Courchene has, in the course of this answer, created his own either-or when he adopts the distinction between "citizen" and "Indian."[37]

Dave Courchene closed with an appeal for Canadians to learn some traditional Indian values in order to avoid duplicating "the destruction in the southern half of the North American continent where pollution is a real disaster now."[38] Finally, he stressed a point to which all members of the Committee, might have interpreted each according to their own lights, "I hope that we can find a new direction *together* as Canadians."

MR. TOM EAGLE (VICE-PRESIDENT, MANITOBA MÉTIS FEDERATION):

Tom Eagle focused heavily on the economic condition of his constituents and pleaded for a devolution of power "to assist the junior governments with the burdens of an even more complex society by increasing local government control."[39] This argument is all the more striking in light of his having initially asserted that "the majority of Métis have a strong Indian identity, and other than in legal terms most of us are as much Indian as those who are covered by treaty."[40]

Mr. Hogarth (Liberal, New Westminster) was concerned that the kind of equalization of which Mr. Eagle had spoken could not be accomplished by passing a law. He went on to "suppose you would [not] go far as to suggest that in a Constitution, which is what we are considering, that there be additional legal rights given to people *in minority ethnic positions,* be they Métis, Doukhobors, Mennonites, Englishmen, Frenchmen, whatever . . ."[41]

The Hon. Walter Dinsdale, in his questions to Tom Eagle, achieved a level of condescension equalled only by his ignorance of the Canadian Constitution. He began his remarks by saying,

"Mr. Chairman, I am interested in *Tom's* emphasis on increasing the powers and responsibilities of both provincial and local governments . . . "[42] In his next question, Mr. Dinsdale addressed the witness directly in the same familiar way, "You are saying then, *Tom*, that actually the Constitution as it stands giving this responsibility to the provinces is adequate if the provinces will accept their responsibility."[43] In 40 years of reading parliamentary committee proceedings I can not recall another instance in which a parliamentarian referred to or addressed a witness by his first name. Dinsdale's question asks Mr. Eagle, who has spoken mainly about economic issues, a question about how the Constitution stands at the moment, after asserting erroneous notions of the constitution's present state.

Mr. Dinsdale then confused status under the *Indian Act* with "Indian" in the constitutional sense of s.91 (24),

> At the moment the treaty people are in the special category that is specifically provided for under the British North America Act, whereas the Métis people who follow *the Indian way of life have no legal status constitutionally* defined.[44] (emphasis added)

Neither Mr. Eagle nor any member of the Committee found it in their interest to point out to Mr. Dinsdale, as it is noted in this Committee's *Final Report,* that Métis are very likely and non-status Indians almost certainly included within the meaning of s.91(24).[45] Mr. Dinsdale then concluded by observing

> [T]he real problem is an educational one, concern at the local community level, an understanding of the special problems of the Métis people, and getting the individual citizen involved in doing something about it. I think this is occurring in Manitoba now. [46]

Mr. Dinsdale was, possibly, grateful that "Tom" had not been so impertinent as to draw a connection between the fraud perpetrated through the administration of Métis scrip and his people's current poverty.[47]

DAWSON CITY, SEPTEMBER 15, 1970

Two references to Indian rights occurred during the Committee's day in Dawson, the capital of the Yukon territory. Erik Nielsen, Progressive Conservative MP for the Yukon related his wish to repeal the *Indian Act* with the desire of "We in the Yukon . . . to see constitutional reform which would result in a blueprint for the gradual emergence of the Yukon as a province in the fullness of time."[48] Just how a blueprint might be embedded in the Constitution was not revealed. Also not apparent were the views of any Indian leaders in the Yukon.

Mr. Normal Chamberlist, Member of the Territorial Council, Whitehorse East, after an original and innovative tour of the Canadian Constitution spoke of the need to repeal the *Indian Act*. When Mr. Hogarth asked if Mr. Chamberlist had "ever advocated on their behalf that the Indian people as of right be represented on the Territorial Council" Mr. Chamberlist was quite forthright in saying, first that "Every Indian person has a right to stand for election." When Mr. Hogarth asked again about special representation, he said, "I do not think they have that right. . . . [I]n my opinion they have no right apart from the fact that they are Canadians."[49] Ironically, this view was offered after he told the Committee

> When I say this [the repeal of the *Indian Act*] it should be in consultation with the Indian people because they are affected and, after all, the Royal Proclamation of 1763 already lays out certain inherent protective rights

> in the Constitution and this is a constitutional thing that has been left out.[50]

Contradictions such as this are not altogether unusual in committee testimony but they are rarely pursued by questions from the parliamentarians.

This may be the first time that the word "inherent" appears in the *MacGuigan-Molgat Proceedings.* The second is Prof. Noel Lyon's reference to the government's "inherent paternalistic attitude."[51] Chamberlist's remarks seem also to be the first reference to the *Royal Proclamation of 1763.* How exactly Mr. Chamberlist arrived at the conclusion that there were no treaty or Aboriginal rights while, at the same time, describing the effect of provisions of the Royal Proclamation as *inherent protective rights* was one of the lesser mysteries of parliamentary history. And if the consultation he envisions with "the Indian people" involves some kind of consent on their part to the abolition of their rights, that proposition is an axiom of the same mystery.

NOEL DOUCETTE (PRESIDENT, UNION OF NOVA SCOTIA INDIANS, SYDNEY, N.S.)

Noel Doucette, President of the Union of Nova Scotia Indians (UNSI), appeared before the Committee on Wednesday, October 21, 1970, during their hearings in Sydney, Nova Scotia. He began by saying that the *White Paper* had "brought into public focus all of the fundamental issues relating to *Canada's native* population"[52] including its (sic) existence as an identifiable entity." [53] Although he wanted the Committee to reflect on the "Several value judgments of far-reaching significance implicit in the *White Paper* he also said that "The past has too often seen misunderstandings and misinterpretations of Indians rights and liabilities."[54]

Noel Doucette set out to give the Committee a brief tour of Maritime Canadian history from a UNSI point of view. He introduced the notion that at Confederation his people "were considered a vanishing race."[55] Doucette did not introduce MicMac terminology; instead he used the terminology of each of the colonial regimes. He reminded the Committee that "Early treaties in [New] France and later in Nova Scotia were peacekeeping in nature and designed to insure the status quo of the Indian people."[56] His history culminated in a discussion of the federal responsibility under s.91(24) of the *BNA Act.* He reminded the Committee of the Government's efforts to remove itself from those responsibilities in the *White Paper* and offered the alternative of making changes to ss.91(24):

> Resources in the tangible form of funds and in the intangible form of "grassroots" involvement . . .
>
> Indian associations and/or band councils must have Indian people appointed to liaison positions at the ministerial levels of government, to insure effective consultation and communication and dissemination of information.
>
> Indian people must be given a chance to work to realize their problems and to work these problems out for themselves, at their own pace, in their order of priority.
>
> Indian people must have open all the choices of Canadian citizenship on the federal, provincial and municipal levels of government.[57]

When Andrew Brewin, a New Democratic MP from Toronto, asked Noel Doucette if he had specific constitutional recommendations to make, Doucette went back to his recommendations about grassroots education.

> [W]hat this Committee could recommend is that first of all the Indian people must be made aware of what the BNA Act is.
>
> There are, in Nova Scotia, believe it or not, Indian people that do not fully understand English. . . . It will take time. . . . . . . We are saying, first, of all, that we must be given the opportunity to tell our people what is in these acts and translated into the language that is understandable to the Indian people.[58]

Certain members persisted in looking for opportunities to play "Gotcha," to challenge the *bona fides,* if not of the witness then of his national and inter-regional relationships. From this perspective it was, perhaps, fortunate that those who used their time in this manner had usually not done their homework:

> **Mr. Dinsdale:** . . . I wonder if the witness who has made an excellent presentation here this morning could indicate to the Committee whether his association was consulted in connection with the response of the National Indian Brotherhood, I believe to the government's *White Paper.*

> **Mr. Doucette:** Yes, sir, we were consulted. Here again the Red Paper of Alberta, you must understand, is the Red Paper of Alberta. It is not necessarily a paper for all Indians of Canada. We were behind the Indians of Alberta in making their presentation to government because *who are we,* in Nova Scotia *to say to Alberta Indians that this is not what they want.*[59] (emphasis added)

The sense of humour reflected in this delightful squelch, as well as the values underlying the statement, may be as characteristic of Doucette's culture as a relationship with the land and a sense of place. From the perspective of First Nations relations we might speculate whether federal Ministers of Agriculture encounter particular difficulty in mastering such nuances.

In contrast to Noel Doucette's notion of grassroots input, Mr. Dinsdale also continued to imagine that the Commissioner might be the person who would do the studies, have ideas and make recommendations:

> **Mr. Dinsdale:** Do you think the appointment of a Commissioner to study treaty rights has gone far enough in dealing with the problem that has been neglected over the years, as you point out in your brief here?
>
> **Mr. Doucette:** I think you will understand, sir, that the National Indian Brotherhood and its member organizations have decided that they will not work through the Commissioner but rather through the Committee of the National Indian Brotherhood, particularly the Committee on Treaty and Indian Rights.
>
> **Mr. Dinsdale:** Have there been any consultations with the Commissioner?
>
> **Mr. Doucette:** None whatsoever, sir.[60]

Walter Dinsdale recognized the direction in which Doucette was heading but he also continued to trip over his own condescension while introducing two words which do not occur at any earlier point in the *Proceedings,* "self-determination" and "consultation."

> **Mr. Dinsdale:** I notice your brief comes down very heavily on the principle of self-determination and consultation. Do you think that the Indians have had an opportunity for consultation and self-determination?

> Do you feel that there has been sufficient representation on various committees now engaged in studying the Indian problem (sic)?[61]
>
> **Mr. Doucette:** If you could define "consultation" then maybe we could answer your question.
>
> **Mr. Dinsdale:** Let us say then the appointment of spokesmen from the Indian community as approved by the National Brotherhood. Is it the feeling of your Nova Scotia Brotherhood (sic) that there has been adequate representation of official spokesmen, approved by the National Brotherhood, on the various committees now dealing with the Indian question (sic)?
>
> **Mr. Doucette:** The reason I asked you what you meant by "consultation" is that you probably remember prior to the Indian policy coming out there was consultation with Indian people right across Canada. We had one day with the Indian affairs Minister—and this was one day for all the Indian people in the Maritimes.[62]

It was characteristic of Noel Doucette's sense of compassion that he asked Mr. Dinsdale to say what he meant by "consultation" but not what he meant by "the Indian problem." More significant is Mr. Dinsdale's response that consultation might consist of "the appointment of spokesmen [presumably by the Government] from the Indian community as approved by the National Brotherhood." Between the Dinsdale vision of consultation and the Doucette notion of grassroots participation there is a very wide gap.

Martial Asselin (PC—Charlevoix) remarked on the diversity of needs and observed, "that these needs change according to the province with regard to the Indians' needs and with regard *to their knowledge of their rights.*[63] Oblivious to the irony of his observation, Martial Asselin pursued the idea of a transfer to provincial jurisdiction—a *White Paper* concept soaked in a Conservative rationale:

> Under these circumstances, could the witness tell us whether he objects strongly to this whole question of Indian affairs being handed over to the provinces, because I think the provinces have the type of government that is closer to the people and knows more of the needs of the people. Would the Indians be more adequately served if they could turn to the provinces. With a federal-provincial agreement, the provinces could administer the *Indian Act*. Could the witness answer that?[64]

The notion that the provinces might be closer to the people was the very reason given by a British Commons Committee in 1831 for keeping Indian affairs *out of provincial control.*[65]

Noel Doucette gently explained that there are, in fact, different legal regimes across Canada according to the presence or absence of different types of treaties. By and large, Indian people wanted more time because they wanted to understand the rights previously guaranteed to them and they wanted an indication that these would be honoured and respected under a new Constitution. Committee members persisted in wanting to know the conclusions likely to be reached at the end of the studies, grassroots discussions and consultations not yet having been undertaken.

Osler grasped the idea that Indians might need to take charge of their own collective lives but persisted in the need to cast such an idea in temporary terms:

> I think that other Canadians would be very suspicious of creating a nation within a nation but that does not to my mind mean that a group of Indians elected by Indians should not be involved in a specifically Indian affair, at least on a temporary basis—and when I say temporary if may be 50 years or 100 years. Is this the kind of concept you are thinking of?[66]

What is, perhaps, most interesting about this statement is not that it introduces the term "nation" but does so as something which Canada might *create*, not as something which has an existence prior to "any imperial legislative or executive act."[67]

MR. WALTER GORDON, RESEARCH ASSISTANT TO CHIEF DAVID AHENAKEW OF THE FEDERATION OF SASKATCHEWAN INDIANS

Walter Gordon addressed the Committee in Saskatoon at the Arts Building of the University of Saskatchewan, at its fourteenth meeting. His title understates his standing. Walter Gordon was a well-respected scholar and orator in his own right. Nonetheless, the decision of the head of the Federation of Saskatchewan Indians to absent himself remains striking.

Walter Gordon's was the first statement to the Committee from an Indian leader to speak in bold and direct language. Unlike Dr. Courchene, Mr. Gordon did not talk of reconciliation as a first step. Nor did he speak of education as a first step. Walter Gordon began with what Chief

Justice Dickson would, some years later, describe as "the honour of the Crown:"

> [T]he Federation of Saskatchewan Indians submits that the Indian treaties made between the federal government of Canada on behalf of Her Majesty Queen Victoria and the Indian people are inviolate. These treaties must be strictly adhered to and must be embodied in the Canadian Constitution now and at any time of revision of the Constitution of Canada.[68]

Gordon was the first witness to introduce the terms "racial and cultural genocide" into these proceedings. He related the honour of the Crown to the health and well being of Indian communities and individual people including their capacity to learn:

> The Indian people have been frustrated in every way during the past 100 years in their attempts to better their life conditions. The Indian identity has borne the brunt of these attacks. Intense pressures were brought to bear upon the Indians to systematically destroy their identity which awakens conscience and which enables each man to see his own self, his culture, his family, religion and history. Taking away the identity is taking away the sense of oneself. Every Indian needs such a sense of value and individuality. It is the real source of all of their motivation in life. Their identity is something that cannot be purchased nor can it be manufactured. However, it can be stolen and it can be lost. The conditions on which their identity depends have all but been destroyed. Their history which gives them roots and a knowledge of what Indians can accomplish has been distorted. their culture which teaches a way of living, learning together, has been ravaged. Their identity is stolen when the conditions necessary for individual development and self-respect are destroyed as a result of a deliberate policy on the part of stronger society and institutions *intent upon racial and cultural genocide.*[69]

The central constitutional recommendation was clear, short and, at least grammatically, simple: "The Canadian government can do no less than keep those treaties in the Canadian Constitution for all time." Walter Gordon addressed the issue of assimilation by stressing its inauthenticity and its impossibility, "As Indian people, they know that no one nation or culture can assimilate other cultures. It can only denature, suppress or alienate them."[70]

In a curious turn of phrase Walter Gordon spoke of the FSI, "in the past two or three years (having risen] to the mammoth task of rebuilding the Indian nation." He spoke of the organization having "their own unique approach to the problems of being human."[71]

> It is not a question of restoring vanished nomadic and tribal societies. It is a matter of allowing Indians of every background to realize their own identity without sacrifice of benefits, of acknowledging that racial and cultural gifts of the Indian are essential to the welfare of the whole. These racial and cultural gifts must be preserved.[72]

Walter Gordon was certainly the first presenter to tell the Committee that honouring the treaties and helping to preserve Indians' sense of national, cultural and individual identity also served a Canadian interest.

After explaining the education and medicine chest provisions of Treaty Six, Walter Gordon concluded with an expression of confidence that this Committee would

> work so that Parliament will reaffirm its intent to carry out the terms of treaty agreements with the Indians of Canada. . . . This reaffirmation can only be made by the embodiment of the treaties of Canada between the Crown and the Indians in the Canadian Constitution.[73]

THE PARLIAMENTARIANS' RESPONSE TO WALTER GORDON'S REMARKS

The question of how Walter Gordon's remarks were received is quite central to the evolution of the discourse. Did a more forthright presentation which made explicit demands and pointed to enduring aspirations of nationhood elicit a different response from the parliamentarians as the immediate auditors? In addition, how was their response to Walter Gordon different from their response to Dave Courchene or Noel Doucette?

Looking at the first page of an exchange between Walter Gordon and Walter Dinsdale, one sees fewer prefatory comments and questions that are more direct. If this is a sign of closer attention being paid, the closer attention does not run so far as to exempt the Federation of Saskatchewan Indians from being called "the Saskatchewan Brotherhood."

Mr. Dinsdale persisted in his effort to promote the role of the Indian Commissioner. It is not clear, however, whether he had grasped whether the role of the Commissioner is judicial, advisory or administrative.

> **Mr. Dinsdale:** Does the Saskatchewan Brotherhood (sic) feel that this Claims Commissioner is an adequate way to deal with a long-standing problem of' unresolved settlement of claims under treaties?
>
> **Mr. Gordon:** The Federation of Saskatchewan Indians and the National Indian Brotherhood have no right to tell the government what to do on the government's part, and this is a government appointment, not an Indian appointment. We believe that we have a voice in the kind of' appointments that are made with regard to the rights of Indian people.
>
> **Mr. Dinsdale:** I wonder if perhaps I did not make myself quite clear. Do you feel that the appointment of a Claims Commissioner is adequate to deal with *a very complex problem* of this kind . . . ?
>
> **Mr. Gordon:** For 100 years the Indian nation has been considered *a complexity'* by the white people and their Government and *it truly is not,* and I cannot say again or speak for the government and say that we like this appointment or we dislike this appointment. All that I could say now at this time is that the new Chrétien Indian policy brought out on June 26, 1969, . . . the Indian people rejected and rejected all it stood for, along with a commissioner, because the Indian people were not consulted in the new Indian policy and the appointment of a commission.[74] (emphasis added)

The corollary of the Indian organizations' rejection of the Indian Commissioner's role—that Indians might do their own research—appeared to be equally difficult for Mr. Dinsdale to fully grasp:

> Does Mr. Gordon feel that *the Indians themselves should have the funds, the wherewithal* to investigate the treaties, and are they proceedings along these lines to do just that?[75] (emphasis added)

The idea of Indians themselves having "the wherewithal" falls directly in line with Martial Asselin's observation about Indian needs rising directly with their knowledge of their rights. Walter Gordon met this concern in his usual direct fashion:

> Yes, we are proceeding to investigate and research the claims that may be made, the abrogations that have been made and the bad things that have been done to Indian people.[76]

Warren Allmand intervened for the first time with, in use his own term, a series of "dilemmas":

> [H]ow do we put it in the Constitution so that it will not do harm to *the Indian* (sic) rather than help him (sic)? And I want to put to you some of the dilemmas that we face. On the one hand, there is the suggestion that we recognize the principle that the Indians be treated equally as all other Canadians, and on the other hand, to do that without destroying *the Indians'* desire to live as a distinctive people. I personally see a dilemma there in our search for a formula so that we can provide for equality and also provide for the type of life that the Indians want to live.[77] (emphasis added)

He, too, however, was limited in his capacity to work through those dilemmas both by the language he and his colleagues were formulating; and, by a correspondingly incomplete understanding of the witnesses' conviction that Aboriginal and treaty rights, as Chief Justice Dickson would later say, were part of a "unique contemporary relationship,"[78] .." . to give the Indians the things that *they ask for* in the treaties[79] and at the same time try to avoid some of the paternalism that has taken place over the last 100 years." Warren Allmand's progress from "the Indian" to "the Indians" within this paragraph may, in this context, be highly significant of the intellectual ferment taking place as he spoke.

Warren Allmand's dilemmas could also be noteworthy examples of *burden shifting* from a scholarly parliamentarian who would as Minister of Indian Affairs and, later, as a member of both the Standing Committee on Indian Affairs and Northern Development (the Standing Committee) and the Penner Committee on Indian Self-Government become particularly sensitive to the interplay of appropriate language and equitable relations. By taking treaties at face value, Allmand makes *a presumption in favour* of the Indian treaty parties and *extends the benefit of the doubt* to their ostensible beneficiaries. In doing this he extends both common decency and the rule of law to Indian witnesses in a way which was still quite novel in Canadian parliamentary practice.

Warren Allmand would surely have agreed, if not at that time then soon thereafter, that treaties are agreements and not instruments of request. He would also recognize that treaties did not particularly *give* anything to Indians except, (1) the right to retain a portion of what a treaty party formerly had or (2) to receive other goods or services in partial payment for what was surrendered and (3) the promise of the Crown to protect that which is to be retained. In that sense, "the honour of the Crown" [80] may be said to be the very essence of a treaty. Without the honour of the Crown neither the compensation nor the protection have currency and, indeed, the prospect of retaining a portion, as is evident throughout the history, is all too slight.

Douglas Hogarth, the Liberal MP from New Westminster, B.C., did not suffer from dilemmas. He was concerned that it was "an unjust criticism to say that the *White Paper* is all wrong merely because Indian people were not consulted in its compilation."[81]

> It appears to me also that the native peoples, with the greatest respect, should come up with proposals for the Government of Canada. I have heard, for instance, about your treaties now for 2 ½ years and I have never seen a comprehensive document presented on behalf of Indian people detailing the treaties, detailing the injustices, details the specifics of what is required. . . . We have heard from Harold Cardinal. We have heard from your people in Saskatchewan and Mr. Courchene in Manitoba and the people from Eastern Canada, but never have we had a comprehensive policy proposed by the Indian people over which we could get into a rapport with them. It appears to me that perhaps it is time to do that.[82]

Hogarth seems to have held the view that the Privy Council's Platonic Republic for Indians might be challenged if only the Indians would get together and design their own final solution. Hogarth's presumption that there is not a comprehensive proposal is a variation on the *argumentum ad ignorantiam*. He does not, however, ask if they may already have presented such a proposal in a forum established for that purpose.[83] Far from seeking a dialogue he uses tactics that resonate with those observed in cross-examinations.

This was a tremendously clever exercise in burden shifting. Dr. Courchene had emphasized the need for research. Noel Doucette had spoken of the need for translation and for social education. Walter Gordon had spoken of the need of the general population to become sensitive to Indian values. Hogarth complains that there is no overall plan.

All of these recommendations required time and money, with which to do research and to do social education among the mainstream culture, immigrant communities and Indian communities, each of which were discussed.

Hogarth may have been correct in one narrow sense. There had not been, at that point, a national, i.e., a Canada-wide or N.I.B. position statement. It had, however, been explained to the Committee that there were, in fact, a range of legal relations between Indian nations and the Crown. However, it is not clear that this Committee was the appropriate forum for a comprehensive alternative to the *White Paper*. Cardinal had presented the Alberta *Red Paper* to the Minister of Indian Affairs the previous summer. Manuel argued that such a comprehensive plan had been laid out both before the Andras Task Force and the National Indian Advisory Council prior to the *White Paper*.[84] Although there were regional variations comprehensive positions might be found in submissions to the Joint Committee on Indian Affairs of 1960–63 and 1946–48.

The issue of whether there had been consultation before the *White Paper* surely hangs not on whether hearings were held but on whether what was said by Indian speakers was actually considered. Such a close consideration, one in which these points of view are not only given careful thought but the grievances and objectives stated are directly addressed, are integral parts of the most traditional definitions of consultation.

CONSULTATION

> 1. a. The action of consulting or taking counsel together; deliberation, conference.
>
> 2. a. A conference in which the parties consult and deliberate; a meeting for deliberation or discussion.[85]

Note that in each definition, the *OED* anticipates a degree of collegiality or *mutual deliberation*. This element has been lacking in almost every event described by the Canadian Government as a "consultation" with a First Nations organization. "Consultation" has been a point of debate within the N.I.B.-AFN since its earliest days. In 1975, the Executive Council adopted a resolution defining their meaning of "consultation." The elements the Executive Council required were those found in the *OED* and missing in the conduct of the Government.

PARLIAMENTARIANS' EXCHANGES WITH WITNESSES AND INNOVATIVE PROCEDURE

One of the striking features of the exchanges between parliamentarians and Indian and Native witnesses is their brevity. The exchanges with Noel Doucette, allowing for interruptions for procedural matters, could not have run more than 25 minutes. The exchanges with Walter Gordon extended for approximately 20 minutes. In addition to the four parliamentarians who intervened during this period, there were three interventions from the floor.

A variety of difficulties were encountered by the Committee in its effort to experiment with innovative procedure that, in turn, limited the exchange between parliamentarians and presenting witnesses. Among these difficulties was a significant reduction in the time available for direct exchanges between Indian leaders and parliamentarians. For those who wished to discuss government-to-government relations, treaty obligations and constitutional guarantees such as the *Royal Proclamation of 1763*, this reduction represented a significant intrusion. So far as some parliamentarians evidenced attention deficits or were easily distracted, intrusions from community activists and representatives of community and interest groups during the appearance of Indian leaders represented a shortcoming in the new procedures.

PROFESSOR NOEL LYON, FACULTY OF LAW, MCGILL UNIVERSITY

Noel Lyon addressed the Committee on November 26, 1970. He was the first non-Indigenous person to address Aboriginal issues. He described that part of his presentation as "Indian lands and self-government." He also spoke of the need to bring together a global, possibly even a "holistic" view of the Constitution together with a more pragmatic view. He drew on his experience teaching constitutional law to French Canadian civil law students having come from a common law background. Students coming from a Francophone civil law background, Lyon said, "tend to have this preference for a global view which is quite a different one to that of the Anglo-Saxon person." Lyon thought that "this does not happen only in the legal profession.[86]

Professor Lyon had also spent a part of the previous summer camping with Mohawk people from Akwesasne and other friends of theirs during the reclaiming of Stanley and Loon Islands. No other academic demonstrated a sense of the Constitution as a living instrument with which the full variety of Canadian societies need to enter into dialogue.

Prof. Lyon envisaged "a declaratory document, which does not have legal effect but which, nevertheless, would serve to guide a constitutional process in the future."

> What the document is called would not particularly matter, but I think it would have to be a document that would attempt to cover the full range of fundamental human values that we are concerned with when we talk about reform of the Canadian Constitution, and it would also deal with the basic constitutional principles and institutional

> organization and practices which we are committed to . . . the rule of law, the supremacy of Parliament and the traditional constitutional principles that now operate within our Constitution and, I suggest, ought to continue to operate under any future Constitution.[87]

Lyon was, almost certainly, the first person to present the concept of worldviews to a parliamentary committee and relate it to the framing of a new Constitution. His common law focus on cases and instances is evident in the midst of this global perspective. He, first, recommended Mr. Justice Sissons book, *Judge of the Far North* as an illustration of how it is possible for a man coming from one cultural background to recognize and take into account the profound differences in the cultural background of other people when it comes to applying legal or other standards.[88]

If members of the Committee had allowed themselves to think in these terms they might have responded to the Aboriginal witnesses much differently. The Committee appears to have heard from witnesses on a first-come, first served basis rather than, for example, hearing academic witnesses first so as to have the benefit of their thought when hearing from Aboriginal political leaders.

Prof. Lyon spoke of "the plight of native peoples,"[89] by which he appears to have meant *the forces pushing Native peoples to the margins of Canadian society*. He also addressed the issues that would have obliged Indian leaders to prove not only their entitlements but even their civility. "[T]he test of our capacity in the future to develop an adequate Constitution and *to call ourselves a civilized nation* will depend upon the state in which our native peoples find themselves."[90] Noel Lyon was the only non-Aboriginal witness to direct the attention of this Joint Committee to the proposition that *the civility of the Canadian nation, as the foundation of the Constitution, depends in significant part upon the state of "our native peoples."* His idea that a people might "find themselves" as a result, at least in part, of their neighbours' civility offers an important measure of autonomy and self-government.

He then reflected something of what he, himself, had learned from Indian culture by telling a story of an instance in which he was somewhat humbled. Possibly he hoped that his parliamentary auditors might share a little of the humbling:

> I had never heard of the *St. Regis Islands Act*. I was at a band council meeting being asked questions and they asked me if I had ever heard of the *St. Regis Islands Act*. I said "no" and they showed me a copy and I could not believe it when they told me its background. There had been this case in the courts in which a lease was challenged.

> The lease was for 999 years. The rental was pitifully small. It was going to the federal crown in trust for these people and then back to the members of the band to share. The lease was found to be illegal because the band or chiefs had not had authority to make it in the circumstances. Therefore the lessees, who by this time were numerous under subleases and who had built cottages on the Islands, were naturally very upset about this decision in the court. They no longer had the right to possession of this island which happened to [be] the Thompson Islands in the particular case I am talking about. Within a year, an Act was run through Parliament and the preamble stated that *whereas these Islands would be of greater benefit to the Indians in their present park-like form, used for summer cottages, than if the Indians were allowed to come to cut wood for firewood and use the land according to Indian custom.*
>
> Therefore the superintendent of Indians was authorized by the Act to deal with these Islands without consulting the Indian band. One decision that the Indians did manage to get out of the courts in their favour was immediately reversed by an Act of Parliament.[91] (emphasis added)

I have emphasized Lyon's summary of the preamble to the *St. Regis Islands Act* because it so fully captures the historic attitude of Parliament, an attitude which allowed Parliament to over-ride the courts' decision in favour of Indian property rights. Noel Lyon was prepared to explain to the parliamentarians some features of their constitutional legacy with which they might want to come to terms in the interests either of Dave Courchene's notion of reconciliation or Walter Gordon's idea of justice; or, indeed, Mark MacGuigan's notion in the *Final Report* that a Constitution was something to be loved.

Noel Lyon also used this story to illustrate the difficulty of participating in the Canadian Constitution for people who have been violently and repeatedly excluded from it.

> I sensed that the idea that it was open to them to take initiatives was something new to them. Then I began to realize the extent to which these Indian peoples——*even the more advanced groups, like the St. Regis tribe*—- had come to view themselves as passive and helpless in the hands of a paternalistic government in which they have no real chance to determine their own future, to determine their own lives and their own rights.[92] (emphasis added)

Lyon's account of the reclaiming of Stanley and Loon Islands includes an instructive exercise in cultural perspectives and bias in language,

> The thing to note is the extent to which those who share our cultural background regarded this as [an] invasion of outsiders. Indians coming back to claim land which they believed to be theirs under their reservation were being regarded as foreigners invading land which properly belong to the White (sic) cottagers.[93]

PARLIAMENTARIANS RESPONDED TO PROFESSOR LYONS' PRESENTATION

Senator Lamontagne displayed some discomfort when he asked if this was not a matter "of more direct concern with other parliamentary committees or especially with the Department of Indian Affairs and Northern Development."[94] Lyon had sought to link his analysis to the notion that a Constitution needed to elicit love and respect. Senator Lamontagne, despite being a product of a Québec education, clearly missed the point when he suggested shunting Lyon's concerns to the Indian Affairs Committee.

The notion that a Constitution is as much about an attitude and a world view as about an amending formula was not going to come easily to parliamentarians who already had their own agenda. Noel Lyon, in contrast, told the Committee that "Any amending formula that is acceptable to all the provinces and to the central government is going to be adequate."[95]

NORTHERN DEVELOPMENT, EVOLUTION OF THE YUKON & SELF-DETERMINATION

The appearance of Jean Chrétien, then Minister of Indian Affairs and Northern Development, was the only occasion when Indians were a subject of discussion without the presence of an Indian organization, a legal scholar or a territorial council. If, as *The Final Report* would argue, Indians as "the first Canadians" ought to be memorialized in a Constitution that needs us to love it, then the complete lack of mention of "Indians" by other witnesses is certainly striking.

More interesting than the Minister's opening statement about federal Indian policy was the discussion initiated by Erik Nielsen (PC, Yukon) while Jean Chrétien was in the witness chair, in which he argued that *the Government favoured Indian organizations over the Yukon Territorial Council:*

> If the Minister can give money to Indian brotherhoods (sic) in the millions of' dollars and not require them to account and trust them with their responsibility of spending it, why can we not trust the Territorial Council, at least to the extent of the revenues they raise themselves?[96]

Nielsen and Dinsdale were both taken with the form of argument, "If they can have something why can't we?" Dinsdale, however, elevated the discussion from mere money to *self-determination:*

> We make quite *a fetish of the principle of self-determination* with respect to newly emerging countries and we even go so far as to support through our International Development Association (sic) the economies of these countries, but we ignore this principle in Canada. I think this is what gets under the skins of the people who have sufficient vision and the pioneering courage to go into *the last frontier.*[97] (emphasis added)

Walter Dinsdale was the first MP to use the term "self-determination." He did so in reference to the northern territories, the Yukon and the North West Territories. Even though he seemed to think that Canadian agencies were overly enthusiastic about self-determination elsewhere, he related it domestically only to the Yukon and not to Indian nations. Dinsdale does not appear to observe the distinction made in international usage between *self-government* (the enjoyment of a set of institutions capable of a wide measure of independent policy making and constituting a significantly sovereign state) and *self-determination* as *a principle entitling a people* to create their own governmental institutions. He did, however, emphasize that it is a right *belonging to those who "go into the last frontier,"*[98] i.e., presumably to settlers rather than to Indian people. In keeping with the idea of the Yukon as a frontier, Dinsdale may implicitly have been describing the Yukon, exclusive of European settlement, as a *terra nullius.*

This contrasts sharply with Osler's question as to why, when the Committee was in the Yukon

> no Indians appeared before us and that is the only place where there are Indians of any substance (sic). I wondered whether they were in such poor shape they would be incapable of doing that, or were they so neglected or had they such an inferiority complex. Are they any worse there than anywhere else?[99]

Mr. Osler seemed to be referring to the hearings of the Standing Committee three years earlier. When Mr. Chrétien said "I cannot comment on their attitude. They are organized like other groups of Indians," Mr. Nielsen replied "They were not then." Mr. Chrétien agreed:

> They were just starting to get organized. There was no Indian organization really working three years ago and it is only since that time that we have helped them to organize and some think we are helping them too much.[100]

Mr. Osler's notion that the Yukon Indians "were organized like other groups of Indians" might have been less remarkable if his colleagues had not had difficulty learning that some organizations were federations, others were associations and only a few were described by their members, directors, or legal charter as "brotherhoods."

ERNEST BENEDICT (UNION OF ONTARIO INDIANS)

Mark MacGuigan's introduction of Ernest Benedict exemplifies the difficulty of finding appropriate and respectful language encountered even by the most thoughtful parliamentarians. MacGuigan introduced Benedict as "a Mohawk Indian from the St. Regis Reserve, a member of the Board of Directors of the Union of Ontario Indians and a part-time instructor in the Indian-Eskimo studies Program (sic) at Trent University."[101] The practice of following the names of Aboriginal nations by the term "Indian," e.g., "Mohawk Indian" still frequently encountered today, is yet another example of the use of a different grammar invoked in discourse about Indians than is commonly used in discourse about other cultures. Are there any Mohawks who are not "Indians" as the word was used at that time? It is an error both of logic and grammar to use a qualifier when there is no distinction to be made. Grammatically, this is equivalent to "Jewish rabbi" or, perhaps, "French European."

The term "St. Regis" has fairly withered away over the last two or three decades. Akwesasne was known as St. Regis from the time a church of that name was built on the point in the village in the latter part of the 18th century. The Mohawk term *Akwesasne* gained acceptance beyond the Longhouse, for whom the use of the term was an act of resistance as well as a factual answer, only very slowly. One of the earliest promotions of the use of the Mohawk name of this Mohawk community was in the name of the newspaper *Akwesasne Notes* in which Ernest Benedict played a significant role.

The use of "Indian-Eskimo Studies" for an academic program that would later become known as "Native Studies" is a further measure of the limitations imposed by language use. So far as it was a term created and accepted by an academic community with great good will, it is an indication that at least some of the difficulties encountered by parliamentarians were representative of their time and place.

Ernest Benedict's discourse on sovereignty and history as a way of envisioning the future may have been well beyond the comprehension of his immediate audience. The Committee members may, on the other hand, have come, by then, to understand a small part of what Benedict meant when he said, "the Indian people have a unique part in the constitutional history of Canada."[102] Most were not likely familiar enough with *The Royal Proclamation, 1763* to understand how "their [the Indians'] special role is reflected in the primary constitutional documents from *The Royal Proclamation, 1763* to the *British North America Act of 1867*.[103] It is even less likely that the immediate audience of parliamentarians comprehended the prophetic nature of the statement with which he ended his opening paragraph:

> It showed no sense of history and therefore no acceptable view of the future. As Indian people we will always see our special status and legal rights as flowing from the original sovereignty of our nations.[104]

Ernest Benedict gave a short course on Aboriginal and treaty rights which he began with a summary of the significance and constitutional status of the Royal Proclamation of 1763 in a single paragraph including a reference to the 1956 Saulteaux adhesion to Treaty 6, then the most recently signed treaty. He pointed out that section 91(24)

> was not enacted, as seems popularly believed, out of a paternalistic concern for Native peoples. It was enacted to make clear the power of the federal government to engage in colonial expansion in the West. The phrase "lands reserved for the Indians" [in ss.91 (24) of the *British North America Act*] included lands not ceded by treaty as of 1867 (which, for Ontario, comprised By far the greater part of the present territory of the province).[105]

Having explained that "[t]he treaties are constitutional documents," Ernest Benedict prefigured an oft-quoted statement of Chief Justice Dickson's when he said that "To violate these documents is to compromise the integrity of the Canadian legal system." He then discussed the *Migratory Birds Convention Act* and three cases pursuant to that Act (*Regina vs. Sikyea,* 1964; *Regina vs. George,* 1966; and *Daniels vs. White and the Queen* in 1968) which "to Indian people, represent violations of basic legal commitments.[106]

Benedict introduced two arguments which were innovative at least as they applied to Indian relations. First, he said that "Indian people have . . . more than any other group in Canada, suffered from the technical preoccupation of the courts and politicians with regard to the division of powers."

Secondly, "Federal jurisdiction over Indians was designed to serve colonialist ends, not to protect Indians. Later, it was used as an excuse for isolation and ignoring native peoples." Benedict laid the foundation for a novel argument for self-government when he suggested that the item "Indian" in the list of federal powers be treated in a wholly different way.

> In other words, the unique constitutional status of Indians in Canada has never been seen by government as an opportunity to be used. We suffered as your embarrassing wards for long enough, you are now to be called to account and required to live up to the constitutional responsibilities you drafted for yourselves.[107]

Benedict cited three specific issues which, he told the Committee, "discredit the integrity of constitutional government in [the] eyes [of Indian people."[108] Each of these three things "is being done secretively:" (1) the imposition of local property taxation when Indian land is leased to a non-Indian; (2) the transfer of policing from the RCMP to provincial police by federal-provincial agreement; and, (3) the transfer of medical care for Indians from federal administration to provincial administration.[109]

Benedict went on to say that the medical records created through band councils were being used "to supply information on income level of band members for use in determining medical indigency. Those bands who co-operate in good faith end up paying premiums."[110]

Education was cited as the best-known example of

> transfer of jurisdiction . . . accomplished without our consent and in such a way as to integrate Indian students as a minority into schools over which Indian people have no control. The public schools are usually culturally insensitive to native people. They are often hostile to the development of native pride.[111]

Clearly, Ernest Benedict's critique of the *status quo 1970* sowed the seeds for institutions constituting a high degree of First Nations' autonomy. He pointed out that

> Our exemption from income tax on income earned off reserve was unilaterally removed in 1952. Our rights under the Jay Treaty to free movement across the border have not been recognized and implemented by the federal government.[112]

Lastly, he suggested that the documents to which he had referred were clear enough on their faces that "the treaties themselves, should be recognized and the government should go on record as recognizing them even without an investigation. *I do not see how an investigation could change a government policy.*"[113] (emphasis added)

This parting shot was clearly calculated to prompt the parliamentarians to ask themselves just what they might hope to accomplish by such an investigation.

THE PARLIAMENTARIANS' RESPONSE TO ERNEST BENEDICT'S PRESENTATION

Walter Dinsdale, the Manitoba MP who had addressed the Vice President of the Manitoba Métis Federation as "Tom," began the questioning of Ernest Benedict by indulging in a parliamentary game, one the author of *Games People Play,* might have called "Gotcha!" Dinsdale invited Benedict to go beyond the scope of his paper: "The problem of Aboriginal rights is even more difficult than treaty rights, because treaty rights . . . are more or less specifically defined . . . How far would Mr. Benedict go in claiming Aboriginal rights, in terms of territorial claims?"[114] Aboriginal rights had not been mentioned in Ernest Benedict's brief for the Union of Ontario Indians, perhaps because Aboriginal rights, as distinct from treaty rights, were not a primary point of contention in the areas represented by the Union of Ontario Indians.

Mr. Benedict was careful to answer within the framework of his own brief:

> If then the government is willing to use the documents and the subsequent treaties, and the methods that were used, that could be justified under that proclamation, then I think the question of Aboriginal rights should be fairly clear.[115]

Mr. Dinsdale asked whether "very detailed consultation with the Indian people" was being urged "before any change in Section 91(24)[116] and whether the Union of Ontario Indians is "the properly constituted body to carry on these negotiations or should these consultations go beyond the Union?" When Mr. Benedict replied that "each of the tribal groups should be consulted," Dinsdale said, "I presume you are speaking for the Six Nations here this afternoon rather than the Brotherhood. Is that it?"[117] Whether Conservative MPs expected that Mr. Benedict was referring to the Six Nations because he was Mohawk, even though the Six Nations were not members of the Union (mislabeled "the Brotherhood" by Walter Dinsdale), or whether Mr. Dinsdale had simply ignored Mr. MacGuigan's introduction of Ernest Benedict remains unclear. Also unclear is whether Dinsdale had come to the hearing without doing his homework or whether he suffered from poor oral comprehension in his mother tongue.

Warren Allmand focussed his questions on clarification of what Ernest Benedict had actually said:

> Were you suggesting in the new Constitution there should be recognition of the special status of Indians in Canada and the rights of Indians to certain lands and so forth; is this what you were suggesting?[118]

This allowed Benedict to give an initial response of "Yes" and then to elaborate in response to supplementary questions: "I believe the Constitution as it stands now recognizes the special status of the Indians. Whether the government recognizes it or not is another topic."

> Yes, I would, and to a certain extent it is entrenched now. If the Royal Proclamation of 1763 is accepted as a basic document and part of the Constitution, then there is a foundation on which to work, unless you want to throw it out. If you are willing to keep those principles and enlarge on them to fit the present date I think Indians would be receptive to negotiations.

The Joint Chairman then called for comments from the floor while Mr. Benedict was still on the stand. However participatory, this was a practice which would not survive the integration of community and parliamentary styles of representation. In fact, no questions were forthcoming. On the other hand, the anticipation of comments from the floor closed off more intense questioning by the parliamentarians.

In the absence of other interventions, Mr. Allmand posed a question with which Mr. Benedict concluded his presentation. Allmand's question was whether in addition to "a comprehensive bill of rights . . . I understood from most of the Indians we heard already that they would not be satisfied with this but that they would want special reference in the Constitution to their own special place in this country."[119] Ernest Benedict agreed with that impression:

> Yes, I do believe that the Government of Canada has made certain promises to Indians and I am confident that whatever the government has promised it will do. Some of the promises are incorporated in the Proclamation of 1763 again. Since then under the terms of that document certain treaties have been negotiated. These treaties did give, I submit, special rights and special status to the Indians. The government recognizes those rights do not give a special legal status to the Indians, it only says that just like anybody else the Indian will get what the government says he is supposed to get.[120]

DELBERT GUÉRIN, A STATEMENT FROM THE FLOOR

The Committee held hearings in Vancouver on January 7 and 8, 1971. Delbert Guérin, later to achieve fame by lending his name and leadership to *Guérin v. The Queen*,[121] was one of the members of the audience who was invited to make a comment. Mr. Guérin[122] said that he found "it kind of amusing that in 1971 we are looking at these sorts of changes . . . providing these sorts of special concessions to minorities in regard to language and cultural heritage" when a hundred years ago the government had dedicated itself to "trying to break the cultural heritage and take a language of a people away from them." He went on to say, "I only raise the point that it is too bad we did not at that time have stronger immigration laws."[123]

On that day, three MPs, all apparently Liberals—McNulty, Whelan and Osler—were replaced by three other Liberals newly named to the Committee—Leonard Donald Hopkins, Pierre De Bané and Maurice B. Foster. Even interviews would be unlikely to establish how much effort each made to catch up with previous testimony.

DONNA TYNDALL (UNION OF BRITISH COLUMBIA INDIAN CHIEFS)

Mr. McQuaid, the Acting Chairman, first introduced Donna Tyndall who was to speak "on behalf of the Union of British Columbia Indian Chiefs."[124]

Mr. McQuaid began by telling the Committee that they would "hear the two briefs by the Department of Indian Affairs, the Indians."(sic)[125] Since the *Proceedings* capitalized departmental names it is evident that the *Hansard* reporters thought that it was *the department that the acting chairman confused with the people*. Apparently, some parliamentarians, in the winter of 1971, still presumed that *Indian thought* was an artifact of *Indian Affairs*.

Mrs. Tyndall reciprocated by speaking in her own language. *Hansard* (i.e., the stenographers and editors of parliamentary debates) dealt with this apparently unprecedented feat by identifying her, not by her title as all other witnesses were identified, but by her exceptional behaviour. Although every other witness's name is followed by a bracketed statement of title and organization in bold, Donna Tyndall's name is followed by the statement, "Commences to speak in an Indian dialect." [126] The reference to "dialect" is contrary to Mrs. Tyndall's own first statement in English:

> Am I going too fast for the Chairman, please? I introduced *my language* here just for a bit of variety and also because I am getting tired of the French, English arguments going on in this room here, but I guess I must present my letter in English. My own language is too beautiful, too complex to be recognized as an official language in Canada.[127]

There are, apparently, moments when sarcasm is the sincerest form of witness.

Mrs. Tyndall's other prefatory comment was that "we do not feel that we have had sufficient time to prepare our exact line and position . . . " [128] The sense that witnesses needed to come to the Committee's hearings with "an exact line and position," it need hardly be said, was not likely to help Aboriginal witnesses feel at ease. Such a request also suggests that when the Committee decided to open their hearings to community participation they had not given much thought to processes appropriate to such an experiment.

The Union of B.C. Indian Chiefs' (UBCIC) position read into the record by Donna Tyndall called for a constitutional provision which "would specifically recognize the unique status of Indians and the contributions of the Indian culture to the development of our country."[129]

Mrs. Tyndall then demanded a response from the Committee to the UBCIC request for adequate time to prepare their statement: "We are not, at this time, however, prepared to make a formal submission, but we submit this letter as a notice of intent to file a formal submission at a later date."[130]

> We request sufficient time to develop a complete and comprehensive submission.
>
> We request from this Committee a response to our notice of intent and an acknowledgement of our request for sufficient time to prepare our exact position.[131]

At the end of her statement, Mr. McQuaid, the Acting Chairman, responded in much the same tone:

> Thank you very much, Miss Tyndall. If you have a further presentation to make, as I believe you have, you can mail it to the House of Commons Constitutional Committee (sic).[132]

Mr. McQuaid appears to have been unaware of either the name or the nature of the committee over which he was presiding.

The major innovative contribution from the UBCIC brief was a proposal for a national conference:

> We propose that a national constitutional conference be convened comprising Indians and the two senior governments to discuss the important position that Indians should occupy in our method of government, and that all future Federal Provincial Constitutional Conferences include Indian participation.[133]

More instructive than the contributions to the formal discourse of First Nations self-government, but well within the broader discourse of First Nations' autonomy was the response to Mrs. Tyndall's expression of personal frustration in her closing statement. "In all due respect to this Committee, I find it very depressing to look about and notice the overwhelming absence of Indians."[134]

> **Mr. Hogarth:** I would just like to mention to the witness that Len Marchand who is a native Indian and a member of Parliament for Kamloops was to sit with us in Vancouver but unfortunately he was called back to Kamloops to go to a funeral of one of his friends and that is the reason he is not here.

The idea that Mr. Marchand's presence during the testimony of B.C. Indians would make the event either less overwhelming for the witnesses or more fruitful for the Committee appears, at first glance, to defy analysis. Such an expectation may verge, however, on the realm of a self-negating prophecy.[135]

At the very least, it reflects, on the part of Mr. Hogarth, the kind of bold honesty which was much less likely to appear on the record ten years later when parliamentarians had learned to be more civil and more obscure.

Mr. Hogarth, the only MP to respond to Mrs. Tyndall, focussed on a "What do we do now?" strategic defence of the Government:

> [I]t is quite apparent to all of us, or it should be apparent to all of us, that the way in which governments of Canada *in the past* have dealt with the Indian people from Newfoundland right to Vancouver Islands and the Queen Charlotte Islands, certainly I would describe it only as disgraceful. The big problem that we are constantly faced with . . . the great problem is to try and find out what we can now do, just how can it be corrected. It is so difficult for me to suggest *how to correct* 100 years of *mistakes* and just *transform the situation overnight*.[136] (emphasis added)

Hogarth's argument exemplifies a certain kind of prevarication. His statement culminated in a kind of question—how to solve "the Indian question" overnight—to which there is never an answer. The search for "a final solution" is always a cause for alarm.[137] Further, the suggestion that the problems were in the *past* was a disingenuous permission to ignore the problems that were current.

CHIEF JOE MATHIAS (SQUAMISH INDIAN BAND COUNCIL)

Later the same day, January 8, 1971, Chief Joe Mathias, representing the Squamish Indian Band Council made a presentation in which he asked that

> If . . . a Canadian Charter of Human Rights entrenched in the Constitution is accepted by the Canadian people, then it should include a section setting out certain rights possessed by the Indian people . . . among others, a recognition of their Aboriginal rights on a broad scale and the fact that as original occupants of the country

> whose situation today is most unsatisfactory, they are entitled to particular services.[138]

Chief Mathias appeared not to have been aware that earlier witnesses had spoken of the need for Aboriginal and treaty rights to be in an additional part of a new Constitution *outside the Charter*. Chief Mathias's parody on the question of whether "Indians and lands reserved for the Indians" ought to be in the list of federal powers or the list of provincial powers, integrated his indignation with his capacity for legal analysis.

> Under Head 24, Section 91 . . . We thereby take our place, with some trepidation, alongside the public debt, the postal service, the census and statistics and the other heads enumerated under Section 91 including beacons, buoys, lighthouses and Sable Island. In the long run this may turn out to have been somewhat preferable to the alternative under Section 92 which would have placed us among saloons, taverns and the establishment, maintenance and managements of hospitals and asylums. As one of the heads enumerated under Section 91 for greater certainty, Indians quite understandably have some interest in the proposals to provide Canada with a new Constitution and to find an acceptable method of amending it.[139]

The *coup de grâce* to this parody came at the end of the following paragraph on the difficulties of interpreting the Indian provisions of the *BNA Act*:

> Interpreting the *BNA Act* has never been simple for Canadians but we are unable to see how or why head 24 should be interpreted other than to mean that where the Parliament of Canada legislates for Indians, and lands reserved for the Indians, then that field is occupied to the extent of the legislation and that otherwise provincial legislation applies to all citizens of a province including Indians. Perhaps that is too simple to be attractive.[140]

This is the effect of section 88 of the *Indian Act* which provides that all laws of general application in the province apply on reserves except so far as they are inconsistent with a treaty or with a federal statute.

Mathias's brief, in addition to its wit, parody and legal analysis, stands for the forthcoming style which runs through almost all the Indian presentations. Mathias devoted considerable time to the presentations made by his band to the Minister during the period immediately preceding the *White Paper*:

> [Our] delegates to the National Conference on the *Indian Act* held in Ottawa in May of 1969 made very clear their belief that the *Indian Act* should be retained but with a number of important amendments. We consider that the repeal of the *Indian Act* by the federal government would be *an abdication of its responsibilities* under Section 91, head 24, of the *BNA Act* and . . . it would be a breach of faith with the Indian people . . . and in addition it would be unconstitutional. At the same time we believe that *most of the administration* under the Act should be carried out *by the Indian people themselves* through their band Councils and their organizations.
>
> In the Squamish Band's brief to the Minister at the Chilliwack Conference on the *Indian Act* held November 18 through 22, 1968, we set out our beliefs in part as follows:
>
> The delegate of the Squamish Indian Band representing the sixteen bands comprising that band is pleased to present the views of the band with regard to the *Indian Act* and *the future of the Indian peoples in Canada*. The Indian *people* are made up of many separate nations with great differences in historical and cultural background and cannot be considered as a homogeneous group.[141] (emphasis added)

This paragraph also emphasized the extent to which Indian leaders were struggling to find appropriate language to describe their own vision of their proper place in the world. The underlined phrase, "the Indian peoples in Canada," refers to many peoples and would appear to equate "peoples" with "Nations" in the second sentence. There was, at this time, however, significant pressure both within the Indian communities and from non-Native political leaders, thoroughly evidenced in the parliamentary committee proceedings under examination, to speak and think of "*an* Indian people." Similarly, there is a difficulty in finding or creating an appropriate taxonomy for Indian political institutions, some of which were bands established under the *Indian Act* while other organizations, whether traditional or contemporary, have more indigenous roots.

Chief Mathias finally broached certain aspects of self-government, by describing ingredients which, taken together, could produce increasing autonomy. First, he recommended that the *Indian Act* "never again be 'closed' for a period of years as has been the case in the [recent] past."[142] Instead, he called for "A permanent legislative Commission composed of Indians and Whites . . . to advise the Federal Government of necessary changes . . . The Band recommends the present name of the Act be continued."[143] (capitals in the original.)

Secondly, he made a statement which strongly identified "maturity" with autonomy:

> If the Indian people are to progress and develop into mature citizens, we and our institutions must be given more decision-making power together with the responsibilities that flow from the exercise of power.[144]

Surprisingly, Chief Mathias immediately attenuated his call for "decision-making power," "As a result, *a delegation of authority* should be made to band councils and band economic corporations at a rate and to the extent they are able to absorb such increased power and responsibility." It is also unlikely that the parliamentarians grasped the reference to "band economic corporations," a concept intended, among other things, to combine the tax exemption granted to Indian persons under the *Indian Act* with the advantages of incorporation particularly for band agencies.

Finally, Chief Mathias identified his band's two key priorities as "improved education" and "the assumption of responsibility and control over our own affairs."[145]

Chief Mathias concluded with a denunciation of the 1969 Indian Policy statement as being "illogical when it speaks of the anomaly of treaties between groups within society and the government of that society."[146]

Even though Joe Mathias had attempted to set a tone which combined an intellectual challenge with grace, wit and charm, at the conclusion of his remarks Mr. McQuaid, the acting chairman, quickly voided that happy climate with a call for expediency:

> In view of the fact that we have four more briefs to hear this evening and because we have to be out of this room by 6 p.m., I am going to confine the questions to two members from the Committee and not more than three from the floor, *if we can possibly get away with that few.*[147] (emphasis added)

THE PARLIAMENTARIANS' RESPONSE TO CHIEF JOE MATHIAS

Colin Gibson (Liberal, Hamilton-Wentworth) wanted to know if "Indians" really wanted "their rights entrenched in a charter of human liberties?" Chief Mathias clarified his position by saying "what I really meant to say was that the rights of the Indian people in British Columbia and across Canada should be included in the Constitution.[148]

Marcel Prud'homme was primarily concerned with persuading Indians to accept his Liberal agenda for bilingualism. He seems to have been audibly disappointed with a witness who was concerned with Indian rights rather than with French rights:

> The question that really puzzles me, and I would like to know your feeling, concerns the two official languages of Canada. *Is it something that is accepted*? Is it something to do with the concept of Canada being multicultural, but being officially bilingualism$_3$? What is the feeling in general? . . . *Do they refuse to see it*?[149] (emphasis added)

Chief Mathias attempted to remain gracious while encouraging these seemingly recalcitrant students to look at the text before them: "The problems and the difficulties our Indian communities face are not concerned with governments' bickering over who should speak what official language."[150]

Finally, Marcel Prud'homme tried to befriend the teacher without acknowledging the need to do one's homework:

> Would you say in essence that French Canadians in their desire for recognition could be the greatest ally of the Indians or vice versa, the Indians who desire to have their lives recognized and rightly so could be the greatest ally of French Canadians.
>
> **Mr. Mathias:** This is possibly true. I never (sic) thought of it in those terms.[151]

FEBRUARY 9, 1971: THE THIRD WORKING SESSION OF THE CONSTITUTIONAL CONFERENCE

The Joint Committee published the "Statement of Conclusions" of the Third Working Session of the Constitutional Conference (a conference of senior officials and ministers) as an appendix to its *Proceedings*.[152] Much of the *Final Report* of the Joint Committee is devoted to a review of the same amending formula discussed in the Third Working Session. The extent to which the First Nations and other Aboriginal communities had not yet made their presence felt in the constitutional debate is reflected in the lack of any reference to Aboriginal issues in the report of The Working Session.

PROFESSOR KEN LYSYK (FACULTY OF LAW, UNIVERSITY OF TORONTO)

Prof. Ken Lysyk—who would later write a report on a least harmful route for bringing gas south from the Beaufort Sea and was subsequently appointed to the B.C. Supreme Court—offered the Committee "some observations upon what the Constitution now provides, what a revised Constitution might be made to provide, with respect to the natives peoples of Canada."[153] Prof. Lysyk, although heading toward a call for enhanced constitutional recognition, fell into a series of language traps at the outset of his remarks:

> I would like to address myself next to constitutional provisions relating to Indians and Eskimos. To save time . . . I will use the term "Indians" in its constitutional sense, which includes Eskimos.[154]

There is no indication that parliamentarians such as Mr. Dinsdale who had earlier expressed the view that there was no constitutional basis for recognition of Métis interests actually appreciated this passing reference to the very wide scope of "Indians" in ss.91 (24) as distinct from the very narrow definition in the *Indian Act*.

Professor Lysyk's submission on "native peoples" worked up to a diplomatic argument against the *White Paper* by focusing on the "question whether this special federal authority ought to be preserved." [155] Section 91(24) supported the trusteeship role of the federal government. Outright repeal of the clause would mark the end of the Indians' special relationship with the federal government. Prof. Lysyk then quoted from the same speech of President Richard Nixon—*Self-Determination Without Termination*—from which Dr. Dave Courchene had quoted at length. Lysyk's first two arguments ran parallel to those which had been made by most of the Indian witnesses to date, particularly Dave Courchene and Noel Doucette. Lysyk's professorial voice lent credibility to these arguments, in the minds of the Committee. His third argument took the Joint Committee into new territory: forced termination is counter-productive not only for those who are terminated but even for those who retain status but lose confidence in their relationship with the government.

Lysyk took this argument a step further when he told the Joint Committee "Any step that might result in greater *social, economic or political autonomy* is regarded with suspicion by many Indians who fear that it will only bring them closer to the day when the federal government will disavow its responsibility and cut them adrift."[156] Lysyk introduced the concept of autonomy by saying that *termination is a threat to the desired goal of autonomy.* For proof that autonomy is desirable Lysyk returned to Nixon's speech,

> As a means of breaking away from the pattern of paternalism it is proposed to move in the direction of transferring the right to control and operate federal programs to the Indians themselves. *But termination is rejected in no uncertain fashion.* (emphasis added)
>
> The first and most basic question . . . with respect to Indian policy concerns the historic and legal relationship between the federal government and Indian communities.
>
> On the one hand, it has—at various times during previous Administrations—been the stated policy objective of both the Executive and Legislative branches of the Federal government eventually to terminate the trusteeship relationship between the Federal government and the Indian people.[157]

Without referring directly to the *White Paper*, Ken Lysyk argued that

> [T]he policy of forc[ing] termination is wrong. First, the premises on which it rests are wrong. Termination implies that the Federal government has taken on a trusteeship responsibility for Indian communities as an act of generosity toward a disadvantaged group and that it can therefore discontinue this responsibility on a unilateral basis whenever it sees fit. The special relationship between Indians and the Federal government is the result instead of solemn obligations.[158]

Adapting this presidential statement to the Canadian context, Professor Lysysk said, "In terms of our Constitution this Committee may wish to consider whether the consent of the Indians ought not to be a prerequisite for any amendment involving Section 91(24) of the *BNA Act*."[159]

This was a recommendation several Indian witnesses had already made. In addition to credibility, Lysyk added an argument that

> The Canadian Constitution in the broader sense . . . presently has quite a lot to say on the subject of Indian rights. Reference might be made to the Royal Proclamation of 1763; to the clauses dealing with Indian hunting, trapping and fishing rights contained in the *Natural Resource Transfer Agreements* confirmed by the British North America Act of 1930; to clauses in the Ontario and Québec Boundaries Extension Acts of 1912 obligating those provinces to recognize the rights of Indian inhabitants.[160]

Although Lysysk had begun by saying that he would not make recommendations, he spoke warmly of three possibilities for respecting Indian rights in the Constitution.

> First, the subject might receive treatment in the preamble to the Constitution.
>
> Second, the body of the Constitution might contain a statement of obligations or objectives for all governments . . . which obligations could be stated to be *not enforceable by the courts*.
>
> Finally, the Constitution could set out rights which would be enforceable against governments. An example . . . is provided by the hunting and fishing rights guarantee that is presently set out in the Natural Resource Agreements.[161] (emphasis added)

The merit of *non-enforceable obligations* in a Constitution is hard to discern even in a country in which people heeded the admonition in the *Final Report* that *a Constitution was something to be loved.* The *Gage Canadian Dictionary* defines an "obligation" as "a duty under the law" or "a binding legal agreement." If an obligation is bolstered neither by care nor by justiciability it is hard to see that it is an obligation at all.

Conceptually, it is interesting that Lysyk pointed to the hunting and trapping rights in existing constitutional documents as the most substantial example of something enforceable. The notion of an all-embracing "full box" statement which might later be judicially construed as "a promise,"[162] such as eventually emerged in s.35 of the *Constitution Act,*

1982, would only evolve in the course of another decade of study and advocacy.

Lysyk's brief is primarily memorable for the argument that it made that Indian rights already have a place in our Constitution and that they deserve respect in their own right. Lysyk also told the Committee that "the argument from economics . . . misses the point," [163] an idea that ran quite contrary to the prevailing Ottawa wisdom.

> . . . First of all, I do not think you can look at it from a legal or constitutional point of view, as President Nixon has. His terror of termination seems to be based solely on the point of view of the so-called solemn obligation of his government.[164]

Hogarth advanced an argument that because "the solemn obligations we have had have not been too solemn from time to time" we need a view that is "cultural" rather than "legal." His idea of cultural protection, however, consisted of "a law that will ensure that the ultimate cultural destiny will be what they had 200 years ago."[165]

The notion that rights might be both "unique and contemporary"[166] continued to elude the Member from Capilano who seemed similarly undisturbed that many of the most compelling and sacred features of our culture—marriage and professional status are but two examples—are enshrined as much in the law as in our beings. Why Aboriginal rights should be frozen in pre-contact time is never made clear. Chief Justice Dickson took quite a different view in *Sparrow*. John Borrows enlarges on this view in an essay.[167]

There may well have been members of the Joint Committee who knew that Ken Lysyk had given them a wealth of ethical, historical and legal material. The most probable indication of the depth of their response, however, was their lack of direct response.

MRS. CECILIA PHILLIPS DORÉ (PRESIDENT, EQUAL RIGHTS FOR INDIAN WOMEN)

Mrs. Cecilia Phillips Doré appeared before the *MacGuigan-Molgat* Committee on Monday, April 16, 1971 on behalf of Equal Rights for Indian Women. "This organization . . . respectfully asks the Special Joint Committee of the Senate and the House of Commons on the Constitution of Canada why she is no longer an Indian just because she has married a non-Indian (sic)."[168]

Senator Thérèse Casgrain (Independent, Mille Isles) responded by defending herself, defending Parliament and blaming Indian men for the *Indian Act*, "I first want to tell you that I have not changed my mind, and that I have done all I could to help you. But I would like to ask the husbands, the Indian men, to help you."

> **Mrs. Doré:** I think the men are concerned about being men. But we lose and they change. So they cannot help us.
>
> It is your *Indian Act* that makes the men . . .
>
> **Senator Casgrain:** I fully agree that the *Indian Act* is made to satisfy the Indian men. But we are doing all we can about it.[169]

Mrs. Doré had not said that "the *Indian Act is made* to satisfy Indian men." For all her supposed independence, Senator Casgrain fit well into the mold of Liberal women parliamentarians pretending that the *Indian Act* reflected the wishes of *Indian men*.[170] There is no evidence that any Indian men participated in the drafting of portions of the *Indian Act*. In fact, until 1951, men who became self-supporting were also forcibly enfranchised under a parallel provision.

Mr. Raymond Rock (Liberal, Lachine) pointed out that he had had a private members' bill on this matter before the House of Commons for the past three sessions. His concern was whether or not the organization was aware of his support for their cause.[171] Sen. Casgrain and Mr. Rock both saw Mrs. Philips presentation as something that might be made to focus more on themselves rather than on those whose identity and land rights were actually at stake.

The essential issue would remain unremarked by parliamentarians until the Subcommittee on Indian Women and the *Indian Act* of 1982. In 1976, Starblanket told another Joint Committee on the Constitution that he would support reinstatement of enfranchised women provided that Parliament supported a proportionate increase in both the land base and the financial base of reserve communities. The demand for *equal rights* for Indian women can only have as much value as the protection being accorded to "Indian rights" in general. Even then, the argument was framed as a response to Liberal women parliamentarians who were accusing the N.I.B. of hostility to the reinstatement of Indian women.[172] Between 1970 and 1981, no woman parliamentarian extended her support for Aboriginal women so far as to challenge existing legislation and government policy as they affected the general economy of reserve communities and the capacity of indigenous institutions to act on their own communities.

MISS BOOTH (NATIONAL ADVISORY COUNCIL ON THE STATUS OF WOMEN)

When the National Advisory Council appeared before the Committee, a week after Equal Rights for Indian Women, Douglas Hogarth suggested that "your council may take this up, because this is one of the greatest [indictments] of law against women . . . if an Indian woman marries a white man she loses her property." Mr. Hogarth appears to have been quite unprepared for the answer he was given.

> **Miss Booth:** We were going to put that in but we were sort of semi-unofficially advised that the Indians would prefer to bring these points forward themselves rather than have them brought forward by a group such as ours.
>
> **Mr. Hogarth:** I know they would certainly appreciate your assistance in getting that changed.
>
> **Miss Booth:** They asked us not to bring it up.[173]

DR. A. R. M. LOWER (PROFESSOR EMERITUS OF HISTORY, QUEEN'S UNIVERSITY, KINGSTON, ONTARIO)

There was one striking exception to the general lack of discussion of Aboriginal matters in the absence of Aboriginal witnesses and associated law professors. Senator Paul Yuzyk (PC, Manitoba), possibly the first parliamentarian to introduce the term "multiculturalism" and a longtime supporter of Aboriginal rights, observed that Prof. Lower had not made any mention at all of an Aboriginal presence in Canadian history. He commented, "Canada, in this organic concept of growing into a nation, has been fusing into itself other elements and these include the Indians and the Eskimos to whom you made no reference."

Prof. Lower first defended himself by saying "A brief has to be limited." Yuzyk pursued the matter, pointing out that Lower's plea for "unity of all the elements" had focused on "the two founding peoples" without mention either of allophones or of indigenous peoples. When

Sen. Yuzyk told him, "I would like to be included," he conceded "I will do that in my next brief, sir."[174]

PROFESSOR PETER CUMMING (OSGOODE HALL LAW SCHOOL)

When Peter Cumming appeared as the principal speaker on behalf of the Indian-Eskimo Association (IEA), the title by which he was introduced in the *Proceedings* was not one which referred to the role in which he was appearing but one which gave him status and credibility with the Committee. The Indian-Eskimo Association went on to become the Canadian Association in Support of Native Peoples and subsequently the Canadian Association in Solidarity with Native Peoples.

The rhetoric of the IEA, as it was reflected in Cumming's speech to the Joint Committee, falls between the stools: It aspires toward a new rhetoric but it appears to be in touch neither with the work of the Joint Committee nor with the work of the nascent Indian organizations:

> We emphasize that it is pertinent that this brief is made in respect of *Canada's very first citizens*, the Aboriginals and that, somewhat paradoxically, they had had far less opportunity . . . to participate generally the decision-making processes affecting their lives and rights.[175] (emphasis added)

The sentimental ends served by the fiction that Aboriginals were the first citizens of Canada were counter-productive to any constructive end. To claim an historical Canadian citizenship for Aboriginal people to a parliamentary committee when Parliament had so consistently denied full citizenship to First Nations peoples over many decades[176] obscured the fact that "Canadian citizenship" did not exist until 1947.[177]

Cumming's pretension to speak on their behalf, unlike Ms. Booth of the Council on the Status of Women, overlooked the considerable number of Indian witnesses who had already appeared and others who were scheduled to appear. Indeed, Cumming's opening paragraph epitomizes the tenuous relationship between the IEA and the N.I.B. during these years.[178]

Cumming went on to outline the well-worn arguments for retaining ss.91(24). Unfortunately, he repeatedly referred to "the native people" in the singular, "The native people consider that Head 24 was incorporated into the Constitution because it was the Crown that was entering into treaty with the native people." Cumming was on stronger ground later in his brief when he objected to the *White Paper* recommendation to repeal ss.91(24).[179]

Cumming blunted an otherwise valuable point about the relationship of Indian nations through treaties to the Crown by continuing to refer to "the native people" in the singular and seeming to collaborate in the denial of the diversity of "Indian nations":

> I want to emphasize that *the native people* see head 24 as following from what took place historically, and this goes back to the constitutional roots of this country of course, namely that they had dealings with the Crown which resulted in treaties with approximately half of the native population of this country.[180]

When Cumming asked, "Would anyone consider changing the constitutional position of *the French-Canadian* without consultation and consent" his dubious use of the zero plural[181] highlighted the intractable nature of both matters. He also overlooked the distinction between those who have significant power and those who do not. Nonetheless, when Cumming coupled *consultation* with *consent* he introduced an idea of self-determination, however obliquely. The government notion—from Robert Andras' hearings to Robert Nault's invitation to send him email—not only separated *consultation* from *consent*, it also omitted the need to listen on the part of those being addressed.

Cumming would have done well to have reviewed the testimony both of Indian witnesses and of the two distinguished professors interested in Native rights who preceded him. Cumming's discussion of what he called "the psychological factors" clearly exceeded his competence:

> I emphasized the psychological factor involved on the part of the native people to deny them their claims their historical, moral and arguably legal claims is psychologically debilitating to put it fairly euphemistically, I suppose, with the result that there is *a virtual refusal to talk about* some of the things which non-Indian people might think to be more important, such as social, economic, educational problems.[182] (emphasis added)

Cumming made an important distinction between the Commissioner to whom the Indian organizations would not talk and the one which had been recommended by two previous Joint Committees of Parliament. The Commissioner's office at dispute at that time had been created by an

Order-in-Council. Its mandate imposed severe limitations as to the claims it might adjudicate as well as restricting its role to making recommendations. [183] In contrast, Cumming said, the Joint Committees on Indian Affairs had recommended a commissioner such as that in the U.S. with judicial independence and quasi-judicial authority.

Had the IEA done their homework, they might have considered the merit of other positive constitutional amendments, such as the recognition of Aboriginal and treaty rights recommended by Mathias and others.[184]

Georges Lachance (Liberal, Lafontaine) raised a previously unexplored question when he asked, "If there were any cash settlement arranged, who would be the recipient of this money?" Cumming looked to "the Alaskan approach . . . a native development corporation which would receive a percentage of the mineral royalties over say, 10 years, and all of the native people would be shareholders, with shares on a per capita basis."[185] The notion of a corporate structure stood over against the entire underpinning of a treaty relationship. The 10 year limitation emphasizes the extinguishment orientation of this brief.

Cumming also advised the Joint Committee that a claim in the NWT would have to be limited "to people alive and living in the Territories."[186] This view would seem to have little to support it from today's vantage point.

Ultimately, Cumming revealed a position that was confused and contradictory. He might have supported a situation in which Indians had exactly the rights of every other citizen but he also wanted "a restoration of rights."[187]

> My view is that over a long transition it would be best from everyone's standpoint *if the native people were full citizens in every sense, not special citizens*. The crucial thing, though, is that that should not be imposed upon them without their consent and it should not take place except at the end of a long, long transition period, during which time *there is a restoration of rights*.[188]

The starkly opposing views of Native rights in these two sentences are not capable of reconciliation. It is regrettable that no one appeared to have put this point to Mr. Cumming at the time.

By offering a brief "made in respect of Canada's very first citizens," Cumming set himself up to be asked questions about the states of mind of people with whom he was not in immediate contact.

> **Mr. McQuaid:** . . . Do the Indian and Eskimo people (sic) feel that they are being neglected in this respect, that they are not being given a chance to be heard?

This was the same Mr. McQuaid who could neither arrange for Mrs. Tyndall to return to the Joint Committee nor give her a proper address to which to send a written brief. Any response offered by Professor Cumming would necessarily usurp the voice of those witnesses who had spoken on behalf of particular Indian, Native or Métis constituencies most of whom were quite explicit as to the needs of their people.

MRS. AGNES SEMMLER (PRESIDENT, COMMITTEE FOR THE ORIGINAL PEOPLES ENTITLEMENT)

C.O.P.E. testified when the Joint Committee travelled to Inuvik on Thursday, June 10, 1971. Nothing could be more indicative of the quality of the dialogue between the parliamentarians and the Aboriginal witnesses than Nellie Cournoyer's comment on the date that they chose to visit Inuvik:

> [T]his is an extremely bad time to have a meeting here concerning the native people up in the Mackenzie Delta, mainly because of the fact that this is the shooting season and they are out in the bush right now.[189]
>
> However, the Tuktoyaktuk representation send you their greetings—they said they saw some of you today—also Fort McPherson, Aklavik, Arctic Red River, Sach's Harbour, and Tree River send their regards; the chief from Arctic Red River however cannot make it across the big river because the wind is just a little too high.[190]

Not only did their trip conflict with "the shooting season" but the Mackenzie River could not be crossed during the limited time that the Joint Committee planned to visit the Mackenzie Delta region. This was a kind and loving, if unintended, response to Mr. McQuaid's question to Peter Cumming: "Do the Indian and Eskimo people feel that they are being neglected in this respect?"

When Len Marchand tried to play the Indian card at the same time as the Liberal card he received a straightforward reply:

> [O]ne of the things you have been concerned about as an organization is the so-called Aboriginal right of the people in the Northwest Territories, and I should say that, as an Indian from British Columbia,

> this is a question that we have been very much concerned with as well. . . . we still feel that there must be some kind of settlement of the Aboriginal rights of the province. How do you feel that these rights should be settled in the Northwest Territories?
>
> **Mrs. Semmler:** . . . I am also referring to the Eskimo people in the Northwest Territories. They are entitled to some kind of a treaty or some Aboriginal rights also. They were around at the time the treaty was signed in 1925 with the Indians. . . . One of the beefs of the Committee for Original People's Entitlement is that the Eskimo people were not consulted in any way on Aboriginal rights or treaties.[191]

Marcel Lambert (PC, Edmonton West), who had been the Speaker of the 25th House of Commons, in 1962–63, first asserted that "the settlement of the Aboriginal rights . . . would be with *the Aboriginal people as a whole*" and then asked if the witnesses "envisage[d] also beyond that, the individual entitlements, such as the private ownership of any land by individual Aboriginal people . . . if the individual concerned would be entitled to the compensation." [192] The notions of extinguishment and of a settlement with "the Aboriginal people as a whole" was, apparently, a common ground shared the Conservative caucus and the Liberal caucus. And the tendency to go to class ill prepared was another common ground.

What Agnes Semmler and Nellie Cournoyer wanted was for the MacGuigan-Molgat Committee to do the kind of deep thinking which does emerge in the *Final Report* but which is nowhere evident in the *Proceedings*.

> The Committee for the original Peoples Entitlement places before the Constitution Committee its urgent request that Aboriginal rights and equities in traditional lands be constitutionally defined. The need for constitutional definition of these rights and equities at this point in history is essential if Aboriginal people are to have any faith in their destiny as traditional occupiers of this land.[193]

C.O.P.E. was essentially asking that their Aboriginal rights be entrenched in the Constitution and that they be defined. The merits of having rights "constitutionally defined," as distinct from *recognized* or *affirmed,* are quite debatable; yet, 11 years later s. 37 of the *Constitution Act, 1982* provided for a special First Ministers' Conference which would *identify and define existing Aboriginal and treaty rights.*

Nellie Cournoyer raised two arguments which go to the heart of a treaty-based trust relationship with the Crown:

> It is not enough to say that the Crown will protect our interests. Firstly, we are not certain just what "the Crown" means. Secondly, we are not certain the Crown is the best judge of what constitutes our interests. We are, primarily, people of the land and it is this relationship that we will strive to retain.

Cournoyer laid out principles which would be taken for granted in any urban Euro-Canadian context. Her principles were all derivative of the principle of self-determination:

> If there are mistakes to be made, we want to make them, so that we can learn from these mistakes. If there is direction to be given, we want to give it, so that we can maintain our own leadership. If there is encroachment of our rights, we want redress. If land is taken, we want equitable and fair settlements acceptable to all.[194]

The right to make one's own mistakes is a classic definition of autonomy. The C.O.P.E. brief coupled that right with the right to fair compensation for lands taken, a right which resonated with elements of *Magna Carta*, the English *Bill of Rights* and the U.S. *Bill of Rights*.

The C.O.P.E. brief spoke of "Aboriginal rights and *equities*." The significance of *the concept of equity*—"the application to particular circumstances of the standard of what seems naturally just and right, as contrasted with the application to those circumstances of a rule of law" [195]—has not been sufficiently explored in an Aboriginal context. Yet, it is precisely in respect to property that equity continues to have application. "The main applications of equitable principles in modern law are the recognition and enforcement of equitable interests in property, notably those arising under a trust."[196] Equity is the English way of appealing to "fairness and justice, and the word is used as a synonym for "natural justice" [. . . in contrast to] strict rules of law."[197]

A strict rule of law might allow the Queen a defence in the many loopholes and vaguenesses written into the numbered treaties. Yet "an underlying theory of equity" has existed in English law since it was propounded by St. Germain in the sixteenth century. It has to do with "the idea of conscience. . . . Equity acts on the defendant's conscience."[198] It might, for instance, be salutary if Messrs. Hogarth, McQuaid and Lambert addressed themselves to the question of being done out of their land, their livelihood and their culture by reason of clever wording in a foreign language over against basic rules of fairness which would require that the same property principles apply to all persons, clans and communities. Their steadfast refusal to consider whether the experiences related by Indian witnesses would be ones that *they would find hateful if they were done unto themselves*[199] is exactly what postcolonial discourse regards as "othering." Stannard and Drinnon relate it to a longstanding tradition that regards "native" as something other than fully human. I have related it to burden shifting and to prevarication.

Ian Watson a Liberal MP from Laprairie, Québec and the chairman of the Standing Committee on Indian Affairs and Northern Development wanted to know C.O.P.E.'s position on mineral rights. He also wanted a response to the argument advanced by the Jean Chrétien, the then Minister of Indian Affairs and Northern Development "that the resources of the Northwest Territories and the Yukon belong to all the people of Canada and they are thus distinguished from the resources of the province." Agnes Semmler replied, "We are not asking for all the resources; we are just asking for a percentage and then the rest of it for all Canadians."[200]

In 1973, when Watson's own Standing Committee on Indian Affairs and Northern Development attempted to come to grips with a definition of Aboriginal rights—the very thing requested by COPE—Ian Watson distinguished himself from other ostensibly sympathetic MPs by arguing that the benefits from Indian lands should go into a common pool for all Indian communities.[201] Watson appears to have shared this position only with Marcel Lambert, the Progressive Conservative MP from Edmonton. This position does not seem to have attracted the support either of other parliamentarians or of any First Nations or other Aboriginal leaders.

Pierre De Bané put a question that would have been no less insulting in French than it was in English. "I would like to know if we can say that in your opinion, a native, an Eskimo or an Indian born in this Territory today has equal opportunity with the white people, or is it a tragedy to be born an Indian or an Eskimo in 1971?" [202]

Nellie Cournoyer, in characteristic humour, pointed him toward a more nuanced way of appreciating the policy and constitutional dimensions of culture, "I do not think it is a tragedy to be born an Indian or an Eskimo, mainly because I think every Indian and Eskimo should be proud of what he is. The fact is that the native industry would be hard pressed if everyone was Indian and Eskimo."[203]

De Bané also wanted to know if COPE was "now large enough to constitute a political force . . . or are you not yet powerful enough?"

Nellie Cournoyer tried, once more, to explain what happens when a Native organization starts to work with the local municipal council:

> [W]e seem to be attending to roads that are for big trucks, which no Eskimo owns, or roads that come in from the south to bring I do not know what, because no one is asking for anything, or building great, massive schools which we do not really have much need for. Perhaps we need smaller schools with more quality inside those schools.[204]

MR. GEORGE MANUEL (PRESIDENT, NATIONAL INDIAN BROTHERHOOD)

George Manuel, the President of the National Indian Brotherhood, appeared before the MacGuigan-Molgat Committee on Tuesday, June 15, 1971 with Marie Smallface Marule, the Executive Director of the N.I.B., and James O'Reilly, his legal counsel.

Manuel began by saying that the brief which they were submitting at that time was "an interim position only" and, at the same time indicated that "we, as Indian people, are especially recognized under the *British North America Act* . . . as Indian people." Manuel's request to make "an interim presentation,"[205] and to return later, was similar to the request made by several previous Indian witness groups. Dave Courchene of the Manitoba Indian Brotherhood and Walter Gordon of the Federation of Saskatchewan Indians and Noel Doucette of the Union of Nova Scotia Indians as well as Donna Tyndall on behalf of the Union of B.C. Indian Chiefs had made similar requests.

This request is significant for our purposes because it demonstrates a tentativeness with which parliamentarians were likely unfamiliar. This tentativeness resonates with the need for further research before stating a complete position. It also demonstrates the very limited mandate that Indian leaders held from their electorates and the lack of previous decisions, at that time, on constitutional issues.

The recurring request for additional time for further research offers a key to understanding the situation in which the nascent Indian organizations found themselves at the time of the MacGuigan-Molgat Committee. There are, I think, three main factors underlying this recurring request. First, Manuel's own reason for presenting an interim position is stated quite clearly:

> [T]he National Indian Brotherhood [has been provided with funds] to set up a Claims Committee to do research into Indian rights and

> treaties and this research has begun work now, both at the national level and at the provincial level.[206]

The National Indian Brotherhood, having been born out of the National Indian Advisory Council about the time of the *White Paper*, and having moved to Ottawa just the year before this presentation had only just begun to do research.

Secondly, Manuel quite clearly wanted to put the shoe on the other foot:

> I think you are aware that Indian rights through treaties, Indian rights through Aboriginal rights claims of Indian people have been a continual problem of the Canadian people. Indian people have made presentations from away back in 1912 up to this point. As a result of these presentations to the Joint Parliamentary Committee in 1926 and 1927 and up to 1949, I think, or 1960, the claims have been submitted by Indian people that they have Aboriginal rights and that their claims in relation to treaties conflict with those interpreted by government.[207]

In this oblique way, Manuel pointed out to the Joint Committee that Indians had a long history with joint parliamentary committees before whom they had appeared in efforts to explain the nature of Aboriginal and treaty rights. He stopped short of reminding MacGuigan-Molgat of the repressive recommendations which emanated from some of its predecessor joint committees including the criminalizing of these very discussions.[208] In short, Manuel was asking the MacGuigan-Molgat Committee if they were more open to the fundamental concepts of Aboriginal and treaty rights than their predecessors had been.

Thirdly, there was, here, the nascent beginning of the two-fold meaning of research which would run through the use of the term "research" in N.I.B./AFN-Government relations throughout the period in question and beyond. In part, the N.I.B./AFN had in mind, by research, a scholarly but practical assembling and studying of documents relating to the historical claims to Aboriginal and treaty rights. But it equally had in mind a process for feeding back the information and analyses gained through such study both to the leadership and to the communities.

In a First Nations context, these two meanings are bound together in ways which may not have been fully appreciated by parliamentarians in 1971. The idea that research includes not only "digging up" new information but also "feeding it back" into the community is, quite possibly, one reason why Indian political processes often appear to move glacially. It is, nonetheless, an idea which no public inquiry or special Parliamentary committee can altogether avoid.

Although there were certain fundamental concepts, such as the recognition of Aboriginal and treaty rights, the substance of the research necessarily varied from one First Nation to the next. If there were common factors beyond the need for a more equitable and honest relationship with the Crown, those factors needed to be identified locally before they could be articulated confederally, i.e., with each provincial or territorial organization or traditional Indian nation setting out its own historical research and its own program for rectification.

In short, the N.I.B. visualized research as an adjunct of a community development process in which researchers collaborated with elders, teachers and local community activists and leaders and out of which the Brotherhood hoped penultimately to articulate a confederal or Canadian-national consensus.

Having indicated that they were prepared to do no more than to state an interim position, Manuel proceeded to outline to the *MacGuigan-Molgat* Committee certain basic principles:

> However, we do outline that we were the original people of this country and as such there were special provisions mentioned in the Constitution of Canada; that the Indians were recognized through the *Indian Act* of Canada; that there were treaties negotiated with the various tribes across Canada; and that there were territories definitely recognized and controlled by Indian people in the days when Indian people were the ruling bodies of Canada. [209]

Manuel's introduction was then followed by brief statements by Bill Wilson of the Union of British Columbia Chiefs, Anthony Francis of the Union of New Brunswick Indians and a longer statement by James O'Reilly, Legal Adviser, National Indian Brotherhood.

Bill Wilson was intent upon telling the Joint committee that "[W]e want you to know that we realize what our rights are *as given to us* by that Constitution, just as the French-Canadians realize what their rights are as given them by the Constitution."[210] In addition to the uncertain strategic value of such a statement, Wilson's statement is memorable mainly because it conceded that rights were *given* by the Constitution rather than asserting *sui generis*, inherent and "pre-existing any legislative act of the imperial power."[211] No less surprising was that Wilson, representing a province where treaties cover a very tiny proportion of the total land mass ended his remarks by saying "We people are very concerned about [the Constitution], [we want] to be involved, not only involved in the token kind of involvement that has very often happened in the past, but we want maybe even at some point [to] incorporate treaties into a Constitution.[212]

Anthony Francis was then erroneously reported as being the "President, Union of Nova Scotia Indians." Francis, very briefly, spoke of the "feeling in New Brunswick that Indians never made any land settlements with the French people" and that "There were documents which said that if you remain peaceful with the British you will maintain your hunting and fishing rights." [213] Francis's statement was neither broad enough to stand on its own nor sharp enough to serve as a clear instance of an argument being made more generally by the N.I.B. . [214]

James O'Reilly then spoke for about five minutes, a brief speech but significantly longer than any of the "Indian" presenters who preceded him. He began by pointing out that although there were rights belonging to Indian peoples in various parts of Canada, "the Parliament of Canada can abolish these rights at their whim, subject to a certain number of protected agreements such as the . . . *Natural Resources Transfers Act.*"[215]

He told the Joint Committee

> I think that often there has been a lot of confusion about what kind of rights the Indian people are claiming and that often there is an equation of absolute sovereignty with public ownership of all lands; that because the Indian people claim that they are sovereign people, they own all of Canada.[216]

O'Reilly explained, perhaps for the first time before a parliamentary committee, that the rights in question were "private rights of ownership," a significant concession away from any claim of self-government, self-determination or autonomy.

Lastly, he argued the reality of First Nations' titles.

> We are not talking about an ethereal type of ownership . . . the rationale behind the treaties . . . was that these areas [Robinson Huron and westward] were situated in what was known as the Indian territory . . . the Indians had a right and title in and to the land . . . and it was by these treaties that they surrendered or had their rights extinguished.

He implied, but did not quite say, that treaty rights are the means by which the Crown paid for Aboriginal rights which have been extinguished and that the payment must be as real as the rights which the Crown acquired.[217]

Lastly, O'Reilly told the Joint Committee that the Constitution required that "even parts of Québec where there are no treaties but . . . was originally part of Rupert's Land . . . be settled in conformity with the same equitable principles which had governed the British Crown in its dealings with the aborigines."[218] This argument would become the basis for *Kanatewat et al*,[219] the longest trial in Québechistory, in which O'Reilly would represent the nine Cree bands of northern Québec, before the Superior Court of Québec,on an application for a permanent injunction against the James Bay Project.

THE PARLIAMENTARIANS' GRASP OF THE N.I.B. PRESENTATION

Colin Gibson put the first question. He asked for a "comment on what our attitudes toward the Métis people should be." [220] This question, entirely unrelated to the initial statements of the four witnesses raised doubts not only about the capacity for concentration of parliamentarians but about their sense of common courtesy.

George Manuel, nonetheless, moved in on the opportunity presented:

> I think this was one of the reasons we took a very strong stand against the *White Paper* policy proposed by the federal government in 1969. . . . We felt that such a change of legislation does not rectify problems. . . . Also we felt that our brothers, the Métis have had the same privileges as were recommended in the *White Paper*, and they have done nothing for the Métis people at all.[221]

Gordon Fairweather distinguished himself by citing a local scandal which provided a prism through which to reflect on national policy:

> I am struck particularly in the Tobique situation . . . It will not help to go back to it except to discuss the position of the Indian agent who, in a sense as trustee, alienated Indian rights because he was employed by a government that wanted the benefits of those rights.[222]

The introduction of the concept of trustee enabled James O'Reilly to say that "The conflict is between the Crown in right of Canada as trustee for Indians and the Parliament of Canada acting for the people of Canada."[223] This was the first time that the conflict between the Crown's two roles—as trustee and as one of the three parts of Parliament was clearly articulated in parliamentary committee proceedings. Fourteen years later, in *Guérin*, the Supreme Court would rule that the Crown may be held liable for the harm caused to a First Nation by an Indian agent.[224]

Warren Allmand finally asked a question that returned the discussion to the main thrust of the N.I.B. presentation.

How will we know the will of the Indian people on these important questions, on what they would like done with respect to the Constitution and what they would like done with respect to changes in Indian rights, Aboriginal rights, and all these things? Is the National Indian Brotherhood a body which fully represents and expresses the will of the Indian people in Canada?

> **Mr. Manuel:** I think there is one thing you have to appreciate, this, the fact Indian people have been involved in their own affairs full-time very recently. It is very recent, in the last three years, and it has really developed in the last two years, this year particularly, and I think it will continue to develop. They have never had a national organization before and national policies are something new to the organization.[225]

Lastly, the issue of representivity[226]—a term not yet then coined—led Manuel to reflect on his experience working concurrently for the Indian Association of Alberta and the Alberta Métis Association.

> I worked in Alberta for almost three years for the Indian Association of Alberta and at the beginning I worked both for the Indian Association and the Métis. I chaired the meetings of the Indian Association annual conference and also chaired the Métis annual conference the first year I worked there. They needed more interpreters for the Métis annual conference, they are non-registered Indians' annual conference, [than] the Indian Association did with its membership.[227]

A declining need for interpreters was taken by Manuel to be a measure of acculturation.

What is most interesting about this comment from the viewpoint of a study of the vocabulary of First Nations' autonomy, is that George Manuel put before the *MacGuigan-Molgat* Committee an appreciation, if not a definition of Indianness, based not on race and not on legal status but on the use of traditional languages. Manuel, under whom the N.I.B. would later intervene in support of the *Indian Act* provisions enfranchising women who "married out" here offered a concept of membership, i.e., of belonging based on that element which most certainly shapes lifestyle and embodies it.

CONCLUSIONS

A very detailed account of the testimony before the *MacGuigan-Molgat* Committee has been necessary to demonstrate the nature of the discourse at the outset of the period in which political and social change began to escalate and the idea of First Nations self-government became both an idea that could be discussed in public and one that had the possibility of realization.

Several themes arise in the interchanges throughout this narrative.

Perhaps the most frequent theme is the inability of the parliamentarians of that day to enter into genuine dialogue with Indian leaders. Time and again questions are non-responsive to the presentations. Parliamentarians appear to travel across the country with their own favourite issues packed with their shirts and ties. The same questions are likely to be asked regardless of the opening statements of witnesses or their areas of expertise.

The parliamentarians' *dialogue of the deaf*[228] might better be understood as a failure, particularly on the part of the parliamentarians to give full weight and credence to the testimony of Indian witnesses. Their difficulties are exacerbated by an attitude in which "native" resonates with "naïf.' Parliamentarians exhibit a difficulty crediting these witnesses with the full range of intellectual talents. The idea that the provincial political Indian organizations from the three prairie provinces each chose a different descriptor—the Manitoba Indian *Brotherhood*, the *Federation* of Saskatchewan Indians (as it then was) and the Indian *Association* of Alberta—because their founding leaders made certain distinct organizational choices was hard for certain parliamentarians to credit. Even Mark MacGuigan appeared awkward in introducing Ernest Benedict. The notion that a Mohawk might represent a predominantly Ojibway political organization was difficult for some members to grasp.

The most consistent feature of these misunderstandings is not so much a placement of emphasis as a disbelief that these are people who make complex and polyvalent statements. Both the basic point and the humour of Joe Mathias's parody of the role of Indians in the Canadian Constitution completely escaped the parliamentarians (as far as one can tell from the record). This, however, may not be entirely a racial attitude. There was also no response to Noel Lyon's observations about his experience, as a professor, teaching Constitutional law to civil law students in contrast to common law students. Comparing Mohawk iron workers to francophone students did not appear to endear Lyon to francophone parliamentarians.

A second indicator is the incapacity to ask questions related to the brief that had just been presented to them. Warren Allmand's question to Ernest Benedict appears to be the first question to an Indian witness to be directly responsive to the witnesses' presentation.

A third, is the need to assert unfounded facts. Tactically, this serves not only to derail the discussion but to assert that the group in question do not have a real history. The assertion that no Indian organization had made a comprehensive proposal was a burden shifting accusation.

A fourth is the tendency to apply standards which do not have application elsewhere: for example, the proposal of Marcel Lambert, that all Indian parties with claims against the Crown might be merged into a common pool. No Conservative leader would make such a suggestion regarding other persons' property rights.

The MacGuigan-Molgat Committee concluded its hearings on June 29, 1971, two weeks after they heard the National Indian Brotherhood. None of the organizations that had requested an opportunity to make an additional submission were given an opportunity to do so. If any organization made an additional written submission, it is not part of the printed record. Neither were any of the later witness groups, such as the N.I.B., told, in response to their requests for more time, that the Committee was about to conclude its hearings.

On the other hand, the MacGuigan-Molgat Committee had held 94 hearings over three parliamentary sessions after having first received its mandate in January, 1970. The Committee had been ambitious in attempting to accommodate a number of major innovations in the ways in which it gathered testimony. At the same time, it lacked not only the experience but also the technical competence and the support of its membership necessary to make effective use of these innovations. The Committee's willingness to innovate was not matched with either the capacity to invest extra effort in meeting non-conventional witnesses nor the discipline to come to hearings well prepared.

Indian witnesses used the MacGuigan-Molgat Committee to test the parliamentary waters. By and large, they presented briefs which graciously, sometimes even elegantly, integrated a pragmatic Canadian approach with a principled concern for their Aboriginal and treaty rights. The witnesses who chose to testify were strongly committed both to the revival of their own nations and to the reinvigoration of the Canadian

Constitution. Indian witnesses, by and large, spoke with the assumption that these were mutually supportive principles, the antithesis of the fundamental assumption of William Lyon Mackenzie King and Pierre Elliott Trudeau.

Parliamentarians were generally ill prepared and did not demonstrate notable listening skills. They sought to use the appearance of Indian witnesses for their own political ends without on the other hand having invested themselves significantly in the situations with which they were being presented. Perhaps two or three MPs distinguished themselves from this general rule. Women parliamentarians tended not to grasp the idea that extending equal rights for Indian women essentially requires preserving and enhancing Aboriginal and treaty rights. Many women parliamentarians supported their government's program of assimilation while also pretending to support "Indian rights for Indian women."[229]

Procedural difficulties tended to reinforce the obstacles to communication. The innovation of having speakers from the floor while Indian witnesses were presenting briefs on behalf of representative organizations suggests (a) that the committee's procedures were in the process of change; and (b) that the urge toward innovation was not well thought out. There also does not appear to have been a similar conflict when the committee was hearing testimony from distinguished scholars or provincial cabinet ministers.

When Courchene referred to his ancestors signing treaties "without the full knowledge of the ramification of those treaties and often without any knowledge of the meaning of the words" he is pointing to a behaviour, on the part of the Crown, that, twelve years later, the Court would describe, in *Nowigijick*,[230] as "sharp practices were." In doing so, Courchene was raising issues with which parliamentarians not equipped to deal. So far as David Courchene, Walter Gordon, Nellie Cournoyer and George Manuel were all appealing to the conscience of parliamentarians—much as equity is said to appeal to the conscience of a defendant—few parliamentarians exhibited such a sensibility during the 1970–72 period.

The idea that laws should be drafted so as to have significant "reference to the interpretation placed upon these documents by the other signatory, the Indian people themselves"[231] asks that Indian peoples be treated with a standard of respect that Parliament and Government conventionally show to major interest groups whose conduct is subject to government regulation. It is also a standard that John Borrows argued, convincingly, was the reason for Governor Johnson's convening the Niagara Conference in 1764, viz., to discuss the meaning, significance and application of the *Royal Proclamation*.[232]

The historic unwillingness or refusal to recognize the fundamental humanity of Indian people and "Indian nations" is recapitulated or maintained in the responses of parliamentarians in this period by their inability draw upon the same ethical and legal standards in responding to First Nations' grievances that would operate in hearing similar grievances from representatives of the dominant cultures.

It is the very nature of *recognition* that one accepts a certain set of responses as a given. Such an assumption comes into play only with a very few of the parliamentarians on the MacGuigan-Molgat Committee. The hurt and outrage manifested by Dave Courchene, for example, did not evoke a corresponding expression of sympathy or support. So far as a denial of any proper place for First Nations in Confederation had been a practice from the beginning (and possibly was implicit in ss. 91(24) of the *British North America Act, 1867*), there is very little in the parliamentarians' responses to suggest that they have experienced the kind of transformation that makes change irresistible.

Although the *Final Report* will speak of the need for a Constitution to gain a people's love as well as their respect, there is nothing in the *Proceedings* to suggest that such feelings on the part of First Nations are deeply desired by Canadian parliamentarians.

The persistent pursuit of the game "Gotcha" by some parliamentarians[233], challenging the *bona fides* of Indian witnesses in a way which simply does not occur in their treatment of other witnesses. At the very least, remarks of Dinsdale and others challenged the witnesses' representativity, i.e., whether or not he represents his constituency. Often, they went further. A significant part of the limited time allocated for questioning is diverted into grandstanding.

When Dinsdale asked Doucette whether or not he and the Union of Nova Scotia Indians were consulted with regard to the N.I.B. statement, Dinsdale appears to have been looking for ways to discredit the N.I.B. . His question gave Doucette very little credit either for basic intelligence or for political savvy. Doucette responded by pointing out the then major recent response to the *White Paper* had been the *Red Paper* of the *Indian Association of Alberta*. It is doubtful that, in a non-Aboriginal context, Dinsdale would have wandered down a path from which there was no safe return.

What Dinsdale attempted was to repeatedly shift the burden on to Doucette with an expectation that Doucette should have demonstrated his competence, his right to appear and to speak for his electorate. Dinsdale entered into the dark side of the discourse not so much by statements but primarily by his search for "a final solution." "Do you think that the Indians have had an opportunity for consultation and self-determination? Do you feel that there has been sufficient representation on various committees now engaged in studying the Indian problem?" The question, itself, belies a belief that if the magic words could only just be found and uttered that the "Indian problem" would disappear.

The linking of "consultation" with "self-determination" suggests a speaker who is either unfamiliar with these terms or who ascribes to them wholly different meanings when speaking to an Indian than he might elsewhere. These are concepts that are not only mutually exclusive they are in some sense reciprocally antagonistic. If a people achieve genuine self-determination the obligation *to consult* them goes beyond an obligation to ask for input, beyond the obligation to listen in good faith, to the obligation to gain a *bona fides* consent.

The need to explain to a Joint Committee on the Constitution that there are different legal regimes according to the presence or absence of different treaty provisions suggests a high level of ignorance amongst the parliamentarians and a consequent willingness to acquiesce in the government's perspective of First Nations relations. The idea that the *Royal Proclamation* and the treaties may have a constitutional significance does not appear to resonate with their study of constitutional renewal. Sen. Lamontagne, for instance, asks whether or not these matters might better be dealt with before the Indian Affairs Committee.

Osler's statement to Doucette that "other Canadians would be very suspicious of creating a nation within a nation" confounds *creating* with *recognizing*.

Hogarth's assertion, "It is so difficult for me to suggest *how to correct* 100 years of *mistakes* and just *transform the situation overnight* begs the question that it does not ask. The supposition that the mismanagement of the Crown's fiduciary obligations were **"mistakes"** already pre-casts the answers that he might find acceptable. The catalogue of First Nations grievances will not be well addressed by regarding them as **the moral equivalents of typographic errors** in need of correction.

The accusation that the Indian organizations have failed to produce a comprehensive solution is another example of burden shifting. His complaint that the N.I.B. had not developed a Canada-wide position on Aboriginal rights, exemplifies how a statement, although factually correct, enters into the **discourse of prevarication** when it is *used primarily for deception*. If Hogarth did not have an intention to shift the burden onto the Indian witnesses and to deceive listeners about a lack of positive proposals he certainly was not extending to Indian political leaders the respect for regional diversity that is almost universal amongst Canadian politicians.

Would any other situation, comparably catastrophic to the population collapses of the various First Nations evoke a question about an *overnight transformation*? The very idea of this question is calibrated *to deny* the nature and extent of the damage suffered by First Nations as a result of the conduct of officials ostensibly acting on behalf of the Crown. **Denial** is *a well-established form of prevarication*. Couching the denial in terms of a desire for overnight transformation does not move the question out of its fundamental category.

The failure to view the *Royal Proclamation* and the treaties as legal instruments and constitutional documents may reinforce the belief that there is a lack of positive suggestion. After all, the most recurring theme from Indian witnesses is that Aboriginal and treaty rights should be entrenched in the Constitution, that treaty rights should be respected and that the constitutional status of the *Royal Proclamation* should be recognized. None of these suggestions, although put forward by numerous witnesses is ever explored in any depth by any parliamentarian.

Dinsdale's later question to Ernest Benedict asking "How far would Mr. Benedict go in claiming Aboriginal rights," as a lead question that diverted attention into a field not mentioned in the presentation was, at the very least, an adversarial move. There is no indication that Ernest Benedict had made any constitutional proposals beyond honouring proclamations and treaties. The suggestion that Benedict was speaking on behalf of the "Six Nations" and not the Union of Ontario Indians was calculated to discredit his testimony. This kind of statement also serves a prevaricating, deceptive purpose.

THE MACGUIGAN-MOLGAT *FINAL REPORT*

Noel Lyon's testimony is significant to the discourse because his purpose is to affirm both the First Nations and the Constitution and to develop means whereby they might become mutually affirming. Lyon discusses the need for a holistic view in terms of his experience as a common law jurist teaching civil law students. It would also establish that the preference for starting with the holistic and seeing details within the context of a larger purpose is not the result of a "primitive mind" such as witnesses before earlier parliamentary committees had suggested. There is no indication that this idea caught the imagination of any of the Committee members.

Noel Lyon told the Committee that "[t]he test of our capacity . . . to develop an adequate Constitution and *to call ourselves a civilized nation* will depend upon the state in which our native people find themselves." The *Final Report* of the MacGuigan-Molgat Committee said

> What is essential is that a people should understand, accept and even love their form of government. Without the understanding of its people a constitution is meaningless. Without their affection it is dead.

These two thoughts are corollaries of one another. It would be difficult to think of a form of government (or a constitution) that was understandable but unjust and that commanded affection while it also continued to visit injustices to the indigenous peoples of the land. (Arguably, both the English and the American Constitutions come to mind as examples of constitutions that are understandable, command the affection of *parts of the populace*, yet are unjust. Briefly, both these Constitutions achieve this paradoxical situation by appealing to the citizenry to acquiesce in overlooking or failing to include those persons—Black slaves and Indians, for example—to whom the law applies in its prohibitive statements but to whom citizenship and other positive benefits are not extended. The understanding, acceptance and affection of those who are excluded are, of course, not sought. Gaining acceptance in all corners of the country is what requires serious consultation, negotiation and concession.) Yet there is a strong disconnect between these fine sentiments and the committee's discussions. Perhaps more important from an historical perspective, is that these fine sentiments were not successful in persuading the Government to include any of the Committee's recommendations regarding recognition of First Nations ("Native peoples") in the texts of proposed constitutional revision, either in 1978 or in 1980. The most that can be said for the influence of this Committee's hearings and its *Final Report* is that a range of ideas dealing with constitutional recognition and with First Nations' self-determination and self-government were introduced to parliamentarians.

The idea that a Constitution is something to be loved would not have been surprising to Walter Bagehot, the author of *The English Constitution*, a study published in 1867, the year of Canadian Confederation to which reference continues to be made. Neither would the idea have been strange to the characters of Baldwin and Lafontaine, two "Fathers of Confederation" who John Ralston Saul considers to have set the tone and character of the Canadian Confederation.[234] Neither would the idea be strange to anyone educated in the Haudenosaunee tradition of the Great Law of Peace, the Constitution that the Mitchells and Thompsons were following, in 1970, when they reclaimed the Islands seized under the *St. Regis Islands Act*, 43 years earlier.

There is, however, a need for the "just reconciliation" of which Dave Courchene spoke, if First Nations and the dominant cultures are to love the same Constitution. *MacGuigan-Molgat* made significant strides by including an entire chapter devoted to acknowledging First Nations and by introducing the social dimension of a constitution. However, the disconnect between the parliamentarians discussed here and First Nations requires that the historical repression, the variety of civil or legal disabilities imposed on First Nations by Parliament be acknowledged. Although the *1982 Constitution Act* entrenches Aboriginal and treaty rights and, through the *Charter of Rights and Freedoms* protects First Nations from a renewed imposition of civil disabilities, the failure to acknowledge the past continues to hobble the potential of a just reconciliation.

One of the ways in which the disconnect is most evident is the incapacity of Canadian political leaders and government officials to speak in straightforward terms about a renewed and healthier relationship with the First Nations. The use of the term "first Canadians" for the same peoples whose autonomy had been suppressed under the *St. Regis Islands Act* and under the 1927 *Act to Amend the Indian Act* is hard to fathom. However good the intentions of the authors of that phrase, its effect is to further deceive Canadians about the history of their relations with First Nations rather than to confront that history and to bring about genuine and lasting change.

Ernest Benedict's statement, "As Indian people we will always see our special status and legal rights as flowing from the original sovereignty of our nations" resonates with the need for a Canadian Constitution that is capable of being "understood, accepted and even loved." It also resonates with the descriptions of Aboriginal rights formulated by the Supreme Court of Canada in a line of cases beginning with *Sparrow* in 1990. Although the Court has grasped and endorsed Benedict's message, successive governments have continued to "read down" the Court's interpretations of section 35 of the *Constitution Act, 1982*.

Mr. Hogarth's statement to Donna Tyndall from the Union of B.C. Indian Chiefs (U.B.C.I.C.) that "Len Marchand who is a native Indian and a member of Parliament for Kamloops was to sit with us in Vancouver but unfortunately . . ." was, undoubtedly intended as a show of good will. It was, in reality, a kind of tokenism. Even the term "native Indian" suggests a difficulty getting a handle on mutually acceptable terminology. If Marchand would have "sat with" the Committee while indigenous people from B.C. were testifying, where would he have been when it came to drafting a report? Marchand, himself, expressed some discontent with government policy regarding Aboriginal rights, albeit in a most mild and gracious manner, "We still feel that there must be some kind of settlement of the Aboriginal rights of the province."[235]

Were Donna Tyndall given to suffering fools gladly she might have mistaken Hogarth's reference to Marchand for a significant concession. If she had been following the work of the Committee she would have known that Mr. Marchand had not participated otherwise and was not in a position to carry a brief for the U.B.C.I.C. had he been inclined to do so.

> Under Head 24, Section 91, We thereby take our place, with some trepidation, alongside the public debt, the postal service, the census and statistics and other heads under Section 91 including beacons, buoys, lighthouses and Sable Islands.

Chief Joe Mathias's parody will be readily recognized as a satirical illustration of the extent to which Indians were objectified and treated as pawns in the power brokering exercise in the drafting of the *British North America Act*,

The several "Indian nations" as George III referred to them in the *Royal Proclamation*, are human entities and are not properly made the objects of other peoples' power brokering. It does no good to say that this reflected the "spirit of the times." The spirit of the times is difficult to distinguish from the will of the majority within the dominant culture.

The well-known tendency of tyrannical majorities to prevail does not move their statements out of the dark side of the discourse of another people's autonomy. Certainly a British Commons Committee of 1837[236] and the minority in *St. Catharines Milling*[237] were aware of what was wrong with this approach. To say that these were minority views begs the question of how the majority was allowed to prevail on such a matter.

"TERMINATION IS A THREAT TO THE DESIRED GOAL OF AUTONOMY"

> Prof. Kenneth Lysyk, Brief to the MacGuigan-Molgat Committee on the Constitution, March 25, 1971.

Professor Ken Lysyk's proposal that "this Committee may wish to consider whether the consent of the Indians ought not to be a *prerequisite* for any amendment involving section 91(24) would appear to have been rejected when the Trudeau Government began to draft patriation proposals. Neither Bill C-60 of 1978 or the patriation resolution introduced by

Trudeau in September 1980 contained any reference to a role for First Nations in amendments directly affecting them.

Lysyk built his argument out of a need for Government and Parliament to gain the confidence of the First Nations by behaving differently and by adopting different policies than their predecessors had pursued. There is no indication in the Committee's *Proceedings* or in the *Debates* of either House that gaining the confidence of the First Nations was a serious objective of Cabinet.

Lysyk's statement that "termination is a threat to the desired goal of autonomy" summarizes the entire body of testimony of First Nations leaders and their criticism of the Government's *White Paper* and the general attitudes of Parliament. If an intermediary were needed to explain the prevailing First Nations' perspective Lysyk might have filled that role admirably. Lysyk highlighted the ironic tension and contradiction between the Government's desire to end their responsibilities for First Nations while being unwilling to allow the Fist Nations to acknowledge the First Nations desire to be more autonomous and to take responsibility for their own affairs.

It is not *the termination of wardship* that is abhorrent but *the termination of Aboriginal and treaty rights*. Recognition of Aboriginal rights would also terminate, or at least substantially curtail wardship. Once patriation—the goal of both the Trudeau Government and the Joint Committees—is achieved, the courts will weigh in with guidelines as to how wardship might be ended while rights are regarded as a promise renewed in the *Constitution Act, 1982*.[238]

Senator Casgrain's statement, ostensibly in response to Mrs. Doré, "I fully agree that the *Indian Act* is made to satisfy the Indians [men]" is so far fetched that one hesitates to pursue an analysis at all. Nonetheless, it embodies a propensity to shift the burden from Government and Parliament to "Indian men," a class of persons long prohibited from assembling as a result of the very *Act* for which they are here being blamed. The statement is all the more striking for Senator Casgrain's lifelong devotion to progressive causes. However, a progressive reputation does not offset a failure to do one's homework before coming to class.

When Agnes Semmler explained to the Committee that June was "an extremely bad time to have a meeting" in Inuvik, she was highlighting the Committee's failure to consider a fundamental reality of the Mackenzie Delta. It is unlikely that a parliamentary committee would seriously ask southern farmers to divert attention from their fields at the height of the harvest to attend a meeting. The failure to extend the same consideration to the Inuvialuit suggests that the Committee either lacked an advance team or failed to heed its advice on a basic question. A well-run committee does careful analyses of the local factors in planning a trip to hold hearings. Failure to consider such basic factors as the feasibility, in terms of river navigation and the spring hunt certainly starts the Committee's relationship with far northern communities "on the wrong foot." Nellie Cournoyer's statement, "We are, primarily, people of the land and it is this relationship that we will strive to retain" is something that an advance person might have included in the briefing book Committee members might have been given to read on the plane from Ottawa to Yellowknife.

The need, as seen by C.O.P.E., for Aboriginal and treaty rights to be constitutionally protected coincides with the views expressed by most southern Indian witnesses as well as by Prof. Lysyk. The C.O.P.E. brief, however, introduced a concept not previously discussed in these proceedings, "that Aboriginal rights and *equities* in traditional lands be constitutionally defined." I had not seen the term "equities" used to describe the Aboriginal interest before. Nor have I seen it elsewhere as a plural noun parallel to 'rights." I do not think that "equity" had the widespread currency in political discourse in 1971 that it came to assume at a later time. Yet the term is worth re-visiting.

Her doubt as to "whether the Crown is the best judge of what constitutes our interests" is a deep insight into the constitutional relationship between the Crown and First Nations and an invitation to the parliamentary committee to think about the nature of the Crown's fiduciary duties. Her statement might also be seen to pre-figure Dickson's observation in *Guérin* that "their interest in these lands is a *pre-existing right* not created by Royal Proclamation . . . or by any other executive order or legislative provision."[239] It may more likely be that they were drawing on the same notion of equity and fairness which influenced Marshall to describe Aboriginal rights as "preexisting" in *Worcester v. Georgia.*[240]

The inability of several of the parliamentarians on this committee to walk a mile in the shoes of the Indigenous witnesses is often described as the result of a cultural gap. I think it may be more than a cultural gap. Messrs Hogarth, McQuaid, Dinsdale and Lambert have a difficulty crediting the Indian witnesses who appear before their Committee with the intellectual attributes they credit to other witnesses.

When the historian A.R.M. Lower was before the Committee, Sen. Paul Yuzyk, a Conservative from Manitoba and the founding chairman of the Slavic Studies Department at the University of Manitoba remarked that Prof. Lower's historical view had no place for Aboriginal people or for settler communities who were neither French nor English. A *cultural gap* is one which has to be bridged to understand those with whose customs we are unfamiliar. *Prejudice* is the prior decision that appreciating a particular culture is not important.

Assumptions of a lack of intellect and sophistication resonate with the root of the word "naïf" in "native,"[241] and a corresponding presumption of incompetence. If these are not "real people," or if these "natives" are not fully human, then it is not necessary to lend full attention to their words. It is certainly not necessary to consider when they might be harvesting. There is, after all, an interest in denying that they have the qualities of organization attributed to real agriculture. Persons possessed of such attributes would have to be considered civilized, in Locke's terms. In short, their whole way of encountering these witnesses reflects a prejudice similar to Prof. Lower's and their nominal show of interest is deeply prevaricating.

SOME POSITIVE OUTCOMES

In the face of many challenges, including the cultural gaps, limited preparation sporadic attention, perceptual handicaps and personal agendas discussed here, the Committee broke new ground both from the perspective of its own mandate and from the perspective of the discourse of First Nations' autonomy.

This Committee ran over three sessions. It produced a report that called for some inclusion of Aboriginal and treaty rights in the Constitution. In the final analysis, *something of what was said was also heard.*

The concept of self-determination was introduced—however cautiously and circuitously. The recognition that quoting Richard Nixon was an effective way of communicating strange and new ideas to Canadian parliamentarians reflects a profound pedagogical insight on the part of Dave Courchene.

Others who followed in his footsteps, reinforced this tendency.

Most of the Indian witnesses recognized that the value in providing parliamentarians with very elementary introductions to the history, philosophy and legal principles with which they—like most Canadians—were abundantly unacquainted. This was not only a wise strategy. It also demonstrated a high level of sophistication about the dominant culture and its institutions on the part of those who were speaking from the margins and asking that their cultures and communities be included in the Canadian mosaic.

The first step toward inclusion was for Canadian parliamentarians—at least a few—to learn *to talk with* First Nations political leaders as respected colleagues. If there this is an *episodic* quality to this account, it is the result of attempting to tell the story of re-socializing of groups of ostensible adults in positions of responsibility. In a more mature political culture than Canada's the basic outline of this story would have been known much earlier.

I trust that I have also introduced some of the significant parliamentary actors of that day. I hope that this digest of the volumes of *Proceedings* tells the story of political leaders from a dominant culture and a colonized culture learning to talk to one another and that it also introduces the reader to a rich and much neglected resource.

Chapter Four
The Middle Period: A Minority Parliament and a First Patriation Bill

A PREVIEW OF THIS CHAPTER: "INDIAN CONTROL," ABORIGINAL

RIGHTS & PATRIATION

This chapter takes the emergence of the vocabulary of First Nations self-government through the years 1972 to 1978. There were two parliaments during this six year period: the 29th Parliament and the 30th Parliament. The 29th Parliament elected on October 22, 1972, elected four years and four months after the first Trudeau Parliament, produced a minority government that lasted until 1974. (See Glossary.)

This is of particular interest to the story told here because a number of events that occurred in the Commons Standing Committee on Indian Affairs and Northern Development (the Indian Affairs Committee) were facilitated by the Government's lack of the control enjoyed by a Government with a majority in the House of Commons.

Possibly the most important event, in terms of its long lasting effects, followed the invitation by the Committee to George Manuel, the president of the National Indian Brotherhood (N.I.B.) to present an N.I.B. position paper entitled *Indian Control of Indian Education*. When the Minister of Indian Affairs and Northern Development, Jean Chrétien, appeared immediately after Manuel, the Minister told the Committee that the N.I.B. paper would become Government policy.

Later in the 29th Parliament, when the N.I.B. presented a position paper on *Aboriginal title*,[1] Flora MacDonald and Joe Clark, two leading Conservative MPs, moved that the Committee recommend that the N.I.B. position paper on Aboriginal title become government policy.[2]

During the 30th Parliament, which was elected on July 8, 1974, Prime Minister Trudeau introduced a bill to patriate the Canadian Constitution, i.e., the bill set out an amending formula which would have replaced the practice of returning to the British Parliament for amendments and which included a *Charter of Rights* and several other highly significant amendments.

This bill was referred to a Special Joint Committee on the Constitution (MacGuigan-Lamontagne) and it is the testimony of First Nations and other Aboriginal leaders before that Committee which will be the primary interest from the 30th Parliament in this chapter.

During the 30th Parliament the Indian Affairs Committee continued the practice developed in the preceding parliaments of inviting the N.I.B. and provincial and territorial Indian organizations to make presentations on the annual estimates. The major event, from the perspective of this study, in the Indian Affairs Committee of the 30th Parliament, was the public discussion of the 1976 collapse of the Joint N.I.B.-Cabinet Committee on the *Indian Act* revision.

BACKGROUND ON INDIAN AFFAIRS COMMITTEE

The Indian Affairs Committee (renamed the Aboriginal Affairs Committee in the 1990s), among other references, during the period under review, was mandated in almost every parliamentary session to study the Annual Estimates of the Department of Indian Affairs and Northern Development.

The presentations submitted to the Indian Affairs Committee by the N.I.B. and various regional First Nations varied widely: some focused on local grievances; others dwelt on the failures of the Indian Affairs Branch to provide services promised by treaty or by the minister. Later in the decade, the N.I.B. began to develop alternative estimates.

The Indian Affairs Committee was an important arena for the discussion of First Nations self-government during this period because much of the vocabulary of First Nations self-government emerged into the public domain in presentations of First Nations leaders before that Committee. What lends complexity to this vocabulary is that it grew out of an interweaving of very practical issues and pragmatic thinking with a larger constitutional vision.

ABORIGINAL RIGHTS: DRAWING ON A BODY OF LAW PRE-EXISTING EUROPEAN CONTACT

The introduction of Aboriginal rights into the public discourse, in significant part by the presentation of the N.I.B. position paper of March 1973 introduced the idea to the public record that First Nations enjoyed certain rights because they had exercised those rights within their territories and over their people before any European contact and *before any executive or legislative act of Britain* or any other European imperial power.

Aboriginal rights as a concept based on *a body of law pre-existing European contact* required non-indigenous people who were interested in understanding Aboriginal rights to take a view of First Nations that would be much more complex and much more respectful than the attitudes of most Canadians in the early 1970s, including, for example, the parliamentarians on the MacGuigan-Molgat Committee discussed in the previous chapter.

When Aboriginal rights are understood as rights based on a pre-existing body of law,[3] self-government is seen as the most fundamental Aboriginal right. Some years later this concept was given some recognition in the first case in which the Supreme Court of Canada explored the recognition of Aboriginal rights in section 35 of the *Constitution Act, 1982* in *Sparrow*.[4] In that decision, Chief Justice Dickson observed that "the fishing right had always been regulated, *albeit self-regulated*." In other words, Edward Sparrow's pre-contact ancestors did not have an unfettered right to fish whenever they felt like it. The right to fish belonged not to individuals but to the community or the First Nation. Individuals participated in that right through their citizenship in that nation. The Chief Justice's term "self-regulated" accepts the idea that the First Nation made regulations (or laws) stipulating when individuals or groups might fish, where they might fish and the means by which they might fish.

The 1973 Clark motion,[5] like the testimony of Chrétien and Manuel, later in the same session, served both to lend legitimacy to the N.I.B. perspective and to identify N.I.B. position papers as the mainstream of Indian thought on such matters. This was the first time in Canadian parliamentary history that parliamentarians had a source of ideas as well as of information other than DIAND and the Privy Council Office. The fact of an Indian source of Indian policies began a process of deligitimization of DIAND on the part of Ottawa watchers without strong partisan or ideological affiliations.

Although the Clark motion was sidestepped by the minority government, it did serve to consolidate an understanding of the issues among the MPs on the Standing Committee and to further their relationship with the N.I.B. A few years later, the same committee, still composed largely of the same MPs, would draw on this understanding and the growing well of political cognitive dissonance to challenge the minister over the deaths of several children from dysentery in James Bay Cree communities.

The N.I.B. position paper did not produce a definition of Aboriginal rights which would withstand the test of time and be widely quoted ever since. It did, however, produce *general agreement on a coherent definition* by members of the N.I.B. General Assembly and particularly delegates from Aboriginal rights areas, i.e., areas in which Aboriginal rights had not been supplanted by treaty rights.

INDIAN CONTROL OF INDIAN EDUCATION: THE 1971 WATSON REPORT ON INDIAN EDUCATION AND THE 1973 N.I.B. POSITION PAPER

Much of the advancement of self-government has come not through the advancement of the concept as a whole but through the advancement of specific fields of legislative jurisdiction. In this sense, Indian education has been on the cutting edge of the self-government debate since the *Watson Report*.

In 1971, Ian Watson, the chairman of the Standing Committee on Indian Affairs had received a mandate for a subcommittee to study the state of Indian Education. The *Watson Subcommittee* produced a report that concluded that the dropout rate among Indian students remained around 94% whether the schools were run by the federal government, provincial governments, or churches. Watson suggested that the one strategic move that had not yet been made in an effort to reduce the dropout rate of First Nations students was to allow First Nations communities to play a greater role in the running of their own schools. The *Watson Report* can be said to have prefigured the N.I.B. paper *Indian Control of Indian Education*.

The *Watson Report on Indian Education* had lent credence to the proposition that, contrary to the White Paper approach, changes in education policy should be made only with the consent of the parents of the community concerned:

> The Committee has noted both in testimony received . . . and during visits . . . *a unanimity of Indian opinion* that no transfer of Indian children into integrated schools or into provincial schools takes place except with the consent and at the request of the majority of Indian parents in the communities concerned.

> . . . the education of Indian and Eskimo young people, and in particular Indian young people, has suffered from the day-to-day, year-to-year improvisation attitude of successive governments which regarded Indian education as a passing thing, soon to be handed over to the provinces.[6] (emphasis added)

The *Watson Report* was cited in the MacGuigan-Molgat *Final Report* on patriation of the Canadian Constitution as a model of gaining the participation of First Nations citizens in the running of their own communities. Both reports represent important rejections of the 1969 *White Paper* not because they contain an explicit rejection but because they contemplate an enhanced role for First Nations governments with a degree of constitutional recognition of First Nations' place in Confederation.

In examining the emergence of the vocabulary of First Nations self-government, several important events, of which the *Watson Report* is a good example, did not particularly introduce new lexical units so much as they lent credence to the application of concepts such as self-government and autonomy to First Nations. The idea of First Nations autonomy was hardly new at the beginning of this era but it was not much discussed beyond First Nations circles and was, very often, discussed in First Nations languages. On those few occasions when First Nations leaders made statements in favour of self-determination, self-government or autonomy, such attention as their speeches received were often reported with a note of sarcasm and a studied incapacity to correctly note the names of the speaker, the place and occasion and his actual statements.

George Manuel, the president of the National Indian Brotherhood responded to the *Watson Report* with a statement saying that the committee had rejected the federal "Termination Policy."[7] "The implications of the report go far beyond formal education. It laid down three basic principles that could form a blueprint for an alternative "Indian Policy." He described the Committee's proposed "models of excellence" as an alternative to the Government's "final solution." Two weeks after Watson tabled the *Report on Indian Education*, on June 30, 1971, Manuel asked the General Assembly of the N.I.B. to set up a Task Force on Education whose primary aim would be "to lay the groundwork for the three principles [recommended by the Watson Report] 'at the community level and through the provincial and territorial Indian organizations."[8]

In light of the role of Indian education as the cutting edge of *Indian Control* and hence, of self-government, it is worth quoting the Minister's endorsements of this paper extensively:

> The staff of my department and I consider the Brotherhood's paper a significant milestone in the development of Indian education in Canada. I have given the National Indian Brotherhood my assurance that I and my department are fully committed to realizing the educational goals for the Indian people which are set forth in the Brotherhood's proposal. In consultation and co-operation with the Indian organizations, my department will begin immediately to effect the educational changes for the Indian people that they have requested.
>
> To achieve our objectives, gentlemen of the Committee, new policies and programs must be developed. The new philosophy must be convey to our education personnel at every level. Attitudinal changes in our personnel and in society at large will require full co-operation of the Indian people in a concerted effort.
>
> Accordingly, to the extent that the Band Councils and local Indian education committees desire, they can assume the control of the Indian education program and can give it the direction they wish with assistance and support from the Department.[9]

George Manuel outlined the highlights of the paper from which he quoted only brief excerpts of which two are most fundamental.

> Indian parents must have FULL RESPONSIBILITY AND CONTROL OF EDUCATION. The Federal Government must adjust its policy and practices to make possible the full participation and partnership of Indian people in all decisions and activities connected with the education of Indian children. This requires determined and enlightened action on the part of the Federation (sic) Government and immediate reform.
>
> We want education to provide the setting in which our children can develop the fundamental attitudes and values which have an honoured place in Indian tradition and culture. The values that we want to pass on to our children, values which make our people a great race, are not written in any book. They are found in our history, in our legends and in the culture. WE believe that if an Indian child is fully aware of the important Indian values he will have reason to be proud of our race and of himself as an Indian.[10] (emphasis in original)

ABORIGINAL AND TREATY RIGHTS IN THE COURTS DURING THE 29TH PARLIAMENT

During the period of the 29th Parliament, 1972–74, three important judicial decisions came down—*Calder*, *Kanatewat*, and *Re: Paulette*—each of which had a significant effect on the position of the government in regard to Aboriginal rights and, in turn, affected the position of the various First Nations organizations and the work of the Indian Affairs Committee.

First, in the *Calder*[11] decision the Supreme Court was unanimously of the opinion that Aboriginal title was an established element of the common law. The Court had then divided evenly as to whether or not the Nisga'a title had been extinguished by pre-Confederation British Columbian legislation. Although this was a very qualified victory it clearly challenged the view frequently expressed by Prime Minister Trudeau that Aboriginal title was too vague a concept on which to base negotiations. At a meeting, some months after the decision, Trudeau told the Nisga'a leaders, "I guess you have more rights than I thought you had." [12]

The *Calder* decision had another important effect in terms of the emergence of self-government. Hall J. described the stereotypical attitude of First Nations—in a phrase coined by U.S. Chief Justice John Marshall in 1832 and widely quoted with approval by Canadian courts, "fierce Indian savages whose occupation was war"[13]—as "ill-founded." Such an observation did not have an immediate or direct effect either on government policy or popular attitudes but it put lower courts in Canada on notice that they could no longer lean on this epithet in refusing to recognize Aboriginal or treaty rights and, thereby, also legitimized the campaign of First Nations organizations to overcome such stereotypes and to gain both public and constitutional recognition for Aboriginal and treaty rights.

Both Trudeau's apology and Hall J.'s recognition of the humanity of indigenous nations were truly remarkable events in the history of First Nations relations in Canada. Trudeau's acknowledgement that the basic assumption on which his *White Paper* policy had been based was without justification may also have encouraged progressive parliamentarians who were not attracted by the dead centre of the political spectrum to move ahead of the position of the Supreme Court.

Secondly, the James Bay Crees, as they were then known, brought an application for an injunction against Hydro Québec to halt the construction of the James Bay Project, a gigantic power dam that would flood their traditional lands in and around the La Grande River system and re-route several other rivers. At the end of the longest trial in the history of Québec, Mr. Justice Malouf granted the injunction. A few weeks later, the Québec Appeal Court overturned his decision and canceled the injunction.[14]

Thirdly, about the same time, Mr. Justice Morrow decided in favour of the Dene in *Re: Paulette*[15] regarding the interpretation of Treaty 8 and the inclusion of oral promises based on the recollection of the surviving translators. This decision was also reversed on appeal.

None of these cases was a clear win for a First Nation. Each of them, however, lent credibility to First Nations claims and put the government on notice that a claims process outside of the courts would be to the advantage of all parties. One result was a policy for settlement of land claims announced in August 1973. From a First Nations perspective this land claims process was deeply flawed. Nonetheless, it allowed that First Nations land claims needed to be taken seriously. The flaws—keeping the process within the Indian Affairs Branch and subject to the discretion of the cabinet so that the minister's representatives were both judge and defendant were plain for all to see.

The new policy on land claims was also, in part, the result of Lloyd Barber's four years as Indian Commissioner. Although many of the First Nations leaders of the day counted Barber as a friend none would cooperate with his office so long as it did not have any of the trappings of an independent, quasi-judicial body.

Each of these events, both the succession of gains in the courts and the revision of the land claims policy provided new grist for the mill of the Indian Affairs Committee and fostered a closer working relationship between the Committee and the First Nations organizations.

THE STANDING COMMITTEE ON INDIAN AFFAIRS AND NORTHERN DEVELOPMENT, 1977–78

The principal way in which Indian organizations were able to appear regularly before the Indian Affairs Committee was by making a presentation during the Committee's study of the annual Estimates of the Department of Indian Affairs and Northern Development. A brief review of some of the highlights of the Standing Committee on Indian Affairs and Northern Development, in the third session of the Thirtieth Parliament, in 1977–78, will provide an opportunity to observe a continued deepening of the relationship between the Members on the Indian Affairs Committee and the N.I.B. leadership and staff.

This was also the same session in which a second Joint Committee on the Constitution was established. This Joint Committee was mandated to study Trudeau's Bill C-60, *the Constitutional Amendment Act*, the first patriation proposal to be presented in a legislative form. The work of this Joint Committee significantly coloured the work of the last session of the 30th Parliament as a whole.

The relationship in which Jean Chrétien had enthused about the *Indian Control of Indian Education* as "a significant milestone" prepared by "our good friend George Manuel"[16] began to fizzle shortly after the Trudeau Government was returned with a solid majority in 1974. The N.I.B.'s relationship with the Government revived, for a while, following the arrival of the Indian Caravan on Parliament Hill in time for the Throne Speech opening the new Parliament in the fall of 1974.

For the first time, the RCMP riot squad was brought onto Parliament Hill. As the RCMP prepared to attack the placard bearing Indians, the militia behind them fixed their bayonets while howitzers behind the infantry stayed at the ready. The much battered Indians, with whom the N.I.B. had conspicuously refused to meet, went into a passive resistance mode and set up an "Embassy" in a long-deserted old stone building on Victoria Island—ironically the mid-point between two bridges joining Ontario and Québec.

The Government, much in need of some Indians with whom they could speak offered to set up a "Joint N.I.B./Cabinet Committee," as it became known. During its first two years the N.I.B./Cabinet Committee had some substantial successes. A working group of civil servants and N.I.B. technicians[17] was established. Treasury Board approved sectoral program funding. *The James Bay and Northern Québec Agreement* was signed. A formal Review of the *Indian Act* was instituted.[18]

In September, 1976, Noel V. Starblanket won the presidency of the N.I.B. by acclamation. Starblanket had attended the Lebret Residential School at the File Hills Reserves. He had been a film-maker with the NFB Challenge for Change series and a liaison officer for the N.I.B. in 1970. He had been elected chief of his band at age 24. In 1975 he had been re-elected vice-president of the Federation of Saskatchewan Indians. At 29, Starblanket brought a new leadership approach to the N.I.B. .

An overview of Starblanket's first term, unearthed under *Access to Information* from the Ministry of State for Social Development, for whom it was probably prepared by policy analysts in DIAND offers the following appraisal:

> In contrast to Manuel's emphasis upon the internal development of the Indian community in Canada, Starblanket brought with him an

> emphasis upon the development of a technically-proficient Indian staff—youthful, energetic, and possessing a high degree of formal education which would make N.I.B. a strong and effective Indian lobby on Parliament Hill.
>
> . . . central themes of the Starblanket era: . . . 1) the issuing of the demand that Indians be involved to their satisfaction in developing policy for Indians; 2) the decision to change the priority of the *Indian Act* Consultative Study to the advancement of Indian band government, and 3) the emergence of a new concern with the Canadian Constitution as it relates to Indian rights.[19]

Starblanket's earliest change to the structure of the N.I.B. was the addition of a Council of Elders together with a resident elder. The Parliamentary Liaison Unit set about regularizing communications with all political parties in both Houses both for the N.I.B. and for member provincial and territorial organizations as well as tribal councils.

Starblanket also established a Canadian Indian Constitutional Commission to consolidate Indian views on the Constitution. The Commission promoted the conviction that was by then rapidly growing amongst Indian leaders, that Indian rights needed to be enshrined in any patriated or revised Canadian Constitution.

In the same month in which Starblanket took office as President of the N.I.B., Warren Allmand became Minister of Indian Affairs. Indian Affairs was riding a crest of public attention associated with two events which had transpired only a few months earlier: the highly-publicized southern Canada hearings of Thomas Berger's Mackenzie Valley Pipeline Inquiry, and the shocking act of protest-by-suicide of Nelson Small Legs, Jr. in southern Alberta. Papers from both the PCO and DIAND claimed that the Government, in 1976, was prepared to encourage "native efforts toward self-determination and self-management" and joint participation in policy and program development.[20] The Government would, however, continue to insist that it would define the scope of this "self-determination and self-management."

A further paper on Government-Indian relations, released to all Indian associations and band chiefs, clearly acknowledged the continuation of Indian status and the adoption of "a policy of *partnership approach*"[21] to encourage and assist all Indian groups to find and take their place as "Indians within Canadian society." Ostensibly, this meant that assimilation, *per se*, had ceased to be an objective of government policy, but autonomous or parallel Indian government was also rejected by Cabinet. Following this paper's rejection at the N.I.B. Whitehorse Assembly, in September, 1976, the N.I.B. Indian Constitutional Commission continued to consolidate Indian views on the Constitution, reflecting the growing conviction that Indian rights should be enshrined in any patriated or revised Canadian Constitution.

Although this paper was rejected at the N.I.B. Whitehorse Assembly, in September, 1976, its approach continued to be followed by DIAND. Shortly after Starblanket took office, the N.I.B. Executive Council vehemently rejected the government's secret policy paper outlining "aspects of a native policy for Canada."[22]

What the paper was advising was a so-called "devolution policy" which would grant (sic) such areas of responsibility from the federal government to bands and tribal councils as the government was willing to grant. The devolution policy established administrative structures to enforce federal and provincial laws and policies, while not recognizing government structures and institutions of (what the chiefs-in-assembly would soon call *First Nations*. This imposition of a series of strict regulatory guidelines would soon provoke an equal and opposite reaction.

The press coverage of the time consistently reported that the N.I.B. and affiliates were *withdrawing* from government committees and *rejecting* government offers. One might well ask why the shoe was not represented on the other foot. *Government rejected every recommendation on which there was widespread support amongst First Nations leaders.* Although ministers insisted that they wanted Indians to be part of Confederation, governments consistently introduced constitutional measures which did not include them. As Indian leaders talked increasingly about autonomy, self-determination and self-government, government officials developed positions of municipalization.

STARBLANKET PULLS OUT OF N.I.B./CABINET JOINT COMMITTEE

On February 27, 1978, Starblanket, appearing before the Standing Committee on Indian Affairs and Northern Development, confirmed that "we have withdrawn from the Joint N.I.B./Cabinet Committee discussions."

Starblanket told the Committee that the N.I.B. had "worked for five years . . . in good faith hoping something could really be accomplished for Indian people by working within the system in this way."[23] Starblanket related the withdrawal to "the refusal of Cabinet to respond to our comprehensive proposals and particularly to recognize aboriginal and treaty rights."[24] From this perspective, Starblanket's address to the Committee integrated constitutional and administrative issues and related them both to self-government:

> Our other resolution responds to funding cutbacks. *There is a real relationship between the question of rights and the question of funding.* We believe recognition of Indian rights is the most assured way of establishing a healthy relationship between our people and the government. We believe establishing those rights in the revision of the Constitution and the *Indian Act* is the surest way of ending the economic, social and cultural state of siege that has surrounded Indian people in the past century. These latest cutbacks suggested that the government is willing to continue its activities a little longer.[25] (emphasis added.)

Starblanket told the Committee that there were "bilateral negotiations . . . underway currently with a number of provinces [which] will result in further federal program cutbacks." On this basis he charged that current government policy was, in effect, reviving the *White Paper* policy of "transferring programs and services to other agencies,"[26] including provincial agencies.

He concluded his charge by saying "we have withdrawn recently from these co-called joint consultative arrangements because that process was *neither joint not consultative.*" (emphasis added) Based on his complaint Starblanket asked the Committee "to the limits of your authority . . . to undertake the following:

> To seek a clarification of the budget of the Department of Indian Affairs to determine the actual funds which reach Indians in the communities and at the reserve level.
>
> (b) To restore to Indian communities all programs which have been curtailed or cut.
>
> (d) To identify federal moneys which were intended for Indians and which have been diluted in the appropriations of other departments so that these funds can once again be clearly earmarked for Indians.
>
> (e) To stop all transfers of federal funds designated for Indians to provinces and restore these to the Department of Indian Affairs.
>
> (f) To undertake a general and complete review of previous Committee recommendations to determine whether any have been implemented, and if so, the way in which they are reflected in departmental appropriations. [27]

MR. SOL SANDERSON (FIRST VICE PRESIDENT, FEDERATION OF SASKATCHEWAN INDIANS)

Sol Sanderson, who had succeeded Starblanket as Vice President of the F.S.I.,[28] appeared with him before the Committee in February, 1978. It is unlikely that any other Indian leader mastered the bureaucrats' own jargon as well as Sanderson did while also developing his own rhetoric of Indian government. He could happily integrate the two into the same sentence, sometimes to the befuddlement of listeners on all sides of the issue:

> I would also request that this Committee take time out to review the *A level* that excludes band control or Indian government operations and *the statutory obligations under the A level authority* at the moment must be redefined to include Indian government jurisdictions. (sic) I know there is a real fear amongst everybody about relating and discussing the existence of Indian government jurisdiction but it is real and it is here and, as soon as that is addressed and those jurisdictions are ironed out and cleared up, many of the symptom kind of problems that we are dealing with daily will disappear. I think the average Canadian, including all politicians, are going to have to adjust to the term "Indian government" because it is real. You are familiar with municipal, provincial and federal government today *but from now on you will be hearing more about Indian government.*[29] (emphasis added)

Sanderson's position was quite different from Starblanket's. Sanderson had, undoubtedly, been developing his own vocabulary of Indian government for quite some time. Other Indian leaders had a good comprehension of federalese but rarely used that vocabulary. Sanderson's was a rhetoric waiting for an argument. Given the on-again, off-again nature of federal fiscal policies[30] and DIAND officials' way of consulting with Indian leaders, there were better than even odds that just such an occasion would arise before long.

Starblanket's role as national president, in contrast, obliged him to articulate a consensus among the PTO heads from every province and territory. It was the Executive Council, and not he alone, who had chosen to withdraw from the N.I.B./Cabinet Committee, a decision which would cost them the funding that was attached to the studies mandated by the Cabinet side of the Committee.

Frank Oberle (PC, Prince George) agreed that "Political development is something that frightens all of us" and went on to compare "what the Dene Nation wants" to apartheid. If that were granted, Oberle predicted "the United States would probably impose economic sanctions on us as we do on South Africa."[31] This was a comparison that Oberle would continue to raise until he achieved a degree of satisfaction somewhere during the Penner Committee hearings in 1982–83. Oberle asked, on this occasion and many more to follow, the question which surely perplexed many interested outside observers,

> [I]n one breath you are saying you cannot work with the government any more, the *Indian Act* is no good . . . and you have no relationship with the ivory-tower people here, the guys in the regions will not talk to you . . . But on the other hand you are saying that 1969 *White Paper* is an example of what they are trying to do to you; but in 1969 they suggested they would abolish the Department of Indian Affairs and hand over the administration to you.
>
> What is it going to be? What is your objective? . . . if we burned down the ivory tower over here and scrapped the Department of Indian Affairs we could pay each Indian family $12,000 a year. . . . [W]ill you not agree that maybe that is what we should do?[32]

The idea that the *Indian Act* needed to be replaced by something which was written by Indian leaders and which recognized those rights for which Indian speakers had been advocating for the past century seemed a difficult concept to convey. But the *White Paper* had not suggested handing the administration of Indian lands and programmes to Indian administration. On the contrary, the *White Paper* proposed to hand "Indian affairs" over to the provinces.

Oberle distinguished himself from most parliamentarians, perhaps from most Canadians, by continuing to ask difficult question for many years.

On May 9, 1978, The Committee received and published in its *Proceedings* "Draft Notes for Statement by the Minister, Hon. Hugh Faulkner." The Minister's "Notes" said that the government regretted the N.I.B. decision but that, despite the lack of proper notice, the decision had come as no surprise "because the Ministers concerned were themselves dissatisfied with the lack of solid progress on substantive issues." The Minister emphasized that "our discussions tended to be blocked by rather rigid assertions of rights from the N.I.B. side."[33]

The Minister also said that the N.I.B. had written to him about "alternative mechanisms for consultation" but that "until new arrangements are worked out, the Department is not proceeding with funding of the N.I.B. which was tied to the processes under the N.I.B.-Cabinet Committee."

Hugh Faulkner agreed that discussions which he described as "tripartite working arrangements" including provincial Indian associations had been taking place with the provinces. He claimed "Indian leaders in all parts of the country increasingly see advantage in this tripartite approach."[34] He then concluded his remarks with a reflection on local government:

> Finally, in the same constructive vein, I should mention with approval the developments which are taking place to strengthen the capacity of Indian bands and other groups to take charge of their own local government. We now have in Ontario, local government development agreements with bands in both Treaty 3 and Treaty 9 areas.[35]

In his oral evidence, Faulkner stated that *Indian Act* revision work would continue within his department *with or without* the cooperation of the Indian leadership. "I am going to still work on it and I would like to see some arrangement develop pretty quickly that would allow us to get this thing back on track." To that end he was circumventing the N.I.B. and had had "some discussions with some of the provincial leaders."[36]

The very limited time that the Minister afforded the Committee (and the Committee's inability to command the attention of the Minister) produced a conflict. Members had to decide whether to pursue matters of major national policy, such as the conflict raised first by Starblanket and then by Faulkner, or to deal with matters of urgent and pressing importance to Indian constituents. Cecil Smith (PC, Churchill, Manitoba) chose to pursue a line of questions preoccupying the Northern Flood Committee, representing communities which had recently lost most of their lands and waters.

Keith Penner (Liberal, Kenora-Rainy River) asked about federal support for the Saskatchewan Indian Federated College, a matter of great and abiding interest, particularly to Sol Sanderson, but not directly responsive to Sanderson's discussion of "Indian Government jurisdiction." The Minister, however, detailed both federal and provincial moneys which would be available to the only Indian college in Canada.

Dr. Robert Holmes (PC, Lambton-Kent) pursued the discussion of the Federated College in terms which did touch on Indian Control. Dr. Holmes pursued a reference by a departmental official that "a program [had been] imposed on the College using a formula dictating that the

Province must contribute 50 per cent of the College's total budget before the Federal Government contribution was made."[37]

In short, federal support for a Federated Indian College was dependent upon its acceptance as part of the provincially chartered university. The federal government was not prepared to make a creative use of s.91(24) of the *BNA Act*, "Indians and lands reserved for the Indians" to promote Indian control of Indian education. The funding available to this college was the funding available to any college within a provincially chartered university.

THE MACGUIGAN-LAMONTAGNE JOINT COMMITTEE ON THE CONSTITUTION, 1978[38]

A brief observation about the mandate, the membership and the political climate in which this Joint Committee worked will serve to set the context.

The order of reference or mandate of the MacGuigan-Lamontagne Committee does not simply refer to Bill C-60, the *Constitutional Amendment Act, 1978*, the measure which was, in fact, the patriation proposal put forward by the Trudeau Government to the Committee for study. The order of reference also contemplates additional references:

> to examine and report upon proposals that have been made and in the future are from time to time made public by the Government of Canada on subjects related to the Constitution of Canada.[39]

A reading of the *Proceedings*, however, leaves the impression that the witnesses, the Committee members and the Chairman were all clearly focused on the *Constitutional Amendment Act, 1978*. Indeed, remarks of the Chairman to the Inuit Taparisat when they appeared, motions to end the hearings by Flora MacDonald and the opposition of the most distinguished constitutional minds amongst the Senators on the Committee all arose from the Committee's preoccupation with Bill C-60. The tenor of the 1978 Committee frequently verged on a partisanship that was not evident in the 70–72 Committee.

It is also striking that few of the key players in the earlier *MacGuigan-Molgat* Committee continued into the MacGuigan-Lamontagne Committee of 1978. Of those who were a strong presence during discussion of Indian issues in the earlier committee, only Mark MacGuigan, Sen. Eugene Forsey and Sen. Jacques Flynn, the Leader of the Opposition in the Senate carried into this committee. In short, the Joint Committees on the Constitution was not a strong repository of collective memory. Committee members did not demonstrate an awareness, in their published *Proceedings*, of the work of their predecessor committee. They were notably unfamiliar with the historical concerns and current positions of Indian organizations. Neither witnesses nor parliamentarians referred to the chapter of the *MacGuigan-Molgat Final Report* devoted to "Native Peoples."

Indeed, the only other person whose work continued from one committee to the next was Barry Strayer. In 1971, Strayer, was the "Director of Constitutional Review, Privy Council Office" and was also "Director of the Constitutional Law Section, Department of Justice on loan to the Privy Council Office together with Dr. Jules Léger who became Governor General in 1974."[40] It was Strayer and Léger who had directed the preparation of the "Background Papers on Fundamental Rights" for the Secretariat of the Constitutional Conference. In August 1978, Strayer appeared before the MacGuigan-Lamontagne Committee with Roger Tassé, the Deputy Minister of Justice and Marc Lalonde, the Minister of State for Federal-Provincial Relations.

Marc Lalonde began his opening remarks to the Joint Committee by saying that their work would be "a significant factor . . . in the decision that will have to be taken by the people of Québec in the course of the coming months as to whether they want Québec to continue to be a part of Canada or not."[41] The Government, Lalonde told the Committee, was prepared to be quite flexible on the proposals contained in Bill C-60.[42] Marc Lalonde reinforced the Government's flexibility by acknowledging that

> [T]he use of a bill as the form in which to consolidate the government's thinking led to the impression on the part of some that the government intended to go ahead without full discussion with the provinces and with all other interested parties. That is not the case. The Prime Minister outlined to the Premiers the form in which it was planned to take this initiative when he visited each of them separately toward the end of 1977. . . . A meeting of First Ministers to discuss the proposals has now been arranged for October 30–31, November 1 next.[43]

Finally, Lalonde made a classic Trudeau appeal that "Parliament must be able to act in the national interest in areas where it legally can, with agreement of the provinces if at all possible, but without being the helpless prisoner of a province if agreement is impossible."[44] This statement foreshadowed, or rationalized, the departure from the Victoria Formula and the *MacGuigan-Molgat Final Report* both of which would have preserved a veto for any province which had, at any point in its history, 25% of the total Canadian population.[45]

Once the Minister had thrown down the gauntlet, the Chairman, Mark MacGuigan opened discussion. Flora Macdonald (PC-Kingston and the Islands) said that "The Conservatives had been asking for a joint committee on the Constitution for a year and a half." She also pointed out that Pépin-Robarts (a royal commission into national unity) was not scheduled to report until after the time allotted for the Committee.[46]

Ed Broadbent (national leader of the NDP) described the purpose of Bill C-60 as "a constitutional proposal which in itself will be regarded as sufficient to head off the forces of separation or independence in the Province of Québec in time for the debate on the referendum. The *Charter*, Broadbent argued, "fails [an] historically crucial test." Allowing the *Charter* to be overridden by such limitations "as are justifiable in a free and democratic society in the interests of public safety or health, the interests of the peace and security of the public, or the interests of the rights and freedoms of others . . ."[47] left it without much force at all.

Aboriginal concerns were not mentioned at all in the opening statements. Neither does the index to the *Proceedings* make reference to "Indian," "Native" or "Aboriginal." The only references to Indians, or to Native people, were, apparently, on the days on which the National Indian Brotherhood, the Native Council of Canada and the Inuit Tapirisat testified.

N.W.T. AND YUKON COUNCILS, CONSTITUTIONAL DEVELOPMENT COMMITTEES

On Tuesday, August 22, 1978, the *MacGuigan-Molgat* Committee heard from the chairmen of the Constitutional Development Committees of the Northwest Territories and of the Yukon. Their testimony is significant largely as a marker for the actual constitutional developments which were to follow over the next decade in respect both to First Nations self-government and to other matters with which self-government is inextricably intertwined.

ARNOLD MCCALLUM, CHAIRMAN, CONSTITUTIONAL DEVELOPMENT COMMITTEE OF THE NORTHWEST TERRITORIES

Arnold McCallum, one of the elected members of the legislature of the Northwest Territories and Chairman of its Constitutional Development

Committee, appeared before the MacGuigan-Lamontagne Committee on August 22, 1978, at its fourth sitting. In contrast to the earlier committee, there appeared to witnesses to be some difficulty gaining an invitation to appear before this committee. McCallum for example, said that had it not been for his "acquaintanceship with Mr. MacGuigan I doubt seriously whether this opportunity [to appear before the Committee] would have presented itself."[48]

McCallum took the Committee back to the 1966 Carrothers Commission on the development of government for the Northwest Territories which, he told the Joint Committee, had said that "every citizen of Canada has a claim to participation in the institutions of responsible government under the Canadian Constitution." Under Bill C-60, McCallum said, people in the N.W.T. "cannot hope to aspire to the rights and privileges under the Constitution that other Canadians enjoy."

Arnold McCallum identified "three basic issues of prime concern to the Northwest Territories."[49] All of them had to do with the failure of C-60 to enhance the place of the N.W.T. in Confederation.

McCallum was concerned that C-60 "argues for responsible government without talking about adapting the Upper and Lower Canadian hallmark of quasi-democratic procedure to the actual conditions of the N.W.T. "[50]

None of McCallum's concerns entailed affirming Aboriginal or treaty rights or what the Dene would soon come to call "public government," i.e., ways of entrenching the protection of Dene rights within the Constitution of the North West Territories or its successors. Nothing in McCallum's submission indicates that he is speaking three years after the Dene Declaration was adopted by the N.W.T. Indian Brotherhood or that the Brotherhood had metamorphosed into the Dene Nation under the presidency of Mona Jacobs of Fort Smith.

On the other hand, his notion of those "actual conditions" also led him to object to the slim protection of Native rights which was contained in the bill .." . references to native rights under Clause 26 are so broad that they make many of the guarantees of the *Charter* virtually ineffectual in the North."[51] Clause 26 was described in the margin notes as being about "Rights not declared by Charter, including those of native people under Royal Proclamation. It stated as follows:

> **26.** Nothing in this Charter shall be held to abrogate, abridge or derogate from any right or freedom not declared by it that may have existed in Canada at the commencement of this Act, including, without limiting the generality of the foregoing, any right or freedom that may have

been acquired by any of the native peoples of Canada by virtue of the Royal Proclamation of October 7, 1763.[52]

It is noteworthy, in considering the emergence of the vocabulary of First Nations' self-government that, as late as 1978, the chairman of the N.W.T. Legislature Committee on Constitutional Development could hold that while the lack of responsible government could be blamed on the federal government, the lack of charter rights in the north was the fault of the Indians.

From McCallum's point of view, it was in recognition of the difficulty of reconciling land claims to constitutional development that Prime Minister Trudeau had appointed Bud Drury to head a commission which would deal with the constitutional development of the N.W.T., thus making land claims an issue separate from constitutional development.

McCallum, speaking for the Council of a territory in which a majority of the people were Dene, in the year in which the Dene Nation constituted a political organization, contributed a Northern neologism, "ethnic variability"[53] to the discourse. He argued "references to native rights under Clause 26 are so broad as to make many of the guarantees of the Charter virtually ineffective in the North.

Sen. Alastair Grosart (PC, Pickering, Ont.) asked McCallum to clarify his statement that Charter guarantees would be made ineffectual by the protection of native rights in clause 26. He replied, " . . . unless the Northwest Territories is to be considered a larger reserve, and people are moving away from it, I would suggest to you that our comment is valid."[54]

MR. WALT LENGERGE (CHAIRMAN, STANDING COMMITTEE ON CONSTITUTIONAL DEVELOPMENT, LEGISLATIVE ASSEMBLY, GOVERNMENT OF THE YUKON TERRITORIES)

Walt Lengerge tabled a document entitled "Some Constitutional Aspects of the Government of the Yukon Territories" prepared for the Land Claims Secretariat of the Yukon.[55] He said

> I understand that you had some difficulty deciding on the merits of hearing the view of the Yukon and N.W.T., and on reading the unedited transcripts of the proceedings of this Committee it appears that some of your members think that the concerns of the Territories are rather trivial and not important enough for you to hear.[56]

Ironically, in terms of the provisions for the admission of new provinces which eventually became part of the new Constitution, a major concern of the Yukon, with C-60, was that "the proposed bill permits Parliament to alter the territorial limits of a territory at will."[57] Lengerge went on to relate this provision to "an agreement in principle between the Government of Canada and the Committee for Original People's Entitlement (COPE).[58] Lengerge cited, as an example, a recent "withdrawal of 15,000 square miles of northern Yukon" ostensibly for the protection of the Porcupine Caribou herd but which at "[a] later date we were to learn . . . was to allow the Inuvialuit exclusive rights to Yukon's north slope with no consultation with the Yukon."[59]

It would be difficult to imagine a clearer example of an emphatic distinction between "us" and "other" in which "us" is interchangeable with the name of the Territory and, therefore, the "other" is outside the Territory. Mr. Lengerge wanted to know "Where does this end?"[60] Lengerge could see no difference between "giving" Yukon lands to the Natives and giving them to B.C.

Bill C-60 had proposed to bring the Charter in at a later time than the amending formula and other provisions. David Elliot, introduced by Walt Lengerge as the person who had prepared the Yukon brief, was concerned that the *Canadian Bill of Rights* was to be repealed in the first phase of the Constitutional Amendment Bill while the Charter would only come in later. Sen. George van Roggen (Liberal, Vancouver-Points Grey) saw that Mr. Elliott's concern for responsible government in the Yukon was bound up with the possibility of "an inordinate amount of mineral and fossil fuel oil and gas and other resources [belonging] to such a small number of people—the number of people that might fit into one office building in Toronto."[61] He failed to observe that much of the mineral wealth was already owned by the people occupying a very few buildings in downtown Toronto, Calgary, Edmonton and Vancouver.

PROFESSOR W.R. LEDERMAN (PROFESSOR OF LAW, QUEEN'S UNIVERSITY)

Prof. Lederman's view prefigured the decision of the Supreme Court of Canada in the *Patriation Reference*:[62] "I do not see how any meaningful amending process affecting the basics of the federal Constitution, the federal union of the country, could really go ahead in the face of the singular dissent of Québec, of Ontario, of Alberta, or of British Columbia."[63]

Prof. Lederman also pointed out that although the federal government claimed authority to effect patriation with an amending formula, nonetheless, " . . . the Government of Canada . . . acknowledge that to go all the way to special entrenchment they require the concurrences of the provinces for a constitutional amendment." The view Lederman offered in his 1978 testimony was consistent with the opinion rendered by the Supreme Court on the *Patriation Reference* in 1981.[64] Lalonde's stated opinion that bill C-60 was intended only to invite discussion, was not grasped either by Committee members or leading legal scholars.

Lederman's opinion reinforced all the worst fears of the N.I.B. leadership. They were offended by the failure to include recognition of Aboriginal and treaty rights in the patriation proposal. The N.I.B. leadership also knew that asking the provinces would be akin to asking the fox to baby sit the chicks.

HARRY DANIELS (PRESIDENT OF THE NATIVE COUNCIL OF CANADA)

Harry Daniels, President of the Native Council of Canada, was accompanied by three advisors: Prof. Victor Vallantine, Special Adviser in the NCC Land Claims Department; John Weynsteyn, from the Directory of Land Claims Research; and Jay Roberts, Executive Director. Harry Daniels opened his remarks with two particularly noteworthy arguments.

> I firmly believe the Métis, as one of the founding peoples of this nation, should be invited to participate in constitutional revisions on the same basis as provincial premiers.

> A third ethnic dimension exists in the Constitution in the form of "Indians" who are identified as having a direct relationship with the Crown.[65]

Daniels statement appears to be the first direct and explicit expression of a right of an "Aboriginal people" to sit at the table of Confederation on an equal footing with provincial premiers. Statements made to the earlier Committee may have laid the groundwork for moving in this direction. Daniels' appears to be the first statement from an Aboriginal leader to set out these demands in plain and unequivocal language.

Daniels scored a number of points around the distinction between the *Indian Act* definition of "Indian" and the *British North America Act* definition:

> It is our contention that the generality and diffuseness surrounding the reference to "Indians" in the Constitution has not served the native

> people well in the years following Confederation. . . . There has been too much faith placed in the inherent feelings for freedom and justice which our forefathers understood to be deeply ingrained in the institutions and people of Canada. The passage of time has seriously eroded this faith.
>
> The absence of explicitness in the Constitution in its reference to Indians means that the courts might concede the unconstitutionality of certain government measures but regard them as being, nevertheless, legal.[66]

Daniels' solution to this grievance was "that the constitutional amendments should spell out the intent which the original provision was intended to reflect at the time of Confederation."[67] Although many status organizations would argue that Canada had obligations in law and in equity arising from treaties and from Aboriginal rights, no one else advanced an *Originalist* legal argument, i.e., no one else said that using the occasion to repeat and elaborate the intentions of the founders, enshrined in the *B.N.A. Act, 1867* would benefit Indians. Daniels went further than offering an Originalist argument; he argued that there was *an obligation on the part of contemporary legislators* to repeat those same intentions. If it were shown that the founders intended to subject Aboriginal peoples to a colonial rule would Daniels still argue that there is an obligation on contemporary legislators to reaffirm that intention?

Daniels, speaking for the Native Council, representing Métis and non-status Indians, spoke repeatedly of "an Indian collectivity"[68] recognized in the Constitution. The N.I.B. had not yet emphasized the collective nature of Aboriginal and treaty rights. Although they had referred to recognition in the *Royal Proclamation of 1763* they had not claimed that these rights were also recognized in the *British North America Act, 1867* (renamed the *Constitution Act, 1867* in 1982). Daniels also charged that the government had helped "to create hopelessly confused jurisdictional tangles" which it has used "to deprive native people of badly needed services."[69]

Although the N.I.B. would agree that the *BNA Act* was written within the context of the Royal Proclamation, for that very reason they emphasized that local autonomy was also reflected in the phrase "the several Indian nations." Manuel and his co-presenters at the time of the Aboriginal Title paper, in 1973, were quite emphatic that the N.I.B. could only reflect a federal consensus on Canada-wide matters and did not attempt to trump whatever position the "several Indian nations" might take. One would be hard pressed to point to a time when there was *an* Indian collectivity.

The one source of tacit support for a native collectivity in the *Proceedings* of the committees reviewed is the advocacy of Ian Watson and Marcel Lambert for a distribution of land claims compensation through a common pool *as though the title had been held* by an Indian collectivity rather than by "the several Indian nations" acknowledged in *The Royal Proclamation*.[70]

Daniels elaborated on the idea of a Native collectivity:

> The concept of a native Collectivity: In re-affirming for native people a special place in the Constitution and a special role in the development of a Canadian identity, the foundations would be laid for a policy which would include some of the following elements:
>
> (i) All native people would be included in such a reference, including Métis, Indians and "non-status" Indians.
>
> (ii) Special status under the Constitution would provide the opportunity for native groups in their various regions to exercise the rights of self-determination within the framework of Confederation to develop as "nations" in a cultural and linguistic sense.
>
> (iii) Consistent with this aim, native people would exercise the right to possess and use lands needed to ensure their economic self-reliance.
>
> (iv)Native people would also have the right to practice and preserve their languages, traditions, customs and values, and to develop their own special institutions.
>
> (v) As a "nation," each native group that achieves this development would have full jurisdiction over a specific geographic area as a form of government within the framework of Confederation.
>
> (vi) The federal government, in keeping with its special responsibility for native people, would facilitate and finance the development of such native "nations" as an integral new dimension to Confederation.[71]

Of these six propositions, only (v) coincides with a position taken by First Nations political organizations. Daniels speaks of nations that might yet *develop*, not as something that exists presently and possesses a history. Daniels' nations would achieve jurisdiction not by virtue of their present and historic existence but through a recognition of their development by the federal government. Daniels would include Métis as one of his nations; he does not reconcile this with the decision of most of the Métis of the Red River, following the Red River Rebellion, to accept scrip intended to finance individual, rather than community land holding.

Perhaps what is most important about Daniels' language is that it reflected an intermediate stage between what we might call the old language and the language that was about to emerge. He spoke of a right to self-determination within Confederation and "to develop as 'nations' in a cultural and linguistic sense." Daniels included "the right to practice their languages, traditions, customs and values" and, then, assigned a political role to these same "nations" by saying that those who "achieve this development" would then "have full jurisdiction over a specific geographic area as a form of government within the framework of Confederation." Daniels discussion of nationhood—because it is contingent upon "native peoples" *developing* in the opinion of the federal government—appears to concede a delegated authority.

Daniels offered an amendment which would allow a "native people . . . to include all persons in their number by virtue of Indian blood or by marriage or adoption." "Blood," as distinct from descent, is not a term that occurs in earlier Canadian Indian legislation. His amendment set out a series of entitlements:

> entitled to representation in Parliament; entitled to executive councils and to a native legislature which shall have the same relationship to Canada as provincial legislatures; authority over specific areas of jurisdiction, including the power to make and administer laws in a class of subjects not covered by the Parliament of Canada; the right to make laws and administer programs specifically in relation to education.[72]

Daniels' amendment effectively described a form of self-government with jurisdiction similar in scope to provincial powers. So far as he adopted a language of entitlement in an amendment to the Constitution, he steered a middle course which neither conceded delegation nor demanded recognition. What truly distinguished Daniels' amendment was its focus, consistent with the brief which preceded it, on a *single people* with entitled to a single "native legislature" and the lack of reference to historic "native" nations.

THE JOINT COMMITTEE'S RESPONSE TO DANIELS' BRIEF

Sen. Joan Neiman opened the discussion by saying that she "must agree with the submission . . . I cannot really see a Constitution of Canada being formulated and finalized which does not fully take cognizance of the contribution and the identity of our native peoples. I think this is essential to our Canadian identity and to our cultural origins in this country."[73]

Whether the senator from Ontario who then chaired the Liberal caucus and would soon chair the Legal and Constitutional Affairs Committee of the Senate fully understood the brief to which she was agreeing is open to question. Her own substantial support for Indian rights ran throughout her time in the Senate to an extent which was often unappreciated by witnesses such as Daniels and Starblanket. On the other hand, her own open-ended questions may have helped them to suspect her of a naiveté that was not borne out by her staying power.

In response to a question as to whether Métis should have the same kinds of rights as Indians, Daniels explained why he preferred the term "'Native'" as a generic term, "because the term 'Indian' is alien to my language and is alien to the Canadian native people." He then went on to say, "[Y]es, we should be all treated the same as having aboriginal rights in this country, a special status in this country above and beyond what the normal citizen would have." [74]

Flora MacDonald dwelt on *A Time for Action,* the white paper which the Government had issued at the time that it presented the *Constitutional Amendment Bill*, from which she quoted at length a statement about the place of "native rights" in the patriation process:

> Evermore bitter was the experience of Canada's native peoples, and even more pressing the need to recognize fully their dignity and their right to equal opportunity, a right they have yet to enjoy.
>
> **Full respect of native rights**
>
> The renewal of the federation . . . must fully respect the legitimate rights of the native peoples, and recognize their rightful place in the Canadian mosaic as the first inhabitants of the country and give them the means of enjoying full equality of opportunity.[75] (Bold heading in original)

One could suspect that Ms. Neiman and Ms. MacDonald periodically exchanged places with one another. Sen. Neiman appeared to be more critical and Ms. MacDonald more protective of the Government at times in these *Proceedings*. Unless this were truly the case, Ms. MacDonald was inviting Mr. Daniels to say something about his confidence that the government would fulfill a statement which had the earmarks of a solemn undertaking.

Sen. Eugene Forsey missed the forest for the trees (and possibly the nation for the state) when he corrected Harry Daniels on the two different *Manitoba Acts* of 1890 which Daniels had apparently confused, one abolishing French as an official language, the other abolishing Catholic schools. Forsey did not directly address the claim that Daniels represented the inheritors of the tradition of disenfranchisement embodied in the conjunction of these two disabling acts.[76]

NOEL STARBLANKET (PRESIDENT, NATIONAL INDIAN BROTHERHOOD)

> It is also my reading and my feeling of the Indian people's political status at this moment, their own political development, that the Indian people do want to stay within Confederation, but we would rather define and elaborate upon existing constitutional rights, indeed establishing a whole new satisfactory or mutual relationship with the government of this country.[77]

Noel V. Starblanket, President of the National Indian Brotherhood, appeared before the MacGuigan-Lamontagne Committee later the same day, accompanied by Arnold Goodleaf, Dave Monture and Michael Posluns (the author of this narrative).

Starblanket, in his introductory remarks, turned Daniels' notion of being a founding people on its head to gain perspective on Bill C-60, "the original people of this land, Indians and Inuit, were not party to that 1867 arrangement. Apparently this government also does not intend to make us part of the new arrangement."[78]

Starblanket went directly to the three ways in which C-60 insulted the body politic of the peoples he represented:

> Bill C-60 is not only inadequate in guaranteeing and protecting our Indian land base, it also fails to properly recognize aboriginal and treaty rights. The bill nowhere acknowledges that Indians have political authority over their lands. . . . The bill, in fact, misrepresents the effect of the Royal Proclamation of 1763. The bill erroneously implies that the proclamation granted, rather than confirmed, already existing Indian rights.[79]

He then put forward an argument that the Indian nations had a sovereignty that existed *sui generis:*

. . . three simple points. First, we are a sovereign people. At no time did the Indian nations that are within the geographical territory now claimed by Canada agree to surrender their sovereignty, and nowhere is it written. Further, that sovereignty continues to reside in each nation.

The nature of this sovereignty is that it exists in and of its own right. I believe there is a legal term that refers to that kind of right. It might be better said that it is a gift to each nation, as a nation, from the Great Spirit, our Creator.[80]

Starblanket then went on to make two corollary points:

> The second point we would like to make is that Indians are now prepared to consider the negotiation of the terms and conditions upon which we will develop our future relationship with Canada. As we have already noted, we have been systematically excluded from taking our place at the table of Confederation by the nature of the present constitutional arrangements.
>
> Third, our rights, which accrue from aboriginal occupation, including those which were affirmed by treaty agreements, shall remain unaltered.[81]

The statement that "we have been systematically excluded from taking our place at the table of Confederation" is fundamental to Starblanket's statement that the Indian nations are "prepared to consider . . . the terms and conditions [of a] future relationship." It could, possibly, be argued that this statement complements Daniels' statement about being a founding people on the basis that there was an idea of "our place at the table." It is a much more substantial and concrete view of history. It is clear that Daniels and Starblanket represented quite opposing views both of history and of the future.

Two features about the third point—"rights . . . which accrue from Aboriginal occupation, including those which were affirmed by treaty agreements, shall remain unaltered"—are crucial. First, that the government's position that recognition solely for the purpose of extinguishment is not on the table. *Recognition requires that Canada allow Indians to live as Indians.* Secondly, treaty rights flow from Aboriginal rights.

Starblanket did not speak explicitly of self-government but he was certainly describing all the conditions in which it is likely to emerge. Indeed, he responded to Marcel Prud'homme who, on the previous joint committee had asked Chief Joe Mathias to agree that "in essence . . . French Canadians in their desire for recognition could be the greatest ally of the Indians or vice versa." Starblanket replied that "if French Canadians can make such an argument, Indians can surely make the same argument more justly." [82]

Starblanket also set out, briefly and secondarily, a philosophic underpinning for acknowledging Indian nationhood, under the Constitution, within Confederation:

> But we are people who are different in philosophy, culture, world view, social values, and language from non-Indians. Our concept of time, for example, is not linear and singular like yours, but rather cyclical and holistic. For us, what is important is not the quantity of a length of time, but rather the quality of a phase of time.

These basic philosophical differences result in different concepts of government, property ownership and relationships with other people and the environment. the aforementioned philosophical differences make it necessary for us to assert our sovereignty in order to continue our way of life.[83]

In retrospect, one could have a sense that all that remained for Starblanket to speak explicitly of self-government was to take the next step.

THE JOINT COMMITTEE'S RESPONSE TO STARBLANKET'S BRIEF

> **Senator E. Forsey:** I must confess that one of my great disappointments when I read Bill C-60 was that there appeared to be absolutely nothing in it about Indian rights except for the extraordinarily iffy Clause 26.16.
>
> **Mr. Starblanket:** That is correct.

Starblanket agreed that he was "asking us to accept the principle of the sovereignty of an Indian nation or nations." Forsey, then, instead of being open to the prospect of the very negotiations for which Starblanket had asked, was quick with the logical reply as to why this position was unacceptable, "If we accept that then we are accepting a tremendous lot and that will not do because that does not conform with the principle of sovereignty. . . . we have a feeling we are being asked to sign a blank cheque." [84]

The good news was that Forsey did pick up on the question of whether "an Indian government" really meant only one. Starblanket, for the first time in the *Proceedings* I have examined, equated the need for self-government with the variety of Indian languages:

> What we are talking about, of course, is something like 55 Indian dialects in this country, aside from the French and English that these Indian people speak, some rather diverse Indian confederacies that existed before the European came to this country. [85]

On the other hand, Starblanket also set out a Confederacy concept which could allow for a single Canada wide entity for dealing with the Crown while allowing for great internal diversity. "There should be no reason why Indian nations cannot gather in a confederacy and develop their own geographical likenesses and things that they believe in together that conform into confederacies." [86]

Flora MacDonald told Starblanket that "I have not heard 'aboriginal rights' equated with 'sovereignty' before." This led to her "Are you saying now that this has changed? To me, 'aboriginal rights' had implied formerly, from definitions I had heard from your spokesman in the past, certain basic rights, but I am not sure that ever included sovereignty."

Starblanket's response is instructive:

> Aboriginal rights in the legal context, I suppose you refer to them as certain basic rights, and that is fine from a superficial and a legalistic point of view. But what we are talking about there in a conceptual framework is the basic philosophy that aboriginal rights emanate and evolve from sovereignty, from the right of a people to govern themselves, and that it is an elaboration of the whole legal question of aboriginal rights and aboriginal title which in the context of the Royal Proclamation was confirmed, and even that is not acceptable in certain legal jurisprudence today. So what we are saying is that we are going even further than just the basic question of aboriginal rights, rather into the whole question of Indian self-determination, the ability to govern one's own people, which has not happened in Canada at the time of the making of this Confederation.[87]

Starblanket, himself, stated that "we are going even further" and that Aboriginal rights includes "the ability to govern one's own people."

Aboriginal rights are the constituent parts of a sovereignty which (unlike any more material construction) pre-existed those individual rights and, he told MacDonald, there needed to be acknowledged for the full recognition of those rights.[88]

DISCRIMINATION UNDER SECTION 12 OF THE *INDIAN ACT*

Both Flora MacDonald and Joan Neiman wanted some kind of undertaking from Noel Starblanket regarding discrimination under s.12(1)(b) of the *Indian Act*, i.e., the sub-section which declared ineligible for Indian status and band membership women who married men who were not band members. It appears to have been difficult for women parliamentarians to refrain from using their power, influence and authority as parliamentarians to impose their solutions to this problem and, thereby, perpetuate the tradition of parliamentary definition of Indian status. In short, what they had difficulty grasping was the need to have parliamentarians leave it alone. Starblanket told the Committee:

> It is a question on which we have finally come together with the Indian women's representatives in this country to a point at which both Indian organizations, which are predominantly dominated by men, and also Indian women's organizations are saying basically the same thing: that Indians should identify and define who Indians are. This brings us right around the circle, of course, to who are Indians and who should be Indians?
>
> Though I am not disagreeing that Indian men are also capable of being chauvinistic, I am saying that non-Indian people are now saying: Well, we are going to try to undo this wrong that we have done.
>
> The government is putting forward the view that Indian men are fighting Indian women. But the Indian men and women are now saying: We are not fighting; it is the non-Indian people who are trying in the media to make us look as though we are fighting.[89]
>
> **Senator Neiman:** But are you prepared at least . . . That the provisions of that particular section of the *Indian Act* should be suspended?
>
> **Starblanket:** No, we cannot agree to that at this point—for the simple reason that there is no guarantee from the Government of Canada that,

> with the influx of a few thousand, or any number, more Indians on the registration roles of the registrar of the Department Indian Affairs there will be an equal increase in the number of dollars and land resources, acres, services in the administration capabilities of the federal government. Until we get that agreement from them we cannot agree to have more Indians placed on our rolls.[90]

Starblanket succeeded in persuading his own people of the need for a change of attitude and of law; this consensus surfaced again two administrations later, under Dr. David Ahenakew at the time of the Commons Subcommittee on Indian Women and the *Indian Act*. What neither Starblanket nor Ahenakew, nor indeed, the parliamentary committees were able to accomplish was a commitment from the Government of Canada that the reinstatement of large numbers of Indian people would be accompanied by proportionate increases in the Indian land base and in funding for social and community services.

MR. ERIC TAGOONA (PRESIDENT, INUIT TAPIRISAT OF CANADA)

The day on which the President of the Inuit Tapirisat came to testify before the Joint Committee on the Constitution, August 19, 1978, began with a procedural motion from Flora MacDonald. She moved that the Committee report to the Houses that the Committee could not justify continuing hearings on Bill C-60, in light of jurisdictional questions raised by legal scholars, and that the *vires* of certain elements of the bill be referred to the Supreme Court. [91]

Mr. Tagoona then introduced the staff accompanying him, viz., "Mr. Tagak Curley from Coral Harbour; Mr. John Amagoalik from Frobisher Bay, he is the Director of the Land Claims Commission; Mr. Peter Ittinuar my Special Assistant."

Eric Tagoona told the Committee that government presence had only come to dominate his people's lives in the past twenty years. "All of you here today will recognize in what I have said the twin processes of colonialism and assimilation." He then went on to challenge the *bona fides* of the Committee:

> I am aware of the very tight schedule set for this Committee . . . Nevertheless, if it is true that the Inuit are permitted one oral submission and then must have all written submissions before this Committee before early October, I must say to you that this hardly seems to provide for, as your booklet phrases it "close and on-going discussions with native peoples."[92]

The phrase had been used by the Prime Minister's office in correspondence with various Aboriginal organizations.

> Mr. Chairman, it is simply not humanly possible, and I ask this Committee either to consider alternative arrangements which would offer us a fair opportunity to research, discuss and present our position to it, or to recommend to the Government of Canada that no amendments to the Canadian Constitution that directly affect us be made without our full involvement.[93]

The term "directly affects" appears to have originated with the Prime Ministers' Office in statements which assured Aboriginal participation in constitutional matters that *directly affected* those Aboriginal people. There is no indication that the PMO intended anyone other than themselves to decide when a matter *directly affected* an Aboriginal people. While allowing the government to appear to be saying "yes" to the request for seats at what Starblanket had called "the table of Confederation," the invitation is rapidly narrowed to instances when the one at the head of the table decides whether native peoples are directly affected.

Indeed, so restrictive is this expression that it would become the ground for a series of exchanges. Tagoona's willingness to adopt the phrase could allow the impression that he was giving ground and submitting to the restrictive meaning except that he immediately made clear just what he meant by the term:

> This means Inuit directly be permitted to represent themselves within the constitutional process rather than the government, provincial or territorial inquiries and so-called sovereignty association options within Canada. On this point I ask the Committee to be guided by the recommendations of its immediate predecessor, the Special Joint Committee on the Constitution of Canada, which in 1972 advised that "no Constitutional changes concerning native people should be made until such time as their own organizations have completed their research . . ." And that "no jurisdictional changes should be made in administrative arrangements concern Indians and Eskimos without prior consultation with them." [94]

At a time when the Opposition were moving to have the bill referred to the Supreme Court, the request to exempt Inuit and Indians from the effect of the bill until they were properly consulted was in keeping with the general tenor of the Committee. The Opposition demand for a reference was all the more reasonable given that Prof. Lederman's views were upheld by the Supreme Court both on the reference case on the Senate provisions in this bill[95] and on the *Patriation Reference*.[96]

More important is the need to ask, "How else are Aboriginal peoples or First Nations to be admitted to the 'table of Confederation' except by making them welcome when they are ready?"

Tagoona sought to explain to the Committee that land claims and self-determination were inextricably intertwined:

> Today it is not accurate to refer to our claims as strictly land claims. We must certainly continue to assert title to our lands but we are also and even primarily claiming our right to self-determination. And it is this principle that forms the basis of my submission to this Committee.[97]

Successive governments would seek to sever these two matters and to see both as somehow separate from the constitutional processes. Yet, when northern land claims have been successfully settled it was only by dealing with both concurrently. And on one of the rare occasions when a Native leader sought to discuss self-government separate from land, he was asked by a leading constitutional thinker to explain how such a separation was possible.

Quite sadly, even tragically (in the classical sense of a flaw that undermines an otherwise great personality), the Committee was too absorbed in its own increasingly partisan preoccupations to exhibit the grace with which one might ordinarily welcome people to share a table. Much as the mandate of this Committee might have been bound up with a perceived need to preserve Confederation by helping Francophones feel welcome, the thought of encouraging Aboriginal peoples to become welcome was beyond the grasp of the Committee. Tagoona made a most explicit offer:

> We see in this re-casting of the Constitution an opportunity to become full participants in Canadian life, to establish an equitable basis for our formal entry and continued existence within this nation and also to end finally the colonial relationship that exists between ourselves and the Government of Canada. To this end, Mr. Chairman, I am proposing that Bill C-60 be modified so as to acknowledge and enshrine the rights of the Inuit to self-determination.[98]

Given the pressures which were already impinging on the Committee, the pressures which provoked Flora Macdonald to start the day with a motion to cease hearings altogether, the offer to become "full participants" might as well have been shouted into the wind.

It is, nonetheless, noteworthy and likely not much remembered that Eric Tagoona was the first Aboriginal witness to tell a Joint Committee on the Constitution in clear and explicit terms that Aboriginal self-determination should be enshrined in the Constitution. Dave Courchene had used the term and had asked for recognition of treaty rights. Starblanket had asserted that there was a right to self-determination. Tagoona asked that it be enshrined in the Constitution. Tagoona went on for four paragraphs making quite clear that what he meant by self-determination was the right "included in the Charter of the United Nations" and endorsed by Canada "outside the traditional colonial setting in the Helsinki Declaration." Indeed, Tagoona explicitly related self-determination to self-government:

> What does self-determination mean to us? It means, first of all, a constitutional recognition of the Inuit as one of the *original peoples* of this nation with an assurance of our right to continuing existence; it means forms of self-government which return political initiative to the Inuit.[99] [Emphasis added]

THE JOINT COMMITTEE'S RESPONSE TO ERIC TAGOONA'S BRIEF

Mark MacGuigan led the questioning with an agenda which he would later make quite explicit:

> [If] in the constitutional changes that take place here over the next few years the constitutional status quo were maintained with respect to you, and that your position could be developed sometime further in the future, would you feel that this would prejudice you in any way?

> . . . Suppose we were to go ahead and make the changes that are now proposed. Suppose there were no change, even, and they all just go through. Would you lose from that? You still have an opportunity in the future because these changes do not affect you directly.[100]

This was the same dismissive offer that the Mulroney Government would make when First Nations objected to having been left out of the Meech Lake Accord. It must surely have been clear, at that time, that if Aboriginal and treaty rights were not entrenched as part of an omnibus constitutional amending package, they were unlikely to attract majority support entirely on their own. In light of the requests of Daniels, Starblanket and Tagoona, each in their own quite different words, that their people become part of Confederation, the Chairman's statement that the patriation proposals "do not affect you directly" might charitably be described as "deeply offensive."

Any remaining presumption of good will was dissipated by Sen. Sarto Fournier (Liberal, de Lanaudière). He asked, in French, if "you people exercise some kind of trade to earn their life (sic)?" Mr. Tagoona did not understand.

> **Mr. Tagoona:** Trade to earn their life?
>
> **Mr. Fournier:** . . . Besides hunting and fishing?
>
> . . . Well, I can hardly imagine that you must have many plumbers because it is not the place for that, or people to repair refrigerators, but some kind of way to earn your living, such as by making business, trades, commerce.[101]

When Mr. Tagoona explained that "evolution has taken us to this point, that we do take advantage of [the] wage economy," Mr. Fournier hit upon "the receipt of social benefits for health, unemployment or poverty" as a reason to avoid what had been said so explicitly.

Mr. Goodale (Liberal, Assiniboia, Sask.) recognized that the objectives set out by Eric Tagoona might be sought through a number of channels, "[A]re you really staking all your case upon a new kind of political orientation or organization in the Northern part of Canada and are you really ruling out a greater role at the centre of the country in the national government?"[102]

Robert Stanfield asked whether beyond the irrelevance of the present proposal might it also do some harm to the Inuit cause in some way:

> I would like to know very precisely whether they regard this measure as not only inadequate from their point of view, and, in a sense, irrelevant from our point of view but whether there is anything in the proposed bill which in their judgment would put them in a worse position than they are today.[103]

Senator Forsey, who had had rallied much of the Liberal caucus against this bill,[104] and was generally well disposed toward some rectification of First Nations relations, asked, "Would you give me some more precise idea of whether you are thinking of an area with some kind of political jurisdiction?"

By the end of his question it started to come clear that what he actually wanted to know was whether, by having a single political jurisdiction that "your people . . . would be taken out of those particular jurisdictions [Québec, Labrador, and the N.W.T.]" and concentrated in a single place.[105]

AN UNDERLYING AGREEMENT BETWEEN PROFESSORS W.R. LEDERMAN OF QUEEN'S UNIVERSITY AND LÉON DION OF LAVAL UNIVERSITY

Professor Lederman was the only witness to be invited to return to expand on his earlier submission. It had been on the basis of his initial testimony at the eighth sitting of the Committee that Flora MacDonald brought her motion, of August 30, 1978, that the Committee cease its hearings.

Prof. Léon Dion of Laval University, appeared four sittings after Prof. Lederman's return and was able to seize on the serendipity of poor drafting quality and nationalist aspiration. "Bill C-60 is so badly drafted and so out of sync with Québec aspirations that it does not even arouse discussion. [106]

The underlying agreement between Professors Lederman and Dion, whose constitutional views were otherwise quite opposed was that Bill C-60 was framed with so little regard to convention and existing constitutional law as not to merit further study.

CLOSING THE PROCEEDINGS ON C-60: THE PARLIAMENTARIANS' RESPONSE IN SUMMARY

Two opposing tendencies occurred through the presentations of Aboriginal witnesses before the MacGuigan-Lamontagne Joint Committee of 1978.

The one tendency was the movement of Aboriginal organizations to focus on constitutional issues and to develop a degree of competence in presenting culturally grounded constitutional arguments. In this area, two sets of relations were furthered. First, they found an issue on which they could open discussions amongst themselves without having to agree on matters which were specific either to the *Indian Act* or the Métis culture or to Inuit aspirations in the Arctic. Secondly, the Aboriginal organizations furthered their relations with those parliamentarians who were interested in a genuine dialogue.

The second tendency was the one in which parliamentarians discredited themselves by displays of ignorance and hostility. What is most striking about these Proceedings is not so much what is found in the testimony of the Indian witnesses and the responses of the parliamentarians as what is missing.

What is missing is any indication that the arguments and propositions submitted to the Committee on Aboriginal matters had been discussed at times other than when Indian witnesses were making presentations. From that point of view, whatever the greater good will of this Parliament from those of the 1920s or 30s or 40s, it nonetheless remained a maxim in the 29th and 30th Parliaments that when Indians were out of sight they were also out of mind.

When the idea of self-determination was put to the Joint Committee on the Constitution in 1978, the Senators and Members responded with sarcasm, derision, and incredulity. The Chairman told the Inuit that the patriation proposal did not affect them directly. The former Leader of the Opposition said that their aspirations were irrelevant to the Constitution. Any sense that their proposal for self-determination within Confederation was consistent with what other witnesses had been saying since 1971was absent. The parliamentarians appeared to be as unfamiliar with the Aboriginal dimension of their own *Proceedings* as they were with the history of First Nations relations in general.

The minority 29th Parliament had allowed the N.I.B. and its affiliates to develop a much closer relationship with the Members on the Standing Committee on Indian Affairs and Northern Development. Joe Clark's motion to adopt the Brotherhood's position paper on Aboriginal rights, in March, 1973, lent credibility to the very notions that Manuel had inherited from his mentor Andrew Paull, the notions that were the subject of ridicule by the Joint Committee of 1926.

Manuel's relationship with Watson in the previous Parliament had, undoubtedly, initiated the process in which the Standing Committee and the N.I.B. collaborated to their mutual advantage. Nonetheless, the increasing capacity of the N.I.B. to produce position papers that combined sound research with a solid remedial program, such as *Indian Control of Indian Education*, in May, 1973, and the Aboriginal rights paper a short while earlier, challenged the monopoly of DIAND officialdom. This capacity gave the N.I.B. the material with which to cultivate a reciprocal relationship with those Members who were capable of recognizing the value of the N.I.B.'s materials.

Whether or not there was any sincerity in Chrétien's undertakings before the Standing Committee in regard to *Indian Control* is less important, at least from the perspective of re-shaping the discourse, than his recognition of the value of what the N.I.B. was producing. In fact, what was emerging was one of those situations in which the minister was suddenly obliged to run to get out in front of the parade.

The legitimacy lent to the N.I.B. by Clark's motion to adopt the N.I.B. Aboriginal title paper did not go so far as to shift the burden of persuasion, as to the nature or even the reality of Aboriginal title, from the Indian political organizations to Government but it lent the N.I.B. (and to some extent its member organizations) *a normative status as an authority on their own entitlements*. At least within certain political circles, this was tantamount to a kind of *de facto* license. It would take some further time for the press gallery to begin to lend credence to this license. Nonetheless, it began a process of **moving the concept of Aboriginal title to the other side of the fulcrum** and, thereby, shifting some part of the burden for demonstrating matters of title, at least in this forum, from the Indian side to the Government, side.

The long term commitment of a core group of MPs who continued to serve on the Indian Affairs Committee and who came to form something of a *parliamentary memory* on the issues discussed in the Committee **exemplify intention in a public sense.** Long term commitment cannot, of course, be demonstrated in advance. There may, however, be certain kinds of behaviours which are indicative of a long term commitment.

Trudeau's statement to the Nisga'a leaders admitting that they had "more rights than I thought you had" may appear to be the kind of statement that should be expected from a prime minister. However much we might *want to expect* such a statement, any analysis must begin with the rareness of such admissions. It demonstrates not so much *a new intention* on Trudeau's part as *a renewed intention* to allow his own policy thinking to be influenced by the law, i.e., by the courts. It demonstrates *an intention to place* his own advocacy of rights *ahead of* the ideological content of the *White Paper*. Such an intention is *integral to* Trudeau's own self-image as *a person of reason.*

AN ANALYSIS OF THE INDIAN AFFAIRS COMMITTEE IN THE 30TH PARLIAMENT

The Ministry of State for Social Development (MSSD) summary of Starblanket's administration stresses an emphasis on self-government (although they refer to "the advancement of band government")[107] and on a "new concern with the Canadian Constitution as it relates to Indian rights." These comparisons may be not so much with the previous leadership of the N.I.B. under George Manuel as with the perceptions of the Indian Affairs Branch as they briefed MSSD.

In contrast, Starblanket's appearance before the Indian Affairs Committee, in February 1978, to explain why he had withdrawn the N.I.B. from the Joint Cabinet Committee focused on "the refusal of Cabinet to respond to our comprehensive proposals and particularly to recognize our aboriginal and treaty rights." Not only did Starblanket's administration want a hand in drafting Indian legislation, to the horror of the Indian Affairs Branch, they wanted to discuss overall policy with Cabinet ministers. These demands to shape *the terms of engagement* and to draft legislation represent an effort to elevate (relative to the IAB perception at least) the dialogue between Indian leaders and ministers. The failure to accomplish this objective is what led to the withdrawal from the Joint N.I.B./Cabinet Committee and the testimony before the Indian Affairs Committee.

Sanderson's inclination to run up and down the rhetorical scale[108] confused members of his audience who did not share his capacity for this kind of virtuoso performance. Nonetheless, we can pierce through the "real fear" to which he, himself, referred. As soon as he demonstrated that he has a command of the bureaucratic rhetoric of "A level" funding and "statutory obligations" he moves on from there to saying that there was a need to talk about "Indian government," the very thing that the ministers had refused to discuss.

In one sense, Sanderson was doing what writing teachers recommend when they say, "Show me, don't tell me." He showed the committee that he could match the bureaucratic witnesses who appear before them at their own game and then showed them that that game addresses neither the aspirations of the Indian leadership nor the needs of Indian communities.

Frank Oberle agreed with Sanderson that "Political development is something that frightens us all." Oberle persisted in asking witnesses and staff from Indian organizations how self-government was different from apartheid.[109] His Diogenes-like persistence was at times off-putting but it was coupled with a willingness to ask piercing and straightforward questions. Oberle provided the opportunity to allow Sanderson and Starblanket to make the distinction between Indian legislation drafted by Indian leaders and legislation that continued the imperial impositions of previous parliaments.

In contrast, the Minister of the day, Hugh Faulkner, adopted the rhetoric that could be heard from his successor Bob Nault in 2001, "our discussions tended to be blocked by rather *rigid assertions* of rights from the N.I.B. side." The writer of Mr. Faulkner's notes might best explain the case for a *limp assertion*. What he, possibly, had in mind was that he would have been happier if the Indian organizations would have been willing to be associations of band councils which acted as *agents of the minister*. Such a discourse, once the premise is accepted, would be far more to the government's liking. Since this was a norm accepted by the Indian Affairs Branch, Faulkner's advisors were disinclined to examine it or to re-evaluate the effectiveness of their programs as they would be seen if Indian leaders were shaping policy in response to the expressed wishes of Indian voters.

Faulkner, following a script which may well have come from the middle level of his bureaucracy, distinguished between the demand for a more policy- centred discourse and his own preference for a program-centred discussion by declaring his account to be the "constructive vein," a condescension that was too thin to constitute an actual deception.

However, when he carried on from there to say "Indian leaders in all parts of the country see advantage in this tripartite approach" he was entering into a more clear-cut prevarication. A more astute committee, with more time and resources, might have asked him to document that claim and contrasted those whom he claimed to have onside with those who were supporting Starblanket. No such evidence occurs in the parliamentary record. Nonetheless, it is clear that the withdrawal of the N.I.B. from the Joint Cabinet Committee was a decision taken by consensus of an Executive Council which consisted of the heads of all the provincial and territorial organizations in Canada. This might lead to the conclusion that Faulkner's prevarication was *a disingenuous effort at burden shifting.*

Keith Penner and Bob Holmes both challenged the minister through an indirect method. They pursued the information that had been supplied to them through Sol Sanderson that federal funding for the Saskatchewan Federated Indian College was dependent upon following a provincial curriculum. These efforts to find direction by indirection were astute and clever but not likely to communicate with folks not already familiar with the issue.

Whatever had inclined Penner and Holmes to this indirect route, they had allowed themselves, on this occasion at least, to be drawn into the government's "needs-based" framework on a matter which might better have been discussed in terms of the willingness of the federal government to exercise their full authority under s. 91(24). This far plain sense approach is one to which Penner would rise in the following Parliament both in regard to the non-fulfillment of the *James Bay Agreement* and in the *Report on Indian Self-Government.*

AN ANALYSIS OF THE SELECTED TESTIMONY BEFORE THE MACGUIGAN-LAMONTAGNE COMMITTEE ON BILL C-60, 1978

Harry Daniels' statement "There has been *too much faith placed in the inherent feelings* for freedom and justice which our forefathers understood to be deeply ingrained in the institutions and people of Canada" was a statement meant to appeal to a latent sense of the ethical amongst his audience of parliamentarians. He coupled this with a prefatory sentence stating, in part, "the generality and diffuseness surrounding the reference to "Indians" in the Constitution has not served the native people well." The paragraph as a whole can be assessed by considering the extent to which the various elements work to support one another. The first is an analysis of Constitutional history from a Native perspective. The second is a statement about the Native experience of relying on the supposed *feelings for freedom and justice.* Does the analysis contribute to understanding the origins of the Native perspective that Daniels presents? Does the Adjectival statement of feelings and perspective explain the question he addressed to Constitutional history?

Starblanket told the MacGuigan-Lamontagne Committee that the patriation bill before them "erroneously implies that the proclamation granted, rather than confirmed, already existing Indian rights." This is a plain sense reading of section 26, "any right or freedom that may have been acquired by any of the native peoples of Canada by virtue of the Royal Proclamation of October 7, 1763." Even were one to believe that these rights had been superseded by later legislation, the notion that they were "acquired . . . by virtue of the Royal Proclamation" is not one that is supported by the earlier cases in which the Royal Proclamation is discussed.[110] Were this statement in any other source it would represent a disingenuous analysis of the *Royal Proclamation* in the prevaricating dimension of the discourse. When the statement appears in a bill for the comprehensive amendment of the Constitution prepared by the Department of Justice and sponsored by the Minister of Federal-Provincial Relations, it enters deeply into the duplicitous so far as it describes and conditions the quality of relationship that it proposes Canada to have with the First Nations.

Such a statement, in a patriation bill grates against Noel Lyons' statement, "The test of our capacity in the future to develop an adequate Constitution and to call ourselves a civilized nation will depend upon the state in which our native peoples find themselves."[111] Those who apply this standard will not only fault the drafters and sponsors of section 26 of Bill C-60 for their analysis but will find it instructive as a statement that deeply characterizes that Government's vision of Canada.

Starblanket's statement that "the land is a gift to each nation, as a nation, from the Great Spirit, our Creator" has a distinct element so far as it describes those nations' relationships with their Creator. However, in the context of that paragraph, he is citing these gifts, as a basis for the sovereignty of the First Nations which he has already said, "exists in and of its own right."

Starblanket offered a comparable view when he compared "Aboriginal rights in the legal context" to "a conceptual framework" in which "Aboriginal rights emanate from sovereignty, from the right of a people to govern themselves."[112] The dimension to which he wanted the Committee to pay attention for a while is the dimension in which political ethics is an extension of personal ethics, the dimension in which *the sovereignty describes the nation* and *Aboriginal rights emanate from that sovereignty.*

Starblanket's statement that both Indian organizations and "Indian women's organizations were saying basically the same thing: that Indians should identify and define who Indians are," is another example of a statement that challenges the government's tendency to shift the burden of proof on questions such as "Who is an Indian." The statement "It is normative for a people to define its own membership" characterizes a concept of peoplehood. Likewise, any particular application characterizes a particular people or nation. A plea that this right of self-definition should be recognized also originates in the dimension in which identity and aesthetics and ethics converge. When a principle crystallizes in this dimension it becomes *a standard or guideline or instruction for drafting or construing a legal instrument.*

The term "directly affects" is a major lexical unit on the negative side of the Discourse of First Nations' Autonomy. If the statement is seen as a feint in which a superficial inclusion serves primarily to mask a substantial exclusion, then it is a device designed to prevaricate in the constitutional amending process. So far as Starblanket told the Committee that the Indian nations wanted to take their place at the Table of Confederation, the statement that they would be welcome *on some occasions* and for limited purposes is a dubious welcome.

Eric Tagoona quoted MacGuigan's own 1972 report which had said, "no Constitutional changes concerning native people should be made until such time as their own organizations have completed their research." In context, this was an entirely positive statement. Sadly MacGuigan's view had drastically changed by 1978. "Suppose that we were to go ahead and make the changes that are now proposed . . . Would you lose from that? . . . these changes do not affect you directly" comes perilously close to the condescension shared by Trudeau's and Mulroney's PMO's in their uses of this same term. Nobody else who claimed a right to sit at the Table of Confederation would agree to have patriation, the amending formula, and a *Charter of Rights* adopted on the basis that these matters did not affect them directly. At the very least, these statements jar with MacGuigan's characterization, in his 1972 report, of the "Native peoples" as "the First Canadians." It seems unlikely that it is a position he would have commended to a client (if he took clients) when he was teaching constitutional law.

The claim that section 26 contained an egregious error in regard to the *Royal Proclamation* which, in turn, cast doubt either on the intentions of the Government or on the fundamental competence of their drafters finds support in the underlying agreement between Professors W.R. Lederman and Léon Dion. They both held that the bill failed both for bad drafting and for failing to address Québec's aspirations. Their characterization, like Starblanket's, placed the bill in the Discourse of Prevarication.

One major overview that emerges from classifying First Nations related testimony before these committees is that, by and large, the less sympathetic parliamentarians *perceived* First Nations discourse as being simple, if not primitive while First Nations witnesses were looking to show deep connections between the specific issues they were describing and the quality of their nations' relationships with Canada. The notion that there was a direct connection between the constitutional status of First Nations and their poverty was either not grasped or was scoffed at by most parliamentarians in this period.

The parliamentarians' tendency is evident in the Indian Affairs Committee where the less sympathetic members want to focus on specific issues even while Starblanket and Sanderson are moving through an analysis of recent events toward an argument for self-government. In the Joint Committee on the Constitution, the persistent belief that Indian issues are ones of social service is reflected in the corollary idea that the more elevated aspects of the Constitutional debate are not essential to an understanding of First Nations issues, that First Nations concerns can be postponed until after patriation, and that no direct answer need be given to the question as to the post-patriation status of treaties.

The recurring effort *to hear* First Nations witnesses in terms of needs that could be met by programs is, in part, a self-fulfilling perception: the parliamentarians hear what they want to hear. Behind the self-fulfilling perception is a large dose of cultural conditioning: there is a received mythology as to how Indians think and speak. Because the mythology is widely shared there the self-fulfilling perception appears to flow from an underlying agreement.

The agreement is not the result of negotiation or, in most cases, previous collegial discussion so much as it is the result of shared assumptions. Liberal and Conservative Ministers fall back on the "directly affects" limitation. Women parliamentarians of liberal views in both Houses assume that a net improvement would result from removing the discriminatory provisions of ss. 12(1)(b) *whether or not there are corresponding increases of resources*.

Hugh Faulkner would not have devoted a significant part of his opening address to the Indian Affairs committee criticizing the N.I.B. for its "rigid assertions of rights" if he did not expect to score points for his side by arguing the need to focus on specific instances without forming any kind of overview and *without relating living conditions to issues of colonialism*. In the same Parliament in which Trudeau's first patriation effort is faulted both for its invasion of provincial rights and for its offer of a rather limp *Charter of Rights*, the Indian Affairs Minister asked that Indian discourse be heard in a way quite inconsistent with the general discourse on metapolicy in Canada.

WHAT PROGRESS DID THE DISCOURSE MAKE IN THE MACGUIGAN-LAMONTAGNE COMMITTEE?

The MacGuigan-Lamontagne Committee on C-60 was "neither fish nor fowl," i.e., it did not have the breadth of mandate enjoyed by the earlier constitutional committee. The claim that a bill, although it had received only first reading, might be used to elicit ideas without being seen as a direction in which the Government wanted to move, alienated the opposition parliamentarians, scholarly witnesses and First Nations leaders.

From our perspective—tracking the public emergence of the vocabulary of First Nations' self-government—there was as much ground lost during this Committee's *Proceedings* as there was gained.

The losses were primarily a result of the attitude of the Government, in its proposal and the consequent attitude of various players on the Committee. Mark MacGuigan, having made a major contribution to furthering a First Nations dialogue by devoting an entire chapter of his earlier report to "Native Peoples" did his Committee and himself a great disservice by his remark that "these changes do not directly affect" Aboriginal peoples. That Mr. MacGuigan's remark appeared to repeat a remark with which Mr. Trudeau had already incensed Aboriginal leaders compounded the insult.

The Conservative and NDP MPs were steadfastly opposed to the bill and were primarily concerned to find witnesses who would support their position. The Senators from both sides of the Upper Chamber were united in opposition to the proposal to replace the Senate. Centrist legal scholars agreed with Péquiste political scientists about the shortcomings of the bill. The Supreme Court later agreed with the Senators.[113]

Centrist women parliamentarians had developed their own agenda including an end to the more conspicuous discriminatory provisions of the *Indian Act* but not including the essential corollaries of a genuine reinstatement. Like their male colleagues, they were more prepared to argue their positions than to do the work essential to a genuine dialogue. Ideological considerations resulted in an apparent disinterest in any kind of genuine dialogue. The unwillingness to address the need to accompany large-scale reinstatements to Indian status with proportionate increases in land and financial resources brought this disinterest to a form of prevarication. It allowed the liberal women parliamentarians to pose with a progressive veneer while they continued to shift onto the Indian leadership a responsibility that rests with their own caucuses. This served to challenge the *bona fides* and to impugn the license of the Indian leadership.

In an atmosphere that was hardly conducive to advancing the discourse of First Nations' autonomy, there were some important accomplishments. Where their predecessors had been able to say only that they needed more time to consult with their constituents and to study the issues, Daniels and Starblanket each set out definite positions. The positions of the Native Council and the National Indian Brotherhood were significantly different from one another. The question asked of George Manuel by Marcel Prud'homme near the end of the previous Committee, about the situation of the Métis, could now be answered from the testimony of their own leadership.

Starblanket had carved out a position in which he sought to integrate the reinstatement of forcibly enfranchised women with the regaining of other assets of which First Nations' communities had been deprived: the land base on which a revitalization of the communities must depend and education and social budgets comparable to other Canadian communities. Some parliamentarians began to grasp that he had taken an innovative position and one which would require selling both to his own constituents and to the Government.

Indian organizations faced a challenge in having to give the same message over and over again. The progress made by the Indian and Native organizations during this period was the painstaking development of the vocabulary with which to express their goals and the education of those few parliamentarians interested in entering into a genuine dialogue.

A financier appearing before the Senate Banking and Commerce Committee or the Public Accounts Committee of the Commons would find that the parliamentarians on those committees understood his (or her) professional jargon and was familiar with the basic concepts at issue. This basic competence constitutes a common ground in those committees across party lines. Such a competence was in an early stage of development in the Indian Affairs Committee. It was conspicuously absent in the MacGuigan-Lamontagne Committee.

The lack of this common ground is a serious impediment to discourse. It also leaves parliamentarians particularly vulnerable to misdirection and prevarication by ministers and officials.

Taken as a whole, the main outcome of the C-60 debate was a hardening of attitudes on all sides. Given the lack of progress since the Victoria Conference in 1970, the Government may well have believed that the time had come to move beyond the broad based inquiry conducted eight years earlier. Nonetheless, the failure to incorporate the major concerns of either the Conservative or the New Democratic Party ensured their opposition. The failure to include any substantial recognition of Aboriginal and treaty rights was compounded by a section 26 that, in the opinion of Indian and Native witnesses, added insult to injury.

The *Constitutional Amendment Act, 1978* attracted a condemnation of one kind or another from all the other political parties, all the Aboriginal organizations, the leading political scientists and the Supreme Court. The Government's inability to see a need to enlist the support of any provincial governments or of any grassroots political movement asserts an authority that has not been typical of the Canadian federal government. It escalated (or reduced) an analytical discussion to a discussion of the legitimacy of an array of institutions. Much of the alienation would have been accomplished had the bill been well drafted. The indifference (or arrogance or hostility) to other interests was, as is often the case, interwoven with issues of technical incompetence.

The widespread distribution of "A Time for Action" the promotional booklet accompanying C-60, which spoke of "Full Respect for Native rights," when the bill had no substantial protection, had all the earmarks of a government disinformation campaign. Disinformation is, by definition, a prevarication. This feature of "A Time for Action" exemplified a Great Lie Theory in its shifting of the burden, not only in the popular and journalistic imagination but also in Parliamentary discourse, onto Indian witnesses who became obliged to show *why the Government's claim was false*. In fairness to the Government, the booklet made little effort to substantiate the specious claim to "full respect." The willingness of parliamentarians, journalists and citizens to accept such statements, given the historical record of Canadian governments on such matters, might be described as an ***acquiescent prevarication.***

Given that the role of Parliament is, more often than not, one of consenting to proposals initiated by Government, the greatest opportunity for parliamentarians to prevaricate is in their acquiescence. A re-reading of these *Proceedings* has, however, demonstrated that despite their limited opportunity non-ministerial parliamentarians frequently demonstrated an aptitude at prevarication and a disinterest in genuine dialogue with Indian leaders quite independent of the failures of the Government.

THE ROAD AHEAD

Whether Starblanket's administration was aware of the need to reshape the dialogue during his first two year term that became the focus of his second term. In 1978, he began to work toward reconstituting the National Indian Brotherhood so that it would come under the control of an assembly of all the chiefs in Canada. Until that time, no such body had ever met.

At the same time that the framework for such a body was being negotiated with the provincial and territorial organizations, a parallel discussion was developing as to an appropriate name for the body that would succeed the N.I.B. It was becoming a commonplace, early in Starblanket's second term, that each of the words in "National Indian Brotherhood" was problematic. The resolution to that problem would emerge in tandem with a more deeply entrenched determination to secure a constitutional recognition of Aboriginal and treaty rights.

Chapter Five

Notions of Sovereignty: Self-Help, Self-Confidence, and Individual and Collective Self-Fulfillment

> No, we cannot agree to [the reinstatement of enfranchised women] at this point—for the simple reason that there is no guarantee from the Government of Canada that, with the influx . . . there will be an equal increase in the number of dollars and land resources, acres, services in the administration capabilities of the federal government.
>
> Noel V. Starblanket, 1978 Joint Committee on the Constitution

INTRODUCTION: "INDIAN CONTROL," ABORIGINAL RIGHTS AND PATRIATION

The two Parliaments from 1979 through 1984—the 31st and 32nd Parliaments—constitute the period in which the vocabulary of First Nations self-government emerged into the public domain, and appeared on the parliamentary record in clear and explicit terms.

There are several features which characterize this period, distinguishing it from the period which preceded it and those that followed. First, we can say that this is the period during which the vocabulary became explicit. Secondly, by identifying the point in time, and the political context in which it became explicit, we can suggest some major factors contributing to the explication within the political life both of First Nations and Parliament.

Thirdly, we can identify a secondary or supporting vocabulary which emerged at the same time and which might be seen as essential to the process of becoming clear. Fourthly, although the story of the patriation debate and the First Ministers conferences and such later events as the *Penner Committee*, the *Charlottetown Accord* and the *Royal Commission on Aboriginal Peoples (RCAP)* fall beyond the scope of this study, the vocabulary that had emerged by the end of this narrative, in June, 1980, helped set the stage for these later events.

The Penner Report might be seen, from the perspective of this study, as an extended gloss on the vocabulary of self-government, which began to take shape shortly after the vocabulary had emerged piecemeal in the proceedings of the Standing Committee and the Joint Committee on the Constitution of 1980–81. Indeed, running throughout the *RCAP Report*, in 1996, is a program to fine-tune and make more precise the framework for the discourse which emerged in the late 70s and early 80s.

THE 31ST PARLIAMENT: BACKGROUND TO THE WORK OF THE STANDING COMMITTEE ON INDIAN AFFAIRS & NORTHERN DEVELOPMENT

The 31st Parliament was the minority Parliament during which Rt. Hon. Joseph (Joe) Clark was Prime Minister of Canada. Clark was elected with a minority government of 136 of the 295 seats then in the House of Commons on May 22, 1979.[1] His Government held office from June 4, 1979 to March 2, 1980.

The death of Bill C-60, the *Constitutional Amendment Act, 1978* with the end of the 30th Parliament had put constitutional issues on the back burner in large parts of the country. However, Starblanket and the N.I.B. continued to press their constitutional concerns both with the Liberals in the last days before the election and with the Clark government from the very outset of its brief time in office.

The N.I.B., under Starblanket, convened the first all-chiefs conference in Canadian history from the 3rd to the 5th of April, 1979 in Montreal. The National Indian Brotherhood had an executive council consisting of the heads of its provincial and territorial member organizations (PTOs). It also had a General Assembly consisting of delegates chosen by the provincial and territorial heads on a rep-by-pop basis. This was a structure which had been successful in creating a national voice in response to the White Paper. It was not, however, a structure well suited to serving as the deliberative assembly in which traditional "Indian nations" might come together. Starblanket went so far as to invite both traditional and elected chiefs from reserves which had both kinds of councils.

A DIAND official reported in a memo that

> During the Conference, DIAND and other officials were impressed by the growing coherence of Indian views and the spirit of responsibility and concern which animated them. The Indians, in the main, were trying to come to grips with the notions of *sovereignty in the sense of self-help, self-confidence, and individual and collective self-fulfillment.* The meeting was important in giving shape to Indian views and in providing insights for federal officials concerned with native and constitutional policies.[2] (Emphasis added.)

The conference was billed as "The National Indian Government Development Conference." The name is noteworthy in that it reflects the language that was then in general use and would not raise controversies before the chiefs had gathered. The next year, when Starblanket convened the first national chiefs' conference under the name "Assembly of First Nations" was, in fact, the second time the chiefs had been convened explicitly to discuss self-government.

The term "Self-Government" only came to supplant "Indian Government" somewhat later, though it was introduced and gained acceptance during this conference. By the same turn, the DIAND memo quoted above has a curious ambiguity in its treatment of the discussions of sovereignty at the conference: on the one hand, it lends legitimacy to the discussions by equating them with very practical concerns; on the other hand, it reduces a far-reaching term to concepts within reach of a municipal administration. At that time, Indian Affairs was engaged in promoting what it termed "Indian Band Government Legislation," a municipal model which failed to attract the support of any First Nations. Some time later, after the Penner Report, Indian Affairs would co-opt the vocabulary developed in the Assembly of First Nations and in the Penner Committee until it became a dirty phrase in the ears of many First Nations people.[3]

During the election campaign, on May 8, 1979, Marc Lalonde, then Minister of Federal-Provincial Relations, reached out to the N.I.B. to guarantee the Brotherhood a limited role at the First Ministers' Conference (FMC) then scheduled for the fall. With the change of government, this offer provided a ground from which Starblanket might seek more favourable terms from the Clark Government.

A few days before the National Indian Government Development Conference, Starblanket had written the Queen requesting an audience in the first week of July, pursuant to a resolution of the N.I.B. Assembly the previous August.[4] On June 18, 1979, Government House delivered a message from Buckingham Palace to the N.I.B. in which the Queen, acting on the advice of her Canadian ministers, said that she "fully recognizes the great importance attached to discussions which have already begun . . ." She hoped that sometime this year, the Governor General would receive a delegation of Chiefs and Elders under the N.I.B. .[5]

Two days later, Jake Epp, Clark's Minister of Indian Affairs and Northern Development, met with the N.I.B. leadership.[6] A week later, William Jarvis, the Minister for Federal-Provincial Relations, committed the "government to consultation with Indian and other native people on Constitutional processes and direct participation in Constitutional revision."[7]

In July, the N.I.B. proceeded to take 300 chiefs to lobby the British Parliament on the need to entrench Indian rights in the Canadian Constitution. Starblanket had earlier rejected a Liberal offer to swap the trip for a two-day conference with the Governor General and a delegation of chiefs. Now, however, the N.I.B. adopted the position that the trip would become unnecessary if the Clark Government guaranteed that Indians would be involved as participants in constitutional conferences, and that Indian rights would be enshrined in the Constitution. When the Government refused to make those commitments the chiefs' trip to England went ahead.

Shortly after the trip, a meeting between the N.I.B. Executive Council, the Prime Minister, and several Cabinet Ministers did result in the Clark Government granting the N.I.B. a participatory role at constitutional talks "on matters directly pertaining to Indians." Although the N.I.B. leadership may have recognized this offer as a kind of progress, the qualifier, "directly pertaining" was one which had been used evasively by Trudeau's Government on more than one occasion. It was an offer which had to be refused. The very phrase used by Jake Epp in an effort to appear generous had been denounced by all national Aboriginal leaders when it had been used by Trudeau's ministers.[8]

During September and October 1979, a number of events provided the N.I.B. with some grounds for cautious anticipation of gaining ground in their dealings with the Clark Government. A new Indian Health Policy was introduced in September, advocating transfer to community control of health care programs "in support of the aspirations of Indian people for self-determination."[9]

On October 11, Prime Minister Clark wrote to the N.I.B. saying that their participation in constitutional revision would be funded. On October 15, Clark announced that David MacDonald, the Secretary of State, took on responsibility in cabinet for relations with the Métis and Non-Status Indians. MacDonald had long been known for his support for minority issues and was thought to provide balance to the more traditionally conservative and less inquiring style of Jake Epp, the Minister of Indian Affairs and Northern Development.

THE INDIAN AFFAIRS COMMITTEE IN THE 31ST PARLIAMENT: SOME BACKGROUND

The change in membership in the Standing Committee on Indian Affairs and Northern Development[10] from the 30th to the 31st Parliaments was minimal. Frank Oberle, a Conservative Member from Prince George, who had been active on the Committee in the previous Parliament, took the chair.

The Standing Committee is important here for two reasons. First, it was before the Standing Committee that the N.I.B. leadership explicated the emergence of the AFN and related that emergence directly to the quest for self-government. Secondly and earlier, during the 31st Parliament and early in the 32nd Parliament, a series of issues arose which provided concrete evidence for the necessity of self-government. These issues provided more than the context in which the vocabulary emerged: they provided a series of demonstrations that competent administration was not likely to come to Indian communities until those communities took control of their own affairs.

MR. JAKE EPP (MINISTER OF INDIAN AFFAIRS AND NORTHERN DEVELOPMENT)

Mr. Jake Epp (Minister of Indian Affairs and Northern Development) (Provencher):

> Now that I have been in the portfolio for five months . . . I think it is appropriate to share with members of this Committee some of the insights that I have gained.
>
> Virtually the first contact I made following my swearing-in . . . was with native leaders; the formal aspect of our relationship began June 19 and 20 at a formal meeting of the National Indian Brotherhood Executive Council in Vancouver.[11]

The idea that the Minister of Indian Affairs needed to be seen to consult with the Indian leadership at the outset of his ministry, although being first thoroughly briefed by departmental officials, had been gaining momentum since Allmand's appointment in September, 1976. Allmand's personal style coincided happily, in this regard, with a growing expectation by Indian leaders that they would be consulted. Whether the appearance of consultation was blessed with substance is a question to be answered anew at each turn in the convoluted history of First Nations relations. The pretense of consultation goes to the very heart of the discourse of prevarication.

Jake Epp's opening remarks are interesting in part because he was situated along the far end of the spectrum which we might describe retrospectively as extending from Allmand to Munro and Crombie. It is, however, interesting that Mr. Epp followed in the footsteps of Mr. Chrétien, in referring to his clients as "native leaders"—a term heavily identified with the assimilationist inclinations of the recently defeated Trudeau Liberals. The application of the term "native," uncapitalized, appears to have come into Parliamentary use with a view to diminishing the distinction between people belonging to communities with treaties and people with an undefined indigenous ancestry. The issue of capitalizing the term almost immediately distinguished writers who considered it important to acknowledge that the term refers to a "particular group" of people, the usual definition of a proper noun over those who were neutral on such an affirmation.[12]

Epp identified his priorities as "Indian education, housing and economic development, as well as the dual processes of *Indian Act* amendments and Constitutional renewal."[13] I do not think that any of Epp's predecessors would have volunteered the view, before a parliamentary committee, that *Indian Act* revision and constitutional renewal were twin processes. It is certainly evident in Mr. Chrétien's testimony as the Minister of Justice piloting Pierre Trudeau's patriation resolution through the Joint Committee on the Constitution, that he had not, one year later, seen these as "dual processes." It is also not clear when Epp became the Opposition Constitutional critic, in 1980, that he continued to see these processes as being intertwined as he portrayed them the year before:

> . . . Increasingly more people are looking to Indian band governments with the powers to manage their own affairs and the principle of community-based planning and development for the solutions of the future, and it is interesting to note the similarity between those concepts of community strength and the approach we in the government are also adopting for the North.[14]

Although these concessions would prove to be but small tokens encompassing both the Minister's community consultations and his briefings on the *Optional Indian Band Government Legislation* which his officials were developing,[15] they were also a significant forward movement from the perspective of ministerial statements. Delegated power along municipal lines would not be acceptable to the N.I.B. . The ambiguity of the phrase "directly affects" had a counterpart in the diffuse phrase "to manage their own affairs." Were these affairs to be "managed" under direction from the Minister or was there to be an authentic policy making role in the band's own institutions?

> At several meetings with Indian groups the Prime Minister and I have committed the government to move ahead quickly to remove discrimination against women from the *Indian Act*. This government has asked Indian people to define and articulate the kind of revised *Indian Act* that will achieve their goals. Together we will develop the means to ensure strong Indian participation, both before amendments are introduced in this House and while Parliament is considering them.[16]

It is possible that Jake Epp did not understand how much his own words were calculated (by those who drafted them and put the speech in front of him) to set the teeth of the Indian leadership on edge. An attentive reading will show how this paragraph came down firmly on both sides of the fence leaving a careful reader knowing no more after the reading than before.

The Indian leadership of the day had long favoured ending discrimination. Starblanket had consistently told parliamentary committees that the N.I.B. opposed piecemeal amendments to the *Indian Act* when there was not a willingness to recognize Aboriginal and treaty rights and to revise the Act as a whole in favour of autonomy. The decision which Epp claimed for Joe Clark and himself, first to remove discrimination and then to study revision of the *Indian Act*, avoided addressing the economic dimensions of ending discrimination. From the N.I.B.'s perspective this was a tactic to create the illusion of positive action while effectively downloading an intractable problem onto Indian communities. Starblanket had told the MacGuigan-Lamontagne Committee, in response to a question from Flora MacDonald, only the year before:

> No, we cannot agree to [reinstatement] at this point—for the simple reason that there is no guarantee from the Government of Canada that, with the influx . . . there will be an equal increase in the number of dollars and land resources, acres, services in the administration capabilities of the federal government.[17]

It is unfortunate that Starblanket did not put a more positive slant on this statement; he would support reinstatement of enfranchised women if the Liberal and Conservative women MPs and Senators would support a proportionate increase in funding for infrastructure and social programs and an expedited land claims process. On the other hand, none of the women parliamentarians ostensibly committed to the cause of reinstatement thought to take Starblanket up on his negative statement of the problem, just quoted. Indeed, not one Liberal or Conservative parliamentarian, woman or man, during the next six years chose to pursue the need for proportionately greater resources as a corollary of reinstatement.[18]

Similarly, the statement that "this government has asked Indian people to define and articulate the kind of revised *Indian Act* which will achieve their goals"[19] pretends that this question had not been under study for several years within Indian organizations. Indeed, Epp did not talk about a dialogue with the Indian leadership or with organizations; his reference to "Indian people" gave the impression of continued picking and choosing with whom he would consult, a practice followed by a succession of later ministers.

Lastly, Epp chose not to disclose to the Committee that DIAND had been engaged in drafting *Optional Indian Band Government Legislation*, as they called their work, for over a year at the time of this appearance. N.I.B. staff attending his testimony were well aware of this work and they ensured that the MPs knew what the Minister was not disclosing. Those who knew this work to be in progress would also have found the Minister's promises of strong Indian participation at each stage to be suspect.

Epp did, however, offer one striking assurance. "I wish to reassure Indian leaders that it is not my intention to prejudge or pre-empt Constitutional discussions by proceeding with amendments to the act."[20] Taken to its logical conclusion, he would not proceed with major revisions to the *Indian Act* before constitutional discussions had been held. Epp went on from there to make a commitment about Indian participation in constitutional talks that went beyond the bounds of Trudeau's offer of matters "directly affecting" Native peoples:

> I am very much aware that constitutionally based questions and the constitutional review process itself are now regarded by Indian leaders in Canada as among the top priority issues facing their people today. Our recent discussions with the Prime Minister and the National Indian Brotherhood on the constitutional review process were conducted in a frank and co-operative atmosphere. They resulted in the understanding that Indian representatives would participate fully in all deliberations

> on matters included under the agenda item "Canada's Native Peoples and the Constitution." They will also be involved in other areas of constitutional discussion where there is a clear Indian interest or where the result of such discussions *could affect Indian people significantly*.[21] (Emphasis added.)

Note that this statement speaks precisely of "Indian leaders" and identifies three areas of participation: (1) the agenda item "Canada's Native Peoples and the Constitution;" and (2) where there is a clear Indian interest; and (3) where the result of . . . [constitutional] discussions could affect Indian people significantly." Who is to decide what constitutes a clear Indian interest or affect[ing] Indian people significantly? If these three criteria are to be applied at the sole discretion of the PMO and the PCO, then they are indistinguishable from the evasive and self-serving language of 19th century treaties, e.g., promises of services to be delivered "when the Queen deems wise." If, however, (2) and (3) were to be the subjects of ongoing negotiation with the representatives of those peoples whose interests were at stake, these categories represented significant advances over any previous offer.

Epp then offered to introduce revisions to the *Indian Act* "necessary to provide a legislative base for Indian people to progressively assume control over the education of their children." He cited the N.I.B. paper *Indian Control of Indian Education* and stated " . . . the future of Indian education rooted in a revised *Indian Act*, will likely see new authorities and discretions available to Indian communities, and Indian people will be able not only to operate their own schools but to pass by-laws governing how they might be run."[22] Had legislation providing for Indian control of Indian education been combined with realistic long term financial commitments, anti-discrimination provisions, a quasi-judicial land claims process and the constitutional commitments Epp attributed earlier in his statement to his Prime Minister, Epp and Clark might well have won the hearts and minds of the Indian leadership.

Warren Allmand wanted to know if Jake Epp's "new principle" might mean that he was prepared to "entertain a discussion of all items relating to Aboriginal claims, constitutional questions and so on in which the Dene have been interested and the Nunavut claim."[23] Epp agreed that, while he had been meeting with the President of the Dene Nation, Georges Erasmus, about the Dene view that these issues needed to be negotiated all together as had been accepted in the Yukon, the Government had "not decided to extend the broad range of subjects to the Dene or to Nunavut yet."[24]

Asked about the Kahnawake[25] Peacekeepers, Epp said that he had been asked to deputize them under the *RCMP Act*. He continued, "I will undertake discussions with the authorities of the Government of Québec that they be commissioned under the QPF." The Quebec Police Force wanted assurances that "in no way in that commissioning, should it take place, would they lose any jurisdiction."[26]

When Epp returned to the Committee, two sittings later, Allmand pressed on:

> . . . many Indians are being prosecuted for violating provincial hunting regulations and also for violating the Migratory Birds Convention Act. . . . Several provincial associations have asked the department and the Minister in his role as trustee to reinstate the fund which used to exist to help support defence actions in these prosecutions that are taken against Indians, where it is a conflict between treaty rights and provincial hunting regulations.[27]

Epp passed over Allmand's reference to the Minister's "role as trustee,"[28] a role which had been assiduously denied by Epp's predecessors, insisted upon by Indian leaders and which would be endorsed in *Penner* and, slightly recast as a "fiduciary duty," would be found by the Supreme Court, to be legally binding in *Guérin*.[29] Neither did he indicate that he was ready to provide protection from provincial hunting laws designed for the "sporting" industry and the Migratory Birds Convention, designed in 1912 with the help of the U.S. BIA.

All these were litmus tests about the Minister's capacity to act as much as his willingness to act. It may well have been that the complex of constraints—from his major clientele, the Priorities and Planning Committee and the provinces—tied the hands of a man who in his own mind was marching boldly down the road of good intentions.

The role of the Minister as trustee was, at that time, arising in another context. Band after band was sending to the Minister and to the Auditor General band council resolutions asking that the trust funds held for them by DIAND be audited.[30] Mismanagement extending back as far as Confederation had been alleged by as many as 75 bands. When the Deputy Auditor General responded to certain bands with a letter stating that it was beyond his authority to conduct the audits they requested and to report his findings to them without the express authorization of Parliament, Warren Allmand, a Liberal from Montreal, and Bob Holmes, a Progressive Conservative from southwestern Ontario, co-sponsored a motion mandating the Auditor General to do the requested audits.

The N.I.B. was formulating a position which would hold that breach of trust, particularly about band funds, was a chief cause of Indian poverty. If the monies owing for surrendered lands had first been paid and then well managed so that they had earned the same rates of interest that comparable trusts (funds managed by a provincial trustee for the province and for municipalities, for example) First Nations communities would not be impoverished.

On non-financial matters, DIAND would advance the argument, before the courts in *Guérin*[31] and before the Standing Committee and the Special Committee on Indian Self-Government, that the trust relationship was a mere political trust[32] and, therefore, not one that was legally binding. The political trust argument was least applicable to actual trust funds; a nominally anti-bureaucratic minister without ties to the many decades of Liberal rule might have been thought to be an ideal candidate to support a professional determination of how well these trust funds were managed. Conversely, a reluctance to take up this issue would be a signal that the Minister could not get hold of his department and that he lacked the political will to support good bookkeeping.[33]

A number of other issues were surfacing at this time quite independent of the government of the day. Mr. Allmand suggested that the regional offices of DIAND be moved onto reserve. Senior officials seemed prepared to remain perplexed and to cede the taxation issue to National Revenue. The Standing Committee proceedings are, to my knowledge, the most public discussion of this issue before it reached the Supreme Court in *Nowegijick* in 1983.[34] Like the trust funds, Indian education and hunting rights, taxation goes to the heart of the movement for self-government and the willingness of the federal government to enter into significant dialogue. Epp's expressed desire for dialogue also reminds us that the pretension of "partnership" had not yet been taken up as part of DIAND's rhetoric of prevarication.

Jake Epp responded to further questions before the Standing Committee at its sixth sitting, on November 13, 1979. Warren Allmand questioned Jake Epp about Epp's statement that he would not bring the COPE agreement before Cabinet until there had been a review of the comprehensive claims policy:

> . . . Do you not consider that there has been a legally biding agreement—only in principle, but still a legally binding agreement—between the Government of Canada and the Committee for Original Peoples Entitlement; and if that is the case, to set aside that legally

binding agreement, do you not consider it as having a very negative effect on all claims negotiations?

Mr. Epp: First of all, Mr. Allmand, as you know, it is an agreement in principle, it is not a final agreement; number one.[35]

At the following sitting, when Bill Blaikie, the NDP Member for Winnipeg-Birds Hill, pursued this question, Paul Tellier, the Assistant Deputy Minister, introduced Mr. Blaikie to the Alice-in-Wonderland nature of bureaucratic discourse:

Mr. Tellier: I do not think, Mr. Blaikie, that it would be accurate to say that the government had difficulty with the agreement in principle reached with COPE. I think basically an accurate description of the situation is, as everybody would recognize, it was legitimate for a newly elected government to take the time to review, in a systematic fashion, the claims policy.

Mr. Blaikie: My problem with that response is that if the review that is now going on, or is completed but not yet gone before Cabinet, . . . is not just a review of practical concerns but a review in principle, then you can say on the one hand that the government agrees with the COPE agreement in principle and at the same time undertake a review, unless of course that review is a review of purely practical matters. So the question remains, if you agree with the COPE agreement in principle, what are the practical concerns that are the problem?

Or, if the postponement of the signing of the COPE agreement comes about as the result of the review, then what is the question of principle involved that is under review? Do you see what I mean?

Mr. Tellier: Yes, I do, Mr. Chairman. There is an agreement in principle, but an agreement in principle does not mean that there is an agreement.

Mr. Blaikie: Oh, I have only been here a short while.[36]

The Epp-Tellier view of whether an agreement is an agreement may provide some basis for explaining the inability of the Crown to fulfill its treaty obligations or of governments to heed the words of Chief Justice Dickson and to act in the knowledge that "the honour of the Crown is at stake."

MR. DENNIS NICHOLAS (VICE-PRESIDENT, NATIONAL INDIAN BROTHERHOOD)

> We recognize that 90 per cent of the success or failure of Indian Government will come from us, the Indian people. We are here before your Committee to talk about the other 10 per cent.[40]
>
> (Dennis Nicholas to the Indian Affairs Committee, Nov. 27, 1979.)

When Dennis Nicholas addressed the Standing Committee, on November 27, 1979, he had been blessed with an embarrassment of riches he might pursue. After a brief introduction on the nature and structure of the N.I.B. for the benefit of new Members, Nicholas pulled together the many basic issues which were then current to present two basic arguments. "First, Indian government is the one alternative which still retains any degree of currency."[37] Secondly, he questioned whether Jake Epp had a decision-making capacity: "The problem today is that we need to find out just who the real Minister is."[38]

From Starblanket's and Nicholas's point of view, these two statements were inextricably intertwined. Indian government was the one alternative with any currency because the issues to which the N.I.B. was sensitizing the Standing Committee Members were not about to be addressed by either federal or provincial intervention. The focus of the Starblanket-Nicholas case for self-government was that no other institution would address the issues that committee members saw as intractable.

Nicholas's statement to the Standing Committee was the most explicit argument for self-government to that point. It built on the earlier remarks of Sanderson and Starblanket and went beyond them. At the same time, its strength, and arguably its weakness, was a reliance on pragmatic arguments for self-government.

Nicholas had picked up, even before he spoke of Indian government as the only remaining alternative, on an argument which had first been made in Dave Courchene's address to the *MacGuigan-Molgat* Committee: "our chief purpose has been to ensure that Indian people are allowed to take our proper place within Confederation."[39] Although Nicholas would not have joined Harry Daniels in claiming that his Métis people were one of "the founding peoples of Canada," he would certainly insist, as had Professor Noël Lyon, that the legitimacy of Canada depended upon Indians being welcomed into Confederation. At a time when the major non-financial political preoccupation of Canadians was the secession of Québec, emphasizing that Indian sovereignty could best be achieved within Confederation was an essential introduction to any discussion of self-government if one expected anyone in Parliament to listen.

Nicholas's argument was embedded in pragmatism. His language was also founded in *pragmatics* in that it is a studied effort to take the committee in the direction of relating his objectives to their own. This contributed to his presentation as a whole being deeply conservative. It emphasized the need for Indians to become responsible for themselves in order to identify the conditions under which that would become possible. He told the Committee that:

> Indian bands across the country, and their representative associations, will require from you the legislative authority to assume increasing responsibility for the governing of their own affairs. We will need a financial base which will have to come, in large part, from appropriations passing through this Committee and eventually from an entirely new procedure. Until the time when Indian government is firmly established we will need the co-operation of this Committee, most of all to monitor the work of the Department of Indian Affairs and to curb its excesses.[41]

Nicholas's statement is of sufficient moment to summarize the steps which he set out:

1. The request for legislative authority was not intended to concede the argument about recognition versus delegation but it discretely sidestepped that issue to focus on the need for an act of the federal Parliament supporting the authority of what were not yet being called First Nations.
2. A financial base granted by federal appropriation has, since the earliest times, been a sign that a poorer province is, indeed, part of Confederation.[42]

3. Abundant evidence had been catalogued by the N.I.B., in the preceding four or five years, to suggest that DIAND had a series of other agendas which took higher priority than meeting the needs of Indian communities. Northern Development loomed larger in officaldom than did the Indian Affairs Branch. Gaining Indian compliance with departmentally defined objectives remained the dominant way of thinking within the Branch. A significant line of advancement for DIAND officials led out of DIAND and into central agencies. Dedication to the ostensible client group was a cul-de-sac.
4. Increasingly, the theme of N.I.B. presentations to the Standing Committee was the documentation of DIAND scandals and the need for Parliament to rein in this "permanent government" of Indian affairs. This argument not only provided a role for the Standing Committee in the advancement of Indian Government, it appealed to the very heart of parliamentary democracy for it to become an ally of Indian Government, and, at the same time, opened the way to a critique of the then Minister.

THE STARBLANKET-NICHOLAS CRITIQUE OF THE CLARK-EPP MINISTRY

Starblanket was the first N.I.B. president with a strong affinity for a Canadian political party. He would have liked to have supported the Progressive Conservative party. Given Joe Clark's record in advocating adoption of the N.I.B. position paper on Aboriginal rights during a Liberal minority Parliament, all that stood in the way of consummating this natural alliance was a close scrutiny of the Clark Government in its first months in office.

Nicholas bridged his comments on "Indian Government" and his critique of Epp's early ministry by considering the prospect of participating in an executive committee within the department:

> There is a potential for some success in participating in the executive planning committees of the department, provided the body is actually engaged in real and important work. Our experience in attending those meetings so far is something else. . . . Our general assembly in Whitehorse, in 1976 passed a resolution declaring that all policy development relating to the programs of Indian Affairs be taken over by the proper representatives of the Indian people, and that is the Indian associations across Canada.[43]

This paragraph integrates the mandate Nicholas and Starblanket received at their election with a critique of departmental committees calculated to appeal to MPs.

The system of cabinet committees headed by super-ministers then known as Ministers of State (a term now ironically reserved to refer to "junior ministers") commonly associated with the Trudeau Government but which, in fact, first surfaced with the formation of the Clark Government.[44] This was the first of a number of indications that the Minister of Indian Affairs had a small and decreasing ambit for policy making; it was already well known that the ground within that ambit was largely determined by the Minister's dependence on senior civil servants who, in DIAND, had few pretences of neutrality.

Nicholas raised this issue for the Committee's consideration:

> Hon. members who were here on May 9, 1978, five days after our last appearances, may recall the Minister of that day replying to our protests against funding cutbacks by saying he did not like our strident tones. The present Minister should have no such difficulty. He has promised that he would make his department into a support body for Indian people. If he can convince his Cabinet colleagues that his own humane approach is also good politics, and if he can get the two super-ministers to whom he answers to talk with each other, then he should have no difficulty at all with that concept.
>
> . . . We hope that your inquiries, and the Minister's own initiative, will steadily establish our presence in policy development of Indian Affairs as a matter of right, not as a matter of occasional courtesy.
>
> . . .
>
> The problem today is that we need to find out just who the real minister is. The hon. (sic) Jake Epp issues press releases announcing new policies without consultation with Indian representatives, without specifics and without answers to this Committee. On the other hand, as far as we can tell, he is the only departmental minister who answers to two different inner-Cabinet ministers. . . .
>
> Mr. Epp is a charming gentleman. I have it on good authority that his executive assistant, Mr. Clark's biographer, is no less charming. But, in suggesting that we resume the practice of regular, formal meetings, we have to say that the success of these meetings will depend on having present the ministers who really make the decisions.[45]

Nicholas's comments would later prove to have been as prophetic as they were caustic. As the core members of the Standing Committee became increasingly pro-active, the senior officials of DIAND, with a few notable exceptions, became increasingly resistant. This trend reached its full flower, three years later, in the systematic campaign to undermine the work of the Penner Committee once it became clear that that Committee was not interested in following the agenda laid out by departmental officials. [46]

What was important for the moment was the ability and the willingness of the N.I.B. to present the Standing Committee with a critique not so much of Jake Epp as of a new cabinet system in which the actual role of the Minister of Indian Affairs was cast into doubt. This was a critique which had as much significance for the Committee's role as for the N.I.B. . Whatever the intentions of the PCO officials who designed the system or of the prime ministers who adopted it, no Minister of State for Social Development, as far as I am aware, ever testified before a Standing Committee of either House.

The notion that a minister intent upon making DIAND into a support body for Indian communities, and upon rewriting Indian law in Canada to maximize Indian participation could actually influence the centres of power both in Cabinet and in the department has now been rejected by two parliamentary inquiries and a royal commission Even if Epp had had all the right ideas and pursued them diligently, the formulating of fundamental policy had been moved into the hands of the Ministries of State. If Epp could garner no more influence than Warren Allmand had managed to accumulate in his time as Minister, then some wholly different approach was needed.

The most credible approach would be one which met a set of criteria which had the support of Indian organizations and which had, before 1979, been recommended in several Parliamentary committee reports. Such an approach would include the following: (1) reducing the level of Indian dependency upon government (2) extricating the federal government from the Indian business; (3) ridding the government of a department nobody wanted to defend; (4) not bringing provinces into a role at which they were unlikely to succeed and in which they would not be welcomed by the client group; and, (5) effecting a modest redistribution of wealth through a reallocation of existing resources while emphasizing the need for self-sufficiency. Starblanket's and Nicholas's arguments for bringing "Indian people into Confederation" could certainly be characterized as arguments which were "Made in Canada."

Indeed, Nicholas offered to come back in the spring and respond to the Blue Book, i.e., the Estimates,[48] with a "Red Book" which would demonstrate how the same moneys might be put to better use. [49] For the moment, Nicholas advanced an argument which combined equity,[50] i.e., an appeal to fairness and conscience, with pragmatism, i.e., how much water is required to float the boat:

> First, there is a need for a description of the per capita amounts per citizen in Canada and the amounts spent in Indian communities by the federal government. We are sure that Indian people are not receiving a handout; we are receiving far below the national average.
>
> Secondly, when you consider that a great deal of the moneys voted by the Committee are [destined for] maintenance of buildings in Hull . . . we suggest that the estimate of money actually reaching Indian people be considered as about half of the amounts you are actually asked to approve.
>
> Thirdly, we suggest that a comparison of an equalization formula for funding Indian communities to the amounts now being voted by the Committee should show that even if 100 per cent of the moneys you appropriate reached us we would be far below the national average.
>
> Fourthly, Indian communities must gain control of their own natural resources, not to retard development but to ensure that development is carried on in ways that actually benefit our people and, most of all, to ensure that the resources on our land and beneath our land are used for the development of the people for whom that land has been set aside and reserved.[51]

It is noteworthy that Nicholas's first three principles relate to moneys voted by the Standing Committee and, ultimately, by Parliament for the ostensible benefit of Indian communities while the fourth is an argument for access to natural resources. Although Nicholas was almost certainly unaware of the argument made by Mr. Justice Strong[52] almost 100 years earlier, the basic notion that control of natural resources was the most natural, most feasible and most Canadian way of reducing dependency was apparent to anyone who deeply asked the same questions.

Nicholas ended his remarks by responding to the question which he said had been raised by "one honourable Member of this Committee . . . 'When is it all going to end?'" [53] First, he reminded the Committee that the first claim was submitted by the Nootka chiefs on the occasion of Lord Dufferin's visit with them in 1885. "We, too, would like to ask, 'When it is all going to end'?"[54] Secondly, he reminded the

Committee that its own predecessor had adopted the N.I.B. definition of Aboriginal rights on a motion of Joe Clark in 1973. "This Committee could do no finer service to the Indian people of Canada or to its own record than to help the Right Honourable Joseph Clark to implement that report."[55]

Nicholas then asked for the committee's co-operation in achieving four goals:

> 1. [E]ntrenching the recognition and active protection of Indian rights, both treaty and aboriginal into the *British North America Act*[56] and its successor.
> 2. The burying of White Paper policies of the previous government.
> 3. The dismantling of those agencies which perpetuate those policies in their daily operations.
> 4. Lastly, returning control of Indian life to the Indian people of Canada."[57]

Several features of Nicholas's terminology are interesting in retrospect. Foremost is that he consistently used the term "Indian Government"; the term "self-government" did not appear in his remarks. Indian Government was the term used at the National Indian Government Development Conference in the spring of 1979. The more explicit term does not appear to have come into the public rhetoric of Indian leaders until the founding of the Assembly of First Nations. Neither was the term "autonomy" used, although that was what was at the heart of the N.I.B.'s advocacy.

Secondly, Nicholas spoke consistently of "Indian people." He did not refer to the severalty of the different Indian nations. This was certainly not because the question had not arisen; it appears that he simply did not find an advantage in raising it to the audience he was addressing at that time.

Thirdly, although he did not distinguish between recognition and delegation in discussing the need for legislative authority, in his conclusion he quite explicitly called for constitutional provisions "entrenching the recognition" of Aboriginal and treaty rights.

THE RESPONSE OF NICHOLAS'S PARLIAMENTARY AUDIENCE

Partly as a result of Nicholas's testimony, the Committee adopted a report to the House regarding funding of First Nations communities and organizations. The established practice at that time did not contemplate committees submitting detailed reports from their study of departmental estimates. The decision to stretch the rules in this way arose when Keith Penner made a statement arguing the need for such a report and the inappropriateness of the rules. Frank Oberle, speaking from the chair, agreed with Penner.[58]

This development is noteworthy for the emergence of the vocabulary of self-government for two reasons. First, it furthered the relationship between the Standing Committee and the Indian organizations, although it may also have distanced the Committee from the Government. It certainly established the *bona fides* of the Committee as a centre of inquiry into First Nations relations with significant independence from the Government.

Secondly, the report is important for its all-party critique of DIAND for "effectively freezing funding of economic development initiatives through the Indian Economic Development Fund, by temporarily transferring the power of decision making from the regional offices to the Assistant Deputy Minister in Ottawa, and by making funds available only on an urgent basis."[59] This direction was exactly counter to the need for long term, reliable and stable funding needed for reserve communities to become increasingly self-sufficient.

Thirdly, the Report reminds us that there were frequent spending restraints imposed during this period, contrary to later journalistic recollections.[60]

N.I.B. discussions of Indian education had used the term "Indian Control" since the 1972 paper discussed earlier in this chapter. The offer by Paul Tellier, the Deputy Minister of DIAND, of a place for "Indian influence" offered a valuable insight into the direction in which his Department wanted to move both with respect to education and more generally.

> The orientation of the department is to—well, there is a trend, a movement, towards band-managed schools. The proportion . . . number of schools managed by bands is increasing and has increased very significantly over the last 10 years.
>
> About the curriculum, I would ask the newly appointed Assistant Deputy Minister, Mr. Nicholson, to answer . . . But basically, the philosophy, if I can call it that, of the department in federal or band-managed schools is to provide as many opportunities as possible to the local community to influence the curriculum, especially with the Indian culture in these schools.[61]

This statement quite explicitly sets out the department's alternative to Indian autonomy. The band would *manage* the school on behalf of the Department, much as local school boards manage schools for the Ministry of Education in Ontario. Tellier undoubtedly saw his administration as munificent in its willingness *to allow* local communities *to influence* the curriculum. The N.I.B., having just set out its agenda for Indian Government in the most explicit terms to date, can only have enjoyed the righteous indignation that Tellier's condescension ignited in the Committee.

Tellier's contribution to the evolution of the vocabulary of First Nations self-government was to demonstrate what Indian Government was not. This is quite different from prevarication, though if his audience were not listening they might miss the subtle but essential difference. What distinguishes Tellier's negating vocabulary from one of actual prevarication is that, upon a *careful* listening, and certainly, upon a *close* reading, his intentions were quite explicit. He was not borrowing a vocabulary of autonomy and reading it down or investing it with meanings it did not have elsewhere. He was using a managerial vocabulary and meant by it pretty much what he said. His intention *to allow influence* was a clear indication that he intended not to allow actual authority, as Nicholas had requested, autonomy or power.

The devil in the detail of Epp's statement to the first meeting of the Standing Committee in the 31st Parliament about strong Indian participation, was made evident in Tellier's description of managerial influence.

PATRIATION: THE HAYS-JOYAL JOINT COMMITTEE ON THE CONSTITUTION

On February 18, 1980 Pierre Trudeau won a substantial majority in the election following the vote of non-confidence in Joe Clark engineered for Trudeau by Alan MacEachen.[62] Among the notable features of this election was Trudeau's agreement with his largely Toronto based advisors not to emphasize constitutional issues. On the other hand, he had won the largest majority he had ever held: in a House of 281 seats, the Liberals won 146 seats (from 44% of the popular vote) compared to 103 seats held by Clark's Progressive Conservatives with 33% of the popular vote and 32 New Democrats elected by 20% of the popular vote. Trudeau later said that he took up the reins of office the second time with a conscious need to focus on those few objectives which were essential to him and to subordinate everything else to those objectives.[63]

On May 21, 1980, the day after the federalist forces won the Québec referendum, Trudeau "rose in the House of Commons to announce that he intended to move immediately to keep his promise to patriate and renew the Canadian Constitution. Jean Chrétien was dispatched that very night to the provincial capitals to inform the premiers of his plans to break the country's constitutional impasse."[64]

Although the patriation debate played a major role in the public emergence of the vocabulary of self-government, First Nations' Aboriginal and treaty rights were quite peripheral to patriation. Trudeau had conceived of patriation as part of a larger programme which would address those concerns of Québec that he considered legitimate while drawing Québec away from the corrupt and dictatorial tendencies associated with the late Premier Maurice Duplessis. The patriation resolution as he first introduced it, like all his earlier proposals since the Victoria Charter had no reference to the recognition of Aboriginal or treaty rights.

Trudeau had come to Ottawa to work in the Privy Council Office in 1949 under Gordon Robertson, a civil servant who appears to have become something of a mentor. In the same year, Sen. Arthur Roebuck, (Liberal, Toronto-Trinity) introduced a resolution to amend the *British North America Act* by adding a *Canadian Bill of Human Rights and Fundamental Freedoms*.[65] Roebuck was responding[66] to a report of a Joint Committee of the previous session on the Implementation of the *UN Declaration of Human Rights* which had rejected a a constitutionally entrenched *Charter of Rights*. Although none of the secondary sources relate Robertson's and Trudeau's work in the Privy Council Office to either the 1948 Joint Committee or to Roebuck's proposal for an entrenched *Bill of Rights*, neither one could have been wholly unaware of the other, particularly since Robertson assigned Trudeau the task of considering what would be required to effect a patriation of the *British North America Act*.[67] Indeed, Roebuck epitomized the reform Liberal tradition Trudeau would later emulate.

Trudeau's 1980 agenda was a good deal more complex than a single-minded focus on patriation with a charter of rights. People who attach his name to a view that considers that the *Charter* is solely about individual rights, as well as misconstruing the nature of both rights and charters, also forget that the Trudeau Government proceeded directly from the patriation debate to an equally all-consuming debate on the National Energy Program centred on the *Canada Lands Act*. Although this agenda extends beyond both the scope and the period of our inquiry, it is important for us to keep in mind that there was a social and economic agenda founded on a strong central government paralleling the constitutional agenda. To understand that moment in history we must recall that Canada then had a government which held a three-fold agenda which might have provided a much-enhanced ability both to redistribute wealth domestically and to afford a measure of protection in dealings with powerful neighbours.

It will, I think, prove to be one of the tragedies of this program that the Trudeau Government failed to include the First Nations, as they were starting to call themselves, in any of part of its program. This section is necessarily limited to an examination of the Proceedings of the Joint Committee on the Constitution co-chaired by Serge Joyal (Liberal, Hochelaga-Maisonneuve) and Senator Harry Hays (Liberal, Calgary South) to which was referred the patriation resolution sponsored by Prime Minister Pierre Elliott Trudeau and shepherded through Parliament by Jean Chrétien.

Although history cannot answer the "What might have been" type of questions, neither can it fail to raise them. We cannot properly understand how the patriation process contributed to the focus on entrenching self-government in the Constitution unless we appreciate how overlooked and excluded Indian leaders felt in the face of the many previous expressions of good will both by Trudeau and by Clark. Had the aspirations of the First Nations been seriously included both in the patriation resolution and in the *Canada Lands Act*, they might possibly have become firm allies of the federal government. The Government chose not to seek such an alliance.

Indians were not seen as highly desirable allies: many did not vote; the N.I.B. and its affiliates did not see their role as delivering the vote; large amounts of residual racism in the country made it desirable to be seen with Indians on ceremonial occasions but not to be too closely associated with them. Similarly, the interests which are often described as the primary clients of DIAND— the resource developers and their ideological allies— might be further offended if the evils of the NEP were compounded by recognizing an Indian interest in Canada Lands.

Less obvious, but possibly more cogent, are several much neglected reasons as to why Indians might be desirable allies. Trudeau's vision, embodied in each of his major later projects, required more than anything else, a strong central government with the legislative capacity to protect individual and collective rights from unwarranted intrusion, to ensure a modicum of redistribution of wealth both for the relief of personal poverty and to promote a greater regional equality. Every Indian or First Nation witness emphasized the need for a nation-to-nation relationship with a Canadian government to assist First Nations in regaining an adequate land base, in gaining effective legal and legislative authority to provide for their lands and their people with a sufficient financial and fiscal base to give meaning to the legislative authority. No constituency in Canada had a greater need for a strong, central government than the First Nations. And every Indian speaker who testified during this period emphasized, as Dennis Nicholas had before the Standing Committee, that their goal was for their nations to take their proper place *within Confederation.*

Likewise, witnessing the patriation process and playing some part in its final outcome convinced some Indian leaders to focus their limited energies on gaining a more complete entrenchment of the right to self-government in the Constitution and to postpone the legislated forms of self-government on which the Penner Report would later focus. Penner, himself, later said that he did not campaign with his full energies for the implementation of his report because he chose to support the expressed direction of the First Nations leadership.[68]

On October 2, 1980, Prime Minister Trudeau went on national television to announce that he would proceed to introduce a resolution for the patriation of the Canadian Constitution, which would include a *Charter of Rights*, and an amending formula based somewhat on the *Victoria Charter*. On October 23, largely in response to opposition demands for committee hearings, the resolution was referred to a Joint Committee.

The saga of patriation has been told elsewhere. This brief review is limited to an overview of the Joint Committee's contribution to the public emergence of the vocabulary of self-government. For reasons perhaps unique to the process of constitutional amendment, parties favouring as well as parties opposing the concept favoured full and public hearings as well as a reference to the Supreme Court. The lengthiness of the process greatly enhanced the opportunity for Indian participation and for the evolution of the First Nations rhetoric through this period.

THE INDIAN AFFAIRS COMMITTEE IN THE 32ND PARLIAMENT

The Standing Committee on Indian Affairs and Northern Development in the 32nd Parliament had much the same membership as it had had during the previous Parliament under the chairmanship of Frank Oberle. Dr. Bob Holmes, the long time senior Conservative critic on the Committee, had chosen not to seek re-election. Oberle achieved seniority over some less enthusiastic Conservative Members on the Committee, by reason of being the Committee's past chairman. The other key Conservative was Dr. Lorne Greenaway (PC, Cariboo-Chilcotin) a veterinarian whose riding bordered on Oberle's in the northern interior of B.C. Jim Manly, newly elected NDP Member from Nanaimo-Cowichan-the Islands (the last seat held by T.C. Douglas) combined a capacity for oratory with a personal diligence which allowed him to bond with the longer serving core members: Warren Allmand, Frank Oberle, Keith Penner, Stan Schellenberger (PC,

Wetaskiwin). Also on the Committee were Peter Ittinuar (NDP, Nunatsiaq), René Gingras, (Liberal, Abitibi) and Vice Chairman, Ray Chénier (Liberal, Timmins-Chapleau) the Parliamentary Secretary, Jack Shields (PC, Athabasca, Alberta), and Ian Watson (Liberal, Laprairie, Québec).

The proceedings of the first (and only) session of the Thirty-Second Parliament became unique in a number of respects. The Government's determination to complete the patriation process while carrying on with the rest of their legislative program on which piecemeal progress had been made while the *Canada Act* resolution was before the Joyal-Hays Committee resulted in a single session extending over a three year period.

One result was that the Standing Committee sat for several months before the Joint Committee received its mandate, continued to sit throughout the year and a half that the Joint Committee was sitting and continued for almost another year and a half after patriation. In fact, the Sub-committee on Indian Women and the *Indian Act* on Indian Self-Government, whose work extended from August, 1982 until November, 1983, was part of the same session as the patriation debate. So also was the 1983 First Ministers' Conference for which the Penner Committee suspended its work.

Topically, the work of the Standing Committee during this period fell into three major categories:

(1) The Annual Estimates gave rise to hearings on the working of the department and provided an opportunity for MPs representing Indian constituents to raise issues with departmental officials and with the Minister;
(2) During the earlier part of this four year session, the Standing Committee continued to conduct special hearings in the course of studying the annual Estimates;
(3) a number of significant bills including the *Fort Nelson Indian Minerals Revenue Sharing Act*, and the *Indian Oil and Gas Act* came before the Committee and gave rise to testimony from Indian leaders on both (or several) sides of each bill.

In addition, there was a considerable overlap in membership between the Standing Committee and the Joyal-Hays Committee. Members, such as Warren Allmand, who sat on both Committees had a unique opportunity to integrate their own thinking on the possibilities for protecting Indian interests by entrenching them in the Constitution and the need for collateral legislation. They also often had the opportunity to hear the same Indian speakers address both committees on closely related topics.

JOHN MUNRO, MINISTER OF INDIAN AFFAIRS AND NORTHERN DEVELOPMENT

This section examines proceedings of the Standing Committee during the first two years of the 32nd Parliament in each of the three fields described above and selected for their significance for the evolution of the vocabulary of self-government. Only such additional material is offered as will provide essential background.

The Standing Committee began its proceedings in the 32nd Parliament, on May 8, 1980, with a statement from the new Minister, John C. Munro. Munro was accompanied by most of his senior officials including: his Deputy Minister, Paul Tellier, four assistant deputy ministers, R.J. Fournier (Finance and Professional Services) and J.D. Nicholson (Indian and Inuit Affairs Program), E.M.R. Cotterill (Northern Affairs), Huguette Labelle (Corporate Policy), as well as G.N. Faulkner, the Executive Director of the Office of Native Claims, Raymond Good, the Minister's Special Assistant, Indian Affairs, and Dan Brant, Munro's Executive Assistant.

John Munro was the most senior minister to be appointed to the Indian Affairs and Northern Development portfolio in recent decades. He was also the most colourful and the most controversial. Newspaper stories about the way in which he took care of his constituents had resulted in allegations of libel or slander typically settled in his favour. His abilities as a political negotiator had been established when he had been Minister of Labour from 1972 to 1978. From 1968 to 1972, Munro had been Minister of National Health and Welfare, a portfolio which included the Indian Health Service at a time when there was much discussion about the transfer of Indian health to the provinces.

Munro was, by all accounts, a "politicians' minister." At the same time that he was eager to make deals he was also filled with ambition, not simply to advance himself but also to fulfill an agenda which would put him strongly into the reform camp of the Liberal party (in the days when "reform" still referred to progressive tendencies). During Munro's four years in office there were frequent occasions when his various zeals conflicted with one another. Outcroppings of these conflicts can be seen in conflicts with the Standing Committee, well reported confrontations with his senior officials and heated exchanges with the Executive Council of the N.I.B. These events can all be misunderstood unless Munro is appreciated as a Minister who was willing to be deeply engaged with each of the communities making demands on his office. He was also a Minister who was senior enough and persuasive enough to be remarkably successful in selling his department's program to the two Cabinet committees on which he sat—Social Development (for Indian Affairs) and Economic Development (for Northern Development) as well as to the Priorities and Planning Committee.

MUNRO'S FIRST ADDRESS TO THE STANDING COMMITTEE

> Today, this government, and my department in particular, is seeking to achieve a new and contemporary expression of the unique status of Indian and Inuit people within Canada and of their distinctive relationship with the federal government.[69]

It is instructive to return to the opening statements of Munro and Epp to see how much these statements have in common. In particular, both emphasized the dual themes of "constitutional renewal" and the need for a renewed relationship, either by "participation" (Epp) or by "effective control" (Munro). Indeed, both speeches might be said to read somewhat like "State of the Indian" speeches.

Munro's speech is best distinguished from Epp's first, by seeing them both within this common framework and, secondly, by considering the energy and the credibility that each Minister brought not just to the job as a whole but more particularly to these two themes which relate quite explicitly to First Nations' autonomy:

> These commitments share a common goal: to set the stage for the exercise of effective control by Indian and Inuit people and by all Northerners over the things that most concern these special groups of Canadians.
>
> Indian people in Canada wish to see their special position in Canadian society and in Canadian history, and their special relationship with the federal government, expressed in new and more meaningful ways. This the government fully supports—and I would like to put on record here, Mr. Chairman, what that commitment means in terms of my portfolio.[70]

Munro went farther than Epp insofar as he spoke of "control." It would, however, soon become clear that his officials were handing him essentially the same text that they had given Epp. The unacceptable nature of the *Optional Indian Band Government Legislation* which they were known to be drafting (without Indian participation) remained unacceptable to the N.I.B.

At his first briefing, Tellier had told Munro that he would be the minister to bring in a new *Indian Act*.[71] Within the month of his appointment, Tellier had Munro go to Cabinet with a memorandum requesting approval in principle to develop the legislation that would become known as *Optional Indian Band Government Legislation*. Munro's brief made use of the rhetoric of self-government while calling for modest grants of devolution to band councils.[72]

Soon after his appointment, but not until he had been well briefed by Paul Tellier, Munro had set about meeting with Indian leaders across the country, initially on their own home ground. In that respect, he might have been better placed than any previous minister to say what the "Indian people in Canada wish to see." Whether or not "effective control" was a turn of phrase intended to wave back to the people he had been visiting, or whether it was intended to point to the long, hard road to deliver something that had long eluded them, his willingness to speak in such bold terms caught the imagination of much of the Indian leadership. Although Munro would come under heavy criticism, nobody came before the Standing Committee and asked the Committee to identify "the real Minister of Indian Affairs" as Dennis Nicholas had with Jake Epp. Indeed, Munro's own statement "the government fully supports . . . what that commitment means in terms of my portfolio" could be seen to substantially forestall just such a question.

The warmth of Munro's statements suggesting that Indians were about to be part of a renewed federation probably served to foster suspicion of the government amongst First Nations leaders:

> Constitutional renewal has become more immediate in recent days. For some time now Indian leaders have pressed their case to be part of a renewed federation. Fortunately, the groundwork has been laid for Indian involvement in this process. The nature of Indian involvement was reaffirmed by the Prime Minister in his remarks to the National Chiefs and Elders Conference here in Ottawa on April 29 As the Prime Minister said, Native people will be involved with the federal and provincial governments in the discussion of constitutional changes which *directly affect them*.[73]
>
> (Emphasis added)

The emphasized clause ending this paragraph would, in itself, have been sufficient to sound the alarms among cautious listeners. This was the same qualifier that had caused deep offense when it was used by Epp and by Trudeau ministers before the Clark interregnum. Mark MacGuigan had managed to alienate Indian leaders from the work of his second committee by saying that they were not "directly affected" by the Constitution.

MPs on the Standing Committee had been kept abreast of ministerial correspondence with the N.I.B. and its affiliates. The Prime Minister's letter to which Munro referred became a source of much discussion before the Hays-Joyal Committee on the constitutuion.[74]

Munro's statement that "reform of the *Indian Act* by way of enabling legislation" is "complementary to constitutional renewal and holding similar promise for the fulfillment of Indian aspirations" resonates with the statement given to the Standing Committee the year before by Jake Epp. The term "enabling legislation" clearly refers to the *Optional Indian Band Government Legislation (OIBGL)* of which the Standing Committee would hear a great deal from Indian witnesses, focussed primarily on the failure of DIAND to include them in the process.[75]

> My objective is to find some consensus on those areas of the act in need of revising now. Such revisions would allow the transfer to Indian bands of authority and responsibilities now exercised by myself under the act, while maintaining and strengthening the special relationship between the federal government and the Indian people. [76]

The objective of finding "some consensus" would suggest far reaching discussions, studies and negotiations. Brotherhood leaders had not, however, received any indication of such a courtship. Neither was such a claim entirely consistent with the Prime Minister's continued use of evasive language. The devolution Munro was proposing may not have been very far reaching. It, did, however, suppose that the *Indian Act* was capable of revision and that only a few sections were "in need of revising now," a view which would not survive *Penner*. Munro was being quite forthright in one respect: he was prepared to discuss delegation to the bands of tasks held by the Minister under the existing *Indian Act*. This delegation was the very sort of revision the N.I.B. had already rejected, knowing this rejection had led DIAND to avoid consultation.

The objective of finding "some consensus" also obscured the source of the conflict. Indian leaders at that time were concentrating increasingly on self-government. Within that context, there was widespread agreement on the legislative changes they wanted. These were much the same changes that had been sought since the Andras hearings and before.

Munro raised the ante somewhat as he carried on:

> Indian communities should be given more responsibility over activities that occur on their lands.
>
> Control should be shifted from the Department of Indian Affairs to the level of the community where it belongs. [77]

"Responsibility" and "control," in this context, are ambiguous terms. To whom is a community to become responsible? A band council which was well and truly empowered would be responsible to the community; an empowered community is surely responsible to itself. Is the same council also responsible to the Minister and, through him, to the Canadian Parliament? Does a demand for an elected council to be responsible to two different, and often opposing bodies represent a conflict of interest?

An examination of the working documents of the department, of Munro's discussion of these proposals before the Self-Government Subcommittee, or the Department's handiwork in the eventual drafting of the *Self-Government Recognition Bill*, C-52 in the spring of 1984, suggest nothing which might, in other parallel contexts, be construed as a ceding of actual control.

There is every indication that the Minister's statement was calculated to persuade the least knowledgeable elements of his audience that he had consulted with the Indian leadership and was about to act on their advice. This is a feel-good speech that works better if not too much is asked about its foundations:

> These include the strengthening of the special status of Indian people as *the first citizens of Canada*; recognition of the form of Indian government necessary for the self-reliance of Indian people; a modern definition of Indian land management; the legislative implementation of the mutually adopted policy of "Indian Control of Indian Education;" and the updating or elimination of sections of the *Indian Act* which are no longer relevant to Indian people today.[78] (Emphasis added.)

What can a Minister mean when he describes "Indian people as the first citizens"? Does this statement have a plain sense meaning? Does he suppose that they were the first people to have Canadian citizenship? (The first Canada *Citizenship Act* was passed in 1947 but Indians did not acquire a right to vote until 1961.) Or, that citizenship in an Indian nation brings with it Canadian citizenship? (A significant number of persons are "entitled to be registered under the *Indian Act* but do not have Canadian citizenship.) Or, that Indians were now about to acquire, a special status, one that is a sort of "first among equals" of Canadian citizenship? (But Trudeau's *White Paper* proposed to abolish special status. Only the need to gain the support of other parties led to the protection of Aboriginal and treaty rights in the *Constitution Act, 1982*.) Whom did Munro suppose that he was kidding?

In Munro's favour, it must be said that the position that he outlined in this speech differs radically from that of ministers before and after him. Faulkner's objection to the "rigid assertion of rights" re-surfaced some years later but it is not to be found in Munro's speech. Munro favours "a modern definition of Indian land management" at the same time that he calls for "recognition of the *forms of Indian government necessary" for self-reliance*, a concept that does not occur in any speech of any other minister. When this is coupled with his revival of "the mutually adopted policy of 'Indian Control of Indian Education'" Munro leaves an impression that Indians are no less entitled to assert their rights as individuals and as communities than are other groups in Canada.

How seriously Munro took his own remarks, or whether his officials intended to backwater on them from the start, is less important for our purposes than the legitimacy that he lent these ideas.

Munro included a statement on ending discrimination under 12(1)(b) which was similarly calculated to please everyone who did not examine it too closely. He would end "this type of discrimination in a manner which is acceptable to the Indian people as well as to Canadians generally." Perhaps he hoped to reach an easier accommodation with the next N.I.B. administration than had been possible with Noel Starblanket. Munro gave no indication that ending discrimination necessarily required measures to establish equity.

Lastly, Munro spoke of comprehensive land claims, in the settlement of which, he said, "the government is seeking nothing less than to provide the foundations for a new and equitable relationship between native and non-native Northerners." We need only wonder that such a self-evident principle had not resulted in a different quality of negotiation if not an actual agreement. We might also ask why DIAND continued to instruct its negotiators not to discuss issues of self-government or "public government" with the Dene but to restrict negotiations only to land claims.[79]

THE STANDING COMMITTEE'S RESPONSE TO MUNRO

Warren Allmand's urging of John Munro to help the Indian leadership to feel more secure with the constitutional process resonates in a number of areas. It particularly resonates with the issue of trust for the simple reason that ministers could not come to terms with the idea that trust between their office and the Indian leadership had to be earned. The issue of feeling secure in the constitutional process would be discussed in just those terms by the Inuit Committee on National Issues, seven months later, with specific reference to the same issues discussed before the Standing Committee by Munro and his departmental officials.

Munro was questioned on what the *Proceedings* index described as "Native people role/consultations." He reiterated that they "would be involved directly in the process . . . at the table with respect to matters directly concerning them."[80] Leaving the interpretation of that phrase to the Prime Minister seems implicit in the lack of other definition. The lack of satisfactory definition would become a matter for repeated representations, indeed, for something close to a common front before the Hays-Joyal Committee by the national Aboriginal organizations. [81]

Warren Allmand described how Pierre Trudeau had risen in the House the day after the 1980 referendum and had said that "he hoped that he would have some process in place before the summer adjournment for constitutional discussion and he sent Mr. Chrétien on the road immediately." Allmand suggested to Munro that

> Native people would feel more secure with respect to these discussions if your words, as Minister, that the role would have a wider ambit, was in fact to take place, and if somebody approaches them within the next few days—because I do not think anybody expected that the structure for constitutional discussion would be going so quickly.[82]

There is no indication that Munro had the authority to do what Allmand suggested. Indeed, the difficulty of meeting with the proper ministers would be so exacerbated that it became a subject of continuing discussion before the Hays-Joyal Committee.

Munro responded to questions about comprehensive land claims with a statement that he hoped to avoid "the agonies that were involved on the part of everybody, including yourselves, with respect to the negotiation of COPE, of the James Bay Agreement." He then went into a discussion of the difficulties of pulling multiple government departments into line on an agreement which touched each of their respective responsibilities. He concluded that he was determined that his negotiator would have a wider mandate than had previous negotiations.[83]

FOLLOW-UP TO MUNRO'S APPEARANCE: THE SENIOR OFFICIALS

Tellier and several of the assistant deputy ministers appeared at the second sitting of the Standing Committee, on May 27, 1980, five days after Munro had completed his two-day appearance. (It is quite normal for senior officials to follow up on a minister's appearance before a parliamentary committee to parse the broad ministerial statement and to give an administrative view of a political position which they themselves had a major role in crafting.

In principle, the officials' statements would be more descriptive in nature and would focus on the past and present activities of their respective branches. A more sophisticated theory reckons that, in practice, their description of the present is an assessment of the health, well-being or soundness of their programs. The standard administrative measure of programs is how well they meet policy objectives set out in the program's original mandate.

Nowhere is this overlap between descriptive statements and policy objectives more apparent than in reviewing the Standing Committee's examination of the trust accounts problem within DIAND. Indeed, this issue runs through accounting, treaty obligations, legal principles and other arenas. What is important for our purposes is the direct connection between trust issues and self-government: the nature of a properly managed trust account is well understood. The *Oxford Companion to Law* begins its discussion of "Trust" with a one sentence definition which touches on all the essential elements:

> An arrangement for the holding and administration of property under which property or legal rights are vested by the owner of the property or rights (truster) in a person or persons (trustees) which they are then to hold or to exercise for or on behalf of another (*cestui que trust* or beneficiary), or others, or for the accomplishment of a particular purpose or purposes. The essence of the concept is the separation of legal and beneficial ownership, the property being legally vested in one or more trustees but in equity held for and belonging to others. The obligations involved are equitable and enforceable only in a court of equity.[84]

The failure to keep and maintain records is itself a major breach of trust. Mr. Justice Dickson, as he then was, found, in *Guérin*,[85] that the Crown, in its management of Indian lands and other assets has an enforceable fiduciary obligation that is "trust-like in character."[86] The Court roundly rejected the Crown's pretension that trust language in an Indian context does not mean what it means elsewhere, i.e., that the Crown's obligations are "merely political,"[87] and that it is not enforceable.

This definition is not different from what Indian leaders were telling the Standing Committee needed to be the understanding of the Crown's responsibility for their trust funds, as well as for their bands' other assets.[88] Warren Allmand and Bob Holmes co-sponsored a motion in the previous Parliament, described earlier, directing that an audit be done of the trust accounts of those band councils which requested an audit of their accounts.

> **Mr. Allmand:** On the trust accounts, Mr. Deputy Minister, in the last Parliament we unanimously passed a resolution in the House of Commons to have the Auditor General audit those trust accounts, which would have been the first audit by the Auditor General in the history of those accounts. . . . Could you tell the committee whether in fact any of that auditing by the Auditor General's department has started.
>
> **Mr. Tellier:** Mr. Chairman, I can tell Mr. Allmand that his motion adopted by the House of Commons, has generated a lot of work for both our people in the department and in the office of the Auditor General. No, Mr. Chairman, the work is not on the way. The reason is that . . .
>
> **Mr. Allmand:** I am a bit confused. You said at first, it has generated a lot of work, and now you tell me the work is . . .
>
> **Mr. Tellier:** Yes, let me explain, Mr. Allmand. Perhaps I should state at the outset in the most unequivocal manner that I surely do not want to speak on behalf of the Auditor General who is an officer of Parliament, but there is no reservation whatsoever in the Office of the Auditor General or in the Department of Indian Affairs, in having each and every one of these accounts fully audited. The question is, is it feasible, and if so, how. It is a very difficult technical problem because first of all, a great many of them were audited we have discovered only until 1942.[89]

The admission that 1,100 accounts estimated at 180 million dollars (after many years in the hands of Indian Affairs) had not been audited since 1942 would, in any other trust context, be an admission of a most gross breach of trust. In a First Nations-Crown context, it became an explanation as to why the audit should not proceed and, from there, to the defense that these were not really trust accounts in the true sense of the term.[90]

Warren Allmand raised an issue which had not been raised previously. He asked why it would not be "possible under the *Indian Act* to set up a trust account on behalf of the band in a chartered bank, still maintain the ministerial responsibility for the investment of that fund while at the same time allowing that bank . . . to invest those funds at a reasonable rate of interest?"[91] At a time when short term deposits were yielding 14 to 15%, the federal government was paying closer to 6% on those funds they were able to identify, representing a loss to Indian bands, according to the chiefs with whom Allmand was corresponding, of $10 million a year. Later, more professional calculations suggest that the loss sustained by these trust accounts, as a result of federal policy, was close to $16.2 million.

THE DEPARTMENT . . . AS TRUSTEE FOR INDIAN INTERESTS

The trust question came to the fore in the seventh sitting of the Standing Committee when this question was posed to Paul Tellier by Jim Manly, the newly elected NDP Member from Nanaimo-Cowichan-The Islands.

> Does the department think of itself, or have a mandate for itself to act as trustee for Indian interests beyond those of their land and other assets, such as band funds or trust accounts?[92]

While it would satisfy a personal curiosity to know what Manly had in mind when he said "beyond those of their land and other assets," Paul Tellier to his great credit, dealt with the "concept of trust responsibility" as a whole in his reply:

> Mr. Chairman, I wish I could answer precisely that question. Unfortunately, it is not possible. As you may be aware, Mr. Manly, first of all that concept of trust responsibility has never been clarified up till now by the courts. Secondly, there is now a case which is around that very question, and I am referring to the Musqueam case in British Columbia. That case was heard and judgment is about to be rendered in the near future. And the crux of the matter in that case is whether that fiduciary relationship is one of a legal or political nature. So the question applies, not only under the *Indian Act* but also under legal

instruments such as when there is a surrender instrument which is ratified or endorsed by the Minister and so on.[93]

Tellier did not mention that the Clark Government had given specific instructions to counsel, in *Guérin*, not to use the political trust argument. Neither did he mention that with return of the Liberal Government, counsel were able, once again, to advance an argument which John Fraser and Sen. Jacques Flynn, Clark's Attorney General, had said was so disreputable as to bring "the administration of justice into disrepute."[94]

Jim Manly returned to the question he had in mind in the first place, "In terms of the day-to-day operations, does the department operate as though it had such trust or as though it does not have such a trust?" To this Paul Tellier was able to answer with a strong affirmative, "The department and the Minister surely operate in the context of the existence of such a trust responsibility." In fact, the Department did not operate in the context of a trust responsibility. It operated on the premise that the trust was a "mere political trust" for which its Minister was solely responsible to Parliament.

Tellier also acknowledged "that there is a built-in conflict of objectives" between the role of trustee and the other roles of the Department, particularly with the Office of Native Claims operating as an arm of DIAND rather than as an independent quasi-judicial body.[95]

NOEL V. STARBLANKET (PRESIDENT, NATIONAL INDIAN BROTHERHOOD)

Noel Starblanket, who had first been elected President of the National Indian Brotherhood in 1976, appeared before the Standing Committee on July 8, 1980, at its eleventh sitting, exactly two months after Munro addressed the Committee at its first sitting of the 32nd Parliament. Starblanket was accompanied by Dennis Nicholas, his Vice President; Arnold Goodleaf, his Executive Assistant; Dave Monture, his Special Assistant; Dave Nahwegahbow, Special Legal Assistant; Sharon Venne, Canadian Indian Constitution Commission of the National Indian Brotherhood; Michael Posluns, Parliamentary Liaison Director and Alastair Campbell, Economic Development.

Starblanket had four requests to make of the Committee. These four requests arose directly from the interrelated concerns of patriation and Munro's expressed intention to introduce legislation to revise the *Indian Act* before the patriation process was complete. Starblanket built on the position outlined to the Committee by Nicholas the previous fall and, in light of more recent developments, went several steps further.

> It is timely for us to come before you to talk about the relationship between Indian government and the Constitution at this point for a number of reasons. Not only is the question of the Constitution the foremost question in public discussion in Canada today but it was also the great question with which the Assembly of First Nations, the First nations Constitutional Conference—which was hosted by the National Indian Brotherhood—which gathered here in April, concerned itself.[96]
>
> (Emphasis added.)

Starblanket told the Committee that "The Assembly of First Nations unanimously resolved that Aboriginal rights, treaty rights and Indian government must be entrenched in the Canadian Constitution." This was the first time that a spokesman on behalf of the national organization attributed his mandate to the Assembly of First Nations which, in the previous paragraph, Starblanket had defined as a "First Nations constitutional conference hosted by the National Indian Brotherhood." The Assembly, he said, "would oppose any revisions to the *Indian Act* until that act was made the administrative statute for implementing those rights which must be entrenched in the Constitution."[97]

Starblanket re-emphasized that the recognition that was wanted was being sought within Confederation:

> Our treaties have been recognized as legal instruments, as contracts made between two sovereign powers. Yet, at the same time, those rights guaranteed to us by treaty have not been enforceable by law, and have been subject to every subsequent law-making venture in this country. The irony of this, Mr. Chairman, is that, if we did not wish to develop within Confederation, our treaties would have greater recognition than they have when we have chosen to be among the strongest advocates of a strong and united Canada. Confirming our treaty rights within the Constitution is neither more nor less than your expression of a desire to include the first peoples of this land within confederation, within a strong and united Canada.
>
> Our right to Indian government is our right to create those political institutions which are essential to exercise, maintain and enhance our aboriginal and treaty rights. No people can truly be a people without seeking to give expression to their collective existence, without creating the institutions by which they will govern their own affairs. It is condescending double-speak to say that we may be "a sociological nation" but that we do not require the political rights corollary to

> nationhood. And that double-speak has been the position of the Prime Minister and the government of this day. That concept, incidentally, is called suzerainty.[98]

He pointed out that friendly MPs had asked him the same question which had been raised by elders, "whether our treaties would continue to have force if the Constitution is patriated."

> A pat answer, a ministerial assurance, is no answer at all on such a fundamental question when it is seriously raised by both Indian and non-Indian statesmen.
>
> Any government which is unwilling to entrench our aboriginal and treaty rights in the Constitution must be seen by Indian people as hostile to the maintenance and enhancement of those rights. [99]

On this basis, Starblanket asked the Indian Affairs Committee to support the AFN position through four means:

> First, we are asking you to support our demands for entrenching Indian rights within the Constitution of Canada before or concurrent with patriation.
>
> Second, we are asking that, if the Minister of Indian Affairs introduces his bill to amend the *Indian Act* or to provide parallel legislation on Indian government, before entrenching Indian rights, that this Committee refuse to deal with any such bill.
>
> And third, we are asking that you not act on the proposal which has recently been touted in these halls to study the recent departmental report, Indian Conditions, but that you instead undertake (a) a study of ways and means to entrench Indian rights in the Constitution; (b) ways and means to transfer control over Indian resources from the Minister of Indian Affairs to Indian bands and (c) ways and means, including equalization, to guarantee adequate funding for Indian government, while stopping the waste of taxpayers' money that is inherent in the operation of the Department of Indian Affairs and Northern Development.
>
> Fourthly, we are asking that this committee form a partnership with the Assembly of First Nations to undertake the research and the

> draftsmanship of the necessary constitutional amendments. We will work with you [to] develop a common understanding among your colleagues and your constituents.[100]

THE SIGNIFICANCE OF STARBLANKET'S STATEMENT: THE FIRST EXPLICATION OF THE RELATIONSHIP BETWEEN ABORIGINAL AND TREATY RIGHTS AND SELF-GOVERNMENT

Starblanket's statement is the first explication of the relationship between Aboriginal and treaty rights and self-government. Although Nicholas had spoken of self-government or "Indian government" the previous fall, Starblanket's speech made links which were only just being made when Nicholas spoke. He spoke not only with the greater authority of being President of the N.I.B., but with the benefit of a new mandate from the all-chiefs' Assembly adopted in anticipation of Trudeau's renewed effort at patriation. Taken together, Nicholas's and Starblanket's statements set out before a parliamentary committee for the first time the aspiration which they continued to call "Indian Government" but which would soon take on the term "self-government."

Starblanket's requests can, themselves, be read both as a measure of the N.I.B.'s relationship with the Members on the Standing Committee, and as his own commentary on the connection between the need to entrench Indian rights during the patriation process and the legislative program for revising the *Indian Act*.

The decision to ask the Standing Committee to refuse to deal with any bill to amend the *Indian Act* generated by DIAND without consultation and before entrenchment of Aboriginal and treaty rights was both bold and carefully considered. While various practical considerations increased the chances that the Committee might respond positively, his proposal was basically that the Standing Committee form a common front with the N.I.B. against the Department and, in a limited way, in opposition to the Government.

Indian Conditions was a departmental study of the continuing poverty conditions of Indian communities. Former associates of Munro have suggested that this study was seen as a ploy to obtain greater funding from Cabinet. The Department was eager to have the Standing Committee invest its energy in hearings around DIAND's own study. The N.I.B. anticipated that such hearings would go no further than a "Gee, ain't it awful" consensus. Transferring resources from DIAND to Indian bands, in contrast, represented significant political change. It also reflects a continuing pragmatic appeal to the need for "stopping the waste of taxpayers' money."[101]

The request for "a partnership" is noteworthy in part for the early use of a word which would later lose much of its currency. Starblanket sets out his agenda for such a partnership: research and drafting of the necessary constitutional amendments and working to develop "a common understanding among your colleagues and your constituents."[102]

Starblanket went on to define the ambit of Indian government:

> While Indian government is not exactly parallel to a province, it must have the same sovereignty, the same right to come to the bargaining table of Confederation and the same right to make its own laws, including its own internal Constitution.[103]

Starblanket then carefully distinguished between the proposals DIAND was urging Munro to bring forward and the Indian government which he had been mandated by the AFN to advocate:

> The Indian government now being talked about by the minister of Indian affairs has nothing to do with the recognition of Indian rights. Their very need to call it self-government is a need to put a label where there is no reality. Every discussion paper produced on this subject by the Indian Affairs branch creates some municipal institutions sponsored by the federal government. Municipal institutions are not governments, and calling a thistle a rose will not make it any easier on the touch.
>
> Indian government has a right to shape its own internal Constitution for the same reason that any other government in Canada has that right. Any body which cannot do that, and any body which does not enjoy exclusive and original jurisdiction over its areas of competence is not a government within Confederation. It is at best a subordinate law-making body.
>
> Indian government is not subordinate to any body. It is *a third order of government within Confederation*. It is our heritage as sovereign Indian peoples, whether you allow us in Confederation or not.
>
> An Indian administration created by amendments to the *Indian Act* or other parallel legislation without entrenching Indian rights will remain a creature of Parliament just as municipal institutions are creatures of

> the provinces. This is what the chiefs of Canada assembled together in this city rejected. Any minister who introduces a bill specifically rejected by 385 elected leaders from Indian bands in every corner of Canada should at least be congratulated for sheer gall and utter contempt of the people he is sworn to serve.[104]

Finally, Starblanket offered a backhanded compliment to John Munro while again urging the Committee to strengthen its alliance with the N.I.B:

> In fact, we rather expect that this present minister will not stoop to the level of the advice he has been receiving, but should our optimism be mistaken, we are asking you to do the courtesy of lifting him out of that slough. For those of you who do not know what a slough is, it is a putrid pond.[105]

Starblanket told the Committee that "Indian government has a spiritual base and a historical base." The historical base he outlined in some detail. The spiritual base he did not describe beyond reminding the Committee how often the Department had taken on a mandate "to assault our spiritual and political structures in order to get at the economic resources underlying them." In his closing remarks, Starblanket elaborated on the spiritual base of Indian government.

> Mr. Chairman and honourable members, Indian government is a gift of the Creation which came to us when the land of which we are the Aboriginal inhabitants was given to us. Indian government is as fundamental to our aboriginal rights as the land itself.[106]

Starblanket told the Committee that much of the funding of Indian government could be accommodated through equalization. The significance of this remark does not depend so much on long term accounting as on the desire to illustrate whole other ways of thinking of the money voted by Parliament for Indian programs and to emphasize the idea that Indian government is financially compatible with existing redistributive programs which allow poorer provinces to exercise considerable autonomy within Confederation.[107]

Lastly, Starblanket addressed the concern about discrimination against Indian women by challenging the *bona fides* of those focusing only on the discrimination against women while not having a corresponding concern for the discrimination against the many other Indians who were forcibly enfranchised including Indian veterans and those whose status had been lost under the double mother clause, 12.(1)(a)(iv) of the *Indian Act*. Starblanket also told the Committee that he had proposed to the Minister that the Minister "use his power under ss.4(2) to suspend the operation of both 12(1)(a) and 12(1)(b) on the resolution of a Band Council," a proposal the Minister did, in fact, act upon at least in respect of Indian women.[108]

Starblanket summarized his views of the Trudeau Government's promise to allow Indian participation in words which have a particular application to this study.

> Mr. Chairman, a government that is willing to protect Indian rights, "*if the provinces agree*," is just not good enough. It is in fact, no protection at all. In 1831, a Westminster Commons' committee said that Indian affairs should remain an imperial power because the provinces' assemblies primarily served the interests of settlers and could not be expected to protect Indian interests. What has changed since 1831 is the language, not the reality. A government which makes *fulfillment of their constitutional obligations subject to other parties' consent* is not very intent on fulfilling their responsibilities.[109]
>
> (Emphasis added.)

THE STANDING COMMITTEE RESPONSE TO STARBLANKET'S SPEECH

The Standing Committee had on its agenda a report to the House asking for a reference of study enabling it "to study the recent departmental report, *Indian Conditions*." In response to the N.I.B. request, Warren Allmand offered an amendment "to adopt the requests that were made in this brief . . ."[110]

Jack Shields (PC, Athabasca) argued, on the contrary, that "the information that would be gathered firsthand by travelling to the areas I feel would be most beneficial to this group," presumably to the Standing Committee. Shields argued that "It would not detract in any way from working with the National Indian Brotherhood on their submission today."[111]

Dr. Greenaway (PC, Cariboo-Chilcotin) supported the amendment for two reasons related to his disposition of the moment: "I am personally tired of looking at reserves and the mess that they are in. I would just as soon sit here and get the job done as tootle around the country; that is how I feel about it."[112]

Stan Schellenberger, the official PC critic, came down firmly on both sides but, on balance, he did not want to be caught taking a strong position:

> Now to say that we should reject that, to accept another area proposed by the National Indian Brotherhood, I think, requires more study by our steering committee. I do not think we can accept this just now and say that this committee should be involved in somehow determining what amendments should be brought forward for the national Indians of this nation (sic) as far as the Constitution is concerned. I do not know whether that is part of the role that this committee should be playing.[113]

Jim Manly argued that *Indian Conditions* did "not produce anything new . . . it is a compilation of previous studies" while, in contrast, "the Indian people . . . have set out some of their own objectives and I think it is time that we began to deal with some of the agenda of the Indian people." He particularly endorsed "the need for Indian people to have some control over their own lives." [114]

Allmand and Manly were clearly agreed on certain principles about the role of the Standing Committee and how it might best serve both the Indian people and their conception of the public good. The Conservatives were divided over the adoption of these same principles.

Schellenberger did, however, tell Starblanket that his party had "moved a number of motions suggesting to the House that the National Indian Brotherhood be at the table . . . how [their] rights should be placed in the Constitution at the meetings that have started yesterday." Starblanket replied that he had not been invited to those meetings but that he had just met with Munro who had undertaken to attempt to set up a meeting between the Prime Minister and the N.I.B. Executive Council.

Starblanket went on to say that the N.I.B. lobby in London had indications that British parliamentarians might be prepared to hold up a Canadian patriation resolution which did not provide for Aboriginal and treaty rights. He also pointed out to Stan Schellenberger that the Conservative Party was much more supportive when it was in opposition than it had been when it was in government.

Jim Manly read a press release in which Trudeau stated that Indian leaders should have only two more years to resolve how to remove "non-legal discrimination against Indian women. Has Mr. Trudeau responded to the suggestion that there be lands and funds made available . . ."[115]

> Mr. Starblanket: We have gone to the extent of preparing an order in council for the Minister of Indian Affairs to act on Sections 12.1 (1)(a) and 12.1 (1)(b), the question of the double-mother clause as well as

> the question of an Indian woman losing her status upon marrying a non-Indian, and all to no avail. The minister has responded only by saying that he will agree to take it under advisement and he has not gone beyond that.[116]

Jim Manly also pointed out that the treaties which Starblanket had said he wanted entrenched in the Constitution often reflected a non-Indian understanding of agreements. Starblanket tacitly agreed that this needed to become the basis of "negotiations that we would like to hold with the Canadian people, through their representatives."[117]

In response to another question from Manly, Starblanket elaborated on the difference between negotiating from "need" and negotiating from "right":

> . . . those of you who were around in 1974 . . . will remember that there was a major confrontation on Parliament Hill in September 1974 between Indian people [and] the R.C.M.P. . . . That violent clash resulted in the joint National Indian Brotherhood-Cabinet committee which functioned, although in fits and starts, from 1974 [until] 1977, and we intended to negotiate with the Cabinet—at that time, the Liberal Cabinet—on the whole question of rights.
>
> It finally broke off in 1978 . . . we pulled out of the Cabinet committee—N.I.B. process simply because of the fact that they refused to recognize the basis of our position as being that of aboriginal and treaty rights. They were quite prepared to recognize in Cabinet . . . that Indian people would be given resources on the basis of need—in other words, sociological needs and all of the other needs that require some form of assistance from the Canadian government—but nothing in the way of recognizing, fully, aboriginal rights and treaty rights, either in terms of legislation or in terms of support to Indian bands, Indian organizations in this country so that they would be able to implement those right.[118]

Suzanne Beauchamp-Niquet, a Liberal from Roberval, Québec, asked Starblanket what he meant by "local power" and by "exclusive power." When he pointed out that he was borrowing those terms from s.92 of the *BNA Act* the matter was not pursued.

Jack Shields asked what was meant when Starblanket had said "the Indian people would determine who was an Indian and who was not an Indian. Surely, is that not determined at birth in the same way as who is a

Canadian." Unfortunately, Starblanket agreed, that that was the case under the *Indian Act*.[119]

Shields also pursued the question of the massive delegation of 350 chiefs Starblanket had led to London. Shields thought such a move "would be blocked by whatever federal government was in power." Starblanket replied at considerable length, beginning and ending his remarks with the assurance that "We conducted ourselves in the most respectable manner while the British "press and media people took to us like a bunch of flies because they had intended to see us as 'Red Indians.'"[120]

A RETROSPECTIVE REVIEW OF THE NARRATIVE CHAPTERS

What continuities can be found through the various committees that have been reviewed here from the perspective of their role in the public emergence of the vocabulary of First Nations' self-government?

Throughout the decade from the beginning of the Watson and MacGuigan-Molgat committees until Starblanket's presentation to the Indian Affairs Committee in June of 1980, Indian and Native leaders were trying to engage parliamentarians in a dialogue on Aboriginal and treaty rights and their relationship to the Canadian Constitution. The effort to engage parliamentarians in this dialogue took place against an historical backdrop of significant political repression. The most blatant forms of this repression had ended in the early 50s when the leadership of the early 70s were beginning their political apprenticeships. The continuing economic and social disadvantage of First Nations and the steadfast refusal of the Crown to fulfill its fiduciary obligations was widely seen, by First Nations leaders, as a remnant of the same policies. Indeed, the *1969 White Paper* has been identified as a continuation of the attitudes of Mackenzie King and Duncan Campbell Scott.

The vocabulary that emerged at the end of the decade had been struggling with a process that was calculated to work against the emergence of a new language. Throughout these *Proceedings* parliamentarians had few, if any, incentives for active listening. By active listening I mean the kind of listening that gives rise to questions that are directly responsive to the opening remarks offered to a committee by a witness. In contrast, I have pointed out, especially in my account of the MacGuigan-Molgat Committee, in Chapter Three, the many questions put to witnesses by MPs and Senators that have all the earmarks of having traveled across the country ready to be pulled from a brief case more or less regardless of the witness's submission to the committee. This is, I suggest, the parliamentary version of a phenomenon that Jean-Paul Sartre characterized as *un dialogue des sourds*. The exception occured when the N.I.B. and its affiliates began to provide a service to MPs who were interested in holding the Department responsible for its programs.

One minister after another is seen to speak enthusiastically about a desire for a close working relationship with Indian communities. Words such as "consultation" and even "partnership" come up time-and-again. Yet each time that Indian organizations made a statement to the Indian Affairs Committee the Indian leadership focus on the lack of substance underlying these terms.

The greatest single obstacle to the emergence of a new language was the steadfast refusal of ministers and their officials to negotiate in good faith, as evidenced by the N.I.B. decision to withdraw from the Joint N.I.B.-Cabinet Committee. The second greatest obstacle might be seen as one instance of that lack of good faith, viz., the lack of diligence and preparation on the part of parliamentarians sitting on these committees. By and large, those sitting on the Joint Committees on the Constitution were particularly ill prepared. Quite possibly Indian and Native presentations were, to their minds, more occasions of endurance than of engagement.

The inability of certain parliamentarians on the *MacGuigan-Molgat* Committee to develop a command of the names of Indian political organizations set a tone that had not quite left the discourse of parliamentarians by the end of the decade, other than for the handful of MPs at the core of the Indian Affairs Committee. Beyond those seven MPs the notion of taking Indian people and their constitutional, political and legal concerns seriously continued to appear slightly "ludicrous and incomprehensible" to senior officials in DIAND as well as to their political masters.

THE ADVANCE OF THE DISCOURSE IN THE CLARK AND LATER TRUDEAU PERIOD AND THE FORMATION OF THE ASSEMBLY OF FIRST NATIONS

The vocabulary of First Nations' autonomy became increasingly explicit through the 31st and 32nd Parliaments. I will now outline several of the factors contributing to this development: The formation of the Assembly of First Nations; the responses of parliamentarians; and the patriotic process.

The recognition, by the National Indian Brotherhood leadership, of difficulties with both the N.I.B. structure and with each of the three words in its name resulted in a movement to reconstitute their organization so as to increase the authority of the traditional nations and their chiefs led to the formation of the Assembly of First Nations. This development, itself, required, in addition to the more visible jobs entailed in creating a new political organization, considerable thought about the use of language. The decision to emphasize that the national body was *an assembly* and that its constituent parts are *First Nations* was a clear and emphatic statement both of the historical understanding these communities had of themselves and of their goal for the future.

This change in structure was, however, not a change in overall policy objectives: an examination of the discussions of the National Indian Advisory Council, the testimony of Indian leaders before the Andras Task Force and the deliberations surrounding the presentation of Harold Cardinal's *Red Paper* show a fundamental consistency. This consistency has continued, with the exception of Phil Fontaine's chieftainship from George Manuel to Matthew Coon Come.

Starblanket's description of the Assembly of First Nations as "our constituent assembly" in a presentation focused on the reasons why self-government was the only course likely to alleviate the apparently intractable problems besetting Indian communities is the point at which the vocabulary of self-government becomes fully explicit. It is unlikely that Starblanket would have made such a presentation without the mandate of the recently constituted AFN.

It is also unlikely that his presentation would have taken the form that it did take had he not been focused on the need for constitutional development since his re-election in 1978. The formation of a Canadian Indian Constitution Commission, under Sharon Venne, soon after his re-election, and the emphasis on the need to include entrenchment of Aboriginal and treaty rights in a patriated Constitution had been central to Starblanket's objectives from the outset.

Starblanket's statement that he was being asked the same question by MPs and by his own elders, "whether our treaties would continue to have force if the Constitution is patriated" is the clearest indication of the role of the patriation debate in the emergence of the vocabulary of First Nations' self-government.

The Liberal Government's 1969 *White Paper* was reportedly retracted in 1971.[121] The Watson Committee had recommended increased control by Indian communities over the education of their own children. The *MacGuigan-Molgat* Committee had recommended recognition of the historic role of Indians and some degree of entrenchment of Aboriginal and treaty rights in a renewed Constitution. These and related developments of the early 1970s led to a reasonable expectation that Indians would receive some significant consideration in a renewed Canadian Constitution.

The decision of the Trudeau Government, in 1978, not to include any provision that lent credence to Aboriginal and treaty rights led to a conviction on the part of the N.I.B. leadership that the *White Paper* attitude continued to characterize the Prime Minister's thinking.

The Clark interregnum was initially welcomed because of Clark's personal record on these matters. The appointment of Jake Epp and the reversion to the Liberal emphasis on Indians being included in matters that "directly affected" them quickly convinced the First Nations' leadership that, whatever Clark's personal inclinations had been as a private Member, he was not likely to stand by them in the hour of patriation.

Trudeau's renewed effort to patriate the Constitution brought with it a renewed failure to extend any intention to include First Nations "at the table of Confederation."

All in all, if the vocabulary was ever to emerge, this was the time that it had to happen.

THE RESPONSES OF PARLIAMENTARIANS

The responses of parliamentarians to the emerging vocabulary were highly mixed. Some, including Frank Oberle, Warren Allmand and Jim Manly appear to have been moved by the mounting evidence around specific issues such as the dysentery epidemic in James Bay Cree communities that nothing was likely to move the federal government to act in the best interests of First Nations communities. Only a wholesale transfer of authority to institutions of their own making was likely to bureaucratic indifference and consequent human suffering.

The number of Members willing to take a position conspicuously different from that of their party leadership was only slightly higher on the Standing Committee than in the Commons as a whole. A number of other factors reinforced the preference for the path of least resistance.

Some Liberal backbenchers showed up at Standing Committee meetings sporadically and used their opportunity to ask questions mainly as an occasion to project interests and preoccupations—including the fostering of French-English bilingualism—quite unrelated to anything said by First Nations' witnesses.

Liberal women—from both the Liberal and the Progressive Conservative party of that day—promoted a women's agenda while few appeared to understand that the constant erosion of Aboriginal and treaty rights, the depletion of the land base of many communities, for example, worked against the interest of the entire community affected, men and women alike. The refusal to demand commensurate increases in funding, housing, and land base concurrent with the reinstatement of forcibly enfranchised women ensured that any reinstatement program would produce as many problems as it solved.

The steadfast failure to understand that, until 1951, every Indian—male or female—who appeared to be self-supporting was liable to be forcibly enfranchised demonstrated the half-heartedness with which parliamentarians approached this issue. The idea that the enfranchisement of men who were stood at attention on parade grounds in England until they signed papers[122] was no more voluntary than was the enfranchisement of the women who married them eluded comprehension by most of the parliamentarians who raised the issue of forced enfranchisement of women during this period. One can only think that they were not paying attention.

A number of Members, such as Lorne Greenaway, were quite willing to wade into specific firefights but were unwilling to think about the possibility that the frequency of such episodes was evidence of the need for far-reaching change. Greenaway, for instance, had led the questioning of the Minister of National Health and Welfare, Monique Bégin, about the Cree dysentery epidemic, but he responded to Starblanket's argument for self-government by saying that he was "tired of looking at reserves and the mess that they are in." This was the kind of insensitive remark to which one can only reply, "Not why be ethical . . . for if someone really . . . poses that as the question to be answered first, he or she is probably beyond the effective reach of ethical concern."[123]

At the end of the day, although there was a growing body of parliamentarians who were interested in a genuine dialogue with First Nations leaders, their influence on their colleagues' thinking remained marginal. Their influence on their parliamentary colleagues became significant only at certain critical moments when they were prepared to take a stand in support of Aboriginal and treaty rights, for instance, and their support was crucial to a larger agenda.

The strongest case for self-government became the inability of parliamentarians to engage in genuine dialogue with First Nations leaders and to direct their energies toward questions of First Nations relations without giving higher priority to other matters such as resource development, provincial relations, bilingualism, financial constraints.

The pragmatic approach which the N.I.B. had followed from Manuel to Starblanket and Nicholas had the benefit that it pulled together the few parliamentarians who were significantly committed to an authentic dialogue across party lines.

The tragedy of this kind of coalition is that serious consideration of First Nations issues in Parliament continued to require epidemics or comparable crises. The rhetoric required for significant social change had emerged into the public domain. The conditions for realizing that change remained elusive.

MINISTERIAL PREVARICATION AND PARLIAMENTARY ACQUIESCENCE

There appears to be an active reciprocal relationship between ministers and their officials and parliamentarians. The kind of prevarication that I discussed in Chapter Two supposes that the speaker is in a position of authority. Ministers and officials have much more opportunity to prevaricate as well as more reason to prevaricate than do other parliamentarians.

The prevarication of ministers and officials, however, particularly on First Nations matters, is only rewarding so far as there is an acquiescence on the part of the parliamentarians who are their immediate audience. Some Members begin by ascribing greater truth value to Ministers' statements that to the statements of First Nations leaders or even to an analysis developed by advanced scholars. Ministers and their officials are able to make far fetched statements to committees when the parliamentarians on the committees lack a familiarity with the current issues, the history and even the basic vocabulary of the matter before them. Heavy reliance on the Minister and his officials combined with a lower regard for First Nations leaders and advisors together with a lack of familiarity with the basic issues and vocabulary has long been characteristic of some Members on the Indian Affairs Committee.

Starblanket's claim to support the reinstatement of women provided that the basic quantum of Aboriginal and treaty rights found proper protection and that the economic base for a realistic reinstatement were part and parcel of the same program surely offered a testing ground for the degree of serious interest on the part of parliamentarians.

Here was an issue on which all parties were said to agree. Indeed, in 1982, at the start of the *Penner* process, the committee produced a report on *Indian Women and the Indian Act* that had the support of all three political parties on the Subcommittee and the three national Aboriginal associations with *ex officio* membership. Their recommendations were consistent with the position enunciated by Starblanket before the MacGuigan-Lamontagne Committee in 1978.

Any parliamentarian might have put both the N.I.B. and the Government to the test. What would have been required would be for parliamentarians interested in pursuing the issue to develop a familiarity with the history of forced enfranchisement, the law as it stood at that time, and the positions of the various parties to the issue.

Each forcibly enfranchised Indian had taken a pro-rated share of their band's assets with them. Starblanket's suggestion basically asked parliamentarians to consider the need to replace those assets. Parliamentarians who supported the slogan "equal rights for Indian women" needed to consider that "equal rights" could be accomplished either by the Trudeau policy of termination and assimilation or by the recognition and affirmation of treaty and Aboriginal rights. If nobody was to have any Aboriginal or treaty rights what was the hurry to ensure that women and others stripped of their rights by previous governments share in the last vestiges of these rights just before they, too, were eliminated?

The same might be said of any number of other issues underlying the demand for self-government: the crisis in Indian health, particularly in northern Quebec in the late 70s and early 80s; the implementation of *Indian Control of Indian Education*; or, the collapse of the Indian fisheries in northwestern Ontario and Manitoba as a result of mercury poisoning. Each of these issues succeeded in attracting momentary attention. None held the sustained attention of even a handful of parliamentarians. What might have distinguished the issue of "Indian women and the *Indian Act*" was that, so far as it rested on a fundamental principle, it was in less danger of bogging down in forensic and scientific detail. It would, nonetheless, require a certain command of the legal history and the issues which Starblanket claimed were bound up with an effective end of discrimination.

What has been consistently lacking is, to borrow a phrase from the *RCAP Report* later used as the title of a Senate Committee Report on implementation of RCAP recommendations, the willingness to honour the importance of *forging a new relationship*. The urge to blame Indians for the *Indian Act* neither requires nor deserves a scholarly refutation. Yet such an attitude recurs from one end of the decade to the other.

A POST SCRIPT ON THE TESTIMONY OF FIRST NATIONS LEADERS BEFORE PARLIAMENTARY COMMITTEES IN THE 1970S

> What is essential is that a people should understand, accept and even love their form of government. Without the understanding of its people a constitution is meaningless. Without their affection it is dead.

> *MacGuigan-Molgat* Joint
> Committee on the Constitution,
> *Final Report*, 1972

The MacGuigan-Molgat statement on the need for citizens to "understand, accept and even love their form of government" is, to my mind, more striking today when Canada has a *Charter of Rights and Freedoms* and a separate constitutional provision recognizing and affirming Aboriginal and treaty rights. It is more striking because when the courts uphold these limits on the authority of legislatures and cabinets it has become popular to complain about the "democratic deficit." As Canadians have come to value these constitutional guarantees of fundamental rights, governments have become intent upon forcing First Nations and others to litigate in order to gain access to their constitutionally guaranteed rights. When the courts have agreed to hear either Charter or Aboriginal and treaty rights cases, as they are required to do under the *Constitution Act, 1982*, scholars and politicians have complained about "judicial activism."

Brian Slattery, in an article entitled, "A Theory of the Charter,"[124] argues that constitutional principles such as those entrenched in the *Charter* and in s.35, require the active participation of drafters, officials and parliamentarians. The courts, Slattery says, are only the third line of defence of such principles. Legal drafters, the officials to whose specifications drafting is done, the ministers who sponsor government legislation and the parliamentarians who supposedly scrutinize government bills all have earlier opportunities, opportunities far upstream from the courts, to ensure that legislation and statutory instruments are consistent with both *Charter* rights and Aboriginal and treaty rights. Yet it is clear that officialdom and successive ministries have, more often than not, set themselves against these constitutional principles rather than as the first and second lines of defence of such principles.

One consequence of constitutionally entrenched rights has been a greater tendency to prevaricate on the part of ministers and officials. Likewise, there has been a corresponding tendency for ministers sponsoring legislation not to accept responsibility for the actual provisions of their bills.

This retrospective look will examine the kinds of prevarication—misleading statements—that were characteristic of the 1970s, the period examined in this study and, particularly, the tendencies that appear to have grown over the years since the enactment of the *Constitution Act, 1982*.

Jake Epp, the Minister of Indian Affairs in Joe Clark's 1979 government, in his statement to the Indian Affairs Committee, attempted to create an air of generosity by identifying three areas of participation in "the constitutional review process." Two of these, however, shift the burden of persuasion onto the "Indian leaders" whose interests he had recognized: (1) "where there is a clear Indian interest"; and, (2) "where the result of such discussions could affect Indian people significantly."

"Significantly" is a word that sets off alarms. As Mr. Epp used the term, it appears to mean *noteworthy to the one speaking*.

Did the minister mean that Indian leaders are welcome to those constitutional talks which are "full of meaning" but not to those lacking fullness of meaning? Or that they will be invited to those meetings with a hidden agenda? Or those which are statistically deviant in some respect?

Whether or not this burden fosters a kind of prevarication depends upon the standard of fairness one applies. If one presumes that "the Crown can do no wrong" and that the government, by dint of its service to the Crown, is always to have the benefit of the doubt, then there is an air of plausibility to Jake Epp's position. If, however, one begins, as the Supreme Court often has, from the premise that, in its dealings with First Nations, upholding the honour of the Crown needs always to be a priority of ministers and officials and that in its dealings with First Nations in particular, "the honour of the Crown is at stake," then the Crown has a duty to avoid even the appearance of "sharp dealings."[125]

Sharp dealings are best avoided when the Crown looks to a combination of the plain meaning of language, the ordinary distribution of burdens and the historical quality of the Crown's relationship with First Nations. Justice Department lawyers have so often denied the existence of *any* First Nation interest that the requirement for a *clear* Indian interest must set off alarms. Where this standard is also integrated with the requirement of "discussions that could affect Indian people *significantly* there is good reason to worry and little reason to anticipate good faith..

In order for Indian leaders to participate they would, by Epp's standards, need to show (a) that there was an Indian interest, (b) that it was *clear*; and (c) that the effects of discussion could be *significant*. The window that Jake Epp is opening for Indian leaders has a striking resemblance to the eye of a needle. So far as he is feigning an inclination to recognize the need to include First Nations and to invite their participation, his statement tilts toward prevarication, not because it is an outright falsehood but because he attempts to appear generous in a way that is deceptive and he shifts a burden of proof onto First Nations that more properly belongs in his own office.

Paull Tellier's statement, " . . . an agreement in principle does not mean that there is an agreement" is, to my mind, a forthcoming and significant disclosure. *As the claims negotiating process has been setup an agreement in principle has no binding effect.* At least in the government's view, it is no more than a framework within which the specific agreements will be negotiated. To the ordinary person this may appear misleading. Should a government claim credit for an agreement in principle without making clear that such an agreement has no binding force or effect that may well be a kind of prevarication.

Mr. Blaikie, the NDP MP, as well as any number of community people who might have heard of this view, might, quite understandably, view this interpretation as defying the plain sense meaning of agreement. What use is an agreement that does not require performance? *Black's* offers two definitions for "agreement to agree":

> An *un*enforceable agreement that purports to bind two parties to negotiate and enter into a contract; esp. a proposed agreement negotiated with the intent that the final agreement will be embodied in a formal written document and that neither party will be bound until the final agreement is executed.
>
> A fully enforceable agreement containing terms that are sufficiently definite as well as adequate consideration, but leaving some details to be worked out by the parties.[126]

Clearly, the government understands land claims agreements in principle to be in the first category. Mr. Blaikie might have come to the meeting thinking that the second category would make more plain sense. The Tellier-Blaikie exchange raises the following questions: (1) Does the First Nation party to an agreement *voluntarily* enter into an unenforceable agreement or is this a condition imposed through a "sharp practice"[127] on the part of the Crown? (2) Would any First Nation voluntarily enter into an agreement with the Crown that could, and might well be, set aside by a succeeding government that considers the agreement in principle to be too generous? (3) Do the relative positions of the Crown and a First Nation make an "unenforceable agreement" inherently inequitable? (4) Is an unenforceable agreement inconsistent with the fiduciary obligations of the Crown?

Arguably, these questions might be answered largely by a discussion of differences of perception, perhaps even the differences between *a bureaucratic culture* and *a social democratic Parliamentary culture*. Although these cultural and perceptual differences are real and important they are not particularly helpful in understanding the clashes over metapolicy. If departmental policy is demonstrably founded on involuntary and inequitable agreements enforced through sharp practices these are not matters to be rationalized as a difference between parliamentary and bureaucratic cultures. Such policies, by applying unstated standards that are not tolerated in other policy arenas, effectively place First Nations, beyond the rule of law.

If the answers to all these questions highlighted a distinctly inequitable dimension to the agreement in principle concept as applied to land claims processes, Mr. Tellier's statement would be even more significant and forthcoming. He had provided the attentive parliamentarian with the very evidence needed to highlight this inequity. His gloss on the agreement in principle highlights the lack of substance characterizing agreements-in-principle as defined by the Crown.

If there is a deception it lies in the then longstanding government pretension that an agreement in principle constitutes something less ephemeral that it actually represents. Given the government's long record of recidivism this may well be a matter in need of remedy. The fact of agreements in principle being jeopardized by changes of government is particularly in need of reconsideration. These, however, are not defects in Mr. Tellier's statement in these *Proceedings*.

Dennis Nicholas, in his 1979 testimony before the Indian Affairs Committee, dealt extensively with the Indian Affairs Branch Estimates. His effort to combine arguments of equity with pragmatism and accuracy epitomizes the position of the N.I.B. throughout this period. *Pragmatism*—"the philosophy that tests the value and truth of ideas by their practical consequences"—is often characterized by a concurrent appeal both to *a principled analysis* and *a plain sense foundation*.

The primary test of equity is whether or not a certain conduct "offends the conscience," presumably the conscience of the court. Whether or not a given account offends or gratifies the conscience depends largely upon the truth of the statement on the most basic level. If, as Nicholas charged, much of the money that the government claims as a benefit to Indians is paying for the "maintenance of buildings in Hull" so that the actual amount "reaching Indian people [should] be considered as about half of the amounts [Parliament is] actually asked to approve," a reasonable parliamentarian might well (a) be offended, (b) feel deceived, (c) prefer to see the Estimates re-written in clearer and more straightforward language before they are approved. Similarly, whether or not there is an issue of equity in the funding of Indian communities can be argued by a comparison to the amounts flowing into economically comparable non-Indian communities under equalization and other transfer programs. Indeed, Nicholas invokes a nationally accepted standard and then argues that there is a statistically *significant discrepancy*.

The ethical response in each of these instances depends upon the application of a known or agreed standard to a given or stipulated fact situation. The moneys Parliament is being asked to vote fail to remedy critical problems in First Nations communities, Nicholas argues, because (a) a large proportion never goes to a First Nation community; and, (b) the amounts considered necessary to address comparable problems elsewhere is much greater.

The decision of the Committee to issue a statement to the House, in part as a result of Nicholas's testimony, broke new ground and reversed a trend in which the reference of Estimates to Standing Committees was used to avoid or curtail debate of the Estimates in the Chamber.

The Estimates, as a penultimate version of the votes that will appear in an *Appropriation Act* are descriptive of programs and of the moneys required for those programs. A report to the House from a Committee making recommendations may be expected to have two distinguishable parts, however they may be arranged: (1) The critique of the Estimates referred to the Committee combines a description with a critical analysis; and, (2) recommended changes that are prescriptive of behaviour.

Paul Tellier's offer of an opportunity for *Indian influence* in shaping Indian education was a clear statement of the direction in which he intended to take the Indian Affairs Branch. First Nations leaders and advisors deeply committed to developing *Indian control* would quickly recognize the shortfall. Few of the MPs on the Indian Affairs Committee in 1979, when Tellier was offering opportunities for "Indian influence" were present at the joint Manuel-Chrétien testimony of 1973. However, the issue of Indian government more generally had been raised in the previous Parliament by Starblanket and by Sanderson and, only shortly before, in this same session by Nicholas and by Starblanket again. An MP who made an effort to learn the historical context which lends such statements their actual meaning would recognize that this was not a significant concession. Citizens encountering brief and incompletely digested reports of such testimony might well be told that concessions were being made. A person does not rise to the rank of deputy minister without an appreciation of how his testimony before a parliamentary committee will play. A reasonable parliamentarian might well think that the deputy minister intended either *to mislead* the committee or *to inform them obliquely* that the position put forward by the N.I.B. and its member organizations had been roundly rejected. *An oblique statement* might be defined as *one calculated* to *slip by the listener* without provoking an immediate reaction.

If we supposed that a deputy minister seeking approval of his annual estimates had an obligation to full disclosure such statements would constitute *a type of prevarication*. If we suppose that an oblique admission of renewed federal control is quite forthcoming and that the interpretation of the statement is the obligation of the parliamentarians then the statement remains close to, but nonetheless, outside the realm of prevarication.

If Tellier's remark about "Indian influence," read in an historical context, does not amount to much of an offer, Munro's commitment "to set the stage for the exercise of effective control by Indian and Inuit people and by all Northerners over the things that most concern these special groups of Canadians" comes, on the surface, much closer to the position being enunciated by Indians leaders before the Committee.

Tellier had told Munro at their first meeting after Munro became Minister that he would be the sponsor of a new *Indian Act*. We know from testimony that the *Optional Indian Band Government Legislation* that the I.A.B. had been developing had been done entirely without Indian participation. We are led to question the intentions and the direction of Munro's statement. Its plain sense meaning does not stand up to examination. On hearing this statement, an attentive parliamentarian would have a stronger sense of *déjà vu* than of an impending breakthrough.

Munro's reference to "Indian people as the first citizens" has already been discussed. Such a phrase does not readily disclose a valid meaning. Any effort to redeem it would ascribe an allegorical meaning—possibly as a term of affection or endearment—not widely apprehended amongst either First Nations communities or the general Canadian community. The question then becomes "Are terms of endearment an appropriate rhetoric for a Minister of Indian Affairs on his first appearance before the Indian Affairs Committee?" This question can be turned in a more fruitful direction: The Minister's proper role consists of defending the Estimates that are referred to the Committee by the House, and pursuant to the Order of Reference, to discuss the work of his department current and proposed. *Do terms of endearment devoid of factual content* contribute or detract from this task? A statement that is patently false on the levels on which the discourse belongs is a form of deceptive prevarication.

Munro's statement calling for "strengthening of the special status of Indian people . . . recognition of . . . Indian government . . . a modern definition of Indian land management [and] the legislative implementation of Indian Control of Indian Education may, in part, represent the introduction of *co-option* of Indian rhetoric by Indian Affairs. The *Optional Indian Band Government Legislation* which Munro's deputies intended him to introduce was opposed by the N.I.B. both on substantive grounds (they opposed its proposals for municipalization) and on procedural grounds (they had been excluded). Although the statement is complex and polyvalent, I do not think that it constitutes a prevarication so much as it reflects the style that Munro brought with him from labour negotiations. Unlike most of the items that I have identified as prevarication this is a prescriptive statement and not one that can be shown to be false. It also lacks an essential element of prevarication, i.e., expressions of sentiment that appear to be deceptive insofar as they lack content and are contradicted by the available evidence. A prescriptive statement would be prevaricating if (a) the prescription or the preceding analysis were willfully flawed, as, for example, a program that denies or ignores the preponderance of evidence; or, (b) if the prescription were made for purposes of deception, e.g., to curry favour without *any intention* of acting.

He sets out an agenda that is calculated to deepen his dialogue with the emerging First Nations organizations without abandoning his officials or being unmindful of the Cabinet, and to some extent the caucus, on whose support his program depends. Like a campaign statement, this is not so much a promise as a statement of wishful thinking on which he would like to proceed when there appears to be adequate support.

Any question of his intentions needs to be addressed on several levels. He may have been quite sincere in endorsing this agenda insofar as he would like to proceed with each part when the circumstances are favourable. As a statement by a Liberal, centrist minister to a parliamentary committee there is, in this, no element of deception. As a statement that represents a substantial effort at reconciliation it seeks to convey endearment and even affection. But do these terms of endearment carry real substance?

Allmand resolved the issue of the minister's intentions when he suggested that "Native people would feel more secure with respect to these [constitutional] discussions . . . if somebody approaches them in the next few days." He allowed that nobody had "expected that the structure for constitutional discussion would go so quickly. So far as Allmand may have been asking for something beyond Munro's authority, it might be said that any misleading was not Munro's. Given the well-defined rules or customs regarding cabinet solidarity this is a very weak defence. If Munro's statements to the Committee were calculated to allay First Nations fears and to offer an alternative focus for their, by then, well known constitutional concerns this was yet a further indignity and a form of prevarication.

Starblanket's statement that "The Indian government now being talked about by the minister . . . has nothing to do with the recognition of Indian rights" points quite explicitly to a ministerial prevarication when he goes on to say, "Their very need to call it self-government is a need to put a label on an empty box."

The department failed to consult with the N.I.B. and its affiliates because it anticipated their opposition. There is no sense, amongst departmental officials, that unanimous opposition amongst the chiefs across Canada is an indication that their program may be flawed. In order to achieve their objective by indirection, the department provided the minister with notes which described their proposal, which would remain in outline form only for more than another two years, in glowingly deceptive terms co-opted from Indian rhetoric, a strategy crafted for the purpose of deception. Such a strategy is, by definition, an insult (in the senses both of causing injury and of offending) to the three parties addressed, e.g., the Indian leadership, the Members of the committee and concerned citizens.

The role of senior officials appearing before a parliamentary committee is commonly said to be to provide factual information and a more elaborate description of programs. This, of course, allows a great opportunity for officials to manipulate not only their own minister but also the parliamentary committee. With the increasing role of First Nations political organizations there is not only an alternative political perspective to the minister's but also an alternative source of factual information about programs to that of the officials.

Policy objectives when they occur in a Cabinet document are, like any prohibitive or permissive statement in a statute or statutory instrument, in the imperative register of the plain sense order of meaning. The rationale behind policy objectives, as an analysis of external conditions, current programs and laws is to provide a ground for analysis of the conditions on which a program is intended to act and a ground for review of the program. Ethical and aesthetic judgements about current conditions are allegorical statements that project deeply held values. Facts become value laden when they point to or support a value. In some contexts it might be more helpful to say that "Values inform fact with meaning."

One example of the blending or linking of the descriptive language with value statements was *Indian Conditions*, an Indian Affairs document describing socio-economic conditions in reserve-based communities. One of the earliest indications that the Penner Committee would focus on a First Nations agenda rather than an agenda set by the officials was its decision to adopt that report as a definitive statement of the socio-economic conditions, minimize hearing from experts likely to recapitulate that work, and move on to developing an agenda aimed at reinvigorating the autonomy of those same communities within the context of a supportive Canadian Confederation.[128,129]

The already thin line between analysis of plain sense meaning and analysis of values becomes ever thinner when the statement is a witness's justification about his own decisions. Statements that are commonly described as "self-serving" are allegorical prevarications. Even when they are true they are calculated to mislead. At the very least the description of "self-serving" conveys a sense that the critic feels his attention has been diverted away from the main point. Comparable statements in more personal discourse often evoke the comment, "It's not about you."

In the Crown's argument in *Guérin* and in testimony before the Indian Affairs Committee, the description, of the Crown's obligations to First Nations as "a mere political trust" is a self-serving argument. There are, however, records in the 18th and the 19th century which strongly argued the reality of the trust relationship. These records rely on a plain sense interpretation of the relevant provisions of the *Royal Proclamation of 1763*. Some of them are also premised on the recognition that *without the benefits of a genuine trust relationship* First Nations will neither assimilate and become a part of the larger society nor will they revive as renewed versions of their traditional cultures. The pretension that trust language in an Indian context does not mean what it means elsewhere comes from a very dark place. It resonates with Herman Melville's term "the metaphysics of Indian hating."[130]

The claim to the status of a legal analysis, of the phrase "a mere political trust" in this context, has the quality of a veneer. Its main purpose is to assert the Crown's freedom from suit and to wrap the misconduct of officials in that same mantle while representing Indians as entities not entitled to the full benefit either of promises made to them or of laws proclaiming their protected status.

The failure to keep and maintain records that had gone on for decades became especially evident when the Commons adopted the Allmand-Holmes motion directing the Auditor General to audit the trust accounts of bands which had passed resolutions asking for such audits speaks. [131] If the absence of an opening balance is seen as *shoddy accounting* then it, too, is a form of prevarication. The Crown's claim to exercise authority over First Nations and to substitute its institutions and practices for the practices of a First Nation depends upon the Crown's claim to competence as well as its *claim* to a *capacity* to protect First Nations from the encroachment of settlers. The shoddiness of the Crown's accounting of First Nations assets gives the lie to any claim of competence on the part of the Crown and its officials. The continued assertion of authority rests only upon the Crown's capacity to exercise force and to make fictitious claims about its own competence.

Paul Tellier's reply to Jim Manly, that "The department and the Minister surely operate in the context of the existence of such a trust responsibility" did not extent to any kind of concerted effort to rectify the situation of accounts that had remained without an audit since 1942. Instead, he cites *Guérin's* being before the courts as the most likely resolution of "whether that fiduciary relationship is one of a legal or political nature." If one accepts that the place to resolve the question is, as Tellier suggested, in the courts, then his statement that it was, presently uncertain whether it is a political or a legal fiduciary relationship is a lucid exploration of the situation at that time.

If, however, one follows Slattery in holding that officialdom and Parliament have obligations prior to those of the courts to uphold constitutional principles, then sloughing off the failure to keep competent records is wholly inadequate. In fact, *Guérin* is about a land transaction and would not necessarily resolve the issue of trust accounts. Indeed, if the Crown receives money on behalf of an Indian band and places it in trust account it is surely disingenuous to then say, "We must wait until the Court decides *Guérin* to know if these accounts require an opening balance and a full accounting to the trust beneficiaries." Jim Manly might well have heard this reply as a straightforward prevarication.

Starblanket's statement, of June 1980, setting out the relationship between Aboriginal rights and self-government maintains, to a large degree, the pragmatic thrust of Nicholas's speech the previous fall with one major addition. Nicholas had tied pragmatic arguments to principled arguments. Starblanket, in relating legal and constitutional rights to self-government was essentially making a connection between the legal dimension and the government's claim to legitimacy. Starblanket's request that the Committee refuse to deal with amendments to the *Indian Act* implies an authority superior to that of the Minister on the part of the Assembly for whom he is speaking. This request is based on a challenge to the government's claim of legitimacy based on the counter-claim of the First Nations.

Starblanket's statement that "Indian government has a spiritual base and an historical base" indicates that the foundation of Indian government is an interweaving of the ethical and spiritual legitimacy which the government's assertions of authority fail to address.

Starblanket, in making his request for "a partnership" was clear that he meant, a genuine invitation to take a seat at "the Table of Confederation," a role in the drafting of new legislation to replace the *Indian Act* and to begin Canadian recognition of self-government. We know this because he set out his agenda for the partnership. His use of "partnership" is highly denotative—it has attributes that are specific to the context and that are also consistent with the general dictionary definition of the term—and stands in sharp contrast to the highly connotative use that will come into fashion in ministerial rhetoric several years later. This early and genuine use of the term provides a standard that illuminates the later use as a leading example of an *ersatz phrase* which might set off prevarication alarms in a practiced ear.

The repeated promises of successive ministers of consultation and of partnership suggest that these words were already "enjoying" ersatz application in departmental rhetoric. The inclination of Ministers to indulge in this rhetoric had, by 1980, already been amply demonstrated before the Indian Affairs Committee. The urge to deceive creates an intention to prevaricate.

Manly's observation that the treaties often reflected (as they were written and, perhaps even more, as they have later been read) a non-Indian understanding of agreements points to two different difficulties that might be clarified through a Four Worlds analysis.

First, the notion that the treaties were not, in their plain sense, binding rests, in turn, on two assumptions: (1) that exemptions inserted in qualifying clauses relieve the Crown of duties that it does not care to perform; and (2) that these agreements lack the solemnity ascribed to them by First Nations.[132] To describe the qualifying clauses, e.g., "when the Queen deems wise," as a "sharp practice" in the *Taylor and Williams* sense has been said to be reading later principles back into history. There were, on the other hand, well placed non-Indians—Chief Justice John Marshall of the U.S. Supreme Court and Mr. Justice Samuel Strong of the Supreme Court of Canada for example—who thought that treaties needed to be taken in their plain sense, good faith meanings. The need to honour the treaties is independent of the anticipated outcome: Some who ascribed real meaning to the treaties anticipated that if Indians learned agriculture and educated their children they would assimilate; some chiefs thought that learning agriculture and educating their children would provide a foundation for the rebirth of their nation.

Whatever else the outcome might have been if treaties had been honoured, people would have been better fed and their children would have had real choices and genuine opportunities. The failure to interpret treaties as though "the honour of the Crown was at stake" foreclosed the possibilities that would have resulted from well fed and well educated children. The choices that might have been made will remain unknown.

Secondly, if cavalier practices are licensed by a presumption that an agreement with an Indian nation is less binding than other agreements—a presumption that falls on the spectrum of "the metaphysics of Indian hating" somewhere close to the presumption that "Indians" are less than fully human.

Starblanket argued that negotiations between the Crown and First Nations needed to begin with a proper understanding of First Nations history and a respect for their humanity. When the recognition of treaty rights and Aboriginal rights are entrenched in the Constitution, and when they are read as a *substantive* promise,[133] then it becomes clear that the Constitution, itself, requires that negotiations take place in a context of mutual respect. The requirement of *consultation* on which the Supreme Court has placed so much emphasis in its interpretation of Aboriginal and treaty rights is a corollary of respect.

Although renewed, reinvigorated rhetoric was needed in order to foster new policies, several factors mitigated against such a development. Some of these are elements in the political process: (1) a high turnover on the Indian Affairs Committee between certain parliaments; (2) irregular contact between First Nations leaders and parliamentarians; (3) the effort of senior officials to dominate the agenda of the parliamentary committee.

Other inhibiting elements arise out of the discourse and the interplay of language, policy and ethics: (1) as the submissions of the N.I.B. and affiliated organizations became increasingly specific they moved away from the inherited rhetoric toward a speech better suited to their program; (2) this was, in part, a recognition that the old rhetoric inhibited creative thought on issues that were widely seen as intractable; the effort of Starblanket and others to introduce a new rhetoric resulted in a countervailing movement by parties who opposed "rights based agendas" so that the Committee's discourse became, itself, a contested matter; (4) those with an interest in preserving the colonial relationship continued with the old rhetoric for a time and, later, sought to co-opt the new rhetoric.

The presumption that the Minister might largely set the agenda for committees studying Indian matters extended back at least as far as the Stevens-Bostock exchange in the Joint Committee of 1927.[134] This is in contrast both to the general theory, repeated by innumerable speakers, that a committee, once it has received an order of reference is "master of its own proceedings" and in contrast to the style of the more effective committees both on legislation and on general inquiries. Implicit in the *presumption for the Minister* is the historic disenfranchisement of status Indians and the *presumption of incompetence* on which their disenfranchisement was based.

Starblanket's request that the Committee refuse to deal with the I.A.B. paper *Living Conditions* and, instead, focus on developing a constitutional and legislative program for "Indian Government" had the effect of asking the Committee to *shift the burden* of persuasion *across the fulcrum* and to conduct their inquiries so that the initiative would lie with the Indian leadership rather than with the Minister and departmental officials.

This did not mean that the Indian leadership would not need to persuade the Committee of their case; it did mean that the Committee would extend to them the courtesy and respect of allowing them the initiative. This, in effect, was a very local version of the recognition that Starblanket was seeking from Parliament and from the Constitution. Seen from this perspective, Allmand's amendment to move the Committee's agenda away from *Living Conditions* and toward the N.I.B. agenda supposed a strong collegial bond between the parliamentary committee and the representative First Nations organizations. Starblanket, in effect, asked the Committee to choose where it would place its primary focus—between First Nations communities and Indian Affairs officials.

The process that culminated in the shifting of the burden in favour of the First Nations began not in the Indian Affairs Committee room but in the All-Chiefs' Assembly that constituted itself as the *Assembly of First Nations*. Starblanket's introduction of the Assembly of First Nations, in his address to the Indian Affairs Committee, in June 1980 as "our constituent assembly" forecast the agenda of the organization that had been established earlier that spring at Penticton.

The term "Assembly of First Nations" had grown out of extended discussions, formal and informal, grounded in the beliefs that (1) the N.I.B. structure of an executive council composed of the heads of the provincial and territorial organizations and an assembly appointed by the PTO heads was no longer appropriate; and, (2) that each word in the name "National Indian Brotherhood" was troubling and not properly descriptive. The creation of an assembly in which all the chiefs in Canada had a seat and which, then, claimed authority to represent the "First Nations" was a first step toward asserting a presumption couched in the traditions and customs of the "several Indian nations" and their recognition in the *Royal Proclamation* rather than accepting the limited framework of the *British North America Act, 1867* and the *Indian Act*.[135]

Starblanket's statement that he was being asked both by MPs and by elders "whether our treaties would continue in force if the Constitution is patriated" shifted some part of the burden of answering that question onto the Members on the Indian Affairs Committee and to Parliament in general. The failure of the 1978 patriation proposal, bill C-60 to reflect the recommendations of the MacGuigan-Molgat *Final Report,* and the promises made in the literature accompanying that bill that were not sustained in the bill itself had resulted in hurt, anger and in massive lobbying by Indian organizations both in Ottawa and in London.

Putting the burden on those parliamentarians who professed an interest in renewed First Nations relations, required that they *demonstrate their bona fides* and that they carry out their proper function as parliamentarians by requiring the Government to demonstrate that Aboriginal and treaty rights were not in jeopardy.

This distribution of the burden is far more in keeping with normal procedure. It is consistent, for instance, with the basic intention expressed in the Diefenbaker *Bill of Rights* provision that the Attorney General certify that any bill presented to Parliament by a minister is consistent with existing rights.[136] More important, it is consistent with the general obligation of the one who moves a motion to demonstrate its virtues. The difference is that Starblanket's question sought a presumption that Aboriginal and treaty rights were virtues and required non-interference at the very least.

The tendency of Liberal backbenchers to attend meetings sporadically and then to ask questions intended primarily to advance their own political agendas is a longstanding parliamentary practice. It has several unfortunate effects. There is, at least, the appearance that the practice is indulged even more frequently in the Indian Affairs Committee than in committees commanding more respect amongst parliamentarians. Even if a statistical study were to demonstrate that parliamentarians are equally inclined to sporadic attendance at, for instance, the transportation committees, the consequences, are quite different.

Given the longstanding tendency to treat Indian witnesses as less than competent and to indulge in condescensions of varying degrees, sporadic, ill-informed participation comes to appear as part of the same spectrum of disrespect. The need to command respect constitutes a significant addition to the normal burden of a witness before a parliamentary committee.

Closely related to sporadic attendance and inappropriate questions is the apparent inattention of some parliamentarians. The appearance arises when a parliamentarian responds that he or she agrees with a statement which, in fact, was not what the witness said. When, for example, briefs go to some lengths documenting that men as well as women have been affected by the *Indian Act* provisions for involuntary enfranchisement and the statement is ignored, there is a sense that witnesses are engaging in *un dialogue des sourds*.[137]

Various parliamentarians have chosen to attribute to the N.I.B. an unwillingness to welcome reinstatement of enfranchised women and, have inferred from this a certain chauvinism. Starblanket cites an N.I.B. resolution asking for an order-in-council to suspend the application of s. 12(1)(b) to which he has had, at the time of his presentation, no reply from the Minister. The Minister's failure to respond and, possibly, to use his authority[138] to rectify a situation that all agree is inequitable, while leaving an appearance that the N.I.B. is the culpable party could prove to be a calculated effort *to discredit the N.I.B.* This is an objective that runs throughout the departmental memoranda of this period obtained under *Access to Information.*

Greenaway's assiduous pursuit of Monique Bégin over the Cree dysentery epidemic jars with his aggressive disinterest in traveling around to reserves. If he missed Allmand's amendment to substitute Starblanket's items on Indian Government for a study of "Living Conditions" then he was, very likely, not paying attention. (His reference to not wanting to look at reserves "and the mess they are in" supports this view of his statement. If, on the other hand, he was rejecting Starblanket's request to focus on self-government, then it may appear that he was more interested in the "Who done it" element in a study of Indian living conditions than in a recasting of the fundamental relationship between Parliament and First Nations.

Nicholas's appeal to a pragmatic blend of *reality* and *affirmation* in making the case for self-government finds confirmation in the inability of parliamentarians to direct their energies toward questions of First Nations relations. If only an inner core of the Standing Committee on Indian Affairs troubles themselves to learn the basic vocabulary of the subject area, the prospects of persuading a parliamentary majority is quite remote. Parliamentarians on committees where their performance will be of interest to their own constituents behave differently. The first test of *in*tention is *at*tention. Both require a continuing mindfulness and entail continuing care and consideration.

The handful of parliamentarians pulled together by a common interest in Aboriginal issues were not numerous enough to be described as a coalition. The Members from each of the political parties then represented in the House of Commons faced an ongoing struggle to bring others in their caucus along the route of Aboriginal and treaty rights, and, often enough, even to find others who would take a serious interest in epidemics breaking out in First Nations communities. The predominant view in all parties was one of acquiescence.

The reciprocal relationship between ministers whose statements are demonstrably prevaricating and *parliamentarians' acquiescence* deserves further study. It may be unrealistic to protest MP'a acquiescence when there are decreasing rewards for challenging ministers particularly in areas, such as First Nations relations, in which the required homework would not get done simply in the normal course of events and where unaccustomed alliances would need to be built. Acquiescence becomes at some point, ethically indistinguishable from the prevarication to which one consents. Yet MP's often find that unquestioning support of the government is the one behaviour that brings rewards. Any other standard would be inconsistent with the desire of backbench MPs, for example, to shelter under the umbrella of positive ministerial accomplishments. Where notice can be taken of the difficulties of challenging ministers and often even of challenging officials is in developing a scale for recognizing and crediting resistance.

Possibly the first step on such a scale would be the extent to which a parliamentarian comes to a committee hearing well prepared. Evidence of *parliamentary preparation* is not different from evidence that students have come to class well prepared. The early benefits might also be similar: parliamentarians who come to class prepared will find it easier to remain attentive; being prepared will reduce the incidence of surprise when key witnesses offer statements that distinguish their position from that attributed to them by others. This was, undoubtedly, a factor when Starblanket repeatedly supported reinstatement of *women and others* who had been forcibly enfranchised. The idea that forced enfranchisement was not an exclusively women's domain would have been easier to absorb for those parliamentarians who were not hearing it for the first time. I have belaboured the matter of preparation because more than first sign of non-acquiescence, it is the first proof of serious intention. The application of intention is the hook that unites *performance, with the ethical and aesthetic.*

Forging a new relationship would require *a continuing intention*, as the root of "intent" suggests, *a continual "reaching out."* The intermittent effort that allowed parliamentarians to show up at a committee hearing long enough to ask the questions that were on their minds before the witness arrived does not offer a basis for a new relationship. Such performances expose the vulnerabilities of parliamentarians who indulge in them so that they become increasingly susceptible to the impositions of ministers and officials.

MAIN THEMES GIVING THIS CHAPTER A DIFFERENT CHARACTER THAN PREVIOUS CHAPTERS

Several themes distinguish the quality and nature of the discourse examined in this chapter from that in the previous two chapters:

- First Nations representatives become increasingly explicit;
- Parliamentarians ask more pointed questions of witnesses, demonstrate a greater familiarity with both the bureaucratic and the First Nations rhetorics;
- The incidence of probable prevarications running through the testimony of officials increases;

- The Minister attempted to embrace the goals of First Nations, and placate the parliamentarians while not greatly deviating from the agenda set by his officials.

The statements regarding First Nations self-government became increasingly explicit through the course of this testimony. The adoption of terms such as "First Nations and "self-government"(first among the communities to whom these terms referred and, during the course of the Penner hearings by those MPs with a serious commitment to those communities) was, itself, a move toward greater denotation. These terms stand in contrast with the term "Indian Government" used to describe the first all-chiefs' conference, in 1978. Starblanket's speech in which the goal of First Nations' self-government becomes fully explicit and in which he describes the Assembly of First Nations as "our constituent assembly" followed shortly after the all-chiefs' conference that adopted these terms and gave Starblanket the mandate to make these statements.[139]

The 32nd Parliament brought together a membership on the Indian Affairs Committee which included a core group of Members who had served on the Committee through several previous parliaments and who had a serious commitment to these issues. Several of these Members had large First Nations populations in the constituencies. All of them had developed close working relationships with the leadership and staff of the First Nations political organizations. These relationships and commitments are reflected in their choice of language and the quality of their questions.

The incidence of prevarication in testimony of officials increased as the parliamentarians' questions became more substantial and as the parliamentarians demonstrated increasing sympathy with First Nations, both on specific issues such as the dysentery epidemic in the Cree villages and its possible connection to the non-fulfillment of federal obligations under the *James Bay and Northern Québec Agreement*, and on larger issues such as First Nations' autonomy.[140]

John Munro's 1980 speech to the Committee was quite unlike any comparable speech of his predecessors. He clearly wished to win and maintain the support of the First Nations leadership and of the Commons Committee. He made tangible promises in regard to First Nations' autonomy (Indian control of Indian education), an end to discrimination against women (two years before the enactment of the *Charter*) and expressed a desire to increase consultation with the First Nations leadership while overhauling the *Indian Act.*

Four years later, following the tabling of the *Penner Report*, Munro succeeded in introducing two bills, one, C-47,[141] to end discrimination against

Indian women under the *Indian Act*, the other, C-52, to provide for the recognition of Indian First Nations governments.

C-47 was rushed through the House of Commons with very little study in the hope of enactment before dissolution. The hurry led to a refusal for a required unanimous consent needed for quick passage in the Senate.[142]

C-52 was denounced by the First Nations Assembly for its failure to adequately reflect the *Penner* recommendations it ostensibly sought to implement. Munro had brought a distinguished lawyer, Peter Hutchins and a consultant with long associations with First Nations political organizations Andy Rickard into his office to work on the drafting.[143] They were unable to gain the cooperation of Justice Department officials who drafted much of the later portions of the bill according to instructions from the "permanent government," i.e., career civil servants in DIAND and MSSD while Munro campaigned for the Liberal leadership.

These comments jump to the end of a four year session of which only the first year was examined here. They do, nonetheless, reflect the dynamic that was emerging in the earliest phases of the 32nd Parliament, and particularly the desire of the Minister to appear to please First Nations while maintaining the support of his officials.

The tendency to increased incidence of prevarication in the testimony of the officials arises as they are increasingly asked questions with sufficient denotation that the preferred tactic of obfuscation becomes less and less applicable.

PATRIATION AND THE LOBBY FOR ENTRENCHMENT

What happened during the lobby around patriation—sometimes it was a lobby against patriation and at other times, by other people, it was a lobby to include Aboriginal and treaty rights in a patriated Constitution—is another chapter. It is, perhaps, a more exciting chapter than the three I have offered here. However, it is also one which came after the vocabulary of First Nations' self-government had emerged and could be found on the Parliamentary record.

In much the same way, there was a series of compelling developments which gave rise to First Nations testimony before the Standing Committee during the balance of the 31st Parliament, events which helped to consolidated First Nations thinking and to solidify the relationship between the First Nations political organizations and the Standing Committee. From the perspective of the vocabulary of self-government, these events served to hone and refine the vocabulary which had emerged into the public domain during the opening months of the first session of the Thirty-First Parliament.

Glossary

Aboriginal: "Aboriginal" as it is used in section Part II of the *Constitution Act, 1982* on "the rights of the *Aboriginal Peoples of Canada*" includes "Indian, Inuit and Métis peoples." It is widely held by scholars of Aboriginal and treaty rights that "Aboriginal" in s.35 has the same meaning as "Indian" in s.91(24) of the *Constitutuion Act, 1867*, the provision that gives exclusive jurisdiction to the federal government over "Indians and lands reserved for the Indians." Note that the definition of "First Nation" below is considerably narrower that the definition of "Aboriginal" and, in this sense, does not refer to the same peoples.

Although contemporary journalism follows a popular usage of lower case first letter on "aboriginal" scholarly and legal journals friendly to indigenous cultures tend to treat "Aboriginal" and "Native" as proper nouns corresponding to "North American." The view that "Aboriginal" is a proper noun or adjective is discussed in the *Oxford Guide to Canadian English Usage*, Oxford University Press Canada, Toronto, 1997.

Aboriginal rights: Rights held by a first nation as a continuation of their nation's Aboriginality, i.e., it having existed as a collective entity prior to any European occupation. These rights were recognized by George III in the *Royal Proclamation, 1763* that the "Indian nations shall remain undisturbed in their lands." In 1985, in *Guérin*, Brian Dickson, their Chief Justice of Canada (C.J.C.), said that these rights "pre-exist any British executive or legislative act." Aboriginal rights are often contrasted with *treaty rights*, i.e., rights which derive from and are protected by a treaty with the Crown.

In the 1970s Aboriginal and treaty rights were often described, by Indian leaders, as "Indian rights." "Indian rights was, for instance, the stated theme of the first all-chiefs conference, convened by the N.I.B. in 1979.

Aboriginal title: the title of an Aboriginal or First Nation to its historic lands. This title has been recognized in a series of recent cases beginning with *Guerin v. The Queen* [1984] 2 S.C.R. 335. Aboriginal title is a particular Aboriginal right.

Band: an Indian community situated on reserved lands and established as a band under the Canadian *Indian Act.* More recently, "bands" have tended to identify themselves either as "First Nations" or as "First Nations communities."

Band council is a council chosen, either by a municipal kind of election or by a traditional indigenous method for the purpose of carrying on a local government under the *Indian Act.* Band council resolutions become valid upon the signature of the federal Minister of Indian Affairs.

Bona fides: More than a mere subjective term *good faith intentions*, for purposes of this study, are intentions for which evidence can be found *of significant efforts to develop and implement stated policy objectives.* . Philosophers as different as Martin Buber and Jean-Paul Sartre have stressed the importance of *bona fides.* See also Jacob S. Ziegel, "Good Faith in the Law of Contract," Memorandum by Joint Research Director, LCA Project, Ontario Law Reform Commission, Sept. 10, 1982. This definition is consistent with Buber, Sartre and Ziegel.

***British** North America Acts, 1867—1975* (*BNA Acts*)**:** The *British North America Act, 1867* was a British statute which established the Canadian Confederation. All or most of the amendments to this act were known as the *British North America Act + date* until the *Constitution Act, 1982* under which the various *British North America Acts* were renamed *Constituiton Act + date.* In revising this dissertation for publication I have followed the current usage rather than the usage that was current at the time of testimony. This means that the *British North America Act, 1867* is cited here as the *Constitution Act, 1867.*

Burden of proof: The obligation on a plaintiff or mover of a particular motion to prove the facts of the complaint that they have laid before the court.

Burden of persuasion: The obligation on a plaintiff to persuade the court that the facts as they have made them out have a particular legal significance, e.g., that the defendant caused the damage and should be held liable to make compensation.

Burden shifting: Strategems by which one party shifts the burden which would otherwise fall upon him to another party.

The title of the presiding member of committees of both Houses during the period of this narrative was "Chairman." This title was used, until very recently by both men and women in both Houses. The Commons has currently chosen the term "chair." The Senate has chosen not to adopt this innovation. I use the titles which these persons held during their tenures.

Cognitive Dissonance: The tension produced when a person entertains conflicting ideas, e.g., the stereotypes of Indians common in Euro-American discourse and the idea that there were nations with their own bodies of law existing in North America before the arrival of Europeans and the claims of sovereignty by various European states.

***Constitution Acts, 1867*:** The *Constitution Act, 1982* is said to have "patriated" the Canadian Constitution, i.e., introduced amending formulas under which Canada would no longer have to seek an amendment to the *British North America Act* by the British Parliament. Under the 1982 act, the various *British North America Acts* were re-named *The Constitution Act, + Year.*

***Constitution Act, 1982*:** *The Constitution Act, 1982* as it was finally passed has several distinct parts. Part I is the Canadian Charter of Rights and Freedoms. Part II, *The Rights of the Aboriginal Peoples of Canada*, consists entirely of section 35 and is not part of the *Canadian Charter of Rights and Freedoms*. Part II is better known as "Section 35. Later parts deal with the amending formulas and a revision of the names of various constitutional enactments.

Co-option: persuade or oblige to join one's own system, culture, side in a dispute, etc.; take over.[1] Likewise, one might *co-opt* a vocabulary by using the words while investing them with different, and even opposing meanings.

Department of Indian Affairs and Northern Development (DIAND): The federal department with responsibility for the administration of most (but not all) federal Canadian Laws regarding Indian communities or bands and the reserved lands (reserves) of Indian communities.

Estimates: The Annual Estimates is a large book of the projected spending tabled each year by the Minister of Finance in the House of Commons. The Estimates for each department are referred to the appropriate standing committee of the Commons for study. The Estimates are enacted by the passage of *appropriation acts*. The Indian Affairs Committee during the 1970s used the reference of the Estimates as an opportunity to invite submissions from the National Indian Brotherhood and various regional First Nations organizations.

Governor-General "the resident representative of the Queen in Canada" the Governor General is empowered to carry out all the duties ascribed to the Queen and serves, in effect, as the Canadian head of state and the commander-in-chief of the Canadian Armed Forces. (See *Canadian Encyclopedia* online at http://www.canadianencyclopedia.ca/index.cfm?

Minority Government: A government which lacks a clear majority in the lower house in a parliamentary system and which must, therefore, look to one or another lesser party to provide the votes necessary to maintain the confidence of the lower house. (See *How Canadians Govern Themselves* by Sen. Eugene Forsey. This book may be found on the parliamentary web site at http://www.parl.gc.ca/information/library/idb/forsey/index-e.asp.)

N.W.T. The North West Territories, in the 1970s, was an enormous territory. It encompassed the present N.W.T., centred on the Mackenzie Valley from the Alberta Boundary to the Arctic Ocean plus the present territory of Nunavut, a predominantly Inuit territory extending from the present eastern boundary of the N.W.T. to the Atlantic Ocean, including several major islands north of the mainland of Ontario and Quebec.

Order of Reference: The motion establishing the mandate of a parliamentary committee. Except when the official term is of special value I use the term "mandate." With rare exception committees of the Canadian Parliament can only conduct hearings or produce reports on those matters that have been referred to them by whichever of the two houses to which they belong.

Originalism: *Constitutional law.* The theory that a law should be interpreted according to the intent of those who drafted and adopted it.

Government: In Canada, the term "Government" is typically used to refer to the Cabinet of the day (or of the historic period under discussion). In this sense, "Government" in Canadian political discourse corresponds to "Administration" in American political discourse. This may be a shortening of the term "Executive Government" as it was used in the *British North America Act* and other British documents of the 19th century.

Committee Proceedings Examined: Joint Committee of the Senate and House of Commons on the Constitution, 1970–72, short title: MacGuigan-Molgat. Joint Committee of the Senate and the House of Commons on the Constitution, 1978, short title: MacGuigan-Lamontage. (The same names in italics refers to the proceedings as a publication.) The Standing Committee of the House of Commons on Indian Affairs and Northern Development for various parliaments and sessions. (The specific sessions and parliaments are identified at the start of chapters three, four and five, the three narrative chapters. Also discussed: The 1972 Report of the Commons Subcommittee on Indian Education; The 1980-81 Joint Committee on the Constitution (Hays-Joyal); the Subcommittee on Indian Women and the Indian Act of 1982 and the Special Committee on Indian Self-Government of 1983.

Joint Committee: A committee of both the Senate and the House of Commons. The Joint Committees discussed here are two Joint Committees on the Constitution, one of which sat from 1970–1972 and the second in 1978.

Standing Committee: Standing House of Commons Committee on Indian Affairs and Northern Development for the sessions indicated in the text, short title: Indian Affairs Committee.

Hansard: The name of the first reporter of complete transcripts of parliamentary debates in Britain and, by inference, the stenographers and editors who produce transcripts of parliamentary debates and committee proceedings today. The name *Hansard* is used to refer to the *House of Commons Debates* and the *Debates of the Senate*, the chief products of the Hansard staff.

Inherent rights: rights that are implicit in a given combination of fact and law. The 1992 *Charlottetown Accord*, provides, "41. The Inherent Right of Self-Government The Constitution should be amended to recognize that the *Aboriginal peoples of Canada* have the inherent right of self-government within Canada. This right should be placed in a new section of the *Constitution Act, 1982*, section 35.1(1)." (The 1998 Canadian & World Encyclopedia Copyright © 1997 by McClelland & Stewart Inc.)

"Honour of the Crown": In a long series of cases the Supreme Court of Canada has said that in its dealings with First Nations "the honour of the Crown is at stake" and, as a result any ambiguities should be resolved in favour of the Indians. See Bibliography for citation of *Nowegijick v. R.*, and *Sparrow v. R.*

Native people/Native peoples: Both these terms have been preferred at various times by liberals who endorse ending discrimination without recognizing Aboriginal and treaty rights. Government ministers and their supporters long favoured the singular term, *native people*, typically without a capital "N." . The *Canadian Native Law Reporter* has treated "Native" as a *proper noun* since it began publication in the 1970s. Parliamentary debates have consistently avoided capitalizing "Native" even after adopting the practice of capitalizing "Aboriginal" a term that appears to be synonymous with "Native."

MacGuigan-Molgat's use of the plural, "Native peoples" distinguishes their report from many other government documents of the period. The tendency to avoid the plural has been seen by First Nations critics as an unwillingness to acknowledge that there are a variety of peoples or, as it was expressed in the *Royal Proclamation of 1763*, "several Indian nations." Indian leaders, particularly in the 1970s when Liberal cabinet ministers frequently spoke in benign terms of "native people" used these terms as code for denying or downplaying the nation-to-nation relationship underlying the Crown's historic recognition of Aboriginal and treaty rights

Parliament: Under section 17 of the *Constitution Act, 1867*, the Canadian Parliament consists of three parts: The Queen; the Senate and the House of Commons. It is a somewhat misleading commonplace to say that *all* power has now become concentrated in the House of Commons. For a highly readable discussion see Eugene Forsey, *How Canadians Govern Themselves, http://www.parl.gc.ca/information/library/idb/forsey/index-pdf-e.asp*.

Parliamentarian The term "parliamentarian" includes both Members of the House of Commons and Senators. Members of the House of Commons ordinarily use the title "Member of Parliament" and the initials "M.P." after their names. Because the bulk of the proceedings examined here are from joint committees it is useful to find a common term for "Senators and Members of Parliament."

Political Party References: Of the three political parties represented in the Canadian Parliament during the decade of the 1970s two are often referred to by short forms or initials: the Progressive Conservative Party is commonly referred called "the Conservative Party" or P.C. and the New Democratic Party is widely known as "the NDP."

Prevarication: Derived from the Latin, "to walk a crooked path," prevarication is a statement calculated to deceive. Sissela Bok, among others, argues that an intention to deceive, more than falsehood, is the essence of lying. (*Lying: Moral Choice in Public and Private Life*, London: Quartet, 1980.) If we accept that view "prevarication" is a range of statements that lie.

Reserve: Approximately the Canadian equivalent of the American term "reservation," a *reserve* is a piece of land held in the name of the Crown (the king or queen of the day) and set aside for the use and benefit of a particular band. Many bands or First Nations have several blocks of land each one of which, as a matter of law, is recorded as a distinct reserve. In popular usage, *reserve* tends to mean the land, as a whole, held for or belonging to a given First Nation, e.g., "They grew up on the reserve."

Royal Commission: A more traditional name for a "public inquiry." Public inquiries are inquiries appointed by the cabinet through an order-in-council to conduct a study into a particular issue. The *Public Inquiries Act* sets out two different kinds of inquiries. One investigates allegations of wrongdoing by government officials or others. the other investigates a broad policy area. The inquiries into alleged wrong doing are chaired by a judge and often he (or she) is the sole commissioner. The inquiries into broad policy areas often have a panel of commissioners with expertise in a variety of related areas. In 1990, the Mulroney Government established a Royal Commission on Aboriginal Peoples which sat for five years, mandated a wide variety of studies, traveled across the country and held round table discussions as well as hearings. The National Library of Canada web site has a listing of all the royal commissions appointed by the Canadian governments. Most provinces have similar legislation.

Second Reading: Second reading is defined as "approval in principle." Bills referred to committee after second reading, as is most frequently the case, cannot be amended in any way that affects the principle of the bill. When a general inquiry into the bill is desired it is referred before second reading. The Senate has for some years gone a step further and frequently refers "the subject matter" of a bill to a committee before the bill is sent from the Commons to the Senate.

Standing Committee: A committee established under the Standing Orders of the House of Commons or the Rules of the Senate, in contrast to "special committees" which are struck or established by a motion which assigns the committee a specific mandate and which expires at the end of that parliamentary session.

Special Committee: A committee established by a motion which assigns to the committee a specific mandate; the committee and its mandate expire at the end of that parliamentary session.

House of Commons Standing Committee on Indian Affairs and Northern Development (Subcommittee on Education) *Watson Report*, 1971.

Parliamentarians: Members of Parliament and Senators

Patriate: pa·tri·ate
Canadian terminology. bring (government, decision-making powers, etc.) under the direct control of the people of a given region, nation, etc.: The British parliament voted in 1982 to patriate the Canadian constitution. -'pa·tri'a·tion, n. *Gage Canadian Dictionary*

White Paper: A kind of government document in the British parliamentary tradition in which the government of the day sets out its objectives and the plans and programmes by which it proposes to achieve those objectives.

The name *White Paper*, came to be identified, particularly in First Nations circles, with the Canadian Government's 1969 *Statement on Indian Policy*. In that context it was the emphasis on "White" that struck many First Nations people as a particularly appropriate characterization. For a discussion of the 1969 *White Paper* see Ch Two.

Licensing: Any acts by which a person's special competence to engage in a certain field of work is recognized, formally or informally and authority is, accordingly, granted for that person to carry on that work. Licensing may be formal, semi-formal or informal. Commissions expressing the Queen's confidence and trust are meaningless if they do not carry an expectation that the person will discharge his office in a manner consistent with that trust and confidence.

Patriation: The written portion of the Canadian Constitution was originally a British statute entitled the *British North America Act, 1867*. Although Canada has been completely independent of the United Kingdom since 1931, Canadian federal and provincial governments were unable to agree on an amending formula. As a result the *British North America Act*, remained a British statute which was amended from time to time on petitions received by Britain from Canada. **Patriation** refers to the process of finding an acceptable amending formula. A distinctively Canadian political term, under the leadership of Pierre Elliott Trudeau patriation came to include the adoption of a *Charter of Rights and Freedoms* in addition to the amending formula. In the course of the debate on a patriation resolution introduced into the House of Commons by Trudeau in the fall of 1980 and proclaimed by the Queen as the *Constitution Act, 1982* in April 1982, the *British North America Act, 1867* was re-named the *Constitution Act, 1867*. A series of different amending formulas were included for different parts of the Constitution and, in addition to the *Charter of Rights and Freedoms* in Part I there was a distinct and separate Part II in which "the rights of the Aboriginal peoples were recognized and affirmed."

Prevarication: tantamount to lying so far as the statement serves to deceive. From a Latin root meaning "to walk a crooked path," prevarication stands over against any mode of discourse described by the phrase recurring in many First Nations languages "to walk a good path." An equivalent term occurs in pre-contact English. See also Psalm 23, in the King James Version of the *Holy Bible*: "Yea, though I walk in the *paths of righteousness*." Erica Bok, in *Lying*, says that the essence of lying is not falsehood but deceit.

Treaty rights: Rights secured or guaranteed to a First Nation in a treaty between the Crown in right of Canada (or in right of Britain and inherited by Canada). Treaty rights are based on the Crown's recognition of the aboriginality of a First Nation. However, not all rights found in treaties were customary practices at an earlier period. Formal education expressed in terms of a school house or contemporary medicine, for example, do not necessarily replace traditional education or traditional healing practices.

Reference Question: Canada appears to be unique amongst the English speaking common law jurisdictions in having legislation under which the Governor-in-Council can refer a legal question to the Supreme Court. Such decisions are said to be advisory and not binding.

Victoria Formula: The *Victoria Charter of 1971* was an agreement reached by Canadian heads of government (with the exception of Québec's Premier Robert Bourassa) concerning constitutional reform.[2]

Notes

NOTES TO ACKNOWLEDGMENTS

1. George Manuel and Michael Posluns, *The Fourth World: An Indian Reallity*, Don Mills: Collier-Macmillan and New York: The Free Press, 1973.
2. Arthur Solomon, *Songs for the People: Teachings on the Natural Way*, Toronto: NC Press, 1990-92, ed. Michael Posluns, Cathleen Kneen; and, *Eating Bitterness: A Vision Beyond the Prison Walls*, Toronto: 1994, ed. Michael Posluns and Cathleen Kneen.
3. Prof. McNeil's most recent book, *Emerging Justice: Essays on Indigenous rights in Canada and Australia*, Saskatoon, Native Law Centre, 2001, received the Saskatchewan Book Award of 2002.

NOTES TO THE INTRODUCTION

1. Collier-Macmillan Ltd., Toronto and New York, 1974.
2. The National Indian Brotherhood was founded in 1970. In the period 1980–82, the NIB leadership laid the foundation for the Assembly of First Nations, a deliberative assembly in which the chiefs of all the First Nations communities in Canada are represented.
3. Section 149A, *An Act to Amend the Indian Act*, Statutes of Canada, 1927.
4. "Civil disability" is the opposite of a civil right. See *Black's Law Dictionary*, 7th ed., Bryan A. Garner, Editor in Chief, St. Paul, Minn., West Group, 1999.
5. There is no such word as "potlatch" in any First Nations language. The term is the fruit of Euro-Canadian miscomprehension of a word that is repeated in a giveaway ceremony of one nation which has then been applied more generally.
6. *St. Regis Islands Act*, 1926–27, c. 37.
7. Prior to the R.C.M.P. Canada had a variety of other federally constituted police forces including the Dominion Police and the Royal North West Mounted Police. In 1920 when the R.N.W.M.P. became the Royal

Canadian Mounted Police, the Dominion Police were also absorbed into the R.C.M.P. *The Canadian and World Encyclopedia*, McLelland and Stewart, 1998.

8. *Report of the Royal Commission on Aboriginal Peoples.* (REAP) Georges Erasmus and Associate Chief Justice René Dussault, *Report of the Royal Commission on Aboriginal Peoples, on Seven Generations: An Information Legacy of the Royal Commission on Aboriginal Peoples*, CD-ROM, Ottawa: Libraxus Inc., 1997
9. The mortality rates and other features of the residential schools are discussed below.
10. I use the term "First Nations relations" to refer to the entire history of relations between Canada and "the several Indian nations," as that term was used in the *Royal Proclamation of 1763* (including Indian nations with whom relations began at a later date). I use the term "Indian policy" to refer much more specifically to policies that were (or may have been) at the core of the attitude and role of the Canadian government in these First Nations relations.
11. "Ill-founded" is, I think, the most charitable characterization of Canadian attitudes during the first century of Confederation. Mr. Justice Emmett Hall, in the 1973 Supreme Court decision, *Calder v. B.C.*, described a succession of court decisions that described Indian nations as savages whose chief occupation was war as "ill-founded."
12. This use of language in the period before the decade of the 1970s is examined in some detail in Chapter Three. Similar critiques of contemporary usage can be found in the testimony of First Nations leaders before the Commons Aboriginal Affairs Committee on Bill C-7 and the Senate Committee on Aboriginal Peoples on Bill C-6 in 2002 and 2003.
13. *St. Catharines Milling and Lumber Company v. The Queen*, (1887), 13 S.C.R. 577.
14. *R. v. Sparrow*, [1990] 1 S.C.R. 1075.
15. *Calder v. A-G. B.C.* [1973] S.C.R 313.
16. *Kanatewat v. James Bay Development Corp.*, [1974] R.P. 38; reversed [1975] C.A. 166.
17. A short note on accessing the legal cases dealing with Aboriginal rights in Canada on the Internet can be found in the Bibliography.
18. *Johnson v. M'Intosh* 21 U.S. (8 Wheat.), 1823.
19. The four *St. Catharines* decisions can be found in vol. 1 of the *Canadian Native Law Cases* nos. 37–38 at http://library.usask.ca/native/cnlc/index.html. Successive courts in this case adopted variant spellings of "Catharine." I have chosen to use the spelling that was used in the Supreme Court of Canada.
20. *Calder v. A-G. B.C.* [1973] S.C.R 313. I acknowledge that Hall J. qualifies his remarks by saying "We know *now*" that such views were wrong. I will advance an argument that there was evidence known at the times of these cases that would lead to a more respectful and positive characterization.

21. Ed. Alex Preminger & T.V.F. Brogran, Princeton, N.J: Princeton University Press, 1993).
22. New York: G.P. Putnam's Sons, 1995.
23. Chicago and London: The University of Chicago Press, 1996.
24. *Saturday Night Magazine*, cited in *RCAP Report.*
25. I consider that Martin Buber and Jean-Paul Sartre are fundamentally agreed on the meaning of "genuine dialogue" for purposes of this study. Further, genuine dialogue necessarily entails *bona fides* (honest intention) as it is discussed by Jacob Ziegel in "Good Faith in the Law of Contract," Memorandum by Joint Research Director, LCA Project, Ontario Law Reform Commission, Sept. 10, 1982.
26. Jean-Paul Sartre, *Being & Nothingness*, New York: Washington Square Press, 1956, Transl. by Hazel E. Barnes.
27. Unpublished essay written for John Borrows' course *The First Nations and the Law*, Osgoode Hall, 1996.
28. David Weiss Halivni, *Peshat & Derash, Plain and Applied Meaning in Rabbinic Exegesis*, Toronto: OUP, 1991.
29. *Will-Kare Paving & Contracting Ltd. v. Canada*, 2000 SCC 36 at p.15.
30. "Public" generally describes that part of the population accepted as adult, human, competent and entitled to express their views on "public affairs," i.e., matters affecting the people as a whole. "Public," *Gage Canadian Dictionary*. The ways in which Indians were excluded are discussed throughout Chapters One and Two.
31. Interview of Emily General with the author, circa, 1972, on file in the Posluns fonds at York University Archives.
32. Richard Drinnon, *Facing West: The Metaphysics of Indian Hating and Empire Building.*
33. "Naïve," Oxford English Dictionary on CD-ROM (OED).
34. See, for example, the chapters "We honour our Grandparents," in *The Fourth World: An Indian Reality*, George Manuel and Michael Posluns, Collier-Macmillan, Don Mills, 1974 (Hereafter, *The Fourth World.*).
35. Black's Law Dictionary.
36. Mark MacGuigan and Maurice Lamontagne, co-chairmen, *Final Report*, The Joint Committee of the Senate and the House of Commons on the Constitution, 19700–1972, (Hereafter, *MacGuigan-Lamontagne)* 30 at 5:40. The method for citing Parliamentary committee proceedings is discussed below, on this and the following page under "References and Citations."
37. *Native Rights in Canada*, 2nd Edition, at p.7.
38. *Re: Eskimos* [1939] 2 D.L.R. 417 heading, reproduced in CNLC at "http://library.usask.ca/native/cnlc/vol05/123.html."
39. Basso, Keith. 1970. "To Give Up on Words: Silence in the Western Apache Culture." *Southwestern Journal of Anthropology* 26: 213–30. 1976, "'Wise Words' of the Western Apache: Metaphor and Semantic Theory." *In Meaning in Anthropology* pp. 93–122. Ed. K. Basso and H.A. Selby, Jr. Albuquerque: University of New Mexico Press. Julie Cruikshank, in collaboration with

Angela Sidney, Kitty Smith & Annie Ned, *Life Lived Like A Story*, (Lincoln and London: University of Nebraska Press, 1990).

40. The duty to consult has been elaborated in a series of Supreme Court decisions beginning with *R. v. Sparrow*, [1990] 1 S.C.R. 1075. The "duty to disclose" plans and research upon which a policy decision may be based, as an extension of the duty to consult, is discussed in *Haida Nation v. British Columbia (Minister of Forests)*, 2004 SCC 73.
41. The Department of Indian Affairs and Northern Development has progressed through a series of acronyms. The most recent acronym favoured by departmental officials, INAC, does not, so far as I can discern correspond to the actual name of the Department established by Parliament. See *Department of Indian Affairs and Northern Development Act*, R.S. 1985, c I-6. Hence, *DIAND* remains a preferred acronym.
42. *Forging New Relationships is* the title of a report of the Senate Standing Committee on Aboriginal Peoples regarding the implementation of the *Report of the Royal Commission on Aboriginal Peoples* (*RCAP*). Ottawa: The Senate, 2000.
43. Bryan A. Garner, ed., *Black's Law Dictionary*, Seventh Edition, St. Paul, Minn: West Group, 1999 and *The Oxford Companion to Law*, ed., David M. Walker, Toronto: Oxford University Press, 1980.

NOTES TO CHAPTER ONE

1. *Guérin v. The Queen*, [1984] 2. S.C.R. 335 at p.20 (Henderson's On-line Law Library) "sui generis," *Black's Law Dictionary* at p. 1448.
2. "sui generis," *Black's Law Dictionary* at p. 1448.
3. In contrast, to "First Nations relations" I use the term "Indian policy" (the actual title of the much reviled *1969 White Paper)* to refer to policies that have been imposed on First Nations by Canada, either without consultation, or, as in the case of the 1969 *White Paper*, in defiance of all the testimony gathered through successive hearings.
4. Duncan Campbell Scott quoted in *Seven Generations*, *The Report of the Royal Commission on Aboriginal Peoples*, Libraxus, Ottawa, 1997. See also Diamond Jenness' testimony, *Proceedings* Joint Committee of the Senate and House of Commons on Indian Affairs, Ottawa, Queen's Printer, 1947.
5. Ss. 91(24), *Constitution Act*, 1867.
6. Maureen McPhee, Director General, Self-Government Branch, Indian and Northern Affairs Canada, testimony before Senate Committee on Aboriginal Peoples, May 3, 2005.
7. The British parliamentary model of government is often, particularly in Canadian political science, referred to as "responsible government" meaning that, unlike the clear separation of powers under the U.S. Constitution, the executive branch is *responsible to* the legislative branch and dependent upon the legislature for the confidence votes that keep the executive, i.e. cabinet, in office.

8. See, in particular, William Connolly, *Identity/Difference: Democratic Negotiations of Political Paradox*, Ithaca and London, Cornell University Press, 1992 and *The Terms of Political Discourse*, Princeton, N.J., Princeton University Press, 1984.
9. Consultation is an integral part of the test set out by Dickson, C.J.C., in *R. v. Sparrow*, [1990] 1 S.C.R. 1075. The need for consultation on any proposed law, regulation or application that may interfere with Aboriginal or treaty rights has been developed further in a series of cases culminating with *Haida Nation v. British Columbia (Minister of Forests)*, 2004 SCC 73 in which McLachlin, C.J.C. admonished the Minister of Forests of B.C. that consultations must be conducted in good faith and that, in certain instances, good faith negotiations may require disclosure of information gathered by a Crown agency or government department or submitted to a government department by a corporation engaged in resource extraction.
10. *Cree School Board v. Attorney General* and *Namagoose v. Robinson.*
11. Keith Penner, Chairman, *Report of the Special Committee of the House of Commons on Indian Self-Government*, Ottawa: House of Commons, 1983.
12. Georges Erasmus and Associate Chief Justice René Dussault, Volume 1, *Seven Generations: The Report of the Royal Commission on Aboriginal Peoples on CD-ROM*, Libraxus, Ottawa, 1997. Hereafter, *RCAP*
13. Sen. Gerry St. Germain, in introducing a bill providing for the recognition of First Nations by Canada (S-16 in the first session of the 38th Parliament) pointed out, as did these earlier reports, that it is quite possible that some First Nations might choose some but not all powers from a list of powers available to them in principle. *Debates of the Senate (Hansard)* November 24, 2004.
14. "at·ti·tude, 2 a position of the body suggesting an action, purpose, emotion, etc: She stood there in an attitude of defiance. 3 the position of an aircraft or spacecraft in relation to some line or plane, such as the horizon or the horizontal. strike an attitude, pose for effect." Gage Canadian Dictionary.
15. Audrey Doerr, *The Machinery of Government in Canada,* Toronto: Methuen, 1981.
16. Coleman & Skogstad, "Policy Communities and Policy Networks: A Structural Approach," *Policy Communities and Public Policy in Canada.*
17. William E. Connolly, *Identity/Difference: Democratic Negotiations of Political Paradox*, Ithaca and London: Cornell University Press, at p.9.
18. Perhaps the most far reaching example was the publication of a report by Dr. P.H. Bryce, chief medical officer of the Indian Affairs Branch, in 1907, in which he observed that residential schools had "a higher mortality rate than most wars." After a brief flurry of public interest, the bureaucracy was allowed to carry on the administration of these schools without any significant reform.

19. Interviews for a master's thesis on *The Bureaucratic Response to the Penner Report*, York University, 1993, on file with the author. The use of "pragmatic" to mean a capacity to ignore the Constitution and to set about undermining the work of a parliamentary committee is a much favoured tool of prevarication, particularly among Indian Affairs officials.
20. Duncan C. Scott, "Indian Affairs, 1867–1912," in *Canada and its Provinces: A History of the Canadian People and their Institutions* by One Hundred Associates, ed. Adam Shortt and Arthur G. Doughty (Toronto: Glasgow, Brook & Company, 1914), volume 7, p.615 quoted in "Residential Schools, Systemic Neglect: Administrative and Financial Realities," *The Report of the Royal Commission on Aboriginal Peoples* at Record 1824. This and other ethical features of Indian policy will be examined in the historical overview in the next chapter.
21. See, for example, "Anglicans in Canada asked to lobby . . ." *Episcopal News Service*, October 3, 2000 at www.epsicopalchurch.org.ens/2000–146D.htm
22. *Ox. Comp. to Law* (at p. 362) defines "disability" as "The legal concept of lack of legal power to do something. Thus, persons are normally under a disability from transferring property which they do not own." *The Blackwell Dictionary of Judaica* (at p. 117) offers an important variation, "In Jewish usage the civil and social disadvantages suffered by Jews as a result of restrictive laws and customs." Apparently, then the term has been applied both where a disability occurs by an individual not having acquired a specific right and when a disability has been imposed upon a class or group within society. *Black's* (at p. 474) specifies "civil disability" as "The condition of a person who has had a legal right of privilege revoked as a result of a criminal conviction." Legislation imposing similar disabilities on an entire people might be seen to "criminalize" their culture or ethnicity.
23. Proposals to limit the right of individuals to sue should not be confused with proposals for voluntary mediation. Neither does respect for the right of petition overlook the complexity of the issues.
24. Isaiah Berlin, "The Pursuit of the Ideal" in *The Crooked Timber of Humanity*, Princeton, N.J., Princeton University Press, 1990, at p.2.
25. I largely follow the Richard Gaskins' thesis. Like many other notable legal scholars, Gaskins uses the term *burdens of* proof to include both *burdens of proof* and *burdens of persuasion.* Although I have some sympathy for the view expressed by Sopinka, Lederman and Bryant in *Evidence Law in Canada,* that the difference between these burdens is elusive it is, nonetheless, important to a study of formal discourse.
26. A line on a ship's hull showing how heavily it may be loaded, i.e., loading the ship so that the hull is submerged below the Plimsoll line is an endangerment.
27. 28 USC Appendix—*Rules Of Evidence* Rule 301, Article III. "Presumptions In Civil Actions And Proceedings," http://www.law.harvard.

edu/publications/evidenceiii/rules/301_proposed.htm.(hereinafter, "Rule 301.)

28. Ibid.
29. Ibid.
30. Not all burden shifting is improper. In litigation on the *Canadian Charter of Rights and Freedoms* litigation where the applicant (or defendant) has the burden of persuading the court that a provision (or action) violates a *Charter* right while the Crown had the burden of persuading the court, in response, that any apparent violation is justified under section 1. (Peter Hogg, 35.4 "Charter of Rights, Burden of Proof," *Constitutional Law of Canada, 199*, Carswell: Toronto, 1997 at p.690.)
31. Bill C-6, 2nd Session, 37th Parliament, *An Act to establish the Canadian Centre for the Independent Resolution of First Nations Specific Claims to provide for the filing, negotiation and resolution of specific claims and to make related amendments to other Acts.*
32. *An Act to Encourage the Gradual Civilization of the Indian Tribes in this Province.*
33. See Glossary.
34. In Canada, a *public inquiry* is an inquiry established by an order-in-council under either Part I or Part II of the *Public Inquiries Act* R.S.C., c. I-13.
35. For a most helpful study of policy oriented public inquiries and their procedures see Liora Salter, *Public Inquiries in Canada.*
36. *Burdens of Proof in Modern Discourse*, New Haven & London: Yale University Press, 1992.
37. This is an instance in which Gaskins uses the term "burden of proof" but defines that burden as "the risk of non-persuasion," i.e., in this context, the burden defined by the U.S. Supreme Court as "the burden of persuasion." (Rule 301)
38. Gaskins, at pp.54–57. Gaskins is as critical of the reasoning in *Brown* as he is sympathetic to the outcome.
39. Gaskins at pp.62–69 and p.175.
40. Chapter Five, "The Erosion of Scientific Authority" and Chapter Six, "The Rise of Ethical Authority" *Burdens of Proof* at pp.141 and 169.
41. Gaskins at pp.172–176, 184–185, 192–194.
42. Gaskins at p. xv.
43. "arguments, types of," *Ox. Comp. to Phil.* at p.49, col.2.
44. "*argumentum ad ignorantiam,*" Black's at p.102, col. 2.
45. Gaskins at p. 55.
46. *Mein Kampf* was the book in which Adolph Hitler laid out his National Socialist (Nazi) agenda.
47. "The great masses of the people [. . .] will more easily fall victims to a big lie than to a small one." Adolph Hitler, *Mein Kampf*, quoted by Sissela Bok in "Lying to Enemies" *Lying: Moral Choice in Public and Private Life*, London: Quartet, 1980. Hitler's chapter on "Propaganda" is written as a critique of Allied propaganda in World War I. It serves, in turn, as a statement of his own strategies and tactics.

48. Some objection has been taken to the term "minority" particularly when it is used in regard to populations which are either a majority or a large plurality. I use the term "minority" not as an indicator of a communities' numerical strength but of their political strength, i.e., their power position. In this sense, any identifiable group which can be said to be "disadvantaged" within the meaning of s. 15 of the *Canadian Charter of Rights and Freedoms* and, therefore, entitled to affirmative action, so long as they remain disadvantaged, may also be described as being in a "minority position." The *Canadian Charter of Rights and Freedoms* constitutes Part I of the *Constitution Act, 1982*. Part II of the *Constitution Act, 1982*, more commonly referred to as section 35, deals with "the rights of the *Aboriginal Peoples of Canada*." The *Constitution Act, 1982* can be found at http://www.canlii.org/ca/const_en/const1982.html.
49. Although ministers invariably insist that their policies conform with all existing laws, instances abound in which the courts have found to the contrary. In Canada, the instances in which the courts have declared a ministerial authority to be without a legal foundation tends to be particularly prevalent in those few federal departments that deal with marginalized people, e.g., Indian Affairs, Immigration, Employment Insurance. The one federal department that deals with people of influence that has been criticized by the courts for arbitrary exercise of unsanctioned authority is the Canada Customs and Revenue Agency, i.e., the tax department. The presumption that policy reflects law requires continuing scrutiny. Likewise, it is dangerous to assume that the policy of one department will be the same as that of another in regard to the same issue.
50. A voluminous collection of administrative memoranda together with a sizeable collection of cabinet documents was reviewed in my master's thesis, *The Bureaucratic Response to the [1983] Penner Report*, York University, 1992. I take this collection to be indicative of the workings of the Indian Affairs Branch. This collection will be drawn upon for background to the parliamentary committee proceedings throughout the narrative chapters.
51. Chapter 134, R.S.B.C. 1960
52. Criminal law in Canada is federal. Throughout Canada criminal proceedings are governed by the Canada *Evidence Act*. The Canadian *Criminal Code* and the *Evidence Act* can be found at http://canada.justice.gc.ca.
53. Section 12, *Evidence Act*, Chap. R.S.B.C. 134, 1960.
54. Interview notes, 1971.
55. Quakers have long preferred to avoid taking of oaths precisely because of their "knowledge of God." Many observant Jews take the same point of view.
56. New York: Dix & Edwards, 1857, republished by Airmont Publishing Company Inc., reprinted in conjunction with Ryerson Press, Toronto,

1966. The full title of Chapter 26 reads, "Containing the Metaphysics of Indian-hating, According to the Views of One Evidently not so Prepossessed as Rousseau in Favour of Savages."

57. Minneapolis: University of Minnesota Press,1980.
58. *Facing West* at p.55.
59. Summarized in Appendix "A" at p.60.
60. Brian Slattery, "A Theory of the Charter," *Osgoode Hall Law Journal*, [25] 1987 4, at page 701.
61. Under the parliamentary system of government, unlike the Congressional system all ministers are members of either the House of Commons or the Senate.
62. "Development of Indian Government Options" A Paper prepared for the Deputy Ministers' Committee, July, 1983. L6d4#101. Legisla3.
63. "intend," *Gage*
64. "Golden Rule" *The Ox. Companion to the Bible* at p.257. Jesus statement occurs in the "Sermon on the Mount" in Luke 6:31 and in Matthew 7:12.
65. Quoted from Babylonian Talmud, Shabbat, 31a.
66. "Golden Rule" *Ox. Comp. Bible* offers the view that the distinction often made between the two—that the negative formulation is based on common sense and the positive "on Jesus' higher ethical concerns . . . fails to hold because the positive form occurs in extrabiblical writing . . . and the negative form occurs in Christian literature, such as a variant reading in Acts 15:20." The effort to create religious stereotypes around the two variations ignores the possibility that both statements were deeply textured by the contexts in which they were uttered.
67. "Kant," *Ox. Comp. Phil* at p. 435.
68. Those scientific methods which test hypotheses may also appear to be prospective to the extent that the result becomes known *after* and presumably *as a result* of the experiment, What a scientific hypothesis has in common with an intuition about a person or an ethical issue is that hypotheses are frequently intuitions that come to the scientist's mind after a period of intense study and thought. ("Logic of Discovery," *Concise Routledge Encyclopedia of Philosophy* at p.808.)

    Scientific experiments are, however, quite different from either deep ethical intuitions or self-evident principles in one critical respect. It is central to such scientific methods to hold that the results that are revealed through testing are always true. Descartes went so far as to hold that if there were no such thing as triangles, the laws regarding triangles would still be valid. The expression "law of nature" appears presently out of fashion. The result, nonetheless, is thought to demonstrate something that has *always been true* whenever similar conditions existed. ("René Descartes," *The Encyclopedia of Philosophy* Volumes 1&2 at p.344.)
69. In 1999, for example, in Ontario, the "Children's Bill of Rights" in the *Child and Family Services Act* was re-written to reflect the values of

the Harris Government in contrast to those which predominated in the Ontario Legislature during David Peterson's tenure. (s. 1, *The Child and Family Services Act*, Consolidated Family Law Statutes and Regulations, 2000, Toronto: Carswell, 1999) For a comprehensive comparison of *The Child and Family Services Acts, 1985 and 1999* see Eisenstat and Posluns, Chapter Three, *The Child and Family Services Act Manual*, Toronto: Ontario Federation of Indian Friendship Centres, 2000.)

70. "Future testing" is, admittedly, a figure of speech. We can only truly test a future after it has become part of the past. However, we can and often do make decisions based on predictions of the most likely outcome. When such predictions are stated in substantial terms it is possible not only to test them after the fact but to work toward fulfillment of those objectives during a probationary period and, indeed, thereafter.
71. "privilege," *Gage Canadian Dictionary*. See also "Privilege," *Ox. Comp. to Law* at p.995.
72. "technique," OED.
73. In a disciplinary proceeding there may not be a formal shifting of burdens. Nonetheless, the burden has shifted conceptually by the requirements follow protocols, adhere to standards and keep records identifying his diagnoses, treatments and prescriptions.
74. The outstanding example of an American governmental agencies which has been unable to produce records required by a court is, not surprisingly, the Bureau of Indian Affairs (U.S. B.I.A.). For details see, *Corbell v. Norton*.
75. "Benefit," *OED*
76. Brian Slattery, "A Theory of the Charter," *Osgoode Hall L.J. [25] 1987 4.*
77. *Inquiries Act*, Chapter I-11, *Statutes of Canada*. "Powers of commissioners concerning evidence" for inquiries under Part I are set out in s.4 "Powers of commissioners" for inquiries under Part II are set out in s.7.
78. One excellent and quite recent example may be found in Hon. Fred Kaufman, C.M., Q.C., *The Commission on Proceedings Involving Guy Paul Morin* (Toronto: Queen's Printer, 1998).
79. Indeed, lamenting the practice of granting authority to act through appropriation acts has been a major theme of the reports of the Joint Committee on Statutory Instruments and its predecessors. (Forsey and McCleave, *Fifth Report* of the Joint Committee on Regulations and Statutory Instruments, 1978. Hereafter, *Forsey-McCleave*)
80. The features of policy documentation described in these two paragraphs is particularly characteristic of Canadian Indian policy. These features have had a significant effect on efforts to re-direct policy and to develop institutions of First Nations government. For example, however outdated the *Indian Act* may be, it is not an authority for many areas of federal policy. These effects will be touched on in the narrative chapters and discussed in more detail in the analysis and conclusion.
81. As adopted by both Houses of Parliament in the *Second and Fifth Forsey-McCleave Committee Reports*.

82. Berger, "The Debate at Valldadolid," *A Long and Terrible Shadow* at pp.15–25.
83. *Johnson v. M'Intosh*, 21 U.S. Wheat 543 (1823)
84. See both Chancellor Boyd in the trial court in *St. Catharines' Milling and Lumber* and Lord Watson in the Privy Council. The four *St. Catharines* decisions can be found in vol. 1 of the *Canadian Native Law Cases* nos. 37–38 at http://library.usask.ca/native/cnlc/index.html.
85. Stannard, *American Holocaust* at p.131.
86. *Calder v. A-G. B.C. [1973] S.C.R 313.*
87. Harold Vetter, "The Double Bind Concept," *Language, Behavior and Psychopathology* (Chicago: Rand McNally & Company, 1969) at pp.167–180.
88. Transl. Constance Farrington, *Wretched of the Earth*, New York: Grove Press, 1968. Transl., Charles Lam Markmann, *Black Skin, White Masks*, New York: Grove Press, 1982. Transl., Haakon Chevalier, *Toward the African Revolution: political essays,* New York: Grove Press, 1967.
89. Transl., Eleanor Levieux, *Jews and Arabs*, Chicago: J.P. O'Hara, 1975. Transl., Judy Hyun, *The Liberation of the Jew*, New York: Orion Press, 1966. *Portrait du colonisé*, Montréal: L'Etincelle, 1972.
90. J. Edward Chamberlin and Sander Gilman editors, *Degeneration: The Dark Side of Progress* (New York: Columbia University Press, 1985).
91. J. Edward Chamberlin, *Come Back to Me My Language: Poetry and the West Indians*, Toronto: McClelland & Stewart, 1993.
92. See discussion of Dr. P.H. Bryce and S.H. Blake, Q.C. in chapter 2.
93. *Worcester v. Georgia,* (1832), 6 Peters 515 at 520.
94. *Nowegijick v. The Queen et al.* Reported: (1983),C.T.C. 20, 83 D.T.C. 5041, 46 N.R. 41
95. Mr. Justice Ian Binnie, *Will-Kare Paving v. The Queen*2000 SCC 36 at para.55.

NOTES TO CHAPTER TWO

1. See, for example, Noel Lyon's testimony regarding the *St. Regis Islands Act*, summarized in Chapter Three.
2. *MacGuigan-Molgat* at p. 3:19:52.
3. 17 George V, Chapter 32, *Statutes of Canada*, 1927.
4. Lit., "an argument from ignorance." This kind of argument asserts something as a bald fact unsupported by evidence so that it appears that the burden of proof lies with the responding party. Richard H. Gaskins, *Burdens of Proof in Modern Discourse*, New Haven & London: Yale University Press, 1992.
5. *RCAP Report*, Volume 1, *Looking Back, Looking Forward.* I have replied to this thesis in "Evading the Unspeakable: A Commentary on *Looking Back, Looking Forward, Canada Watch* 5, 5 (1997), at p. 87.
6. Alan Cairns, *Citizens Plus: Aboriginal peoples and the Canadian State*, Vancouver: U.B.C. Press, 2000, at p. 48.

7. In Canada, there are two government departments directly under the Prime Minister: (1) the Prime Minister's Office and (2) the Privy Council Office. The PCO is ostensibly non-partisan and has overall responsibility for coordinating all other departments. It also has overall responsibility for constitutional development and for the machinery of government.
8. "Assimilate," *OED*.
9. The 1929 *Act to Amend the Indian Act* created s. 149A under which it became an offense "to raise funds for the purpose of pressing an Indian land claim." I consider that this is tantamount to making the pressing of the claim punishable.
10. "Assimilate," *OED*.
11. *Looking Forward, Looking Back*, at record 1444.
12. *Ibid.* "The Relationship in Historical Perspective, 8. Extending Measures of Control and Assimilation" at Record 1038, citing J. Leslie and R. Maguire, ed., *The Historical Development of the Indian Act*, second edition, (Ottawa: Treaties and Historical Research Centre, Department of Indian Affairs and Northern Development, 1978) at p.115.
13. *Akwesasne Notes* Spring, 1972.
14. Disability: "Incapacity in the eyes of the law. **Civil disability.** The condition of a person who has had a legal right or privilege revoked . . ." *Black's* at p.474. *Black's* contemplates that a civil disability is imposed "as a result of a criminal conviction." This makes the arbitrary nature of a situation in which a civil right enjoyed by the rest of the community is arbitrarily withdrawn from a particular group, typically a cultural, ethnic or racial group all the more apparent. See also *The Blackwell Dictionary of Judaica*, at p.117 " . . . the usage and social disadvantage suffered by Jews as a result of restrictive laws and customs."
15. The proceedings of this committee are summarized in a chapter of *The Fourth World* entitled "We Honour our Grandfathers who Kept us Alive," pp.83–95.
16. *The Fourth World* at p.95.
17. Section 6, *An Act to Amend the Indian Act*, Statutes of Canada, Chap. 134, 1927.
18. *St. Catharines Milling and Lumber Company v. The Queen*, (1887), 13 S.C.R. 577.
19. CNLC vol. 1, Case 37. http://library.usask/ca/native/cnlc/index.html
20. CNLC vol. 1, Case 40. http://library.usask/ca/native/cnlc/index.html
21. The term "assimilation" has been identified with bad faith dealings for so long and on the part of so many imperial powers that it is difficult to regard the distinction between "positive assimilation" and "negative assimilation" as meaningful. Some proponents of honouring treaty rights and fulfilling trust responsibilities were of the view that the long-term result would resemble what we now mean by "integration." The first of the two *OED* definitions could be a synonym for "integration."
22. A line on a ship's hull showing how heavily it may be loaded, i.e., loading the ship so that the hull is submerged below the Plimsoll line is an endangerment.

23. The common notion that the policies of assimilation reflected the values of the day overlooks the range of views in the 19th and early 20th century that roundly criticized both Canadian and American Indian policy. For a thorough and far reaching discussion of American Indian policy in the same period, and its critics, see Richard Drinnon, *Facing West: The Metaphysics of Indian Hating and Empire Building*, Minneapolis: University of Minnesota Press, 1980.
24. Volume 1 of the *Report of the Royal Commission on Aboriginal Peoples, Looking Forward, Looking Back* is the Commission's view of the history of Aboriginal and First Nations relations with Britain and Canada.
25. *Saturday Night*, November 23, 1907, quoted in *Looking Forward, Looking Back*, at record 1824.
26. "Memorandum to the Hon. Frank Oliver, Minister of the Interior," January 27, 1907, quoted in *Report of the Royal Commission on Aboriginal Peoples*, at record 1825.
27. The Deputy Superintendent General, before 1951, corresponds to the contemporary position of Deputy Minister.
28. "PART TWO: False Assumptions and a Failed Relationship: Veterans," *Looking Forward, Looking Back*. This was also at the core of the brief of the National Indian Veterans' Association to the Standing Committee on Indian Affairs and Northern Development hearings on Bill C-31, in 1985. For a particular instance, see the *Proceedings* of the Standing Committee on the *Fort Nelson Indian Minerals Revenue Sharing Act*, 1980, which provided restitution to a band who were forced off their reserve in favour of non-Indian veterans and, consequently, also deprived of oil and gas revenues to which they would otherwise have been entitled. Displacement of Indian communities in favour of veterans was the basis of *Blueberry River Indian Band v. Canada*, [1995] 2 S.C.R. 387.
29. See *St. Peter's*.
30. I have generally avoided this phrase in my writing. In attempting to offer synonyms for "assimilation" I find few others offered. However, there is support for the equation of "assimilation" and "cultural genocide" in an article entitled "The Case for Assimilation" by Jonathan Kay, in *The National Post* of Dec. 8, 2001. This article carried the banner headline: "Assimilation: Cultural Genocide or Great Leap Forward." The editors seem not to have been aware that the loss of 20 million people in the Great Leap Forward under Mao Zedung, in 1958, had many of the earmarks of genocide, both cultural and physical.
31. U.N.T.S. No. 1021, vol. 78 (1951), p. 277. Resolution 260 (III) of the United Nations General Assembly on 9 December 1948.
32. This becomes evident when one compiles and analyzes the oral traditions of resistance in various First Nations communities.
33. All these leaders were fluent in their own language and English.
34. Chapter Three.
35. Chapter Three.
36. George Manuel's mentor, Andrew Paull, had been the leader whose 1926 petition was an immediate factor contributing to the 1927 *Indian*

Act amendment prohibiting fund raising for the purpose of pressing land claims. Ernest Benedict recalled, in a personal interview, attending meetings in St. Regis village when Fred Loft had come to speak. The meeting, Benedict said, had been interrupted by an R.C.M.P. constable who noticed a concentration of automobiles. Benedict had devoted much of his veteran's charter after WWII to developing a local newspaper at Akwesasne. He took care to produce it at Hogansburg, a non-reservation village surrounded by the New York State St. Regis reservation.

37. Poerksen, Uwe; *Plastic Words: The Tyranny of a Modular Language,* Pennsylvania University Press, University Park, Pennsylvania, 1995.
38. *Gage.*
39. "Indian Policy" were the two enlarged words written across the cover and forming the key part of the official title. Jean Chrétien, *Statement of the Government of Canada on Indian Policy*, 1969, Ottawa, Queen's Printer.
40. *Making Canadian Indian Policy: The Hidden Agenda, 1968–1970*, Toronto, University of Toronto Press, 1981. Weaver details the struggle between PCO and DIAND. In *The Fourth World,* George Manuel examines the consultations held through the National Indian Advisory Council and through the Andras Task Force and the extent to which they were simply disregarded in the writing of the Government Statement.
41. 17 George V, Chapter 32, *Statutes of Canada*, 1927.
42. Section 6, An Act to Amend the Indian Act, chap. 32, 1927. Quoted in The Fourth World at p.126.
43. Mackenzie King's attitude is discussed in *The Fourth World.* The issue arising from government policy is the subject of Chapter 12, "Veterans" in the *RCAP Report.* The request that Aboriginal and treaty rights be integrated with full Canadian citizenship is a recurring theme running throughout the testimony of veterans to the 1947–48 Joint Committee on Indian Affairs. The failure to implement this request culminates in the same view characterizing "Citizens Plus" as that term was used first by Hawthorn and then by Harold Cardinal in his book by the same name.
44. The Fourth World at p.129.
45. Harold Cardinal, *The Unjust Society.*
46. Uwe Poerkson, *Plastic Words.*
47. See Glossary, *Constitution Act, 1982.*

NOTES TO CHAPTER THREE

1. MacGuigan, a Trudeau Liberal, had been elected from the Ontario riding of Windsor-Walkerville in 1968. He had earlier collaborated with Maxwell Cohen and Pierre Trudeau and others on the Special Committee on Hate Propaganda. Lester Pearson had appointed Maurice Lamontagne, an economist who had previously represented Outremont in the House of Commons, to the Senate. Gildas Molgat replaced Lamontagne early in the first of the three sessions during which this Committee sat.

2. In the testimony that I examined for this purpose, none of the elected leader from a provincial or territorial administration or from a non-Indian political or cultural organization was challenged as to his or her representivity. In my 40 years of reading parliamentary committee proceedings such challenges have occurred in a non-Indian context only very rarely.
3. The term "public servant," although it may have been a generic term earlier did not come into common use in Ottawa until the introduction of the *Public Service Employment Act* in 1967. Audrey Doerr, "The Public Service," *The Canadian Encyclopedia*, CD-ROM.
4. The Standing Committee had been the forum for parliamentary approval of the Estimates of the Department of Indian Affairs and Northern Development since it became Commons practice, in 1969, to send the Estimates to standing committees rather than to the Committee of the Whole House. For background on federal Parliamentary committees see C.E.S. Francks, "Committees," *The Canadian Encyclopedia.*
5. Observations of the author while engaged in public relations at the National Indian Brotherhood.
6. "Mandate," *Final Report.*
7. *Final Report,* Joint Committee of the Senate and the House of Commons on the Constitution of Canada, 28th Parliament, 4th Session, Sen. Gildas L. Molgat and Mark MacGuigan, M.P., Chairmen, (Ottawa: The Queen's Printer). (Hereafter *MacGuigan-Molgat Final Report* Committee, 1972).
8. Gerald Beaudoin, "Constitutional Law," *The Canadian Encyclopedia* (Toronto: McClelland & Stewart Inc., 1996, CD-ROM).
9. Stephen Clarkson and Christina McCall, *Trudeau and Our Times, Vol. 1: The Magnificent Obsession* (1990: McClelland & Stewart, Toronto) at p.124. Bourassa's initial acceptance of the Victoria Charter followed by a rejection upon his return to Quebec is strikingly similar to Levesque's initial acceptance and later rejection of the constitutional amending formula in 1981.
10. Keith Banting & Richard Simeon, *And No One Cheered: Federalism, Democracy & the Constitution Act,* (Agincourt, Ont.: Methuen Publications, 1983)
11. *MacGuigan-Molgat* at 2:1:26.
12. *MacGuigan-Molgat* at 2:1:28.
13. F.R. Scott, "W.L.M.K.," *15 Canadian Poets X2*, Gary Geddes, ed., Toronto, O.U.P., 1990, at pp. 46–47.
14. *MacGuigan-Molgat*2:1:43.
15. Conversation with a former executive assistant to Dr. Courchene.
16. *MacGuigan-Molgat*p.2:9:79.
17. Ibid.
18. Nixon's administration was repeatedly cited for a variety of executive misconducts in the trials following 1973 events Wounded Knee. The dismissal of charges against Russell Means and Dennis Banks is detailed in successive issues of *Akwesasne Notes* 1983–1985. Other dismissals are discussed by Peter Matthiessen in *The Spirit of Crazy Horse,* Viking Adult, 1991.

19. Thirteen years later Courchene's argument, which had been considered novel, and even courageous in 1970 was largely adopted by the Supreme Court in *Nowegijick v. The Queen* [1983) 1 S.C.R. 29.
20. *MacGuigan-Molgat*2:9:76.
21. *MacGuigan-Molgat*2:9:78.
22. *MacGuigan-Molgat*2:9:78.
23. *MacGuigan-Molgat*2:9:79.
24. *MacGuigan-Molgat* at 2:9:78–9.
25. *MacGuigan-Molgat*2:9:78.
26. "reconcile," *Gage.*
27. *MacGuigan-Molgat*2:9:79.
28. *MacGuigan-Molgat* 2:9:80.
29. Nixon's statement that "The first Americans—the Indians—are the most deprived and most isolated minority group in our nation" stressed that the people described by that phrase are a part "of our nation," an idea which stands over against both historical policy and those more strongly sovereigntist Native American views. Indeed, this opening line might be read as Nixon's own limit on the self-determination of which he speaks a few paragraphs later.

    When the term "First Americans" was adapted as *the first Canadians,* in the *Final Report,* the conceptual difficulties become much more apparent. One might allow that "America" has become the name of a continent. Or, that there is a tendency amongst United States people to see America as eternal and hence, to conceive that those who were here before the mists of time must be "the first Americans." To adapt that idea to speak of First Nations as "the first Canadians" is to substitute a re-writing of history for a re-forming of policy. The idea that one might be both "Indian" and "Canadian" was explicitly rejected by Mackenzie King in 1947 and was still difficult for some members of the Constitution Committee to grasp in 1971. There is no evidence that the Canadian state had embraced the idea of Indians as Canadian citizens before 1960.
30. *MacGuigan-Molgat* at p. 2:9:78.
31. *MacGuigan-Molgat* at p 2:9:76.
32. *MacGuigan-Molgat* at p. 2:9:88.
33. The zero plural is usually reserved for game animals and fish. "If the animals are being thought of as individuals, the plural form is used. *If they are a category of game, they have a zero plural.*" David Crystal, "Invariable Nouns," *The Cambridge Encyclopedia of the English Language* at p.201. In an earlier era, the zero plural was also used for a variety of non-European cultures. See, for example, Cheyette's Constructions *of 'the Jew' in English Literature and society: Racial representations 1875* to 1945. "Native" cultures appeal to be the one human classification which continues to elicit a zero plural in English. This may be a residue of the earlier distinction between "man" and "Native" as per Stannard.

34. *MacGuigan-Molgat* at p. 2:9:88.
35. *MacGuigan-Molgat* at p. 2:9:88.
36. *MacGuigan-Molgat* at p. 2:9:85.
37. *MacGuigan-Molgat* at p. 2:9:85.
38. *MacGuigan-Molgat* at p. 2:9:85.
39. *MacGuigan-Molgat* at p. 2:9:123.
40. *MacGuigan-Molgat* at p. 2:9:122.
41. *MacGuigan-Molgat* at p. 2:9:129.
42. *MacGuigan-Molgat* at p. 2:9:129.
43. *MacGuigan-Molgat* at p. 2:9:129.
44. *MacGuigan-Molgat* at p. 2:9:129.
45. Under the *Indian Act*, a person is entitled to be registered as an Indian, if he has a male ancestor who was entitled to be registered. The general direction of the membership rules under the Indian Act is to restrict membership with a long term view of eliminating most of those who presently qualify. In contrast, Indians within the meaning of section 91(24) of the *Constitution Act*, 1867 following the Supreme Court's decision in Re: *Eskimos (sub nom. Re Term "Indians")* [1939] S.C.R. 104) appears to include anyone who has ancestral and lifestyle connections to an indigenous community in Canada. Reference question and answer summarized: '"Does the term 'Indians' as used in Head 24 of s. 91 of the B.N.A. Act, 1867, include Eskimo inhabitants of the Province of Quebec?" Answered in affirmative.' Also reported at: http://library.usask.ca/native/cnlc/vol05/123.html.
46. *MacGuigan-Molgat* at p. 2:9:129.
47. "The Relationship in Historical Perspective, 6. Stage 3: Displacement and Assimilation, The Forging of Métis Identity *RCAP* at Record 867. Also Records 7954, 9711. Also "Métis Perspectives," *RCAP* vol. 4 Chapter 5.
48. *MacGuigan-Molgat* at p. 2:13:7.
49. *MacGuigan-Molgat* at p. 2:13:19.
50. *MacGuigan-Molgat* at p. 2:13:19.
51. *MacGuigan-Molgat* at p. 2:16:11.
52. *MacGuigan-Molgat* at p. 3:3:4.
53. *MacGuigan-Molgat* at p. 3:3:4.
54. *MacGuigan-Molgat* at p3:3:4.
55. *MacGuigan-Molgat* at p. 3:3:4.
56. *MacGuigan-Molgat* at p. 3:3:4.
57. *MacGuigan-Molgat* at p. 3:3:7.
58. *MacGuigan-Molgat* at p. 3:3:9.
59. *MacGuigan-Molgat* at 2:3:9.
60. *MacGuigan-Molgat* at p. 3:3:9.
61. *MacGuigan-Molgat* at p. 3:3:9.
62. *MacGuigan-Molgat* at p. 3:3:9.
63. *MacGuigan-Molgat* at p. 3:3:9.
64. *MacGuigan-Molgat* at p. 3:3:9.

65. Quoted in *Native Rights in Canada,* first edition at frontispiece. See also *The Fourth World.*
66. *MacGuigan-Molgat* at p. 3:3:9.
67. Dickson J., in *Guérin* at 132 quoting Hall J. in *Calder* at 390.
68. *MacGuigan-Molgat*3:14:38.
69. *MacGuigan-Molgat*3:14:38.
70. *MacGuigan-Molgat*3:14:38.
71. *MacGuigan-Molgat*3:14:38.
72. *MacGuigan-Molgat*3:14:39.
73. *MacGuigan-Molgat*3:14.
74. *MacGuigan-Molgat*3:14:42
75. *MacGuigan-Molgat*3:14:42
76. *MacGuigan-Molgat*3:14:42
77. *MacGuigan-Molgat*3:14.
78. Dickson, C.J., *Sparrow* at p.44.
79. Emphasis added. Parties to a treaty do not "ask for things" in the treaty. The treaty sets out an agreement, in whole or in part, of the matters on which the parties to the treaty have agreed upon. Whatever requests are noted in the treaty were *requested and agreed upon* prior to the signing of the written treaty. The point deserves emphasis because I doubt that it would have been a point of confusion in a non-Indigenous context.
80. See Glossary for the meaning of "honour of the Crown" and its origin in legal decisions.
81. *MacGuigan-Molgat* at p. 3:14:45.
82. *MacGuigan-Molgat* at p. 3:14:45.
83. Cardinal had presented the Alberta *Red Paper* in the summer before these hearings. Manuel argued that such a comprehensive plan had been laid out both before the Andras Task Force and the National Indian Advisory Council prior to the *White Paper.*
84. These events are discussed in some detail in Chapter Three, "First Nations Relations Before 1970."
85. "Consultation," *OED.*
86. *MacGuigan-Molgat*3:16:6.
87. *MacGuigan-Molgat*3:16:6.
88. *MacGuigan-Molgat*Proceedings at p. 3:16:7.
89. *MacGuigan-Molgat*Proceedings at p. 3:16:7.
90. *MacGuigan-Molgat*Proceedings at p. 3:16:7.
91. *MacGuigan-Molgat*Proceedings at p. 3:16:7.
92. *MacGuigan-Molgat*Proceedings at p. 3:16:7.
93. *MacGuigan-Molgat*Proceedings at p. 3:16:11. Although the *Proceedings* do not allow a capital for "native" or for "Aboriginal," they do allow that "White" is a proper noun. The scale which allows more particularity for "White" than for "Native" is one best known to *Hansard.*
94. *MacGuigan-Molgat*3:16:12.
95. *MacGuigan-Molgat* at p. 3:16:23.
96. *MacGuigan-Molgat* at p. 3:18:36.

97. *MacGuigan-Molgat* at p. 3:18:27.
98. *MacGuigan-Molgat* at p. 3:18:27.
99. *MacGuigan-Molgat* at p. 3:18:34.
100. *MacGuigan-Molgat* at p. 3:18:34.
101. *MacGuigan-Molgat* at p. 3:19:51.
102. *MacGuigan-Molgat* at p. 3:19:52.
103. *MacGuigan-Molgat* at p. 3:19:52.
104. *MacGuigan-Molgat* at p. 3:19:52.
105. *MacGuigan-Molgat* at p. 3:19:52.
106. Parliamentary Committee *Proceedings* in this period, even in their final bound form, did not italicize or underline the names of statutes or legal cases. Where I am quoting I will attempt to follow the original usage.
107. *MacGuigan-Molgat* at p. 3:19:53.
108. *MacGuigan-Molgat* at p. 3:19:54.
109. *MacGuigan-Molgat* at p. 3:19:54.
110. *MacGuigan-Molgat* at p. 3:19:54.
111. *MacGuigan-Molgat* at p. 3:19:54.
112. *MacGuigan-Molgat* at p. 3:19:54.
113. *MacGuigan-Molgat* at p. 3:19:54.
114. *MacGuigan-Molgat* at p. 3:19:54.
115. *MacGuigan-Molgat* at p. 3:19:55.
116. *MacGuigan-Molgat* at p. 3:19:55.
117. *MacGuigan-Molgat* at p. 3:19:53.
118. *MacGuigan-Molgat* at p. 3:19:57.
119. *MacGuigan-Molgat* at p. 3:19:58.
120. *MacGuigan-Molgat* at p. 3:19:60.
121. *Guerin v. The Queen* [1984] 2 S.C.R. 335.
122. The accent does not appear either in the testimony or in the 1984 Supreme Court decision.
123. *MacGuigan-Molgat* at p. 3:26:42.
124. *MacGuigan-Molgat* at p. 3:27:77.
125. *MacGuigan-Molgat* at p. 3:26:77.
126. *MacGuigan-Molgat* at p. 3:26:77.
127. *MacGuigan-Molgat* at p. 3:27:77.
128. *MacGuigan-Molgat* at p. 3:26:77.
129. *MacGuigan-Molgat* at p. 3:26:77.
130. *MacGuigan-Molgat* at p. 3:26:77.
131. *MacGuigan-Molgat* at p. 3:26:79.
132. *MacGuigan-Molgat* at p. 3:26:80.
133. *MacGuigan-Molgat* at p. 3:26:79.
134. *MacGuigan-Molgat* at p. 3:26:79.
135. Variations on this attitude continue. See, for example, discussions on the election of a new chair for the Senate Committee on Aboriginal Peoples in the *Proceedings of that Committee* of Feb. 16, 2000. Upon the resignation of Charlie Watt, Jack Austin, a former Minister of State for Social Development and a Senator from B.C. agreed to take the chair for the

duration of the hearings on the *Nisga'a Final Agreement* bill. Sen. Aurelian Gill, an Innu leader from Quebec took the chair when the Committee returned to its public inquiry role.

136. *MacGuigan-Molgat* at p. 3:26:79.
137. *MacGuigan-Molgat* at p. 3:26:80.
138. *MacGuigan-Molgat* at p. 3:27:80.
139. *MacGuigan-Molgat* at p. 3:27:81.
140. *MacGuigan-Molgat* at p. 3:27:81.
141. *MacGuigan-Molgat* at p. 3:27:83.
142. *MacGuigan-Molgat* at p. 3:27:83.
143. *MacGuigan-Molgat* at p. 3:27:83.
144. *MacGuigan-Molgat* at p. 3:27:83.
145. *MacGuigan-Molgat* at p. 3:27:83.
146. *MacGuigan-Molgat* at p. 3:27:85.
147. *MacGuigan-Molgat* at p. 3:27:85.
148. *MacGuigan-Molgat* at p. 3:27:85.
149. *MacGuigan-Molgat* at p. 3:27:85.
150. *MacGuigan-Molgat* at p. 3:27:85.
151. *MacGuigan-Molgat* at p. 3:27:88.
152. *MacGuigan-Molgat* at p. 3:40, Appendix DDD.
153. *MacGuigan-Molgat* at p. 3:59:4.
154. *MacGuigan-Molgat* at p. 3:59:7.
155. *MacGuigan-Molgat* at p. 3:59:7.
156. *MacGuigan-Molgat* at p. 3:58:8–9.
157. *MacGuigan-Molgat* at p. 3:59:7.
158. *MacGuigan-Molgat* at p. 3:59:9.
159. *MacGuigan-Molgat* 3:59:8–9.
160. *MacGuigan-Molgat* 3:59:8–9.
161. *MacGuigan-Molgat* 3:59:10–11.
162. Dickson, C.J., *Sparrow* at p.13.
163. *MacGuigan-Molgat* at p. 3:59:10–11.
164. *MacGuigan-Molgat* at p. 3:59:11.
165. *MacGuigan-Molgat* at p. 3:59:11.
166. Dickson, C.J., *Sparrow* at p.44.
167. Borrows, *Morality and Law*.
168. *MacGuigan-Molgat* at p. 3:68:40.
169. *MacGuigan-Molgat* at p. 3:68:42.
170. Indian men had been arguing for a rewriting or replacing of the *Indian Act* since the Joint Committee on Indian Affairs of 1947–48. They had, however, said that the *Act* ought not simply to be repealed but that it should be replaced by legislation recognizing Aboriginal and treaty rights. The deliberations of the National Indian Advisory Council and the Andras Task Force are summarized in *The Fourth World*.
171. *MacGuigan-Molgat* at p. 3:68:42.
172. MacGuigan-Lamontagne 30 3: 5:78.
173. *MacGuigan-Molgat* at p. 3:74:40.

174. *MacGuigan-Molgat* at p. 3:75:83.
175. MacGuigan Molgat at p.3:76:4.
176. The demand to allow Indian rights to be integrated with full citizenship is a recurring theme in the Joint Committee on Indian Affairs of 1947–48. The Hawthorn Report coined the phrase "Citizens Plus." Harold Cardinal revived the term "Citizens Plus," originally coined by Hawthorn, in *The Red Paper.*
177. "Citizenship," *The Canadian Encyclopedia.*
178. Interviews with George Manuel.
179. *MacGuigan-Molgat* at p. 3:76:9.
180. *MacGuigan-Molgat* at p. 3:76:5.
Reference to a single view held by "the native people" (sing.) represents at best an archaic and stereotyping rhetoric. Cumming would have been on more solid ground had he told the Committee that *an overwhelming majority of Indian leaders have objected* to the repeal of ss.91(24).
181. "Zero plural" is the use of the singular to refer to a human culture or an animal species *as a whole.* The zero plural was widely used in reference to human cultures in the 19th and early 20th century when social sciences sought to produce astute generalizations that could summarize cultures. Contemporary usage restricts the zero plural to game animals, e.g., "He took two deer today." "Zero plural," *Encyclopedia of Poetics.* See also note 33, p. 292
182. *MacGuigan-Molgat* at p. 3:76:7.
183. *MacGuigan-Molgat* at p. 3:76:7.
184. *MacGuigan-Molgat* at p. 3:76:24.
185. *MacGuigan-Molgat* at p. 3:76:17.
186. *MacGuigan-Molgat* at p. 3:76:9.
187. *MacGuigan-Molgat* at p. 3:76:24.
188. *Mac Guigan-Molgat* at p.3:76:13.
189. *MacGuigan-Molgat* at p. 3:87:28.
190. *MacGuigan-Molgat* at p. 3:87:28.
191. *MacGuigan-Molgat* at p. 3:87:28.
192. *MacGuigan-Molgat* at p. 3:87:28. (emphasis added)
193. *MacGuigan-Molgat* at p. 3:87:29.
194. *MacGuigan-Molgat* at p. 3:87:29.
195. "Equity," *Ox. Comp. to Law* at p.424.
196. "Equity," *Ox. Comp. to Law* at p.426.
197. "Equity," *Ox. Comp. to Law* at p.424.
198. "Equity," *Ox. Comp. to Law* at p.426.
199. "That which is hateful unto you do not do unto others," attributed to Rabbi Hillel in the Babylonian Talmud, Shabbat, 31a.
200. *MacGuigan-Molgat* at 3:87:32.
201. *Indian Affairs Committee*, 29:1:8 at pp.5–6 and 42–4. The notion of *defining* Aboriginal rights was embraced by the Government in s.37 of the *Constitution Act, 1982.* The hazards of defining rights are discussed in the Chapter Five, at p. 216.

202. *MacGuigan-Molgat*3:87:34.
203. *MacGuigan-Molgat*3:87:44.
204. *MacGuigan-Molgat*3:87:45.
205. *MacGuigan-Molgat*3:88:6.
206. *MacGuigan-Molgat*3:88:6.
207. *MacGuigan-Molgat*3:88:6.
208. Section 6, *An Act to Amend the Indian Act*, Chap. 134 1927.
209. *MacGuigan-Molgat*3:88:7.
210. *MacGuigan-Molgat*3:88:9.
211. *Guérin et al v. the Queen* [1985] 1 C.N.L.R. at 136.
212. *MacGuigan-Molgat*3:88:8.
213. *MacGuigan-Molgat*3:88:9.
214. *MacGuigan-Molgat*3:88:9.
215. *MacGuigan-Molgat*3:88:10.
216. *MacGuigan-Molgat*3:88:10.
217. *MacGuigan-Molgat*3:88:11.
218. *MacGuigan-Molgat*3:88:11.
219. *Kanatewat v. James Bay Development Corp.*, [1974] R.P. 38; reversed [1975] C.A. 166.
220. *MacGuigan-Molgat*3:88:14.
221. *MacGuigan-Molgat*3:88:14.
222. *MacGuigan-Molgat*3:88:18.
223. *MacGuigan-Molgat*3:88:19.
224. *Guérin v. The Queen* [1984] 2 S.C.R. 335.
225. *MacGuigan-Molgat*3:88:20.
226. "Representivity" is widely used in Ottawa in bureaucratic discussions as to whether or not government funded NGOs, including Native and First Nations organizations are representative of a particular constitutuency. This preoccupation of senior officials of the Dept. of the Secretary of State and its successors does not appear to merit entries in the leading dictionaries and reference works. The term does not appear in the OED on CD-ROM copyrighted 1994. It also does not appear in the *Gage Canadian Dictionary* 1998 or the *Ox. Comp. to World Politics.*
227. *MacGuigan-Molgat*3:88:20.
228. I borrow the term "dialogue of the deaf" from Jean-Paul Sartre's *Being and Nothingness.* I also want to acknowledge that the inability *to hear* is unrelated to the inability *to listen.*
229. The lack of preparation and the inability to grasp names of major organizations by some parliamentarians on this Committee goes well beyond anything that I have observed in several decades of tracking the major committees of the Senate and testimony on Indian Affairs in both Houses. Some garrulous opinionating is common on most parliamentary committees. That behaviour often appears to be aimed at displaying the prior knowledge of the field brought to the hearing by the parliamentarian. The behaviour here is atypical inasmuch as it does not serve that end but rather suggests that the parliamentarians lacked a grasp of the field represented

by the witnesses. I have long been struck by the ability of politicians of all kinds to recall names, an ability I personally lack. In contrast, I have not seen a tendency to confuse organizational categories, e.g., association, federation and brotherhood by parliamentarians in any other proceedings I have studied in the past 40 years.

230. *Nowigijick v. The Queen* [1983) 1 S.C.R. 29.
231. Courchene, in *MacGuigan-Molgat* at p. 2:9:78.
232. Niagara Conference," *Canada in the Making*, www.canadiana.org/citm/themes/aboriginals/boriginals2_e.html.
233. For an elaboration on mind games that is readily adaptable to Parliamentary events see Eric Berne, *Games People Play: The Psychology of Human Relationships*, New York: Ballantine Books, 1973.
234. John Ralston Saul, *Voltaire's Bastards: The Dictatorship of Reason in the West*, Toronto: Penguin, 1993.
235. *MacGuigan-Molgat* at p. 3:87:28 and p.127 above.
236. Cummings, *Native Rights in Canada*, Toronto, Indian Eskimo Association, 1973.
237. *St. Catharines Milling and Lumber Company v. The Queen*, (1887), 13 S.C.R. 577.
238. *Guérin v. The Queen* [1984] 2 S.C.R. 335clearly distinguished the fiduciary duties of the Crown from any presumption of wardship or First Nations incompetence. *R. v. Sparrow*, [1990] 1 S.C.R. 1075 set out a framework for ensuring that there were bona fide negotiations.
239. *Worcester v. Georgia*, 31 U.S. 525 (1832) USSC at p.543.
240. *Ibid.*
241. "native," *OED*.

NOTES TO CHAPTER FOUR

1. Aboriginal title is a particular kind of Aboriginal right. Aboriginal title, as the name suggests, is an interest in a particular piece of land. In contrast, almost all other Aboriginal rights are rights to certain activities, e.g., hunting, fishing, trapping. See Thomas Isaac, *Aboriginal Law: Commentary, Cases and Materials*. Purich Publishing Ltd., Saskatoon, 2003.
2. Joe Clark became the leader of the Progressive Conservative Party and following the election for the 31st Parliament formed a minority government. Flora MacDonald served as Minister of External Affairs in the short lived Clark Government.
3. The idea that the rights of a First Nation "pre-existed" any executive or legislative act of the British Crown or its successors was clearly laid out by John Marshall, Chief Justice of the U.S. Supreme Court in *Cherokee v. Georgia*.
4. *R. v. Sparrow*, B.C. Court of Appeal, (1986), 9 B.C.L.R., (2d) 300.
5. *Indian Affairs Committee*, Proceedings, 29:1:8:19–40.
6. Ian Watson, Chairman, *Fifth Report*, *Indian Affairs Committee* Subcommittee on the Status of Indian and Eskimo Education, June, 1971.

7. NIB press release, June 2, 1971 and accompanying briefing notes.
8. Press release of July 2, 1971 and briefing notes.
9. *Indian Affairs Committee*, at p. 29:1:18:5.
10. *Indian Affairs Committee*, at p. 29:1:18:13.
11. *Calder v. A-G. B.C.* [1973] S.C.R. at 348.
12. *The Fourth World* at p.225. This connection is also discussed in *Looking Back, Looking Forward*, vol. 1 of the *RCAP Report* at record 1124.
13. *Johnson v. M'Intosh* 21 U.S. (8 Wheat.), 1823.
14. *Kanatewat v. James Bay Development Corp.*, [1974] R.P. 38; reversed [1975] C.A. 166.
15. *Re Paulette et al., & the Registrar of Land Titles*, 39 D.L.R. (3d) 45, [1973] 6 W.W.R. 97.
16. *Indian Affairs Committee* 29 at 3:18:5.
17. "Technicians" was the term used in this period within First Nations organizations to describe staff who, like civil servants in the Canadian tradition, were politically neutral and served which ever political leadership was in office.
18. "Self-Government Chronology, 1975" at p.13. Summary of DIAND Document box L6D6F7.
19. "Self-Government Chronology, 1976" at p.14. L6DF67, 5230.
20. "Self–Government Chronology," 1976, MSSD doc#2 and 43603 L5D6.
21. MSSD Doc#4, MSSDCCBox239.
22. Self-Government Chronology, 1976, MSSD doc#4. 5240, p.16.
23. *Indian Affairs Committee* 30 3:3:5.
24. *Indian Affairs Committee* 30 3:3:5.
25. *Indian Affairs Committee* 30 3:3:6–7.
26. *Indian Affairs Committee* 30 3:3:8.
27. *Indian Affairs Committee* 30 3:3:8.
28. Soon after Sol Sanderson became president the Federation of Saskatchewan Indians became the Federation of Saskatchewan Indian Nations.
29. *Indian Affairs Committee* 30 3:3:24.
30. Major federal infrastructure programs, such as the Trans-Canada Highway, were financed through their own statutes with multi-year authority. Indian community infrastructure was funded exclusively through annual estimates and, hence, subject to Finance Department review from year to year. In 1983, the Special Committee on Indian Self-Government *(Penner)* specifically recommended that this disparity of treatment be ended. *Penner*, "Recommendations," "Fiscal Arrangements."
31. *Indian Affairs Committee* 30 3:3:29.
32. *Indian Affairs Committee* 30 3:3:830.
33. *Indian Affairs Committee* 30 3:4A:4–7.
34. *Indian Affairs Committee* 30 6:10.
35. *Indian Affairs Committee* 30 6:10.
36. *Indian Affairs Committee* 30 3:4:6. Faulkner's determination to proceed "with or without . . . the Indian leadership" resonates in statements of the Minister of Indian Affairs in 2001, Robert Nault. Nault went so far

as to accuse the National Chief of "failing to deliver," a phrase which suggests an expectation of the National Chief that was not previously articulated.

37. *Indian Affairs Committee* 30 3:7:8–12. Capitalization in this sentence occur in the original.
38. References to this Committee will be *MacGuigan-Lamontagne 30*. Since the Committee sat only in the third session of the 30th Parliament no session references is necessary. Hence, page numbers will consist only of the issue and the page number, e.g., 1:68.
39. Minutes of the Proceedings of the Senate of June 29, 1978
40. *MacGuigan-Molgat* at p. 2:3:45. See "Leger, Jules," *The Canadian Encyclopedia* on CD-ROM.
41. *MacGuigan-Lamontagne* 30 1:68.
42. *MacGuigan-Lamontagne* 30 1:70.
43. *MacGuigan-Lamontagne* 30 1:70.
44. *MacGuigan-Lamontagne* 30 1:70.
45. *MacGuigan-Lamontagne* 30 1:72.
46. *MacGuigan-Lamontagne* 30 1:75.
47. *MacGuigan-Lamontagne* 30 1:75.
48. *MacGuigan-Lamontagne* 30 4:10.
49. *MacGuigan-Lamontagne* 30 4:10.
50. *MacGuigan-Lamontagne* 30 4:11.
51. *MacGuigan-Lamontagne* 30 4:12.
52. *Constitutional Amendment Bill*, 1978.
53. *MacGuigan-Lamontagne* 30 4:12.
54. *MacGuigan-Lamontagne* 30 4:12.
55. *MacGuigan-Lamontagne* 30 4:29.
56. *MacGuigan-Lamontagne* 30 4:30.
57. *MacGuigan-Lamontagne* 30 4:31.
58. *MacGuigan-Lamontagne* 30 4:31.
59. *MacGuigan-Lamontagne* 30 4:31.
60. *MacGuigan-Lamontagne* 30 4:31.
61. *MacGuigan-Lamontagne* 30 4:39.
62. *Reference re: Resolution to Amend the Constitution*, [1981] 1 S.C.R. 753,
63. *MacGuigan-Lamontagne* 30 5:14.
64. *Reference re Resolution to Amend the Constitution*, [1981] 1 S.C.R. 753 (*Patriation Reference*).
65. *MacGuigan-Lamontagne* 30 5:40.
66. *MacGuigan-Lamontagne* 30 5:40.
67. *MacGuigan-Lamontagne* 30 5:40.
68. *MacGuigan-Lamontagne* 30 5:40.
69. *MacGuigan-Lamontagne* 30 5:40.
70. See Watson's statement in *MacGuigan-Molgat* 2:87:32 and Lambert at *MacGuigan-Molgat* 2:87:26.
71. *MacGuigan-Lamontagne* 30 5:40.
72. *MacGuigan-Lamontagne* 30 5:40.

73. *MacGuigan-Lamontagne* 30 5:48.
74. *MacGuigan-Lamontagne* 30 5:49.
75. *MacGuigan-Lamontagne* 30 5:50.
76. *MacGuigan-Lamontagne* 30 5:40.
77. *MacGuigan-Lamontagne* 30 5:78.
78. *MacGuigan-Lamontagne* 30 5:66.
79. *MacGuigan-Lamontagne* 30 5:66.
80. *MacGuigan-Lamontagne* 30 5:66.
81. *MacGuigan-Lamontagne* 30 5:66.
82. *MacGuigan-Lamontagne* 30 5:66.
83. *MacGuigan-Lamontagne* 30 5:66.
84. *MacGuigan-Lamontagne* 30 5:74.
85. *MacGuigan-Lamontagne* 30 5:74.
86. *MacGuigan-Lamontagne* 30 5:75.
87. *MacGuigan-Lamontagne* 30 5:78.
88. *MacGuigan-Lamontagne* 30 5:78.
89. *MacGuigan-Lamontagne* 30 5:78.
90. *MacGuigan-Lamontagne* 30 5:78.
91. *MacGuigan-Lamontagne* 30 7:6.
92. *MacGuigan-Lamontagne* 30 7:7.
93. *MacGuigan-Lamontagne* 30 7:8.
94. *MacGuigan-Lamontagne* 30 7:8.
95. *Reference re Authority of Parliament in relation to the Upper House*, [1980] 1 S.C.R.
96. *Reference re Resolution to Amend the Constitution*, [1981] 1 S.C.R. 753 (Patriation Reference).
97. *MacGuigan-Lamontagne* 30 7:9.
98. *MacGuigan-Lamontagne* 30 7:9.
99. *MacGuigan-Lamontagne* 30 7:9.
100. *MacGuigan-Lamontagne* 30 7:13.
101. *MacGuigan-Lamontagne* 30 7:13.
102. *MacGuigan-Lamontagne* 30 7:13.
103. *MacGuigan-Lamontagne* 30 7:13.
104. Eugene Forsey, *A Life on the Fringe: The Memoirs of Eugene Forsey*, Toronto: Ox. Univ. Press, 1990 at p. 157.
105. *MacGuigan-Lamontagne* 30 7:13.
106. *MacGuigan-Lamontagne* 30 12:16.
107. The full quote appears earlier in this chapter.
108. See earlier in this chapter.
109. The remarks quoted on p. 20 jibe with numerous personal observations.
110. See, for example, Marshall, U.S. C.J. in *Worcester v. Georgia*, (1832), 6 Peters 515 at 520.
111. *MacGuigan-Molgat Proceedings* at p. 3:16:7.
112. Chapter Five.
113. *Reference re Authority of Parliament in relation to the Upper House*, [1980] 1 S.C.R.

NOTES TO CHAPTER FIVE

1. *Trudeau and Our Times* at Vol. 1 at p.18.
2. "Self-Government Chronology, 1979" at p.24.
3. See Michael Posluns, *The Bureaucratic Response to the Penner Report*, Master's thesis, York University, Faculty of Environmental Studies.
4. "Self-Government Chronology, 1979" at p.24.
5. "Self-Government Chronology, 1979" at p.25.
6. "Self-Government Chronology, 1979" at p.25.
7. "Self-Government Chronology, 1979" at p.25.
8. Qualified offers to participate in constitutional talked that "directly relate" were discussed before the *MacGuigan-Lamontagne* Committee by Eric Tagoona, President of the Inuit Tapirisat at p.7:6, by Harry Daniels, president of the Native Council of Canada at p. 5:16, summarized in Narrative Appendix "B" at pp.388–389.
9. "Self-Government Chronology, 1979" at p.29.
10. Later reconfigured as the Standing Committee on Aboriginal Affairs, Northern Development and Natural Resources.
11. *Indian Affairs Committee* 31 at p. 1:15.
12. See, for example, Norman Zlotkin, "Aboriginal Customary Adoptions, A Valid Alternative to Statutory Adoptions," Endnote 1 and also Brian Slattery in "Understanding Aboriginal Rights," 66 C.B.R. at 727. footnotes 18 and 175.
13. *Indian Affairs Committee* 31 at p. 1:16.
14. *Indian Affairs Committee* 31 at p.1:17–18.
15. "Self-Government Chronology," 1978, at p.5.
16. *Indian Affairs Committee* 31 at p.1:16.
17. See, for example, *MacGuigan-Lamontagne 30* at 5:78.
18. Having observed these proceedings at that time I also reviewed the committee proceedings and parliamentary debates with regard to this question.
19. *Indian Affairs Committee* 31 at p.1:16.
20. *Indian Affairs Committee* 31 at p. 1:16.
21. *Indian Affairs Committee* 31 at p. 1:16.
22. *Indian Affairs Committee* 31 at p. 1:18.
23. *Indian Affairs Committee* 31 at p. 1:32–3.
24. *Indian Affairs Committee* 31 at p. 1:32–3.
25. The English spelling "Caughnawaga" was still in common usage in 1979. The community later adopted the customary Mohawk orthography, "*Kahnawake.*"
26. *Indian Affairs Committee* 31 at p. 1:34.
27. *Indian Affairs Committee* 31 at p. 3:6–18.
28. *Indian Affairs Committee* 31 at p. 3:6–18.
29. Dickson, J., "The Fiduciary Relationship," *Guérin et al. v. The Queen* [1984] 2 S.C. .R.
30. For a Committee discussion following up the response of the Auditor General see *Indian Affairs Committee* 32 2:25 where Paul Tellier tells the

Committee of the work the resolution created for the Department. Tellier went on to head the Canadian National Railway.

31. *Guerin v. The Queen [1984] 2 S.C.R. 335.*
32. Ibid., Wilson J., paraphrasing of appellant's factum.
33. *Indian Affairs Committee* 31 at p. 3:24–6.
34. *Nowegijick v. The Queen*, [1983] 1 S.C.R. 29.
35. *Indian Affairs Committee* 31 at p.6:7.
36. *Indian Affairs Committee* 31 at p. 7:12–13.
37. *Indian Affairs Committee* 31 at p. 11:8.
38. *Indian Affairs Committee* 31 at p. 11:9.
39. *Indian Affairs Committee* 31 at p. 11:7.
40. *Indian Affairs Committee* 31 at p.11:9.
41. *Indian Affairs Committee* 31 at p. 11:9.
42. The *Constitution Act, 1982* specifically enshrines a practice known as equalization, under which provinces with less than the national average per capita income receive funds from the federal government to bring their treasuries up to the national average. Equalization is over and above any federal subsidies for specific projects such as the Trans Canada Highway.
43. *Indian Affairs Committee* 31 at p. 11:9.
44. *Trudeau and Our Times* Vol. 1 at p.116–117. A list of junior ministers with the title "Minister of State" can be found by googling "Minister of State" and restricting the search to Canada.
45. *Indian Affairs Committee* 31 at p. 11:10.
46. For a detailed account of this campaign see Michael Posluns' *The Bureaucratic Response to the Penner Report*, Master's thesis, York University.
47. The 1983 *Penner Report* on Indian Self-Government found that the Indian Affairs Branch could not be reformed to become a source of support and set out alternative structures through which the federal government might be supportive of First Nations governments. The 1996 *RCAP Report* came to a similar conclusion as did the 2000 report of the Standing Senate Committee on Aboriginal Peoples entitled *Forging New Relationships*.
48. *The Estimates*, in Canada, are often referred to by the term "Blue Book" because of the covers in which they are commonly bound. Estimates are "Statements put before the House of Commons each year stating the grants of money which it is estimated will be required" for each of the departments. "Parliament debates the estimates and the result of its debates is embodied in the annual Appropriation Act which authorizes the expenditure of the total sum of the estimates, appropriating stated sums to each vote."
    "Estimates," *Ox Comp. to Law*, at p. 432.
49. *Indian Affairs Committee* 31 at p. 11:10.
50. "Equity" *Ox. Companion to Law*, at p.426.
51. *Indian Affairs Committee* 31 at p. 11:11.
52. In *St. Catharines Milling and Lumber Company v. The Queen*, (1887), 13 S.C.R. 577 (also reported: 4 Cart. B.N.A. 127).

53. *Indian Affairs Committee* 31 at p. 11:13.
54. *Indian Affairs Committee 31* at p. 11:13. A "final solution theme" might readily be traced through liberal rhetoric on First Nations matters from *An Act for the Gradual Civilization of the Indians, 1857* to speeches of recent ministers. Scott Momaday, in *The Man Made of Words* refers to the term "Indian problem" as dangerous because it suggests that there is a single problem and invites a search for a single solution. Logically *single solutions* tend, in turn, to be an urge toward finality. Well wishers do not wish for final solutions.
55. *Indian Affairs Committee* 31 at p. 11:14.
56. The backbone of the Canadian Constitution at Confederation, the *British North America Act, 1867* was renamed the *Constitution Act, 1867* at patriation.
57. *Indian Affairs Committee* 31 at p. 11:15.
58. *Indian Affairs Committee* 31 at p. 14:3.
59. *Indian Affairs Committee* 31 at p. 14:3.
60. I have been privileged to have had access to a large body of documentation from DIAND regarding attitudes within the Department concerning the work of the Penner Committee and the notion of self-government. Excerpts from this collection are identified by the title "Self-Government Chronology" plus date and page. References to "spending restraints" occur frequently throughout these files.
61. *Indian Affairs Committee* 31 at p. 14:8–9.
62. *Trudeau and Our Times* Vol. 1 at p.180.
63. *Trudeau and Our Times* Vol. 1 at p.188.
64. *Trudeau and Our Times* Vol. 1 at p.245.
65. Motion of Hon. Arthur W. Roebuck, November 3, 1949, *Debates of the Senate*, p.215–216. Roebuck's motion includes the complete draft of a bill of rights. It was structured as a motion because it began with a provision that "The Government be requested to submit to the forthcoming Dominion-Provincial Conference on the Constitution the following draft amendment to the British North America Act."
66. Roebuck's opening statement makes reference to the Report of the Joint Committee on Human Rights and Fundamental Freedoms of the previous session and the report of that Committee presented by the Senate co-chairman, Sen. Gouin (Liberal, De Salaberry, Québec). *Debates of the Senate*, 1949, at p.216–219.
67. *Trudeau and Our Times* vol. 1 at p.251.
68. Interview, 1992, on file.
69. *Indian Affairs Committee*, 32 1:14. Because there was only one session in the 32nd Parliament the pagination includes the Parliament, the Issue and the Page number but not the session.
70. *Indian Affairs Committee*, 32 1:14.
71. Unattributed interview.
72. "Self-Government Chronology, 1980" at p.31.
73. *Indian Affairs Committee* 32 at p. 1:14.
74. *Indian Affairs Committee* 32 at p. 1:14.

75. *Indian Affairs Committee* 32 at p. 1:15.
76. *Indian Affairs Committee*, 32 at p. 1:15.
77. *Indian Affairs Committee*, 32 1:16.
78. *Indian Affairs Committee* 32 at p. 1:15.
79. "Self-Government Chronology" at p.32. Personal notes on Dene land claims negotiations.
80. *Indian Affairs Committee* 32 at p. 1:26.
81. The National Indian Brotherhood, the Native Council of Canada and the Inuit Tapirisat of Canada agreed on a common set of amendments that each would put in their independently written briefs. *Hays-Joyal* at p.16:12–3, 20–23 and 29.
82. *Indian Affairs Committee* 32 at p. 1:27.
83. *Indian Affairs Committee* 32 at p. 1:38.
84. Ox. Companion to Law at p. 1241.
85. *Guérin v. The Queen* [1985] 1 C.N.L.R. at p.138.
86. *Guérin v. The Queen* [1985] 1 C.N.L.R. at p.139.
87. Wilson, J. in *Guérin* [1985] C.N.L.R. at p. 145.
88. Sanders, Nahwegahbow and Posluns, *The Crown and the First Nations: A Study of Trust Relationships* prepared for the Special Committee of the House of Commons on Indian Self-Government.
89. *Indian Affairs Committee* 32 at p. 2:24–25.
90. *Indian Affairs Committee* 32 at p. 2:24–29.
91. *Indian Affairs Committee* 32 at p. 2:25.
92. *Indian Affairs Committee* 32 at p. 7:14.
93. *Indian Affairs Committee* 32 at p. 7:14.
94. *Indian Affairs Committee 32* at p.7:14. The information as to the specific instructions to counsel came from an interview and letter from Hon. John Fraser, Minister of Fisheries in the Clark Government in which he described conversations between himself, Sen. Jacques Flynn, the Minister of Justice and the Crown's counsel in *Guérin* supra en 489.
95. *Indian Affairs Committee* 32 at p.7:15.
96. *Indian Affairs Committee* 32 at p.11:6.
97. *Indian Affairs Committee* 32 at p.11:6.
98. *Indian Affairs Committee* 32 at p.11:7.
99. *Indian Affairs Committee* 32 at p.11:8.
100. *Indian Affairs Committee* 32 at p. 11:8.
101. *Indian Affairs Committee* 32 at p. 11:9.
102. *Indian Affairs Committee* 32 at p. 11:9.
103. *Indian Affairs Committee* 32 at p. 11:10.
104. *Indian Affairs Committee* 32 at p. 11:12.
105. *Indian Affairs Committee* 32 at p. 11:13.
106. *Indian Affairs Committee* 32 at p. 11:14.
107. *Indian Affairs Committee* 32 at p. 11:12.
108. *Indian Affairs Committee* 32 at p. 11:14.
109. *Indian Affairs Committee* 32 at p. 11:8.
110. *Indian Affairs Committee* 32 at p. 11:15.

111. *Indian Affairs Committee* 32 at p. 11:16.
112. *Indian Affairs Committee* 32 at p. 11:17.
113. *Indian Affairs Committee* 32 at p. 11:17.
114. *Indian Affairs Committee* 32 at p. 11:18.
115. *Indian Affairs Committee* 32 at p. 11:11:16.
116. *Indian Affairs Committee* 32 at p. 11:25.
117. *Indian Affairs Committee* 32 at p. 11:25.
118. *Indian Affairs Committee* 32 at p. 11:25.
119. *Indian Affairs Committee* 32 at p. 11:30.
120. *Indian Affairs Committee* 32 at p. 11:31.
121. Emily Dickason, in *Canada's First Nations*, says that the *White Paper* was withdrawn in 1971. A similar statement occurs in the *RCAP Report* of which Ms. Dickason may have had a major hand in the writing of the historical sections. In 2003 I spend several days reviewing agendas for cabinet meetings and found no reference to anything resembling a proposal to withdraw or to retract the 1969 *White Paper*.
122. 1972 interview of Arthur Anderson, by the author. Mr. Anderson had been the secretary of the Longhouse council at Ohsweken in 1919 and 1920 when the troops came home following the end of World War I.
123. *Identity/Difference*.
124. *Osgoode Hall Law Journal (L.J.)*, [25] 1987 4.
125. *Nowegijick v. The Queen* [1983) 1 S.C.R. 29.
126. "agreement to agree," *Black's* at p. 68.
127. *Taylor v. Williams* (1981), 34 O.R. (2d) at p. 367 "the honour of the Crown is always involved and no appearance of 'sharp dealing' should be sanctioned." (Semi-quotes in the original.)
128. This tension between the bureaucracy and the Penner Committee is discussed in detail in *The Bureaucratic Response to the Penner Report* at pp. 42, 95 and 116.
129. This decision, taken in August or September, 1982 arose directly from Starblanket's speech of June 1980, examined here in which the third of his concluding requests was that the Indian Affairs Committee not undertake an inquiry based on *Indian Conditions* but, instead, focus on developing "Indian Government." This request was a response to an item on the Committee's agenda to ask for an order of reference asking for a reference to study *Indian Conditions*. In response to Starblanket's request moved an amendment to that motion that the requests in his brief be adopted.
130. "*Containing the Metaphysics of Indian-hating, According to the Views of One Evidently not so Prepossessed as Rousseau in Favour of Savages.*" is the title of chapter 26 in Melville's, *The Confidence Man. New York: Dix & Edwards, 1857, republished by Airmont Publishing Company Inc., reprinted in conjunction with Ryerson Press, Toronto, 1966. The term was revived as a sub-title by Richard Drinnon in* Facing West: The Metaphysics of Indian-Hating and Empire Building *Minneapolis: University of Minnesota Press,1980.*
131. See earlier in this chapter.

132. Peter Hogg, in *Constitutional Law in Canada* Constitutional Law of Canada, 1997, Carswell: Toronto, 1997, at p. 27.6(c) identifies five qualities that define a treaty between a First Nation and the Crown: (1) Parties: The parties to the treaty must be the Crown, on the one side, and an Aboriginal nation, on the other side; (2) Agency: The signatories to the treaty must have the authority to bind their principals, namely, the Crown and the Aboriginal nation; (3) Intention to create legal relations: The parties must intend to create legally binding obligations; (4) Consideration: The obligations must be assumed by both sides, so that the agreement is a bargain; (5) Formality: there must be "a certain measure of solemnity." Hogg also notes that "The argument that an Indian tribe was not an entity possessing the legal personality or the capacity to enter into treaties was summarily rejected in *Simon* (at 398–401) and not raised again in *Sioui* (fn. 115).
133. *R. v. Sparrow* 1990 S.C.R. 1 at p.25 (HTML conversion to RTF).
134. Chronicled in Chapter Three.
135. Indeed, the ultimate test of the emergence of the vocabulary of self-government set out here would be a parallel chronicle of the proceedings of the N.I.B.-AFN assemblies during the same period and a cross-referencing of related discussions.)
136. This requirement has been described as self-policing. (Russell quoted in Hogg at 32.6 and discussed more fully in Chapter Three at p. 84.) Nonetheless, it established a standard different from simply evading the question.
137. Jean-Paul Sartre, *Being and Nothingness*, Simon and Shuster, Washington Square Press, New York, 1956.
138. The Statutory Instruments Committee challenged the Minister's authority when Munro did, later, begin to suspend 12(1)(b) in respect to those bands which requested its suspension. The SI Committee's argument was that the Minister's authority under section 4 to suspend the application of other sections applied only to narrowing their scope and not to expanding the scope of a provision or to increasing the burden on the Crown. When Munro did accede to the N.I.B. request he asserted, to the Statutory Instruments Committee that he had a legal opinion which he did not disclose. My observation here is limited to the claim, first by the N.I.B. and later by Munro that he had that the authority.
139. Starblanket referred to this Penticton Assembly of April 1980 in his statement.
140. The attitudes of senior officials in DIAND and in MSSD are documented at length in my master's thesis, *The Bureacuratic Response to the Penner Report.*
141. These numbers refer to the 2nd Session of the 32nd Parliament.
142. This procedural failure is on all fours with the later and more famous defeat of Meech Lake in the Manitoba Legislative Assembly.
143. *Bureaucratic Response* and interview with Peter Hutchins.

NOTES TO THE GLOSSARY

1. "Co-opt," *Gage Canadian Dictionary.*
2. For an excellent summary of the long and complex story of the patriation of the Canadian Constitution and an introduction to the key terms of the patriation debate see, "Constitutional Law,"*The 1998 Canadian & World Encyclopedia*, Toronto: McClelland & Stewart Inc.

NOTES TO THE BIBLIOGRAPHY

1. Unless otherwise indicated, I have relied for current federal statutes on the consolidated statutes published on the web site of the Department of Justice.
2. The line between several previous categories including Ethics, Law and History and the category of "Politics and Political Discourse" appears to be a very fine one. I have tried to sort texts here according to the context in which they are discussed in this dissertation.

Bibliography

NOTE:

I have relied extensively on reference works for definitions and background. Below is a list of the articles and entries which I have cited. Under certain headings below, there are reference works, books, and articles. Under each heading, I have grouped those reference entries not attributed to specific authors alphabetically by entry title at the top of each category. Articles and books appear below in by authors' names in alphabetical order.

Within each of the categories by which I have sorted works on which I have drawn I use the following three sub-categories: (1) encyclopedia and reference works sorted alphabetically by entry title; (2) newspaper and periodical articles sorted by title; (3) poems, articles and chapters sorted alphabetically by authors' surnames; (4) books by authors' surnames. There are also two sets of legal cases sorted by the names of the parties.

Here is a list of the reference works on which I have drawn with their full titles and publishing information:

Black's refers to *Black's Law Dictionary*, Seventh edition, Bryan A. Garner, Editor in Chief, St. Paul, Minn., West Group, 1999.

The Cambridge Encyclopedia of the English Language, David Crystal, ed., Cambridge, CUP, 1995.

OED. All references to *OED* refer to the *Oxford English Dictionary Second Edition on Compact Disc,* Toronto: Oxford University Press, 1992.

Gage Canadian Dictionary. All references refer to Gage Canadian Dictionary on *The 1998 Canadian & World Encyclopedia*, Disk 1, Toronto: McLelland & Stewart Inc., 1998.

"*Oxford Comp*. To ____. All such references refer to an *Oxford Companion to* [a given subject]. Here is the list of Ox. Comp. references on which I have drawn:

Oxford Companion to the Bible, ed., Bruce M. Metzger and Michael D. Coogan, Toronto, Oxford University Press, 1993.

Oxford Companion to Philosophy ed., Ted Honderich, Toronto: Oxford University Press, 1995

The Oxford Companion to Law, ed., David M. Walker, Toronto: Oxford University Press, 1980.

The Oxford Companion to Politics, ed., Richard L. Gregory, Toronto: Oxford University Press, 1987.

Princeton Encyclopedia, refers to The New Princeton Encyclopedia of Poetry and Poetics, Frank J. Warnke, O.B. Hardison, Jr., and Earl Miner, Assoc. Editors, Princeton, N.J: Princeton University Press, 1993.

The Blackwell Dictionary of Judaica, ed., Dan Cohn-Sherbok, Oxford: Blackwell, 1992.

ABORIGINAL AND TREATY RIGHTS

Gerald Beaudoin, "Constitutional Law," *the Canadian Encyclopedia* (Toronto: McClelland & Stewart Inc., 1996, CD-ROM).

Alan Cairns, *Citizens Plus: Aboriginal peoples and the Canadian State*, Vancouver: U.B.C. Press, 2000.

Harold Cardinal, *The Unjust Society: The Tragedy of Canada's Indians*. Edmonton: M.G. Hurting, c.1969

Peter Cumming and Neil Mickenberg, "The Theory of Aboriginal Rights," *Native Rights in Canada,* Toronto: The Indian-Eskimo Association of Canada & General Publishing Co. Ltd., Toronto, 1972.

Robert Gehrke, "Missing papers cloud lawsuit over Indian funds," *Boston Globe*, Feb. 14, 2002, p.A3, reprinted on Truthout.com/02.15F.Norton.Lawsuit.htm

Douglas Sanders, "Pre-existing Rights: The *Aboriginal Peoples of Canada*," in Beaudoin and Ratushny, ed., *The Canadian Charter of Rights and Freedoms: A Commentary*, Toronto: Carswell, 1989.

Douglas Sanders, "The Supreme Court of Canada and the 'Legal and Political Struggle' over Indigenous Rights," *Canadian Ethnic Studies*, 22(3): 122–132, cited in Dale Kerr, "Arguments for and against recognizing Aboriginal Rights in Canada," November 21, 1995, Tatlayoko Think Tank, www.childcotin.bc.ca/tt/lcpc.htm#footnote22.

Brian Slattery, "Understanding Aboriginal Rights," 66 *Canadian Bar Review* at 727, footnotes 18 and 175.

Brian Slattery, "A Theory of the Charter," *Osgoode Hall Law Journal (L.J.)*, [25] 1987 4.

H.B. Hawthorn, ed., *A Survey of the Contemporary Indians of Canada: A Report on Economic, Political, Educational Needs and Policies*. Ottawa: Indian Affairs Branch, 1966–1967.

LEGAL CASES

R. v. L. (W.K.) (1991), 64 C.C.C. (3d) 321 at *327–328* (S.C.C.), *R. v. A.(D.)* 11 C.R.R. (2d) 290 (Ont. C.A.), _R. v. MacDonnell, [1997] 1 S.C.R. 305.

R. v. Badger, [1996] 1 S.C.R. 771.
Calder v. A-G. B.C. [1973] S.C.R 313.
Delgamuukw v. British Columbia, [1997] 3 S.C.R. 1010.
Guerin v. The Queen [1984] 2 S.C.R. 335.
Johnson v. M'Intosh 21 U.S. (8 Wheat.), 1823.
Kanatewat v. James Bay Development Corp., [1974] R.P. 38; reversed [1975] C.A. 166.
Namagoose v. Robinson, F.C.T.D., September 10, 1991 F.C.J. No.904, action No. T-451–91.
Nowegijick v. The Queen (1983) 1 S.C.R. 29, 46 NR. 41.
Re: Paulette et al., & the Registrar of Land Titles, 39 D.L.R. (3d) 45, [1973] 6 W.W.R. 97.
Procureur Géneral du Canada v. La Commission Scolaire Crie, Quebec Court of Appeal, Sept. 5, 2001.
Reference re: Resolution to Amend the Constitution, [1981] 1 S.C.R. 753.
St. Catharines Milling and Lumber Company v. The Queen, (1887), 13 S.C.R. 577.
(The four *St. Catharines* decisions can be found in vol. 1 of the *Canadian Native Law Cases* nos. 37–38 at http://laws.justice.gc.ca/.)
R. v. Sparrow, B.C. Court of Appeal, (1986), 9 B.C.L.R., (2d) 300.
R. v. Sparrow, [1990] 1 S.C.R. 1075.
R. v. Taylor, (1981), 34 O.R. (2d) 360.
Van der Peet, [1996] 2 S.C.R. 50.
Haida Nation v. British Columbia (Minister of Forests), 2004 SCC 73.

ETHICS: AUTHENTICITY, GENUINE, GOOD FAITH (BONA FIDES)

"Applied Ethics," *Concise Routledge Encyclopedia of Philosophy* (London: Routledge, 2000).
"Practical Reason and Ethics," *Concise Routledge Encyclopedia of Philosophy* (London: Routledge, 2000).
Brian Slattery, "A Theory of the Charter," *Osgoode Hall Law Journal*, [25] 1987 4.
Coleman and Skogstad, *Policy Communities and Public Policy in Canada.*
William Connolly, "Introduction: The Problem of Evil" *Identity\Difference: Democratic Negotiations of Political Paradox,* Ithaca and London: Cornell University Press, 1992.
William Connolly, *The Terms of Political Discourse*, Princeton, N.J., Princeton University Press, 1984.
Maurice S. Friedman, *Martin Buber: The Life of Dialogue*, New York: Harper & Row, Harper Torchbooks, 1960.
Maurice S. Friedman, Martin Buber's Life and Work: The Early Years, 1878–1923, New York: E.P. Dutton, 1981.
John Locke, *Concerning Civil Government, Second Essay*, Great Books of the Western World, vol. 35, Chicago, Toronto, Encyclopaedia Britannica, Inc., 1952.

Jacob S. Ziegel, "Good Faith in the Law of Contract," Memorandum by Joint Research Director, LCA Project, Ontario Law Reform Commission, Sept. 10, 1982.

INTENTION

"Intention," *Catholic Encyclopedia*. www.newadvent.org/cathen
"Intention," *Gage Canadian Dictionary*.
"Intent," *Ox. Comp. to Law.*
"Intention," *Black's Law Dictionary.*
"Negligent," *Gage Canadian Dictionary.*
Dr. Milton Aron, *Ideas and Ideals of the Hassidim*, Seacacus, NJ: Citadel Press, 1969
Martin Buber, *For the Sake of Heaven*, Philadelphia, The Jewish Publication Society of America, 1946.
Martin Buber, *Tales of the Hasidim,* New York: Schocken Books, 1975.
Maurice S. Friedman, *Martin Buber's Life and Work: The Middle Years, 1923–1945*, New York: E.P. Dutton, 1981.
Max Kadushin, *The Rabbinic Mind,* New York: Bloch Publishing Co., 1972.

FOUR WORLDS THEORIES

"Anagogic," *OED.*
"Figure, Scheme, Trope," Princeton Encyclopedia.
"Influence," Princeton Encyclopedia.
Morton W. Bloomfield, "Interpretation, Fourfold Method" *Princeton Encyclopedia* at p.619.
"Metaphor," *Princeton Encyclopedia.*
Metonymy," *Princeton Encyclopedia.*
"on all fours," *Black's.*
"Pardes," *Ox. Comp. to World Religions.*
"Peshat," *The Oxford Dictionary of World Religions.*
"secular," *OED.*
Harold Bloom, *Kabbalah and Criticism*, New York: The Seabury Press, 1975.
Julienne Ford, *Paradigms and Fairy Tales* (1975) reviewed in Yvonna S. Lincoln and Egon G. Guba, *Naturalistic Inquiry*, London: Sage Publications, 1985.
Aryeh Kaplan, *Sefer Yetzirah: The Book of Creation, In Theory and Practice*, York Beach, Maine, Samuel Weiser, Inc., 1993.
Gershom Scholem, *Kabbalah,* Jerusalem: Keter Publishing House, 1974.
Gershom Scholem, *The Kabbalah and Its Symbolism*, New York: Schocken Books, 1960.

PLAIN SENSE

"Copula," *The Oxford Companion to the English Language*, Tom McArthur, ed., Oxford: OUP, 1992.
"happening," *Gage Canadian Dictionary.*

"History," *Gage Canadian Dictionary.*
"Paradise," *OED.* "Pardes," *The Oxford Dictionary of World Religions*, ed. John Bowker, Toronto: Oxford University Press, 1997] at p.735.
"Reality," *Gage Canadian Dictionary.*
"Shekinah," *The Oxford Dictionary of World Religions*, John Bowker, ed., (Oxford: Oxford University Press, 1997).
"Naïve," *OED.*
"Obverse," *Gage Canadian Dictionary.*
"Public," *Gage Canadian Dictionary.*

ADDITIONAL RABBINIC COMMENTARIES ON PLAIN SENSE

"Seder Mo'ed Shabbat," *Babylonian Talmud*, Transl., Rabbi H. Freedman, Ph.D., New York: Rebecca Bennet Publications, Inc., 1959.
David Weiss Halivni, *Peshat & Derash: Plain and Applied Meaning in Rabbinic Exegesis,* Toronto: OUP, 1991.
Isaac Unterman, *The Talmud: An Analytic Guide to Its History and Teachings*, New York: Bloch Publishing, 1970.
R. Joseph Telushkin, *Jewish Wisdom*, New York: William Morrow and Company, 1994.

LEGAL REFERENCES, WORKS ON PLAIN SENSE

"Plain Sense Rule," Bryan A. Garner, ed., *Black's Law Dictionary* Seventh Edition, St. Paul, Minn: West Group, 1999.
"strict interpretation . . . what the reader thinks that the author must have been thinking at the time of writing and no more." *Black's* at p. 824.
Will-Kare (below) cites a number of reference works and commentaries that deal with "plain sense" at length.
Law Cases on Plain Sense
R. v. McIntosh, [1995] 1 S.C.R. 686.
Victory (City) v. Bishop of Vancouver Island, [1921] A.C. 384.
Will-Kare Paving & Contracting Ltd. v. Canada, 2000 SCC 36.
W. Liebig & Co. v. Leading Investments Ltd., [1986] 1 S.C.R. 70.
Nowigijick v. The Queen [1983) 1 S.C.R. 29.
Reference re Authority of Parliament in relation to the Upper House, [1980] 1 S.C.R.
Reference re Resolution to Amend the Constitution, [1981] 1 S.C.R. 753 (*Patriation Reference*).

RELATED PHILOSOPHIC CONCEPTS

Burden of Persuasion

28 USC Appendix—*Rules Of Evidence* Rule 301, Article III. "Presumptions In Civil Actions And Proceedings," http://lawresearch-registry.org/rule301.htm.

http://www.law.harvard.edu/publications/evidenceiii/rules/301_proposed.htm.
Richard H. Gaskins, *Burdens of Proof in Modern Discourse*, New Haven & London: Yale University Press, 1992.

COHERENCE

"Coherence," and "Practical reasoning," *Dictionary of the Philosophy of Mind*, found at http://www.google.com/search?q=coherentism&hl=en&lr=&safe=off&start=10&sa=N

INTENTION

"Intention," *Black's Law Dictionary.*
"Intention," *Catholic Encyclopedia.* www.newadvent.org/cathen
"Intention, *Gage Canadian Dictionary.*
"Intent," *Ox. Comp. to Law* at p.629.
"Negligent," *Gage Canadian Dictionary.*
Dr. Milton Aron, *Ideas and Ideals of the Hassidim*, Seacacus, NJ: Citadel Press, 1969.
Martin Buber, *For the Sake of Heaven*, Philadelphia, The Jewish Publication Society of America, 1946.
Martin Buber, *Tales of the Hasidim.*
E.H. Carr, *What is History?*, New York: Knopf, 1965 (c.1961).
Claude Steiner, *Scripts People Live: Transactional Analysis of Life Scripts*, (Grove Press: New York, 1971).
Elie Wiesel, *Four Hasidic Masters,* Notre Dame, Univ. of Notre Dame, 1978.

DISCOURSE EXAMPLES, NON-PARLIAMENTARY

"Anglicans in Canada asked to lobby . . ." *Episcopal News Service*, October 3, 2000 at www.epsicopalchurch.org.ens/2000–146D.html
Saturday Night magazine, November 23, 1907, on the report of Dr. P.H. Bryce, ChiefMedical Officer, Indian Affairs Branch. Quoted in *RCAP* at record 1824.
"Invariable Nouns," *The Cambridge Encyclopedia of the English Language.*
Robert Burns, "My Love Is Like A Red, Red Rose," Allan Cunningham, *Burns Poetical Works*, Philadelphia: Porter & Coates, 1876.
Deborah Cameron, & al., *Researching Language: Issues of Power and Method*, London, Routledge, 1992.
Basso, Keith. 1970. "To Give Up on Words: Silence in the Western Apache Culture." *Southwestern Journal of Anthropology* 26: 213–30.
1976, "'Wise Words' of the Western Apache: Metaphor and Semantic Theory." *In Meaning in Anthropology* pp. 93–122. Ed. K. Basso and H.A. Selby, Jr. Albuquerque: University of New Mexico Press.

Julie Cruikshank, in collaboration with Angela Sidney, Kitty Smith & Annie Ned, *Life Lived Like a Story*, (Lincoln and London: University of Nebraska Press, 1990).

The Child and Family Services Acts, 1985 1999 see Eisenstat and Posluns, Chapter Four, *The Child and Family Services Act Manual*, Toronto: Ontario Federation of Indian Friendship Centres, 2000.

Morris C. Shumiatcher, *Welfare: Hidden Backlash, A Hard Look At The Welfare Issue in Canada. What It Has Done To The Indian. What It Could Do To The Rest of Canada*. Toronto: McClelland & Stewart, 1971.

David E. Stannard, *The American Holocaust: The Conquest of the New World*, New York, Oxford University Press, 1992.

Russell Thornton, *American Indian Holocaust and Survival: A Population History Since 1492*, Norman, University of Oklahoma, 1987.

DISCOURSE EXAMPLES, PARLIAMENTARY

Related Reference Works

"Charlottetown Accord," Gage Canadian Dictionary.

Gérald Beaudoin, "Constitutional Law," *The Canadian Encyclopedia*.

"Frontier," *The Gage Canadian Dictionary*.

"Standing Committees," *The Canadian Encyclopedia*.

"Fourteen Points," *The Canadian Encyclopedia*.

NATIONAL INDIAN BROTHERHOOD POSITION PAPERS SUBMITTED TO THE INDIAN AFFAIRS COMMITTEE

"NIB position on Aboriginal title," House of Commons Standing Committee on Indian Affairs and Northern Development, *Proceedings*, 29th Parliament, First Session.

Indian Control of Indian Education, NIB position paper, Ottawa: National Indian Brotherhood, 1973.

CONSTITUTION, STATUTES AND INTERNATIONAL CONVENTIONS DISCUSSED

Canada[1]

A Consolidation of the Constitution Acts, 1867 to 1982, Ottawa, Dept. of Justice, 1989.

Department of Indian Affairs and Northern Development Act, R.S. 1985, c I-6.

Section 149A, *An Act to Amend the Indian Act*, Statutes of Canada, 1927

An Act to Amend the Indian Act, 1985 (C-31).

Indian Act, Chapter 1–5, http://laws.justice.gc.ca/en/I-5/65055.html

The Public Service Employment Act, 1967, R.S. 1985, c. P33.
Royal Proclamation, 1763.
St. Regis Islands Act, 1926–27, c. 37.
War Measures Act.

British Columbia

"Indian Testimony Receivable in Certain Cases," ss. 12–14, *Evidence Act*, Chapter 143, *Revised Statutes of British Columbia, 1960.*

Ontario

The Child and Family Services Act, 1984, Chapter 55, *Statutes of Ontario, 1984*, Toronto.
The (Ontario) Child and Family Services Act, Consolidated Ontario Family Law Statutes and Regulations, 2000 (Toronto: Carswell, 1999) Queen's Printer, 1984.

United Nations

UN Convention On the Prevention and Punishment of the Crime of Genocide' U.N.T.S. No. 1021, vol. 78 (1951), p. 277. Resolution 260 (III) of the United Nations General Assembly on 9 December 1948.

BILLS AND MINISTERIAL STATEMENTS

"Allied Indian Tribes of British Columbia, Joint Committee to Inquire into Claims," *Debates, House of Commons*, 1st Session, 16th Parliament, Volume I, 1926–27, at p. 979.
A Time for Action, Ottawa: Queen's Printer, 1978.
Canada Lands Act, 32nd Parliament, 1982.
Jean Chrétien, *Statement of the Government of Canada on Indian Policy*, 1969, Ottawa: Queen's Printer, 1969.
Indian Oil and Gas Act, R.S. 1985, c.I-7.
Fort Nelson Indian Minerals Revenue Sharing Act, 1980, 1980–81–82–83, c.38.
Ted White, *Plain Language Act*, Bill C-311, "Introduction of Bills," *House of Commons Debates*, November 5, 1999.

REPORTS OF PARLIAMENTARY COMMITTEES AND PUBLIC INQUIRIES

Maxwell Cohen, Pierre Trudeau and Mark MacGuigan, *Report of the Special Committee on Hate Propaganda*, 1966.
Dorothy Dobbie and Claude Castonguay, co-chairs, *Shaping Canada's Future Together,* Joint Committee on the Constitution, September, 1991.
Dorothy Dobbie and Gérald Beaudoin, A Renewed Canada: The Report of the Special Committee of the Senate and the House of Commons, Ottawa: Canada Communication Group, 1992.

Georges Erasmus and Associate Chief Justice René Dussault, *Quebec Superior Court Report of the Royal Commission on Aboriginal Peoples*, on *Seven Generations: An Information Legacy of the Royal Commission on Aboriginal Peoples*, CD-ROM, Ottawa: Libraxus Inc., 1997. This encyclopedic report may also be found online at http://www.ainc-inac.gc.ca/ch/rcap/index_e.html.

Sen. Eugene Forsey & Robert McCleave, MP, Joint chairmen, Standing Joint Committee on Regulations and Statutory Instruments, *Second Report*, Ottawa: Queen's Printer, 1977.

Sen. Eugene Forsey & Robert McCleave, MP, co-chairmen, *Fifth Report,* The Joint Committee of the Senate and the House of Commons on Regulations and Statutory Instruments, 1978.

Hon. Fred Kaufman, C.M., Q.C., *The Commission on Proceedings Involving Guy Paul Morin,* Toronto: Queen's Printer, 1998.

Mark MacGuigan, MP, and Sen. Gildas Molgat, co-chairmen, Joint Committee of the Senate and the House of Commons on the Constitution of Canada, 28th Parliament, 4th Session, *Final Report,* Ottawa: Queen's Printer, 1972.

Keith Penner, Chairman, *Report of the Special Committee of the House of Commons on Indian Self-Government*, Ottawa: House of Commons, 1983.

Jack Burkhart, Chairman, *Report of the Special Committee of the House of Commons on Indian Women and the Indian Act*, Ottawa: House of Commons, 1982.

Ian Watson, chairman, The Report of the House of Commons Subcommittee on Indian Education, Queen's Printer, 1971.

Senator Charlie Watt, Chairman, Senator Janis Johnson, Deputy Chairman, *Forging New Relationships: Aboriginal Governance in Canada*, Report of the Standing Senate Committee on Aboriginal Peoples, February 2000.

PROCEEDINGS OF JOINT, SPECIAL AND STANDING COMMITTEES[2]

Joint Committee on the Constitution, *Proceedings*, Mark MacGuigan, MP and Sen. Gildas Molgat, co-chairmen, 2nd Session, 28th Parliament. (MacGuigan Molgat)

Joint Committee on the Constitution, *Proceedings*, Mark MacGuigan, MP and Sen. Maurice Lamontagne, co-chairmen, 30th Parliament. (MacGuigan-Lamontagne)

House of Commons Standing Committee on Indian Affairs and Northern Development, *Proceedings,* 29th Parliament, First Session, Ottawa, Queen's Printer, 1972–74.

House of Commons Standing Committee on Indian Affairs and Northern Development, *Proceedings,* 30th Parliament 3rd Session, Ottawa, Queen's Printer, 1978.

House of Commons Standing Committee on Indian Affairs and Northern Development, *Proceedings,* 31st Parliament, First Session, Ottawa, Queen's Printer, 1980–83.

PUBLISHED POSITION PAPERS OF THE NATIONAL INDIAN BROTHERHOOD

Indian Control of Indian Education, 1973.
"Aboriginal Rights Position Paper," 1973.

HISTORY AND HISTORIOGRAPHY

"Burger, Warren Earl," *The Canadian Encyclopedia.*
Robert Sheppard, "Constitution, Patriation of," *The Canadian Encyclopedia.*
"koan," *OED.*
"Dawes Act," *Encyclopedia of North American Indians: Native American History, Culture, and Life from Paleo-Indians to the Present,* ed., Frederick E. Hoxie, Boston: Houghton Mifflin Co., 1996.
Audrey Doerr, "The Public Service," *The Canadian Encyclopedia*, CD-ROM.
"Social constructionism," *Ox. Comp. Phil.*
Eric Berne, *Games People Play: The Psychology of Human Relationships*, New York: Ballantine Books, 1973.
Carl Bernstein and Bob Woodward, *All the President's Men*, New York: Simon and Shuster, 1974.
David Biale, *Kabbalah and Counter-history* Cambridge, Mass: Harvard University Press, 1984.
Edward Hallett Carr, What is History?, New York: Knopf, 1965, c. 1961.
Bryan Cheyette, *Constructions of 'the Jew' in English literature and society: Racial representations, 1875–1945*, Cambridge: CUP, 1995.
Winston S. Churchill, *A History of the English Speaking Peoples*, Toronto: McClelland & Stewart Ltd., 1958.
Stephen Clarkson and Christina McCall, *Trudeau and Our Times, Vol. 1: The Magnificent Obsession,* 1990: McClelland & Stewart, Toronto.
Olive Patricia Dickason, *Canada's First Nations: A History of Founding Peoples from Earliest Times*, Toronto: McClelland & Stewart Inc., 1992.
Angie Debo, *And Still the Waters Run: The Betrayal of the Five Civilized Tribes,* Princeton, N.J., Princeton University Press, 1972, c.1940.
Richard Drinnon, *Facing West: The Metaphysics of Indian-Hating and Empire Building* Minneapolis: University of Minnesota Press,1980.
Georges Erasmus and Associate Chief Justice René Dussault, Volume 1, *Seven Generations: The Report of the Royal Commission on Aboriginal Peoples on CD-ROM.*
C.J. Friedrich, *The Philosophy of Law in Historical Perspective,* Chicago: The University of Chicago Press, 1957.
Sander L. Gilman, *Jewish Self-Hatred: Anti-Semitism and the Hidden Language of the Jews.* Baltimore: The Johns Hopkins University Press, 1986.
Louis Hartz, The Founding of New Societies: Studies in the History of the United States, Latin America, South Africa, Canada and Australia, New York: Harcourt, Brace & World, Inc., 1964.

Johann Huizinga, *The Waning of the Middle Ages: A Study of the Forms of LIfe, Thought and Art in France and the Netherlands in the Fourteenth and Fifteenth Centuries*, Harmondsworth: Penguin Books, 1978.
Noel Ignatiev, *How the Irish Became White*, New York, Routledge: 1995.
George Manuel and Michael Posluns, *The Fourth World: An Indian Reality*, Toronto: Collier-Macmillan, 1973.
Peter Matthiessen, *In the Spirit of Crazy Horse*, New York: Viking Penguin, 1991, c.1983.
Duncan C. Scott, "Indian Affairs, 1867–1912," in *Canada and its Provinces: A History of the Canadian People and their Institutions* by One Hundred Associates, ed. Adam Shortt and Arthur G. Doughty, Toronto: Glasgow, Brook & Company, 1914, volume 7.
David E. Stannard, "Sex, Race and Holy War," *The American Holocaust: The Conquest of the New World*, New York, Oxford University Press, 1992.
Claude Steiner, *Scripts People Live: Transactional Analysis of Life Scripts*, Grove Press: New York, 1971.
Voices from Wounded Knee, 1973: The People are Standing Up, Rooseveltown, N.Y., Akwesasne Notes, 1974.
Sally Weaver, *Making Canadian Indian Policy: the Hidden Agenda, 1968–1970*, Toronto, University of Toronto Press, 1981.
Elie Wiesel, *Four Hasidic Masters and Their Struggle Against Melancholy*, Notre Dame: U. of Notre Dame Press, 1978.

POLITICS AND POLITICAL DISCOURSE[2]

Bowdler, Thomas, *Cambridge Biographical Encyclopedia*, David Crystal, ed., at p.133.
Bowdler, *The Canadian Encyclopedia.*
"Influence," *Princeton Encyclopedia.*
"Kant, Immanuel" in *Ox. Comp. to Phil.*
Safire's New Political Dictionary, William Safire, ed., New York: Random House, 1993.
"Unmotivated (Gratuitous) Hatred," Tractate *Yoma*, *Babylonian Talmud*, 9b.
"Public" *Gage Canadian Dictionary.*
Rules of the Senate of Canada, Part IX. "Third Reading," http://www.parl.gc.ca/information/about/process/senate/rules-e/senrulespart9-e.html.
David V.J. Bell, "Power and Influence," *Power, Influence and Authority: An Essay in Political Linguistics*, Toronto: Oxford University Press, 1975, at pp. 15–33.
H.H. Ben-Sasson, ed., *A History of the Jewish People*, Cambridge, Harvard University Press, 1976.
Carl Bernstein and Bob Woodward, *All the President's Men*, New York: Simon and Shuster, 1974.
Sissela Bok in "Lying to Enemies" *Lying: Moral Choice in Public and Private Life*, London: Quartet, 1980.

Richard Drinnon, *Facing West: The Metaphysics of Indian-Hating and Empire Building* (Minneapolis: University of Minnesota Press, 1980.
William E. Connolly, *The Terms of Political Discourse*, Princeton, N.J., Princeton University Press, 1983.
Richard H. Gaskins, *Burdens of Proof in Modern Discourse* (New Haven & London: Yale University Press, 1992.
Sander L. Gilman, "The Language of Thieves," *Jewish Self-Hatred: Anti-Semitism and the Hidden Language of the Jews*, Baltimore: The Johns Hopkins University Press, 1986.
Adolph Hitler, "War Propaganda," *Mein Kampf, http://www.stormfront.org/books/mein_kampf/mkv1ch06.html*
Peter Hogg, 35.4 "Charter of Rights, Burden of Proof," *Constitutional Law of Canada, 1997 Student Edition*, Carswell: Toronto, 1997.
Patrick Johnston, *Native Children and the Child Welfare System*, Toronto: Canadian Council on Social Development & James Lorimer, 1983.
Martin Luther, *Liber vagatorum (Book of Thieves)* in 1512. "Luther . . . claims that this thieves' jargon 'has come from the Jews.'"
Herman Melville, *The Confidence Man*, New York: Dix & Edwards, 1857, republished by Airmont Publishing Company Inc., reprinted in conjunction with Ryerson Press, Toronto, 1966. The full title of Chapter 26 reads, "Containing the Metaphysics of Indian-hating, According to the Views of One Evidently not so Prepossessed as Rousseau in Favour of Savages."
Douglas Sanders, "Pre-existing Rights: The *Aboriginal Peoples of Canada*," in Beaudoin and Ratushny, ed., *The Canadian Charter of Rights and Freedoms: A Commentary*, Toronto: Carswell, 1989.
Douglas Sanders, "The Supreme Court of Canada and the 'Legal and Political Struggle' over Indigenous Rights," *Canadian Ethnic Studies*, 22(3): 122–132, cited in Dale Kerr, "Arguments for and against recognizing Aboriginal Rights in Canada," November 21, 1995, Tatlayoko Think Tank, www.childcotin.bc.ca/tt/lcpc.htm#footnote22.
Brian Slattery, "Understanding Aboriginal Rights," 66 C.B.R. at 727, footnotes 18 and 175
John Ralston Saul, "Victims of Mythology," *Reflections of a Siamese Twin: Canada at the End of the Twentieth Century*, Toronto: Penguin Viking 1997.
Harold Vetter, *Language, Behavior & Psychopathology*, Chicago: Rand, McNally & Co., 1970.
Normal Zlotkin, "Aboriginal Customary Adoptions" *C.N.L.R.* at Endnote 1.

POLITICAL PHILOSOPHY

"Heidegger," Ox. Companion to Phil.
Isaiah Berlin, "The Pursuit of the Ideal" in The Crooked Timber of Humanity, Princeton, N.J., Princeton University Press, 1990.
Frederick Copleston, S.J. "The Doctrine of Forms" A History of Philosophy: Greece and Rome, Vol. I, Part I, Garden City, NY: Doubleday, 1960.

Edwards, John Ll. J. The Attorney-General, Politics and the Public Interest, London: Sweet & Maxwell, 1984.
Victor Farías, Heidegger and Nazism, Philadelphia: Temple University Press, 1989.
Michael Ignatieff, The Rights Revolution: Massey Lectures, 2000, C.B.C. Ideas Series.
Ernst H. Kantorowicz, The King's Two Bodies: A Study in Mediaeval Political Theology, Princeton: Princeton University Press, 1957.
Brian Slattery, "A Theory of the Charter," Osgoode Hall Law Journal, [25] 1987 4, at page 701.

RACE

"Blumenbach," *The Canadian Encyclopedia.*
"Gobineau," *The Canadian Encyclopedia.*
"Race," *The Gage Canadian Dictionary.*
"Race," *The Canadian Encyclopedia.*

"Race," *The Norton Dictionary of Modern Thought.*
"Race," *The Oxford English Dictionary.*

Index

D

E

F

Q

R

Printed in the USA
CPSIA information can be obtained
at www.ICGtesting.com
LVHW010302220424
778064LV00023B/333

9 780415 882613